Literary

A Reader

LITERARY AESTHETICS
A Reader

edited by

Alan Singer and *Allen Dunn*

BLACKWELL *Publishers*

Copyright © Blackwell Publishers 2000

Editorial matter, selection and arrangement copyright © Alan Singer and
Allen Dunn 2000

First published 2000

Blackwell Publishers Ltd
108 Cowley Road
Oxford OX4 1JF
UK

Blackwell Publishers Inc.
350 Main Street
Malden, Massachusetts 02148
USA

British Library Cataloguing in Publication Data

A CIP catalogue record for this book is available from the British Library.

Library of Congress Cataloging-in-Publication Data has been applied for

ISBN 0–631–20868–2 (hardback) ISBN 0–631–20869–0 (paperback)

Typeset in $10^1/_2$ on $12^1/_2$ pt Ehrhardt
by Best-set Typesetter Ltd., Hong Kong
Printed in Great Britain by
T.J. International, Padstow, Cornwall

This book is printed on acid-free paper.

Contents

Acknowledgments

The publishers gratefully acknowledge the following for permission to reproduce copyright material. Every effort has been made to trace copyright holders, but in some cases this has proved impossible. The publishers would be happy to hear from any copyright holder who has not been acknowledged.

The following items are in the order in which the extracts appear in the book.

Extract from Anthony, Earl of Shaftesbury, *Characteristics of Men, Manners, Opinions, Times,* edited, with notes, by John M. Robertson, originally published by Bobbs-Merrill Co. Inc. Published by Cambridge University Press 1999. Reprinted by permission of Cambridge University Press.

Extract from Francis Hutcheson, *An Inquiry Concerning Beauty, Order, Harmony, Design,* edited by Peter Kivy, published by Martinus Nijhoff 1973. Reprinted by kind permission from Kluwer Academic Publishers.

Extract from Karl Marx, Frederick Engels, *Collected Works,* vol. 28, *Marx 1857–1861,* © Lawrence and Wishart, London, 1986. Reprinted by permission of Lawrence and Wishart Limited.

Extract from Georg Lukács, *The Theory of the Novel,* translated from the German by Anna Bostock, published by MIT Press 1971. First published by P. Cassirer, Berlin, 1920. German edition © 1968 by Herman Luchterhand Verlag GmbH. Translation © 1971 by the Merlin Press. First MIT edition 1971. Reprinted by permission of Merlin Press, London and MIT Press, Cambridge, Massachusetts.

Extract by Georg Lukács, in *Marxism and Art: Writings in Aesthetics and Criticism,* edited by Berel Lang and Forrest Williams, published by Random House Inc.

Extract from Walter Benjamin, *Reflections: Essays, Aphorisms, Autobiographical Writings*. © 1978 by Harcourt Inc. Reprinted by permission of Harcourt Inc. and Harvard University Press.

Extract from Herbert Marcuse, *The Aesthetic Dimension*. English version translated and revised by Herbert Marcuse and Erica Sherover. Copyright © 1978. Reprinted by permission of Beacon Press, Boston.

Extract from Theodor W. Adorno, *Aesthetic Theory*, edited by Gretel Adorno and Rolf Tiedemann, newly translated and edited by Robert Hullot-Kentor (English edition published by University of Minnesota Press 1997). English translation © 1997 by the Regents of the University of Minnesota. Original German language edition © 1970 by Suhrkamp Verlag. Reprinted by permission of the University of Minnesota Press.

Extract from Hans-Georg Gadamer, *The Relevance of the Beautiful and Other Essays*, translated by Nicholas Walker, edited by Robert Bernasconi. First published in 1986. Part I published in German as *Die Aktualität des Schönen*, © Phillip Reclam Jr., Stuttgart 1977. English translation © Cambridge University Press 1986. Reprinted by permission of Cambridge University Press and Phillip Reclam Jr.

Extract from Louis Althusser, *Lenin and Philosophy and Other Essays*, translated by Ben Brewster, published by Verso, London, and Monthly Review Press, New York, 1971. Reprinted by permission of Verso, and Monthly Review Press.

Extract from Fredric Jameson, *The Political Unconscious: Narrative as a Socially Symbolic Act*. Copyright © 1981 Cornell University Press. Used by permission of Cornell University Press and ITPS Limited, on behalf of Routledge.

Extracts by Longinus, in *Classical Literary Criticism*, translated by T. S. Dorsch (Penguin Classics 1965). Copyright © T. S. Dorsch 1965. Reprinted by permission of Penguin Books Limited.

Extract from Plotinus, *The Enneads*, translated by Stephen MacKenna, published by Faber and Faber Limited (3rd edn. published by Pantheon Books Inc., New York). Reprinted by permission of Faber and Faber Limited.

Extract from David Hume, *Essays: Moral, Political, and Literary*, edited by Eugene F. Miller, published by Liberty Classics Inc. 1985. Reprinted by permission of Liberty Fund Inc.

by Cornell University. Revised and abridged edition © 1961 by Thomas
Goddard Bergin and Max Harold Fisch. Revised unabridged edition © 1968
by Cornell University. Translation of *Practic of the New Science* copyright ©
1976 by the Johns Hopkins University Press. Used by permission of the publisher, Cornell University Press.

Extract from A. G. Baumgarten, *Reflections on Poetry: Meditationes Philosoph-
icae de Nonnullis ad Poema Pertinentibus*, translated and edited by Karl Aschenbrenner and William Holther, published by University of California Press.
Reprinted by permission of the University of California Press.

Extract from *J. G. Hamann, 1730–1788: A Study in Christian Existence*, by
Ronald Gregor Smith, published by HarperCollins Publishers. Reprinted with
permission of HarperCollins Publishers Limited.

Extract by Johann Gottfried Herder, in *German Aesthetic and Literary Criticism: Winckelmann, Lessing, Hamann, Herder, Schiller, Goethe*, edited and
introduced by H. B. Nisbet, 1985. Reprinted by permission of Cambridge
University Press.

Extract from Friedrich Nietzsche, *Human, All Too Human: A Book for Free
Spirits*, translated by Marion Faber, with Stephen Lehmann. © 1984 by the
University of Nebraska Press. Reprinted by permission of the University of
Nebraska Press.

Extract from Matthew Arnold, *English Literature and Irish Politics*, vol. IX of
The Complete Prose Works of Matthew Arnold, published by the University of
Michigan Press, Ann Arbor, 1973. Used with permission.

Extract from Jacques Lacan, *The Ethics of Psychoanalysis 1959–1960*, edited by
Jacques-Alain Miller, translated by Dennis Porter, published by Routledge and
W. W. Norton. © 1986 by Editions du Seuil. English translation © 1992 by
W. W. Norton & Co. Reprinted by permission of Taylor & Francis Books
Limited and W. W. Norton & Company Inc.

Extract from René Girard, *"To Double Business Bound": Essays on Literature,
Mimesis, and Anthropology*, pp. ix–xii. Copyright © 1978 by the Johns Hopkins
University Press. All rights reserved. Reprinted by permission of the Johns
Hopkins University Press.

Extract from Jacques Derrida, *The Truth in Painting*, translated by Geoff Bennington and Ian McLeod, published by the University of Chicago Press, 1987. © 1987 by the University of Chicago. All rights reserved. First published as *La Verité en peinture* in Paris, © 1978 Flammarion Paris. Reprinted by permission of the University of Chicago Press.

Extract from Monroe C. Beardsley, *Aesthetics: Problems in the Philosophy of Criticism*, published by Harcourt Brace Inc. Reprinted by permission of Mark Beardsley.

Extract by Victor Shklovsky, in *Russian Formalist Criticism: Four Essays*, translated and with an introduction by Lee T. Lemon and Marion J. Reis. © renewed 1993 by the University of Nebraska Press. Reprinted by permission of the University of Nebraska Press.

Extract from T. S. Eliot, "The Social Function of Poetry," in *On Poetry and Poets*. Copyright © 1957 by T. S. Eliot. Copyright renewed 1985 by Valerie Eliot. Published by Farrar, Straus and Giroux LLC, and Faber and Faber Limited. Reprinted by permission of Farrar, Straus and Giroux LLC and Faber and Faber Limited.

Extract from Cleanth Brooks, "The Language of Paradox," in *The Well Wrought Urn*. Copyright 1947 and renewed 1975 by Cleanth Books, reprinted by permission of Harcourt Inc.

Extract from Roland Barthes, *Critical Essays*, translated from the French by Richard Howard. Evanston: Northwestern University Press, 1972. © 1972 by Northwestern University Press. Used with permission of Northwestern University Press and Editions du Seuil.

Extract from Gérard Genette, *The Work of Art: Immanence and Transcendence*, translated from the French by G. M. Goshgarian. Copyright © 1997 Cornell University. Used by permission of the publisher, Cornell University Press.

Extract from Friedrich Schiller, *On the Aesthetic Education of Man*, edited and translated by Elizabeth M. Wilkinson and L. A. Willoughby, 1967. © Oxford University Press 1967. Reprinted by permission of Oxford University Press.

Extract from Friedrich Schlegel, *Dialogue on Poetry and Literary Aphorisms*, translated, introduced, and annotated by Ernst Behler and Roman Struc, published by Pennsylvania State University Press, 1968. Copyright 1968 by Pennsylvania State University. Reproduced with permission.

Extract from Ludwig Wittgenstein, *Lectures and Conversations on Aesthetics, Psychology and Religious Belief*, edited by Cyril Barrett © 1966 Basil Blackwell. Published by University of California Press. Reprinted by permission of University of California Press.

Extract from Kenneth Burke, *The Philosophy of Literary Form*, 3rd edn., revised by Kenneth Burke. Copyright © 1973 Regents of the University of California Press. Reprinted by permission of the publisher.

Extract from Charles Altieri, *Canons and Consequences: Reflections on the Ethical Force of Imaginative Ideals*. Evanston: Northwestern University Press. Pages 346–7. © 1990 by Northwestern University Press. All rights reserved. Reprinted by permission of Northwestern University Press.

Extract from *Selected Writings of the Ingenious Mrs. Aphra Behn*, published by Grove Atlantic Inc.

Extract from *George Eliot: Selected Critical Writings*, edited by Rosemary Ashton (World's Classics 1992). Reprinted by permission of Oxford University Press.

Extract from Virginia Woolf, "Women and Fiction," in *Granite and Rainbow*. Copyright © 1958 by Leonard Woolf, and renewed 1986 by M. T. Parsons, Executor of Leonard Sidney Woolf. Reprinted by permission of Harcourt Inc. and Random House Group Limited.

Extract from Julia Kristeva, *Revolution in Poetic Language*. © 1984 Columbia University Press. Reprinted by permission of Columbia University Press.

Extract from Paul de Man, *The Resistance to Theory*, Yale French Studies 63 (1982). Reprinted by permission of Yale French Studies, Yale University, New Haven.

Extract from Arthur C. Danto, *The Transfiguration of the Commonplace*, published by Harvard University Press 1981. Reprinted by permission of Georges Borchardt Inc., New York.

Extract from Tony Bennett, *Outside Literature*, published by Routledge, London, 1990. Reprinted by permission of Taylor & Francis Books Limited.

Extract from Pierre Bourdieu, *The Rules of Art*, translated by Susan Emanuel. Reprinted by permission of Stanford University Press, California and Polity Press, Oxford.

Extract from Jean-Luc Nancy, *The Sense of the World*, translated by Jeffrey S. Librett, published by University of Minnesota Press, 1997. North American edition Copyright 1997 by Regenets of the University of Minnesota. Originally published as *Le Sens du monde*. Copyright 1993 Editions Gallimard, Paris. Reprinted by permission of the University of Minnesota Press.

We would like to thank Allison Carey, Abdi Hussein and Dax Zimmerman for their generous assistance in this project.

Introduction

Organization of this Volume

It is one of the ironies of contemporary literary study that, as it has moved toward greater interdisciplinarity, it has grown skeptical of the aesthetic. Courses in literary study typically assume that the literary text is a work of art. But far less frequently do they inquire what this means or entertain the proposition that it matters. Even less frequently do such courses examine the historical and conceptual ground upon which the aesthetic character of the text stands. When aesthetics is discussed in the contemporary literature classroom, it is often confused with aestheticism. Teachers and critics usually assume that in order to discuss the aesthetic value of a literary text one must treat it as an autonomous object and isolate it from non-literary values and disciplines. The result is an ironically self-fulfilling judgment: literary aesthetics becomes identified with nineteenth-century notions of art for art's sake and mired in fruitless arguments about the possibility of art's autonomy.

In resisting this trend, this anthology asserts the continuing vitality and importance of literary aesthetics but insists that aesthetic value can be understood properly only in the context of a broader inquiry into human values and cultures. That is, we feel that literary aesthetics must be reintegrated into the widening repertoire of critical practices. The fact is that literary aesthetics, from its inception, has been engaged in the full range of debates generated by what we now call cultural criticism. Unlike the more restricted discourse of philosophical aesthetics, literary aesthetics has explored the ways in which value commitments extend across disciplinary domains by reckoning with the practical concerns of art production and consumption. Therefore the readings in this anthology reach back to classical sources of philosophical aesthetics and forward to the most current accounts of the utility and value of the literary artwork in postmodern culture. The organization of the text is designed to engage the reader in the shaping debates of literary aesthetic theory and to demonstrate their continuing relevance for our understanding of the ways literature sustains and critiques culture.

Community, Culture, Politics

The critics of classical antiquity clearly recognized the important role that poetry played in shaping cultural identities and legitimating political power. This recognition is apparent in Plato's dismissal of the poets from his ideal republic on the grounds that they spread lies about the gods and the afterlife and encourage their audiences to relinquish control of their emotions. Yet classical critics tend to view the political functions of poetry in fairly unproblematic if not simplistic ways; they acknowledge poetry's role in providing a *paideuma* or body of cultural knowledge, but frequently restrict their inquiries into its political implications to an affirmation of its ability to illustrate familiar virtues or of its utility as a source of rhetorical tools for inspiring and manipulating crowds.

With the rise of modern aesthetic theory, however, poetry or literature (as it was soon to become) is assumed to model and embody the logic of various competing forms of political order. Thus, at the beginning of the eighteenth century Lord Shaftesbury, who is sometimes referred to as the father of modern aesthetics, claims that the human ability to appreciate and enjoy beauty proves that human desire is not exclusively or even primarily driven by the selfish need for personal satisfaction as more pessimistic political theorists such as Hobbes had suggested. The delight that we take in the harmony of a work of art, Shaftesbury claims, is analogous to the pleasure we take in a well-ordered society whose members are bound by a common sympathy and respect. In neither case, he insists, is enjoyment derived from selfish calculations of personal gain. Furthermore, the order that we enjoy in each case is not the product of a bland uniformity. Art and society both derive their beauty from their ability to incorporate difference and discord in larger patterns of harmony, and this is nowhere clearer than in literature, Shaftesbury observes, since in literature the author is obligated to balance multiple viewpoints in a single text.

Shaftesbury's criticism anticipated the dialectic theories of art and literature that flourished in the nineteenth century. In the most general terms, these theories claim that art derives its value from its ability to reconcile opposing forces or ideas and, following Kant, especially from its ability to mediate the conflict of the concrete particular with the abstract universal or, in political terms, the interests of the individual with good of the society as a whole. Indeed, in this *Aesthetic Letters*, Friedrich Schiller makes clear the political implications of aesthetic mediation. In the kind of play facilitated by art, he claims, law becomes less tyrannical and impulse loses its merely selfish qualities.

Similar notions of the dialectic function of art are apparent in Hegel's aesthetics and in much Marxist criticism, and a version is apparent even in the politically conservative work of Coleridge and of the New Critics as well. The political differences between these versions of the dialectical model arise from conflicting notions of whether and how art's mediating powers are reflected in social practice. Many Marxist critics, following Lukács and Jameson, claim that literature's powers of mediation will always be a reflection of the society in which it is produced. Thus, they argue, the literature produced by capitalist society will be most authentic when it mirrors the conflict and fragmentation of that society. This logic leads Adorno to the dramatic conclusion that the function of literature in the contemporary world should be essentially negative; it should negate, that is, the images of false reconciliation with which we are surrounded. In this criticism, literature paradoxically commemorates the absence of true beauty from the modern world.

Beauty and Sublimity

The origins of modern ideas of beauty and sublimity can be traced back to classical antiquity. However, the systematic distinction between these two aesthetic qualities dates from the eighteenth century and marks a deep tension in modern aesthetics. According to this distinction, beauty is the product of harmony, symmetry and wholeness, while sublimity is generated by the experience of power and magnitude. Beauty is usually credited with producing feelings of pleasure, well-being, and integration with nature and society, while sublimity is said to inspire feelings of empowerment, autonomy, and even isolation.

In comparison with the ubiquitous discourse of beauty, the development of theories of sublimity is relatively straightforward. All theories of sublimity trace their origin to Longinus' first-century treaties *On the Sublime*. This text languished in obscurity for over a millennium and survived only in a single damaged copy. It was revived, however, in the seventeenth and eighteenth centuries when sublimity became a fashionable term. Longinus claims that mere correctness in literary composition is not enough to produce greatness; for true greatness, he insists, one must have great thoughts and great emotions as well as formal qualities such as effective figurative language and diction, and compositional unity. According to Longinus, sublimity will transport an audience by inspiring it to identify with the exalted emotions and ideas that the poet presents, and this distinguishes sublimity from ordinary rhetoric, which leads an audience along a path of reasoned persuasion. When Longinus was first popularized in France and Britain his treatise was read as an argument for qualities such as elevation and brevity, but sublimity was assumed to be either complementary to or identical with beauty. The relationship between beauty and sublimity was redefined, however, by the influential aesthetic theories of Burke and Kant, who viewed beauty and sublimity as antithetical properties, the former demonstrating the value of human reason and the latter dramatizing its limitations.

Theories of the beautiful are both more numerous and more difficult to isolate than theories of the sublime, but there are two overlapping traditions that have exerted the most influence in shaping critical discussions of beauty. The first is Neoplatonic tradition, which originates in Plotinus' reading of Plato, and the second is the rationalist aesthetics of the neoclassical period. Neoplatonic theories of beauty assume that beauty is created when the chaos of the material world is shaped by artistic form and thus made to reflect higher, spiritual realities. The block of marble, to cite Plotinus' most famous example, is only brute matter until it is chiseled into the shape of the sculptor's ideas. Art thus employs concrete particulars but uses them to embody universal and ideal truths. This account of beauty had understandable appeal to those who wished to defend art on Christian grounds, since it supports the notion that art presents spiritual truths in sensuous form. In literary terms, this means that secular literary texts can be defended as parables or allegories; beneath their worldly narratives, one may expect to find spiritual instruction. Neoclassical defenders of rationalist notions of beauty had little difficulty building on this framework. For Baumgarten, who first introduced the term "aesthetic" in the eighteenth century, beauty is the product of the unifying power of perception that art uses to organize sensuous particulars. As Kant will later formulate it, beauty combines sensuous multiplicity with the unity of reason.

During the nineteenth century, the mention of sublimity becomes increasingly rare, but the standard of beauty retains its importance. For the French Symbolists and the English aesthetes such as Pater and Wilde, beauty is the quality that distinguishes art and insulates it against what these critics see as the increasingly debased quality of life in the everyday world. With the advent of modernism, however, the aestheticism of the late nineteenth century is increasingly attacked for its escapism and otherworldly detachment, and, as Adorno's criticism illustrates, beautiful art is suspected of falsifying the world and of offering bogus consolation for real world problems. Thus it is not surprising that the second half of the twentieth century should see a resurgence of interest in the sublime. For the new postmodern partisans of the sublime such as Lyotard, sublimity presents compelling evidence of the limitations of human reason and human language. As such, sublimity is consonant with the criticism of the Enlightenment found in the work of philosophers such as Heidegger and Derrida.

Truth, Value, Ethics

Perhaps no issue in aesthetic theory is more vexed than the question of whether art does or can tell the truth. In the literary theory of classical antiquity, the battle lines around this issue had already been drawn by Plato's charge in *The Republic*, mentioned above, that poets are liars and should be banished from the ideal state until they can give a better account of themselves. Of course, most critics have disagreed with Plato, but the grounds upon which they have done so have varied widely. Some, like Horace and various medieval rhetoricians, have argued that literature is a rhetorical vehicle for imparting more or less conventional kinds of truth, from historical facts to moral precepts. Starting with Aristotle, however, there is a strong tradition of criticism that argues that the truth found in literature is somehow qualitatively different from the truth as it is presented elsewhere: literary truth is more philosophically general than history and more historically particular than philosophy, to cite one version of this claim. Furthermore, Longinus and many after him have claimed that the truth of literature is not to be found in truth statements as such but, rather, is the product of an audience's dramatic experience of the literary text; that is, the truth of literature lies in the reader's collaborative performance of the text. Thus there are at least three general types of responses that can be offered in reply to Plato's charges. The first type of response is implicit in any attempt to use literature to illustrate truths that are stated elsewhere, while those who claim that literature works at an emotional, precognitive level can be assumed to favor the performative theory of literature invoked in the third response.

The Neoplatonic and Kantian aesthetics discussed above provide clear examples of theories that assume that art possesses a distinct kind of truth. Vico, however, presents an important variation on this argument. He claims that art, and specifically poetry, reveals the constructed or artificial nature of human society, including its values and institutions. According to Vico, human social institutions are imaginative creations just like the various narratives, poetic and non-poetic, from which these institutions derive their authority. For some, such as Matthew Arnold, the kinds of claims that Vico makes about the poetic origins of human values are the grounds for hope. In the future, Arnold predicts, humanity will be able to affirm a set of values simply because they are good poetry, not because they have the authority of science or religion behind them.

Twentieth-century critics, however, have employed Vico's insights to less optimistic ends. By showing us the artificial or socially constructed nature of our desires, values, and social institutions, these critics claim, literature can help us debunk them and discredit their claims to authority; that is, they insist that the truth that literature conveys is that human reality is fictional. Both Girard and Lacan, for instance, turn to literature for confirmation of their claims that human desire is itself constructed through a process of poetic projection and imitation. Following Hegel, they suppose that when we think that we are acting upon our deepest desires, we are in fact only imitating what we take to be the desires of others. For Lacan, the ego and the sense of self that it provides is the foundation for all conventional notions of truth, and, unfortunately, this foundation is completely fictional; the self that I think of as my own is only the product of my unconscious identification with others. The beauty of literature, as Lacan describes it, is its ability to shatter the illusions of the ego. Along similar lines, Derrida claims that art can demonstrate the impossibility of philosophical quests for truth by revealing that such quests are always hampered by the figural and fictional nature of language itself.

Literary Formalism

Literary formalism would seem to be the most apt site for the application of aesthetic principles to literary study. Almost from the beginning, the formal element in literature – such things as its imagery, figurative language, sound and even its printed image – has been assumed to be what distinguishes the artwork as an expressive medium from communication aspiring only to the accurate representation of nature or to the statement of objective facts. Indeed, it is the sensuousness of literary language and its emphasis on the particularity of experience that is supposed to make it a medium for personal expression. Yet Aristotle's anatomy of plot in the *Poetics* argues that literary form is not a simple expression of the freedom of either character or author but rather the record of a conflict between the world of human aspirations and the objective forces that threaten to limit or frustrate human actions. It is no surprise, then, that since Aristotle, critics have argued about whether human desire or the objective facts that constrain that desire should play the predominant role in shaping literary form. They have also disagreed about whether the value of literary form is the product of cultural or authorial prejudice or whether it reflects some objective standard.

Whatever the answers to these questions, literary formalists have consistently made the rhetorical and linguistic features of the literary text prominent in their analysis. Whether they are Aristotleans, Romantics, New Critics, or Structuralists, the formalists are united by their engagement with the multiple dimensions of experience embodied in literary form and their faith that the text must be analyzed on its own terms. Even if those terms turn out to be freighted with the ideological baggage of the social, political, and religious conventions of the culture at large, they provide, by their formal distance, a lever for critical reflection; that is, by making us self-conscious about the formal features of language, literature can also prompt us to think critically about the familiar ideas that language conveys. In that way the formalists always hold out some hope that the originality of the artwork can sow the seeds of social change, even if that transfiguration must originate on the level of the individual sensibility. The range of formalist views of literary art extends from Coleridge's analysis of linguistic structures as reflections of uniquely literary meaning to Barthes's notion that literary language is coded with the non-literary meaning of the larger cultural structures. This diversity of formalist approaches provides useful tools for investigating the ways in which the insights and creative impulses of literature are enacted in everyday life.

Agency, Expression

As the disagreements between formalist critics makes clear, literature has long been viewed as a medium for exploring the possibilities and limitations of human freedom and the notions of agency that freedom makes possible. Critics working in the idealist tradition of Kant and Schiller assume that just as art can embody a kind of ideal mediation between the needs of individuals and the demands of the community, so it can serve as a model of human freedom, a freedom which is won in an analogous way by harmonizing conflicting forces within the psyche. We are most free when we play, Schiller argues, and he describes art as a kind of intensified play in which the conflicting emotional and cognitive forces that shape human behavior are harmonized. However, the harmony that art produces, he insists, is not the result of coercion or repression; it preserves tension and conflict but makes conflict productive and even enjoyable. Thus expressive theories of literature do not necessarily assume that the literary text is the expression of a static ideal; they do not view literature as fixed imprint of the author's godlike will. Even in their most idealistic form, expressive theories presuppose a practical and even unpredictable engagement with the world. To express oneself, to act willfully, is to undertake an experiment, since the force, meaning, and ultimate success of human actions are never simply given. Expressive theories of art, therefore, must presuppose that artistic expression will be a process of negotiation and improvisation, and this is nowhere more apparent than in twentieth-century accounts of artistic expression, especially those influenced by pragmatism. Wittgenstein, Dewey, Kenneth Burke, and Altieri all exemplify this pragmatic attitude in so far as they view art as providing ways of getting on in the world rather than as a repository of ultimate solutions to human problems or as the simple revelation of pre-established identities. What we are is what we do, in Altieri's formulation, and for him literature is an important part of that doing. As all of these thinkers are well aware, however, this acting does not take place in an existential void; it is a response to a cultural world and a potential transformation of the culture to which it responds.

Gender

Those who have championed women's writing have been in general agreement that women's writing deserves a prominent place in the literary canon, but they have differed, sometimes dramatically, in their notions of how women's literature should be judged. Some have argued that writing by women should be judged by the same standards applied to texts by men and that simple fairness in the application of these standards will suffice to establish women in their rightful place. Others have insisted that women's writing should be judged by uniquely feminine standards since women authors are responding to unique social conditions and, according to some, expressing uniquely feminine sensibilities. Thus, on the one hand, Aphra Behn, a successful Restoration playwright, demands fairness, insisting that her plays be judged by the same aesthetic and commercial standards that are applied to plays written by men, while on the other, the twentieth-century critic and philosopher Luce Irigaray argues that women's writing is shaped by a logic and a psychology that is fundamentally different from men's and thus must be approached with a different critical framework.

Interestingly, some of the most important women authors and critics have endorsed elements of both positions. Virginia Woolf, for instance, argues for the importance of a literature that in style and content reflects the realities of women's experiences, experiences which she presumes to be centered on the emotional lives of women themselves and those around them. Woolf, however, also claims that the best writing is androgynous and incorporates both masculine and feminine viewpoints. Of course, to the extent that gender roles are socially constructed and thus subject to revision, Woolf's call for an androgynous viewpoint may be understood as a plea for more human and more livable notions of gender itself.

Aesthetic/Anti-aesthetic

One of the most provoking questions raised by contemporary literary criticism is whether or not the literary artwork ought to be considered in aesthetic terms at all. Why is it important to treat the work of art differently from any other phenomenal experience that warrants interpretation? Such questioning of the most basic assumptions about the literary text arise very directly from the influence of continental philosophy on literary study. This philosophical turn in the course of literary history was first navigated by poststructuralist theorists such as Barthes and Derrida and later sustained through the 1990s in the work of critics such as Bennett and Nancy. It takes advantage of the fact that aesthetics is officially a subset of the discipline of philosophy. Because philosophy is charged to ask questions that transcend the narrow realm of the aesthetic, many poststructuralists have argued that the literary text, in the guise of artwork, ought likewise to be subordinated to broader philosophical questions. On that basis, contemporary theory forces a critical reckoning with the time-honored assumptions that the text embodies ideals of beauty or taste, that it possesses an organic integrity endowed by an authorial subject, that its meaning is governed by the same concepts of totality and unity that give authority to authorship.

In this final section of *Literary Aesthetics*, we sample several contemporary arguments from the debate about whether the literary artwork embodies its own values or represents the values of other disciplines of knowledge. In other words, is there a meaning in the artwork that distinguishes its expressivity from the reigning ideologies of human expression? Each of the readings in this section reveals the complexity of attempting to come to terms with the value of the artwork in the wake of poststructuralist skepticism about the verities of Enlightenment culture, that is, skepticism about the fixity and even the communicability of meaning. Some of the readings endorse the category of the aesthetic as a useful explanatory paradigm for reading literary art. Others adopt the stance that the American critic Hal Foster has called the "anti-aesthetic;"

they reject the proposition that works of art produce types of meaning that are not found in other kinds of human activities. In either case, each of the theorists collected in this section understands that what it means to be a human subject and a maker of artifacts in the twenty-first century can no longer be taken for granted as the legacy of our philosophical past. Each of them therefore contends with the open-endedness of the question, What is literary art? In that way, they serve the most general purpose of this volume: to comprehend the enduring incompleteness of literary aesthetics. Perhaps that is our strongest affirmation of the unbreakable bond between literature and art.

I
Community, Culture, Politics

Lord Shaftesbury

(1671–1713)

Because he was the first to argue that all human beings have an inborn faculty making them sensitive to beauty, Shaftesbury is sometimes referred to as the father of modern aesthetics. Despite the independence that he grants to this aesthetic sense, however, it is important to see the ways in which his notions of beauty are closely tied to both his ethical and political theories. In his ethics, politics, and moral philosophy, Shaftesbury is arguing against Thomas Hobbes's claim that human nature is essentially selfish and that virtuous individuals are those who restrain their selfish impulses because they fear punishment and hope for rewards. In opposition to this pessimistic view, Shaftesbury insists that the pleasure we take in acts of benevolence or in experiences of beauty are just as natural as our more selfish emotions.

Furthermore, Shaftesbury claims, the immediate pleasures that we find in both beauty and benevolence are accompanied by the more complex kind of pleasure we feel when we see the harmony that kindness and the pursuit of beauty produce. This pleasure that we feel when contemplating our nobler feelings contrasts, according to Shaftesbury, with the embarrassment we are likely to experience when contemplating our purely selfish deeds. The harmony that individuals discover when reflecting upon their benevolent emotions is twofold: they discover the harmony and coherence of their own characters as these are defined by benevolence, and they discover the harmony of society as it is held together by a collective good will, by mutual feelings of benevolence.

Just as this process of reflection distinguishes the pleasure that is found in selfish action from the pleasures of virtue, so a similar process of reflection distinguishes mere sensuous enjoyment from aesthetic enjoyment. When we reflect upon aesthetic pleasure, Shaftesbury says, we discover that it is caused not by the gratification of sensuous appetites but by the experience of the order or harmony revealed in the aesthetic object. Like Plotinus, Shaftesbury insists that we are pleased by a statue not because of our fondness for the sculptor's particular materials but because we find pleasure in the form that the materials reveal; it is not marble that pleases us but the human shape which emerges from the stone.

Shaftesbury's republican politics depend on a similar notion of reflection. He imagines public debate and political dialogue as the means for establishing and revealing social harmony. In such exchanges, the individual reveals her or his character (the harmony of actions) and establishes her or his place in the collective order of the social world. Unlike Plato's republic, Shaftesbury's ideal political order is based upon the free exchange of ideas protected from the threat of despotic power. Shaftesbury implies that the discordant harmony of free political dialogue itself is as valuable as the truth of the ideas which the participants express.

Literature plays a pivotal role in this vision, since it is the most obviously dialogic of the artistic genres and therefore less easily assimilated to the platonic model than are the plastic arts like painting and sculpture. This is clear in "Advice to an Author" wherein Shaftesbury methodically blurs the distinction between literature and moral philosophy. The "moral poet" like the moral philosopher must know the "inward form and structure of his fellow creature" (Treatise III, ɪ, iii).

Suggested reading

Peter Kivy, *The Seventh Sense*, New York: Burt Franklin, 1976.

Freedom of Wit and Humour

Treatise II, Part ɪv, Section iii

And thus, after all, the most natural beauty in the world is honesty and moral truth. For all beauty is truth. True features make the beauty of a face; and true proportions the beauty of architecture; as true measures that of harmony and music. In poetry, which is all fable, truth still is the perfection. And whoever is scholar enough to read the ancient philosopher, or his modern copyists, upon the nature of a dramatic and epic poem, will easily understand this account of truth.

A painter, if he has any genius, understands the truth and unity of design; and knows he is even then unnatural when he follows Nature too close, and strictly copies Life. For his art allows him not to bring all nature into his piece, but a part only. However, his piece, if it be beautiful, and carries truth, must be a whole, by itself, complete, independent, and withal as great and comprehensive as he can make it. So that particulars, on this occasion, must yield to the general design, and all things be subservient to that which is principal; in

Reprinted from: Anthony, Earl of Shaftesbury, *Characteristics of Men, Manners, Opinions, Times,* edited by John M. Robertson, Indianapolis and New York: Bobbs-Merrill, 1964, pp. 94–7, 279–82.

order to form a certain easiness of sight, a simple, clear, and united view, which would be broken and disturbed by the expression of any thing peculiar or distinct.

Now the variety of Nature is such, as to distinguish everything she forms, by a peculiar original character, which, if strictly observed, will make the subject appear unlike to anything extant in the world besides. But this effect the good poet and painter seek industriously to prevent. They hate minuteness, and are afraid of singularity; which would make their images, or characters, appear capricious and fantastical. The mere face-painter, indeed, has little in common with the poet; but, like the mere historian, copies what he sees, and minutely traces every feature and odd mark. 'Tis otherwise with the men of invention and design. 'Tis from the many objects of nature, and not from a particular one, that those geniuses form the idea of their work. Thus the best artists are said to have been indefatigable in studying the best statues: as esteeming them a better rule than the prefectest human bodies could afford. And thus some considerable wits[1] have recommended the best poems as preferable to the best of histories; and better teaching the truth of characters and nature of mankind. . . .

Such is poetical and such (if I may so call it) graphical or plastic truth. Narrative or historical truth must needs be highly estimable; especially when we consider how mankind, who are become so deeply interested in the subject, have suffered by the want of clearness in it. 'Tis itself a part of moral truth. To be a judge in one, requires a judgment in the other. The morals, the character, and genius of an author must be thoroughly considered; and the historian or relator of things important to mankind must, whoever he be, approve himself many ways to us, both in respect of his judgment, candour, and disinterestedness, ere we are bound to take anything on his authority. And as for critical truth, or the judgment and determination of what commentators, translators, paraphrasts, grammarians and others have, on this occasion, delivered to us; in the midst of such variety of style, such different readings, such interpolations and corruptions in the originals; such mistakes of copyists, transcribers, editors, and a hundred such accidents to which ancient books are subject; it becomes, upon the whole, a matter of nice speculation, considering withal that the reader, though an able linguist, must be supported by so many other helps from chronology, natural philosophy, geography, and other sciences.

And thus many previous truths are to be examined and understood in order to judge rightly of historical truth, and of the past actions and circumstances of mankind, as delivered to us by ancient authors of different nations, ages, times, and different in their characters and interests. Some moral and philosophical truths there are withal so evident in themselves, that 'twould be easier to imagine half mankind to have run mad, and joined precisely in one and the same species of folly, than to admit anything as truth which should be advanced against such natural knowledge, fundamental reason, and common sense. . . .

This too is certain, that the admiration and love of order, harmony, and proportion, in whatever kind, is naturally improving to the temper, advantageous to social affection, and highly assistant to virtue, which is itself no other than the love of order and beauty in society. In the meanest subjects of the world, the appearance of order gains upon the mind and draws the affection towards it. But if the order of the world itself appears just and beautiful, the admiration and esteem of order must run higher, and the elegant passion or love of beauty, which is so advantageous to virtue, must be the more improved by its exercise in so ample and magnificent a subject. For 'tis impossible that such a divine order should be contemplated without ecstasy and rapture, since in the common subjects of science and the liberal arts, whatever is according to just harmony and proportion is so transporting to those who have any knowledge or practice in the kind. . . .

Concerning Virtue or Merit

Book II; Part 1, Section i

We have found that, to deserve the name of good or virtuous, a creature must have all his inclinations and affections, his dispositions of mind and temper, suitable, and agreeing with the good of his kind, or of that system in which he is included, and of which he constitutes a part. To stand thus well affected, and to have one's affections right and entire, not only in respect of oneself but of society and the public, this is rectitude, integrity, or virtue. And to be wanting in any of these, or to have their contraries, is depravity, corruption, and vice.

It has been already shown, that in the passions and affections of particular creatures there is a constant relation to the interest of a species or common nature. This has been demonstrated in the case of natural affection, parental kindness, zeal for posterity, concern for the propagation and nurture of the young, love of fellowship and company, compassion, mutual succour, and the rest of this kind. Nor will any one deny that this affection of a creature towards the good of the species or common nature is as proper and natural to him as it is to any organ, part, or member of an animal body, or mere vegetable, to work in its known course and regular way of growth. 'Tis not more natural for the stomach to digest, the lungs to breathe, the glands to separate juices, or other entrails to perform their several offices, however they may by particular impediments be sometimes disordered or obstructed in their operations.

There being allowed therefore in a creature such affections as these towards the common nature or system of the kind, together with those which regard the private nature or self-system, it will appear that in following the first of these affections, the creature must on many occasions contradict and go against the latter. How else should the species be preserved? Or what would signify that implanted natural affection, by which a creature through so many difficulties and hazards preserves its offspring and supports its kind?

It may therefore be imagined, perhaps, that there is a plain and absolute opposition between these two habits or affections. It may be presumed that the pursuing the common interest or public good through the affections of one kind, must be a hindrance to the attainment of private good through the affections of another. For it being taken for granted that hazards and hardships of whatever sort are naturally the ill of the private state, and it being certainly the nature of those public affections to lead often to the greatest hardships and hazards of every kind, 'tis presently inferred "that 'tis the creature's interest to be without any public affection whatsoever."

This we know for certain, that all social love, friendship, gratitude, or whatever else is of this generous kind, does by its nature take place of the self-interesting passions, draws us out of ourselves, and makes us disregardful of our own convenience and safety. So that according to a known way of reasoning on self-interest, that which is of a social kind in us should of right be abolished. Thus kindness of every sort, indulgence, tenderness, compassion, and, in short, all natural affection, should be industriously suppressed, and as mere folly and weakness of nature be resisted and overcome; that by this means there might be nothing remaining in us which was contrary to a direct self-end; nothing which might stand in opposition to a steady and deliberate pursuit of the most narrowly confined self-interest.

According to this extraordinary hypothesis, it must be taken for granted "that in the system of a kind or species, the interest of the private nature is directly opposite to that of the common one, the interest of particulars directly opposite to that of the public in general." A strange constitution! in which it must be confessed there is much disorder and untowardness, unlike to what we observe elsewhere in Nature. As if in any vegetable or animal body the part or member could be supposed in a good and prosperous state as to itself, when under a contrary disposition and in an unnatural growth or habit as to its whole.

Now that this is in reality quite otherwise, we shall endeavour to demonstrate, so as to make appear "that what men represent as an ill order and constitution in the universe, by making moral rectitude appear the ill, and depravity the good or advantage of a creature, is in Nature just the contrary. That to be well affected towards the public interest and one's own is not only consistent but inseparable; and that moral rectitude or virtue must accordingly be the advantage, and vice the injury and disadvantage of every creature."

Note

1 Thus the great Master himself in his *Poetics* above cited, viii., διὸ καὶ φιλοσοφώτερον καὶ σπουδαιότερον ποίησις ἱστορίας ἐστιν· ἡ μὲν γὰρ ποίησις μᾶλλον τὰ καθόλου, ἡ δ᾽ ἱστορία τὰ καθ᾽ ἕκαστον λέγει. ("Poetry is both a more philosophic and a more real thing than history; for poetry tells rather the universal, history the particular," Aristotle, *Poetics*, xcvi)

Francis Hutcheson

(1694–1746)

Francis Hutcheson follows Shaftesbury in constructing moral and aesthetic theories based upon the assumption that humans take a natural pleasure in both virtue and beauty. Both philosophers insist that this pleasure is as fundamental and irreducible as any of the pleasures resulting from sensual appetites. They claim, however, that the pursuit of the pleasures caused by beauty and virtue binds people together in natural sympathy rather than fragmenting human communities as selfish pleasures do. Although he rejects Locke's assumption that pleasure in beauty resembles other forms of sensuous pleasure, Hutcheson uses Locke's empiricist philosophy to provide a foundation for Shaftesbury's theories of beauty. Like Locke, he denies the existence of innate ideas, and assumes that all mental phenomena are to be explained as the compounds of various primary ideas, which are the products of sensation.

Hutcheson, however, goes on to assert that besides the external senses, which allow us to perceive such things as colors, tastes, sounds and smells, there also exists an "internal sense," which allows us to perceive certain qualities in complex ideas. Foremost among these qualities is beauty itself. Thus a sense of beauty allows one to apprehend and enjoy the complex configurations of simple ideas that combine to create the beautiful. Like Shaftesbury, Hutcheson insists that the very act of perceiving either good or virtuous ideas produces pleasure. That is, pleasure is a necessary part of the act of perception; we cannot know what true beauty is without taking pleasure in it. Yet Hutcheson's claims raise some difficult questions: if the internal sense that allows people to experience beauty is like the external senses such as sight, touch, and taste, then it does not involve any judgment or reflection at all. We simply become aware of beauty as a sensation of pleasure in the same way in which we become aware of warmth as a sensation of pleasure on a cold day. To many this seems counterintuitive, and philosophers have debated whether Hutcheson's notions of beauty are based upon cognition or sensation and emotion, or both.

Hutcheson distinguishes two types of beauty: original or absolute beauty and comparative or relative beauty. Original beauty is characterized by "uniformity amidst variety." For instance, Hutcheson claims that a square is more beautiful than a triangle because it incorporates a greater variety (a greater number of sides) in its unified symmetrical pattern. Hutcheson's formula for original beauty is the forerunner of Coleridge's definition of beauty as "multeity in unity," but it seems more appropriate as a standard for the plastic arts than for literature. However, comparative beauty, the second type of beauty that Hutcheson distinguishes, seems to have been formulated with literature in mind, since he illustrates it primarily with literary examples. Comparative beauty is pleasurable primarily because of its mimetic accuracy; it is founded on the "unity between the original and the copy" (Sect. IV, i). Hutcheson seems to think of comparative beauty as existing in natural tension with the harmony of original beauty, since he emphasizes that while representation of absolute beauty may be more "lovely" than the irregular scenes found in comparative beauty, the irregular variety of comparative beauty will be more beautiful nonetheless. This means that an accurate representation of a flawed character is to be preferred over the representation of perfect virtue, since "we have more lively ideas of imperfect men with all their passions" than we do of perfect men for whom there are no originals in the world of our experience (Sect. IV, ii). Hutcheson includes one further kind of correspondence under the heading of comparative beauty and that is the correspondence between the text and the author's intention. There is something fundamentally pleasing, he claims, in a well-executed design.

In the following passages from *An Inquiry Concerning Beauty, Order, Harmony, Design*, Hucheson defines beauty and describes the differences between original and comparative beauty.

Suggested reading

Susan Purviance, "Intersubjectivity and Sociable Relations in the Philosophy of Francis Hutcheson," *Eighteenth Century Life* 15 (1991): 23–38.

Section I: *Concerning some Powers of Perception, Distinct from What is Generally Understood by Sensation*

(ix)   Let it be observed that in the following papers the word *beauty* is taken for *the idea raised in us*, and a *sense* of beauty for *our power of receiving this idea*. *Harmony* also denotes *our pleasant ideas arising from composition of sounds*, and a *good ear* (as it is generally taken) a *power of perceiving this pleasure*. In the following sections, an attempt is made to discover what is the immediate

Reprinted from: Francis Hutcheson, *An Inquiry Concerning Beauty, Order, Harmony, Design*, edited by Peter Kivy, The Hague: Martinus Nijhoff, 1973, pp. 34–5, 38–9, 54–6.

occasion of these pleasant ideas, or what real quality in the objects ordinarily excites them.

(x)   It is of no consequence whether we call these ideas of beauty and harmony perceptions of the external senses of seeing and hearing, or not. I should rather choose to call our power of perceiving these ideas an *internal sense*, were it only for the convenience of distinguishing them from other sensations of seeing and hearing which men may have without perception of beauty and harmony. It is plain from experience that many men have in the common meaning the senses of seeing and hearing perfect enough. They perceive all the *simple ideas* separately, and have their pleasures; they distinguish them from each other, such as one colour from another, either quite different, or the stronger or fainter of the same colour [when they are placed beside each other, although they may often confound their names when they occur apart from each other, as some do the names of green and blue.]¹ They can tell in separate notes, the higher, lower, sharper or flatter, when separately sounded; in figures they discern the length, breadth, wideness of each line, surface, angle; and may be as capable of hearing and seeing at great distances as any men whatsoever. And yet perhaps they shall find no pleasure in musical compositions, in painting, architecture, natural landscape, or but a very weak one in comparison of what others enjoy from the same objects. This greater capacity of receiving such pleasant ideas we commonly call a *fine genius* or *taste*. In music we seem universally to acknowledge something like a distinct sense from the external one of hearing, and call it a *good ear*; and the like distinction we should probably acknowledge in other [objects,] had we also got distinct names to denote these *powers* of perception by.

(xi) [We generally imagine the brute animals endowed with the same sort of powers of perception as our external senses, and having sometimes greater acuteness in them; but we conceive few or none of them with any of these sublimer powers of perception here called *internal senses*, or at least if some of them have them, it is in a degree much inferior to ours.] . . .

(xvi) Beauty [in corporeal forms] is either *original* or *comparative*; or, if any like the terms better, *absolute* or *relative*. Only let it be [observed] that by absolute or original beauty is not understood any quality supposed to be in the object [which] should of itself be beautiful, without relation to any mind which perceives it. For beauty, like other names of sensible ideas, properly denotes the *perception* of some mind; *so cold*, [*hot*,] *sweet*, *bitter*, denote the sensations in our minds, to which perhaps there is no resemblance in the objects which excite these ideas in us, however we generally imagine [otherwise.] The ideas of beauty and harmony, being excited upon our perception of some primary quality, and having relation to figure and time, may indeed have a nearer resemblance to objects than these sensations, which seem not so much any pictures of objects as modifications of the perceiving mind; and yet, were there no mind with a sense of beauty to contemplate objects, I see not how they could be called beautiful. We therefore by[2] absolute beauty understand only that beauty which we perceive in objects without comparison to anything external, of which the object is supposed an imitation or picture, such as that beauty perceived from the works of nature, artificial forms, [figures]. Comparative or relative beauty is that which we perceive in objects commonly considered as *imitations* or *resemblances* of something else.

Section IV: *Of Relative or Comparative Beauty*

(i)   If the preceeding thoughts concerning the foundation of *absolute beauty* be just, we may easily understand wherein *relative beauty* consists. All beauty is relative to the sense of some mind perceiving it; but what we call *relative* is that which is apprehended in any object commonly considered as an *imitation* of some original. And this beauty is founded on a conformity, or a kind of unity between the original and the copy. The original may be either some object in nature, or some established idea; for if there be any known idea as a standard, and rules to fix this image or idea by, we may make a beautiful imitation. Thus a statuary, painter, or poet may please with an Hercules, if his piece retains that grandeur, and those marks of strength and courage which we imagine in that hero.

And farther, to obtain comparative beauty alone, it is not necessary that there be any beauty in the original. The imitation of absolute beauty may indeed in the whole make a more lovely piece, and yet an exact imitation shall still be beautiful, though the original were entirely void of it. Thus the deformities of old age in a picture, the rudest rocks or mountains in a landscape, if well represented, shall have abundant beauty, though perhaps not so great as if the original were absolutely beautiful, and as well represented. [Nay, perhaps the novelty may make us prefer the representation of irregularity.]

(ii)   The same observation holds true in the descriptions of the poets either of natural objects or persons; and this relative beauty is what they should principally endeavour to obtain, as the peculiar beauty of their works. By the *Moratae Fabulae*, or the ἤθη [ethos or character. AD] of Aristotle, we are not to understand virtuous [manners,] but a just representation of manners or characters as they are in nature, and that the actions and sentiments be suited to the characters of the persons to whom they are ascribed in epic and dramatic poetry. Perhaps very good reasons may be suggested from the nature of our passions to prove that a poet should not [draw his characters perfectly virtuous]. These characters indeed abstractly considered might give more pleasure, and have more beauty than the imperfect ones which occur in life with a mixture of good and evil; but it may suffice at present to suggest against this choice that we have more lively ideas of imperfect men with all their passions, than of morally perfect heroes such as really never occur to our observation, and of which consequently we cannot judge exactly as to their agreement with the copy. And farther, through consciousness of our own state we are more nearly touched and affected by the imperfect characters, since in them we see represented, in the persons of others, the contrasts of inclinations, and the struggles between the passions of self-love and those of honour and virtue which we often feel in our own breasts. This is the perfection of beauty for which Homer is justly admired, as well as for the variety of his characters.

(iii)   Many other beauties of poetry may be reduced under this class of *relative beauty*. The *probability* is absolutely necessary to make us imagine *resemblance*. It is by resemblance that *similitudes*, *metaphors*, and *allegories* are made beautiful, whether either the subject or the thing compared to it have beauty or not; the beauty indeed is greater when both have some original beauty or dignity as well as resemblance, and this is the foundation of the rule of studying *decency* in metaphors and similes as well as likeness. The *measures* and *cadence* are instances of harmony, and come under the head of absolute beauty.

(iv)   We may here observe a strange proneness in our minds to make perpetual comparisons of all things which occur to our observation, even of those which [are very different from each other.] There are certain resemblances in the motions of all animals upon like passions, which easily found a comparison; but this does not serve to entertain our fancy. Inanimate objects have often such positions as resemble those of the human body in various circumstances. These airs or gestures of the body are indications of [certain] dispositions in the mind, so that our very passions and affections, as well as other circumstances, obtain a resemblance to natural inanimate objects. Thus a tempest at sea is often an emblem of wrath; a plant or tree drooping under the rain of a person in sorrow; a poppy bending its stalk, or a flower withering when cut by the plow resembles the death of a blooming hero; an aged oak in the mountains shall represent an old empire; a flame seizing a wood shall represent a war. In short, everything in nature, by our strange inclination to resemblance, shall be brought to represent other things, even the most remote, especially the passions and circumstances of human nature in which we are more nearly concerned; and to confirm this and furnish instances of it one need only look into

Homer or Virgil. A fruitful fancy would find in a grove, or a wood an emblem for every character in a commonwealth, and every turn of temper or station in life.

Notes

1   Brackets indicate additions subsequent to the first edition.
2   This division of beauty is taken from the different foundations of pleasure [to] our sense of it, rather than from the objects themselves; for most of the following instances of relative beauty have also absolute beauty, and many of the instances of absolute beauty have also relative beauty in some respect or other. But we may distinctly consider these two fountains of pleasure, uniformity in the object itself, and resemblance to some original.

Karl Marx

(1818–1883)

The writings of Karl Marx have helped shape twentieth-century history and have exerted enormous influence on many intellectual fields, including aesthetics and literary criticism. All Marxist criticism starts from the assumption that literature and other products of culture reflect the socioeconomic conditions of the society in which they are produced. These socioeconomic conditions are determined by a mode of economic production such as feudalism or capitalism and by the kind of class conflict which this mode of production makes inevitable. Most famously, the capitalist mode of production engenders conflict between workers and capitalists, and the Marxist critic assumes that modern works of literature can be understood only in the context of this strife.

Beyond these points of general agreement, however, there are many diverse and even antagonistic schools of Marxist criticism, schools which reflect the very different ways in which Marx's political doctrines have been interpreted. A central point of contention among Marxist critics has been how to evaluate literature that has been written without the express purpose of illustrating Marx's insights. Marxist critics disagree, for instance, about whether the literature of the pre-Marxist past should be read as a mere reflection of ruling class prejudices or whether it should be credited – to various degrees – with the ability to diagnose and criticize those prejudices. (See Marx's speculation about the continuing value of Greek art in the excerpt below.)

Marxist critics from the Soviet Union generally advocated the development of an explicitly Marxist workers' literature, which they saw as supporting Soviet Communism. These Soviet critics were critical of literature that deviated from the kinds of plots, characterization, and explicit polemic that they thought should characterize a workers' literature. They suspected such deviant literature of "decadence" and of complicity with capitalist ideology. On the other hand, Marxist critics in the West have tended to view literature as being potentially more independent of its cultural origins and as thus able to criticize and even resist the society which produced it. These critics are likely to stress the way in which art analyzes and illuminates the historical conditions of its time *and* the way in which those historical conditions shape and determine the work of art. Because Marx's comments on art are scattered throughout his writings, they are suggestive rather than systematic and thus leave much room for disagreement.

The first passage below reflects Hegel's influence on Marx. In it Marx describes the way in which all human activity – both cultural and economic – is a form of human self-creation. That is, Marx believes that human identity is both created and recognized in the process by which people transform their physical and cultural environments. Art and literature are simply conspicuous cases of this process of self-creation. Capitalism, Marx insists, distorts people's perceptions of their own creative agency by making it appear as if the world consists of objects and commodities that are somehow independent of human activity. In this way capitalism creates a world of alienation. In the second passage Marx speculates about why literature of the past continues to inspire modern readers even while it reflects a world very different from our own.

Suggested reading

Terry Eagleton, *Marxism and Literary Criticism*, London: Methuen, 1976.
——, *The Ideology of the Aesthetic*, Cambridge, Mass.: Blackwell Publishers, 1990.

The Economic and Philosophical Manuscripts of 1844 (from the Third Manuscript)

The supersession of private property is, therefore, the complete *emancipation* of all the human qualities and senses. It is such an emancipation because these qualities and senses have become *human*, from the subjective as well as the objective point of view. The eye has become a *human* eye when its *object* has become a *human*, social object, created by man and destined for him. The senses have, therefore, become directly theoreticians in practice. They relate themselves to the thing for the sake of the thing, but the thing itself is an *objective human* relation to itself and to man, and vice versa.[1] Need and enjoyment have thus lost their *egoistic* character and nature has lost its mere *utility* by the fact that its utilization has become *human* utilization.

Similarly, the senses and minds of other men have become my *own* appropriation. Thus besides these direct organs, *social* organs are constituted, in the

Reprinted from: Karl Marx, *Early Writings*, translated and edited by T. B. Bottomore, London: C. A. Watts, 1963, pp. 160–2.

form of society; for example, activity in direct association with others has become an organ for the manifestation of life and a mode of appropriation of *human* life.

It is evident that the human eye appreciates things in a different way from the crude, non-human eye, the human *ear* differently from the crude ear. As we have seen, it is only when the object becomes a *human* object, or objective *humanity*, that man does not become lost in it. This is only possible when man himself becomes a *social* object; when he himself becomes a social being and society becomes a being for him in this object.

On the one hand, it is only when objective reality everywhere becomes for man in society the reality of human faculties, human reality, and thus the reality of his own faculties, that all *objects* become for him the *objectification of himself*. The objects then confirm and realize his individuality, they are *his own* objects, i.e. man himself becomes the object. *The manner in which these objects* become his own depends upon the *nature of the object* and the nature of the corresponding faculty; for it is precisely the *determinate character* of this relation which constitutes the specific *real* mode of affirmation. The object is not the same for the *eye* as for the *ear*, for the ear as for the eye. The *distinctive character* of each faculty is precisely its *characteristic* essence and thus also the characteristic mode of its objectification, of its *objectively real*, living *being*. It is therefore not only in thought, but through *all* the senses that man is affirmed in the objective world.

Let us next consider the subjective aspect. Man's musical sense is only awakened by music. The most beautiful music has no meaning for the non-musical ear, is not an object for it, because my object can only be the confirmation of one of my own faculties. It can only be so for me in so far as my faculty exists for itself as a subjective capacity, because the meaning of an object for me extends only as far as the sense extends (only makes sense for an appropriate sense). For this reason, the *senses* of social man are *different* from those of non-social man. It is only through the objectively deployed wealth of the human being that the wealth of subjective *human* sensibility (a musical ear, an eye which is sensitive to the beauty of form, in short, senses which are capable of human satisfaction and which confirm themselves as human faculties) is cultivated or created. For it is not only the five senses, but also the so-called spiritual senses, the practical senses (desiring, loving, etc.), in brief, human sensibility and the human character of the senses, which can only come into being through the existence of *its* object, through humanized nature. The cultivation of the five senses is the work of all previous history. Sense which is subservient to crude needs has only a restricted meaning. For a starving man the human form of food does not exist, but only its abstract character as food.

It could just as well exist in the most crude form, and it is impossible to say in what way this feeding-activity would differ from that of animals. The needy man, burdened with cares, has no appreciation of the most beautiful spectacle. The dealer in minerals sees only their commercial value, not their beauty or their particular characteristics; he has no mineralogical sense. Thus, the objectification of the human essence, both theoretically and practically, is necessary in order to *humanize* man's senses, and also to create the *human senses* corresponding to all the wealth of human and natural being.

Just as society at its beginnings finds, through the development of *private property* with its wealth and poverty (both intellectual and material), the materials necessary for this *cultural development*, so the fully constituted society produces man in all the plenitude of his being, the wealthy man endowed with all the senses, as an enduring reality. It is only in a social context that subjectivism and objectivism, spiritualism and materialism, activity and passivity, cease to be antinomies and thus cease to exist as such antinomies. The resolution of the *theoretical* contradictions is possible *only* through practical means, only through the *practical* energy of man. Their resolution is not by any means, therefore, only a problem of knowledge, but is a *real* problem of life which philosophy was unable to solve precisely because it saw there a purely theoretical problem.

Note

1   In practice I can only relate myself in a human way to a thing when the thing is related in a human way to man.

Economic Manuscripts of 1857–8

As regards art, it is known that certain periods of its florescence by no means correspond to the general development of society, or, therefore, to the material basis, the skeleton as it were of its organisation. For example, the Greeks compared with the moderns, or else Shakespeare. It is even acknowledged that certain forms of art, e.g. epos, can no longer be produced in their epoch-making, classic form after artistic production as such has begun; in other words that certain important creations within the compass of art are only possible at an early stage of its development. If this is the case with regard to the

Reprinted from: Karl Marx and Frederick Engels, *Collected Works*, vol. 28, *Marx 1857–61*, New York: International Publishers, 1975, pp. 46–8.

different arts within the sphere of art itself, it is not so remarkable that this should also be the case with regard to the entire sphere of art in its relation to the general development of society. The difficulty lies only in the general formulation of these contradictions. As soon as they are specified, they are already explained.

Let us take, for example, the relation of Greek art, and that of Shakespeare, to the present time. We know that Greek mythology is not only the arsenal of Greek art, but also its basis. Is the conception of nature and of social relations which underlies Greek imagination and therefore Greek [art] possible in the age of selfactors [machinery. AD], railways, locomotives and electric telegraphs? What is Vulcan compared with Roberts and Co., Jupiter compared with the lightning conductor, and Hermes compared with the Crédit Mobilier? All mythology subdues, dominates and fashions the forces of nature in the imagination and through the imagination; it therefore disappears when real domination over these forces is established. What becomes of Fama beside Printing House Square? Greek art presupposes Greek mythology, in other words, nature and even the social forms have already been worked up in an unconsciously artistic manner by the popular imagination. This is the material of Greek art. Not just any mythology, i.e. not any unconsciously artistic working up of nature (here the term comprises all objective phenomena, including society). Egyptian mythology could never become the basis or material womb of Greek art. But at any rate [it presupposes] *a* mythology. Hence, on no account a social development which precludes any mythological, [i.e.] any mythologising, attitude towards nature, and therefore demands from the artist an imagination independent of mythology.

Regarded from another angle: is Achilles possible when powder and short have been invented? And is the *Iliad* possible at all when the printing press and even printing machines exist? Does not the press bar inevitably spell the end of singing and reciting and the muses, that is, do not the conditions necessary for epic poetry disappear?

But the difficulty lies not in understanding that Greek art and epic poetry are bound up with certain forms of social development. The difficulty is that they still give us aesthetic pleasure and are in certain respects regarded as a standard and unattainable model.

An adult cannot become a child again, or he becomes childish. But does not the naiveté of the child give him pleasure, and must he not himself endeavour to reproduce the child's veracity on a higher level? Does not the specific character of every epoch come to life again in its natural veracity in the child's nature? Why should not the historical childhood of humanity, where it attained its most beautiful form, exert an eternal charm as a stage that will never recur?

There are unbred children and precocious children. Many of the ancient peoples belong to this category. The Greeks were normal children. The charm their art has for us does not conflict with the immature stage of the society in which it originated. On the contrary, that charm is a consequence of this and is, rather, inseparably linked with the fact that the immature social conditions which gave rise, and which alone could give rise, to this art can never recur.

Georg Lukács

(1885–1971)

Georg Lukács was the first great Marxist critic. Before he became a Marxist, he was strongly influenced by the philosophy of Frederic Hegel and the work of German sociologists such as Georg Simmel. Lukács was particularly impressed by Hegel's insistence that philosophy reflects its historical circumstances and by Simmel's claims that modern industrial society destroys social cohesion. These influences paved the way for his decision to join the Communist Party shortly after the Russian Revolution, and helped shape his distinctive form of western Marxism. Lukács's pre-Marxist literary criticism describes the way in which literature reflects either harmony or fragmentation of the society in which it originates. In his *Theory of the Novel*, for instance, he contrasts the wholeness and harmony that he finds in Greek epic with the alienation that he finds in the modern novel. And in *History and Class Consciousness*, his first explicitly Marxist work, he expands on this diagnosis of modern fragmentation, describing the way in which all aspects of culture and especially philosophy itself mirror the divisions and conflicts of capitalism.

Throughout his career, Lukács remains critical of the two dominant tendencies that he thinks characterize literature in capitalist society. On the one hand, he rejects the work of naturalist writers such as Émile Zola on the grounds that their objective descriptions of society record facts and surface appearances but fail to analyze the dynamic logic of history. On the other hand, Lukács is even more critical of modernist writers such as James Joyce who focus not on objective description but on complex experiments with style and point of view. According to Lukács, the modernists retreated into worlds of private fantasy, worlds that reflect the narcissistic and solipsistic perspective of the bourgeois class, which refuses to acknowledge the class struggle in which it is engaged. In place of either naturalism or modernism, Lukács advocates a Marxist-based Critical Realism. In works such as *The Historical Novel* and *Studies in European Realism*, he argues that such realism can not only avoid the fragmented visions of both naturalism and modernism, but in true Hegelian fashion can combine and reconcile the subjective and the objective, the personal and the public. This is possible, Lukács believes, because realism, like all good forms of art, provides what he, following Hegel, calls the "concrete." The concrete is neither an empty abstraction nor a mere isolated particular but a combination of the two.

In the first two passages below, Lukács contrasts the integrated world of the epic with the lonely world of modern drama. In the third, he describes the way in which art, because it is concrete, can overcome the limitations of its historical moment and unify historically fragmented perspectives.

Suggested reading

Fredric Jameson, *Marxism and Form: Twentieth-Century Dialectical Theories of Literature*, Princeton, NJ: Princeton University Press, 1972.

Integrated Civilisations

Happy are those ages when the starry sky is the map of all possible paths – ages whose paths are illuminated by the light of the stars. Everything in such ages is new and yet familiar, full of adventure and yet their own. The world is wide and yet it is like a home, for the fire that burns in the soul is of the same essential nature as the stars; the world and the self, the light and the fire, are sharply distinct, yet they never become permanent strangers to one another, for fire is the soul of all light and all fire clothes itself in light. Thus each action of the soul becomes meaningful and rounded in this duality: complete in meaning – in *sense* – and complete for the senses; rounded because the soul rests within itself even while it acts; rounded because its action separates itself from it and, having become itself, finds a centre of its own and draws a closed circumference round itself. 'Philosophy is really homesickness,' says Novalis: 'it is the urge to be at home everywhere.'

That is why philosophy, as a form of life or as that which determines the form and supplies the content of literary creation, is always a symptom of the rift between 'inside' and 'outside', a sign of the essential difference between the self and the world, the incongruence of soul and deed. That is why the happy ages have no philosophy, or why (it comes to the same thing) all men in such ages are philosophers, sharing the utopian aim of every philosophy. For what is the task of true philosophy if not to draw that archetypal map? What is the problem of the transcendental *locus* if not to determine how every impulse which springs from the innermost depths is co-ordinated with a form that it is ignorant of, but that has been assigned to it from eternity and that

Reprinted from: Georg Lukács, *The Theory of the Novel*, translated from the German by Anna Bostock, Cambridge, Mass.: MIT Press, 1971, pp. 29–30, 66–9.

must envelop it in liberating symbols? When this is so, passion is the way, pre-determined by reason, towards complete self-being and from madness come enigmatic yet decipherable messages of a transcendental power, otherwise con-demned to silence. There is not yet any interiority, for there is not yet any exte-rior, any 'otherness' for the soul. The soul goes out to seek adventure; it lives through adventures, but it does not know the real torment of seeking and the real danger of finding; such a soul never stakes itself; it does not yet know that it can lose itself, it never thinks of having to look for itself. Such an age is the age of the epic.

It is not absence of suffering, not security of being, which in such an age encloses men and deeds in contours that are both joyful and severe (for what is meaningless and tragic in the world has not grown larger since the begin-ning of time; it is only that the songs of comfort ring out more loudly or are more muffled): it is the adequacy of the deeds to the soul's inner demand for greatness, for unfolding, for wholeness. When the soul does not yet know any abyss within itself which may tempt it to fall or encourage it to discover path-less heights, when the divinity that rules the world and distributes the unknown and unjust gifts of destiny is not yet understood by man, but is familiar and close to him as a father is to his small child, then every action is only a well-fitting garment for the world. Being and destiny, adventure and accomplish-ment, life and essence are then identical concepts. For the question which engenders the formal answers of the epic is: how can life become essence? And if no one has ever equalled Homer, nor even approached him – for, strictly speaking, his works alone are epics – it is because he found the answer before the progress of the human mind through history had allowed the question to be asked. . . .

The epic individual, the hero of the novel, is the product of estrangement from the outside world. When the world is internally homogeneous, men do not differ qualitatively from one another; there are of course heroes and villains, pious men and criminals, but even the greatest hero is only a head taller than the mass of his fellows, and the wise man's dignified words are heard even by the most foolish. The autonomous life of interiority is possible and necessary only when the distinctions between men have made an unbridgeable chasm; when the gods are silent and neither sacrifices nor the ecstatic gift of tongues can solve their riddle; when the world of deeds separates itself from men and, because of this independence, becomes hollow and incapable of absorbing the true meaning of deeds in itself, incapable of becoming a symbol through deeds and dissolving them in turn into symbols; when interiority and adventure are forever divorced from one another.

The epic hero is, strictly speaking, never an individual. It is traditionally thought that one of the essential characteristics of the epic is the fact that its theme is not a personal destiny but the destiny of a community. And rightly so, for the completeness, the roundness of the value system which determines the epic cosmos creates a whole which is too organic for any part of it to become so enclosed within itself, so dependent upon itself, as to find itself as an interiority – i.e. to become a personality. The omnipotence of ethics, which posits every soul as autonomous and incomparable, is still unknown in such a world. When life *quae* life finds an immanent meaning in itself, the categories of the organic determine everything: an individual structure and physiognomy is simply the product of a balance between the part and the whole, mutually determining one another; it is never the product of polemical self-contemplation by the lost and lonely personality. The significance which an event can have in a world that is rounded in this way is therefore always a quantitative one; the series of adventures in which the event expresses itself has weight in so far as it is significant to a great organic life complex – a nation or a family.

Epic heroes have to be kings for different reasons from the heroes of tragedy (although these reasons are also formal). In tragedy the hero must be a king simply because of the need to sweep all the petty causalities of life from the ontological path of destiny – because the socially dominant figure is the only one whose conflicts, while retaining the sensuous illusion of a symbolic exis-tence, grow solely out of the tragic problem; because only such a figure can be surrounded, even as to the forms of its external appearance, with the required atmosphere of significant isolation.

What is a symbol in tragedy becomes a reality in the epic: the weight of the bonds linking an individual destiny to a totality. World destiny, which in tragedy is merely the number of noughts that have to be added to 1 to trans-form it into a million, is what actually gives the events of the epic their content; the epic hero, as bearer of his destiny, is not lonely, for this destiny connects him by indissoluble threads to the community whose fate is crystallised in his own.

As for the community, it is an organic – and therefore intrinsically mean-ingful – concrete totality; that is why the substance of adventure in an epic is always articulated, never strictly closed; this substance is an organism of infi-nite interior richness, and in this is identical or similar to the substance of other adventure.

The way Homer's epics begin in the middle and do not finish at the end is a reflextion of the truly epic mentality's total indifference to any form of archi-tectural construction, and the introduction of extraneous themes – such as that of Dietrich von Born in the Song of the Nibelungs – can never disturb this balance, for everything in the epic has a life of its own and derives its completeness from its own inner significance. The extraneous can calmly hold out its hand to the central; mere contact between concrete things creates concrete relationships, and the extraneous, because of its perspectival distance and its not yet realised richness, does not endanger the unity of the whole and yet has obvious organic existence.

Dante is the only great example in which we see the architectural clearly conquering the organic, and therefore he represents a historico-philosophical transition from the pure epic to the novel. In Dante there is still the perfect immanent distancelessness and completeness of the true epic, but his figures are already individuals, consciously and energetically placing themselves in opposition to a reality that is becoming closed to them, individuals who, through this opposition, become real personalities. The constituent principle of Dante's totality is a highly systematic one, abolishing the epic independence of the organic part-unities and transforming them into hierarchically ordered, autonomous parts. Such individuality, it is true, is found more in the secondary figures than in the hero. The tendency of each part-unity to retain its autonomous lyrical life (a category unknown and unknowable in the old epic) increases towards the periphery as the distance from the centre becomes greater.

The combination of the presuppositions of the epic and the novel and their synthesis to an *epopoeia* is based on the dual structure of Dante's world: the break between life and meaning is surpassed and cancelled by the coincidence of life and meaning in a present, actually experienced transcendence. To the postulate-free organic nature of the older epics, Dante opposes a hierarchy of fulfilled postulates. Dante – and only Dante – did not have to endow his hero with visible social superiority or with a heroic destiny that co-determined the destiny of the community – because his hero's lived experience was the symbolic unity of human destiny in general.

Art as Self-Consciousness in Man's Development

. . . for the emergence of every work of art it is precisely the concrete that is crucial in the reality represented. An art, which wishes to transcend objectively

Reprinted from: Georg Lukács, "Art as Self-Consciousness in Man's Development," in Berel Lang and Forrest Williams (eds.) *Marxism and Art: Writings in Aesthetics and Criticism*, New York: David Mackay, 1972, pp. 230–5.

its national bases, the class structure of its society, the stuff of the class war in it, and – subjectively – the stance of the author with respect to these issues, can do this only by asserting itself as art. It is meaningful scientifically to investigate the common, general regularities of an economic structure (indeed of all structures). For every work of art, however, only a certain concrete stage of development of a certain concrete structure is involved as an immediate object of creation. This undeniable truth was obscured for a long time in the idealistic account of the subject of art as the "universally human"; a healthy turn away from this was effected only by historical materialism (and its important predecessors) which called art back theoretically to the reality of its actual activity.

At the same time, an opposite distortion also entered the affair. Vulgar Marxism immediately identified the social genesis of art with its essential character, and thereby came at times to conclusions which were quite absurd, for example, that in the classless society, the great art works of the class societies will be unintelligible and unenjoyable. A neglect of the theory of representation and the meager conception of art as the expression of a certain position in the class struggle underlie this narrowing and distortion of the true facts of the matter. Because it is only with representation as an underlying principle of art that the universality of the substance of art, and with it that of art's form, can be theoretically founded. The social determination of the genesis of any creation and its necessary partisanship, can unfold themselves only given such a universality in the world reproduced and by its potential for being reproduced. Addressing this matter, Marx himself put the issue quite differently from the vulgarized versions. For him, too, the point of departure is naturally the genesis of society. After it is accomplished, however, the real work of aesthetics only begins: "The difficulty is not in understanding that Greek art and poetry are tied to certain social forms of development. The difficulty is that they still hold for us the pleasures of art, and stand in a sense as norm and unattainable ideal."

When the issue is put in this way, the conception of the common substratum emerges naturally. (This shows that the theory of a "common humanity" was a false answer to a legitimate question.) In a materialistic-dialectical conception of the process of history, the answer appears with out much difficulty: this common substratum is the continuity of development, the real transactional relation of the parts in it, the fact that the development does not originate in its entirely at the beginning, but always proceeds through the results of earlier stages which correspond to present needs, and incorporates them. The implications and incongruities of this development cannot be treated here. The bare delineation of the facts referred to indicates, however, the significant moment which the development of mankind makes available to art for articulation; it is precisely the task of that articulation to discover in the conereteness of the national and class-conscious immediate content anything novel which promises to become a lasting possession of mankind and which in fact becomes such a possession.

This definition is, however, not yet sufficiently concrete for the specific problems of art. The continuity of the development of mankind has its own solid, material basis. For art this serves only as a means for fulfilling its assignment: to give form to men, their fate, their behavior – all this understood in the broadest sense. With this the project, for the first time, assumes its true shape: the development brings out changes in the typical which for the most part, naturally, are transitory. Only a limited number of the newly emerging socio-historical types of people and situations are – in the good as well as in the bad sense – preserved in the memory of mankind, incorporated as a lasting possession. This process would be only a contextual selection with respect to which the qualification must still be made that from the standpoint of its "context-type," the object can only be situated relatively between the ephemeral and the perennial. No type belongs altogether to one or the other category; its membership is decided insofar as the artistic representation succeeds in grasping the typical properties in such a way that a moment of this durability – as good or evil – may be expressed. The mass of typical human characteristics preserved in man's historical development is thus surely greater than the number preserved live in the presentations of art. Accordingly, art has an objective basis for the durability of its typology in reality itself; if types of presentation do develop and persist, this is a result of its own activity. . . .

Men experience in great works of art the present and past of humanity, perspectives on its development. They experience them, however, not as external facts which one may acknowledge as more or less important, but as something essential for one's own life, as an important moment also of one's own individual existence. Marx, speaking about Homer's work, generalized this point:

A man cannot become a child again or he becomes childish. But doesn't the naiveté of a child please him, and doesn't he have to strive himself to reach a higher level in order to reproduce its truth? Doesn't its own character – in its natural reality – stir in the child's nature for each epoch? Why should man's historical childhood, where he appears at his most beautiful, transpire as a stage which will not recur, as an ephemeral charm? There are backward children and precocious children. Many ancient peoples fitted these categories. The Greeks were normal children. The attraction of their art for us does not consist in its opposition to the stage of society in which it evolved. It is much nearer the result of that stage and is inextricably tied to the fact that the unripe social conditions under which it developed and by which alone it could develop can never recur.

And it is clear from this alone that these hints of Marx do not refer only to the childhood of mankind, that much more, *every* period which is as such a moment in a peculiar and never recurring past, *can* be experienced.

We have already referred to the fact that the creative personality that figures in the emergence of the work of art is not simply or immediately identical with its everyday identity; that the artist's creating demands from him a generalizing on himself, a movement upward from his particular singularity to aesthetic uniqueness. We see now that the effectiveness of important works, at their most striking – when the formed content is alien in spatio-temporal terms, or in terms of nationality or class – conveys a broadening and deepening, a transcending of the unmediated everyday individuality. And above all, in this enrichment of the "I," stands the felicitous experience which genuinely great art provides.

It is generally acknowledged that the efficacy of art is a decisive moment in the movement upward of the individual enjoying it, a movement from the particularity of the merely subjective to uniqueness. It awakens realities which would have otherwise been inaccessible to him in the fullness presented by the work; his conceptions of man, of his real possibilities for good or evil realize an unparalleled broadening; alien worlds, in space and in time, historically and economically, reveal themselves to him in the inner dialectic of those for us in whose reflection something alien is of course experienced, but also, at the same time, something which can be placed actually in relation to his own life, to his own inwardness. (Where the latter is lacking, there develops an interest in the exotic, in a mere curiosity involving the purely external, often formal or technically artistic – but not, in essence, the aesthetic.)

The real content of this generalization, which (objectively as well as subjectively) deepens and enriches – but never departs from – the individuality, is the social character of the human personality. Aristotle already knew this precisely. It was first in the subjective idealism of the bourgeois epoch that this social substratum of the aesthetic process and of its force was mystified in the most diverse ways. The content of the work and, as a result of this, of its activity, is the experience of the individual in the manifold riches of life in society and – mediated by the essentially new features of clearly defined human relations – his existence as a part and a moment of man's development, as a concise abbreviation of it. This elevation of the particular subjectivity does not of itself produce a purely objective generality; to the contrary, it deepens the individuality, precisely because it brings it into this middle ground of what is unique. The subject in the audience imitates in his aesthetic pleasure every movement which receives objective form in the creation of the individuality of the work: a "reality" which, with respect to differentiation, is more intense than the experienced quality of the objective reality itself, and which in this intensity immediately reveals the essential features concealed in reality. Thus, the individuality of the work provides a basis for such processes. Hegel, in the concept of "pathos," conceives of the elevation of subjectivity into uniqueness on the part of the recipient as similar to the process sponsored by the creator. It is clear, then, that the genuinely aesthetic process depends on the soulful-spiritual-moral level to which the impulse in the work must rise in order to yield a genuinely aesthetic process: the uniqueness in the individuality of the work reflects the tendency toward uniqueness in the aesthetic act of the enjoyment of art.

Walter Benjamin

(1892–1940)

German philosophical thinker, social critic, and aesthete, Walter Benjamin established the persona of the art critic as cultural theorist. He was an associate of the Institute for Social Research at Frankfurt University, the birthplace of the philosophical movement known as the Frankfurt School, of which his friend Theodor Adorno was a leading member. His ideas have significantly influenced contemporary thought about the sociopolitical status of the literary work of art.

Walter Benjamin's reputation as an aesthetic theorist derives from a collection of writings which are focused more on the social, political, theological and philosophical uses of the artwork than they are on faith in an essential aesthetic nature. Benjamin's own theoretical orientation crosses the boundaries of disciplinary order and cultural tradition: his work is a paradoxical mixture of Jewish mysticism, historical materialism, as well as surrealist and Dadaistic subversions of systematic thought. It should come as no surprise that Benjamin's own prose defies conventional forms of exposition and argument, as if to suggest that the subject matter of the written text will not submit to preordained modes of rationalization. Indeed, Benjamin's doctoral thesis on baroque tragic drama (*Trauerspiel*) was rejected by both the philosophy and literature departments of the University of Frankfurt on the grounds of its unintelligibility within the discursive bounds of those fields.

In his work on *Trauerspiel*, subsequently published as *Origin of the German Tragic Drama* (1977), Benjamin discovered the figure of allegory – a form that is antagonistic towards the unitary spirit of the organic symbol – to be an analytical tool especially suited to his critical ambitions. Allegory, by expressing the non-identical relation of mind to nature, obviated the myth of history as a structured totality. It thereby revealed the need of would-be critics to approach the meaning of cultural history through the shocks and dislocations of actual temporal experience. For Benjamin, this subordination of the meaning of history to the destabilizing effect of its most traumatic events, exposed its intrinsically political nature. Likewise, much of Benjamin's life's work is founded on showing how art is political, not thematically, but in its productive capacity. In his famous 1936 essay "The Work of Art in its Age of

Mechanical Reproduction" Benjamin observes that the technologies of photography and the cinema have divested the artwork of its *aura*, its iconic status as a touchstone of historically conferred universality. This makes possible an understanding of artistic production as a cultural labor akin to the historical work of the proletariat. Indeed, Benjamin asserts the socially transformative efficacy of technologized cultural practices. This faith in the prospect for reforming the forms of lived cultural experience buttresses Benjamin's belief in the role of the literary author as a producer who is ethically bound to remake the forms that empower authorship.

In "The Author as Producer" (1934) Benjamin enthusiastically takes up Brecht's coinage of the term *Umfunktionierung* (functional transformation) to designate the means by which the literary artist might serve the class struggle. The bourgeois means of production inherent to the well "educated" forms of high culture might seem to doom any learned aesthetic technique to becoming a tool of regressive politics. But, following Brecht's idealism, Benjamin is decidedly optimistic about the prospect of art transcending its history. He argues that the responsible artist initiates an innovative (which is to say, critical) engagement of canonical aesthetic technique. In doing so, the artist makes formal technique a vehicle for transforming the social identity presupposed within it: "technical progress is for the author as producer the foundation of his political progress." As he goes on to say, the properly innovative artist, the "author as producer," comes to understand "his solidarity with the proletariat" ' and with other producers in the culture who would formerly have been strangers to the enterprise of artistic vision.

Suggested reading

Terry Eagleton, *Walter Benjamin, or Towards a Radical Criticism*, London: Verso, 1981.

The Author as Producer

You will remember how Plato, in his model state, deals with poets. He banishes them from it in the public interest. He had a high conception of the power of poetry, but he believed it harmful, superfluous – in a *perfect* community, of course. The question of the poet's right to exist has not often, since then, been posed with the same emphasis; but today it poses itself. Probably it is only seldom posed in this *form*, but it is more or less familiar to you all as the question of the autonomy of the poet, of his freedom to write whatever he pleases.

Reprinted from: Walter Benjamin, *Reflections: Essays, Aphorisms, Autobiographical Writings*, translated by Edmund Jephcott, edited by Peter Demetz, New York: Harcourt Brace Jovanovich, 1978, pp. 220–1, 228–31, 233–6.

You are not disposed to grant him this autonomy. You believe that the present social situation compels him to decide in whose service he is to place his activity. The bourgeois writer of entertainment literature does not acknowledge this choice. You must prove to him that, without admitting it, he is working in the service of certain class interests. A more advanced type of writer does recognize this choice. His decision, made on the basis of a class struggle, is to side with the proletariat. That puts an end to his autonomy. His activity is now decided by what is useful to the proletariat in the class struggle. Such writing is commonly called *tendentious*.

There you have the catchword around which has long circled a debate familiar to you. Its familiarity tells you how unfruitful it has been, for it has not advanced beyond the monotonous reiteration of arguments for and against: *on the one hand*, the correct political line is demanded of the poet; *on the other*, it is justifiable to expect his work to have quality. Such a formulation is of course unsatisfactory as long as the connection between the two factors, political line and quality, has not been *perceived*. Of course, the connection can be asserted dogmatically. You can declare: a work that shows the correct political tendency need show no other quality. You can also declare: a work that exhibits the correct tendency must of necessity have every other quality.

. . . I should like to show you that the tendency of a literary work can only be politically correct if it is also literarily correct. That is to say, the politically correct tendency includes a literary tendency. And, I would add straightaway, this literary tendency, which is implicitly or explicitly contained in every *correct* political tendency of a work includes its literary quality *because* it includes its literary *tendency*. . . .

For the transformation of the forms and instruments of production in the way desired by a progressive intelligentsia – that is, one interested in freeing the means of production and serving the class struggle – Brecht coined the term *Umfunktionierung* (functional transformation). He was the first to make of intellectuals the far-reaching demand not to supply the apparatus of production without, to the utmost extent possible, changing it in accordance with socialism. "The publication of the *Versuche*," the author writes in introducing the series of writings bearing this title, "occurred at a time when certain works ought no longer to be individual experiences (have the character of works) but should, rather, concern the use (transformation) of certain institutes and institutions." It is not spiritual renewal, as fascists proclaim, that is desirable: technical innovations are suggested. I shall come back to these innovations. I should like to content myself here with a reference to the decisive difference between the mere supplying of a productive apparatus and its transformation. And I should like to preface my discussion of the "New Matter-of-factness" with the proposition that to supply a productive apparatus without – to the utmost extent possible – changing it would still be a highly censurable course even if the material with which it is supplied seemed to be of a revolutionary nature. For we are faced with the fact – of which the past decade in Germany has furnished an abundance of examples – that the bourgeois apparatus of production and publication can assimilate astonishing quantities of revolutionary themes, indeed, can propagate them without calling its own existence, and the existence of the class that owns it, seriously into question. This remains true at least as long as it is supplied by hack writers, even if they be revolutionary hacks. I define the hack writer as the man who abstains in principle from alienating the productive apparatus from the ruling class by improving it in ways serving the interests of socialism. And I further maintain that a considerable proportion of so-called left-wing literature possessed no other social function than to wring from the political situation a continuous stream of novel effects for the entertainment of the public. This brings me to the New Matter-of-factness. Its stock in trade was reportage. Let us ask ourselves to whom this technique was useful.

For the sake of clarity I shall place its photographic form in the foreground, but what is true of this can also be applied to the literary form. Both owe the extraordinary increase in their popularity to the technology of publication: the radio and the illustrated press. Let us think back to Dadaism. The revolutionary strength of Dadaism consisted in testing art for its authenticity. Still lifes put together from tickets, spools of cotton, cigarette butts, that were linked with painted elements. The whole thing was put in a frame. And thereby the public was shown: look, your picture frame ruptures time; the tiniest authentic fragment of daily life says more than painting. Just as the bloody fingerprint of a murderer on the page of a book says more than the text. Much of this revolutionary content has gone on into photomontage. You need only think of the work of John Heartfield, whose technique made the book cover into a political instrument. But now follow the path of photography further. What do you see? It becomes ever more *nuancé*, ever more modern, and the result is that it can no longer depict a tenement block or a refuse heap without transfiguring it. It goes without saying that photography is unable to say anything about a power station or a cable factory other than this: what a beautiful world! *A Beautiful World* – that is the title of the well-known picture anthology by Renger-Patsch, in which we see New Matter-of-fact photography at its peak. For it has succeeded in transforming even abject poverty, by recording it in a fashionably perfected manner, into an object of enjoyment. For if it is an economic function of photography to restore to mass consumption, by fashionable adaptation; subjects that had earlier withdrawn themselves from it –

springtime, famous people, foreign countries – it is one of its political functions to renew from within – that is, fashionably – the world as it is.

Here we have a flagrant example of what it means to supply a productive
apparatus without changing it. To change it would have meant to overthrow
another of the barriers, to transcend another of the antitheses, that fetter the
production of intellectuals, in this case the barrier between writing and image.
What we require of the photographer is the ability to give his picture the
caption that wrenches it from modish commerce and gives it a revolutionary
useful value. But we shall make this demand most emphatically when we – the
writers – take up photography. Here, too, therefore, technical progress is for
the author as producer the foundation of his political progress. In other words,
only by transcending the specialization in the process of production that in the
bourgeois view, constitutes its order can one make this production politically
useful; and the barriers imposed by specialization must be breached jointly by
the productive forces that they were set up to divide. The author as producer
discovers – in discovering his solidarity with the proletariat – simultaneously
his solidarity with certain other producers who earlier seemed scarcely to
concern him. I have spoken of the photographer; I shall very briefly insert a
word of Eisler's on the musician: "In the development of music, too, both in
production and in reproduction, we must learn to perceive an ever-increasing
process of rationalization. . . . The phonograph record, the sound film, juke-
boxes can purvey top-quality music . . . canned as a commodity. The consequence of this process of rationalization is that musical reproduction is
consigned to ever-diminishing, but also ever more highly qualified groups of
specialists. The crisis of the commercial concert is the crisis of an antiquated
form of production made obsolete by new technical inventions." The task
therefore consisted of an *Umfunktionierung* of the form of the concert that had
to fulfill two conditions: to eliminate the antithesis firstly between performers
and listeners and secondly between technique and content. On this Eisler
makes the following illuminating observation: "One must beware of overesti-
mating orchestral music and considering it the only high art. Music without
words gained its great importance and its full extent only under capitalism."
This means that the task of changing the concert is impossible without the
collaboration of the word. It alone can effect the transformation, as Eisler
formulates it, of a concert into a political meeting. But that such a transformation does indeed represent a peak of musical and literary technique. Brecht and
Eisler prove with the didactic play *The Measures Taken*. . . .

Tragedies and operas are constantly being written that apparently have a
well-tried theatrical apparatus at their disposal, but in reality they do nothing
but supply a derelict one. "The lack of clarity about their situation that

prevails among musicians, writers, and critics," says Brecht, "has immense consequences that are far too little considered. For, thinking that they are in possession of an apparatus that in reality possesses them, they defend an apparatus over which they no longer have any control and that is no longer, as they still believe, a means for the producers, but has become a means against the producers." This theater, with its complicated machinery, its gigantic supporting staff, its sophisticated effects, has become a "means against the producers" not least in seeking to enlist them in the hopeless competitive struggle in which film and radio have enmeshed it. This theater – whether in its educating or its entertaining role; the two are complementary – is that of a sated class for which everything it touches becomes a stimulant. Its position is lost. Not so that of a theater that, instead of competing with newer instruments of publication, seeks to use and learn from them, in short, to enter into debate with them. This debate the epic theater has made it own affair. It is, measured by the present state of development of film and radio, the contemporary form.

In the interest of this debate Brecht fell back on the most primitive elements of the theater. He contented himself, by and large, with a podium. He dispensed with wide-ranging plots. He thus succeeded in changing the functional connection between stage and public, text and performance, director and actor. Epic theater, he declared, had to portray situations, rather than develop plots. It obtains such situations, as we shall see presently, by interrupting the plot. I remind you here of the songs, which have their chief function in interrupting the action. Here – in the principle of interruption – epic theater, as you see, takes up a procedure that has become familiar to you in recent years from film and radio, press and photography. I am speaking of the procedure of montage: the superimposed element disrupts the context in which it is inserted. But that this procedure has here a special right, perhaps even a perfect right, allow me briefly to indicate. The interruption of action, on account of which Brecht described his theater as *epic*, constantly counteracts an illusion in the audience. For such illusion is a hindrance to a theater that proposes to make use of elements of reality in experimental rearrangements. But it is at the end, not the beginning, of the experiment that the situation appears – a situation that, in this or that form, is always ours. It is not brought home to the spectator but distanced from him. He recognizes it as the real situation, not with satisfaction, as in the theater of naturalism, but with astonishment. Epic theater, therefore, does not reproduce situations; rather, it discovers them. This discovery is accomplished by means of the interruption of sequences. Only interruption here has not the character of a stimulant but an organizing function. It arrests the action in its course, and thereby compels the listener to adopt an attitude *vis-à-vis* the process, the actor *vis-à-vis* his role. I should like to show you through an example how Brecht's discovery and use of the *gestus* is nothing but the restoration of the method of montage decisive in radio and film, from an often merely modish procedure to a human event. Imagine a family scene: the wife is just about to grab a bronze sculpture to throw it at her daughter; the father is opening the window to call for help. At this moment a stranger enters. The process is interrupted; what appears in its place is the situation on which the stranger's eyes now fall: agitated faces, open window, disordered furniture. There are eyes, however, before which the more usual scenes of present-day existence do not look very different: the eyes of the epic dramatist.

To the total dramatic artwork he opposes the dramatic laboratory. He makes use in a new way of the great, ancient opportunity of the theater – to expose what is present. At the center of his experiment is man. Present-day man; a reduced man, therefore, chilled in a chilly environment. Since, however, this is the only one we have, it is in our interest to know him. He is subjected to tests, examinations. What emerges is this: events are alterable not at their climaxes, not by virtue and resolution, but only in their strictly habitual course, by reason and practice. To construct from the smallest elements of behavior what in Aristotelian dramaturgy is called "action" is the purpose of epic theater. Its means are therefore more modest than those of traditional theater; likewise its aims. It is less concerned with filling the public with feelings, even seditious ones, than with alienating it in an enduring manner, through thinking, from the conditions in which it lives. It may be noted, by the way, that there is no better start for thinking than laughter. And, in particular, convulsion of the diaphragm usually provides better opportunities for thought than convulsion of the soul. Epic theater is lavish only in occasions for laughter.

Herbert Marcuse
(1898–1979)

Herbert Marcuse was a German philosopher and social critic whose name is often associated with the New Left and the youth movements of the 1960s and 1970s. He was born in Berlin just before the turn of the century, and as a college student, he took part in the Berlin Revolution at the end of the First World War. This episode inaugurated his life-long commitment to leftist politics, although he never officially joined the Communist Party. In 1932 Marcuse became a member of the Institute for Social Research, or the Frankfurt School, as the members of the Institute came to be known. By the time Marcuse joined the group, however, they had moved to Geneva in order to escape the newly empowered Nazis, and within a few years the Institute moved on to Paris and then to New York. After the Second World War many members of the Frankfurt School, including Max Horkheimer and Theodor Adorno, returned to Germany, but Marcuse remained in the United States, teaching first at Brandeis and then at the University of California in San Diego. The members of the Frankfurt School generally agreed with Marx's diagnosis of the evils of capitalism and with the principles of Communism that Marx espoused. Yet they were considerably more pessimistic than most Communists of the time because they believed that Russian or Eastern Communism was a totalitarian perversion of true Communism. They felt that modern capitalism had succeeded in managing and controlling the working class, and, consequently, that it would be unrealistic to expect the working class in the West to lead a Communist revolution.

In an influential book entitled *One Dimensional Man* Marcuse describes the techniques of social control through which capitalism has produced what he calls a "totally administered" society. At the heart of this program of social control, he argues, is consumerism. In consumerism, the production and consumption of goods becomes a goal in itself; true human needs and possible satisfactions are ignored or suppressed while false needs are created, often with the help of mass media and advertising, in order to sustain the cycle of production and consumption. The result, Marcuse argues, is a "pattern of *one-dimensional thought and behavior* in which ideas, aspirations, and objectives" that do not fit with the dominant culture are either suppressed or reduced to the logic of that culture (1964: 12). Because the system of social control is so pervasive and complete, conventional political resistance is extremely difficult, if not impossible. This led Adorno and other members of the Frankfurt School to assume that it would be impossible to offer any kind of positive political program in such a social climate. All social critics can do, they said, is negate the false images of happiness that fuel the consumer society. Marcuse, however, remained more hopeful and speculated that positive social change might be brought about by a coalition of social outsiders who have somehow been alienated by the system. It was this vision of a revolution led by a federation of alienated outsiders that inspired the radicals of the 1960s, who hoped that racial minorities, alienated students, and others who had dropped out of the system, might band together to become a political force.

Marcuse was also more optimistic than other members of the Frankfurt School in the way he described the social function of art. In books such as *Eros and Civilization* and *The Aesthetic Dimension*, he argues that art embodies the kinds of true needs and pleasures that consumer culture inevitably suppresses or transforms into an advertised commodity. Drawing on the psychology of Sigmund Freud and the philosophy of Fredrich Schiller, Marcuse claims that art represents the return of repressed pleasures, the return of pleasures that had to be repressed as humanity developed the modern work ethic allowing it to overcome scarcity and hardship. When culture has been freed from scarcity, Marcuse argues, art can illustrate the kind of freedom that will allow humanity to reconcile and reintegrate pleasure and reason. Art not only revives the sensuous pleasures that a fully administered society has repressed, but also shows us how reason can heighten and intensify sensuous pleasures rather than negate them. In the following excerpt from *The Aesthetic Dimension*, Marcuse describes the way in which aesthetic form, the stylization that gives works of art their beauty or other distinctive aesthetic qualities, works to express repressed sensuality. Marcuse describes this process of putting realistic subject matter in artistic form as sublimation. (According to Freud, sublimation works by directing sexual energies toward non-sexual "higher" goals.) However, because artistic form becomes the defining feature of the work of art, it works not to hide reality but to reveal the repressed pleasures of the senses. Hence the paradox: art sublimates reality in order to desublimate human desire.

Reference

Herbert Marcuse, *One Dimensional Man*, Boston: Beacon Press, 1964.

Suggested reading

Robert Pippin, Andrew Feenberg, and Charles P. Webel (eds.) *Marcuse: Critical Theory and the Promise of Utopia*, South Hadley, Mass.: Bergin and Garvey, 1988.

From *The Aesthetic Dimension*

I shall submit the following thesis: the radical qualities of art, that is to say, its indictment of the established reality and its invocation of the beautiful image (*schöner Schein*) of liberation are grounded precisely in the dimensions where art *transcends* its social determination and emancipates itself from the given universe of discourse and behavior while preserving its overwhelming presence. Thereby art creates the realm in which the subversion of experience proper to art becomes possible: the world formed by art is recognized as a reality which is suppressed and distorted in the given reality. This experience culminates in extreme situations (of love and death, guilt and failure, but also joy, happiness, and fulfillment) which explode the given reality in the name of a truth normally denied or even unheard. The inner logic of the work of art terminates in the emergence of another reason, another sensibility, which defy the rationality and sensibility incorporated in the dominant social institutions.

Under the law of the aesthetic form, the given reality is necessarily *sublimated*: the immediate content is stylized, the "data" are reshaped and reordered in accordance with the demands of the art form, which requires that even the representation of death and destruction invoke the need for hope – a need rooted in the new consciousness embodied in the work of art.

Aesthetic sublimation makes for the affirmative, reconciling component of art, though it is at the same time a vehicle for the critical, negating function of art. The transcendence of immediate reality shatters the reified objectivity of established social relations and opens a new dimension of experience: rebirth of the rebellious subjectivity. Thus, on the basis of aesthetic sublimation, a *desublimation* takes place in the perception of individuals – in their feelings, judgments, thoughts; an invalidation of dominant norms, needs, and values. With all its affirmative-ideological features, art remains a dissenting force.

We can tentatively define "aesthetic form" as the result of the transformation of a given content (actual or historical, personal or social fact) into a self-contained whole: a poem, play, novel, etc.[1] The work is thus "taken out" of the constant process of reality and assumes a significance and truth of its own. The aesthetic transformation is achieved through a reshaping of language, perception, and understanding so that they reveal the essence of reality in its appearance: the repressed potentialities of man and nature. The work of art thus re-presents reality while accusing it.[2]

Reprinted from: Herbert Marcuse, *The Aesthetic Dimension: Toward a Critique of Marxist Aesthetics*, Boston: Beacon Press, 1978, pp. 6–11, 16–18.

The critical function of art, its contribution to the struggle for liberation, resides in the aesthetic form. A work of art is authentic or true not by virtue of its content (i.e., the "correct" representation of social conditions), nor by its "pure" form, but by the content having become form.

True, the aesthetic form removes art from the actuality of the class struggle – from actuality pure and simple. The aesthetic form constitutes the autonomy of art *vis-à-vis* "the given." However, this dissociation does not produce "false consciousness" or mere illusion but rather a counter-consciousness: negation of the realistic-conformist mind.

Aesthetic form, autonomy, and truth are interrelated. Each is a socio-historical phenomenon, and each *transcends* the socio-historical arena. While the latter limits the autonomy of art it does so without invalidating the *trans*-historical truths expressed in the work. The truth of art lies in its power to break the monopoly of established reality (i.e., of those who established it) to *define* what is *real*. In this rupture, which is the achievement of the aesthetic form, the fictitious world of art appears as true reality.

Art is committed to that perception of the world which alienates individuals from their functional existence and performance in society – it is committed to an emancipation of sensibility, imagination, and reason in all spheres of subjectivity and objectivity. The aesthetic transformation becomes a vehicle of recognition and indictment. But this achievement presupposes a degree of autonomy which withdraws art from the mystifying power of the given and frees it for the expression of its own truth. Inasmuch as man and nature are constituted by an unfree society, their repressed and distorted potentialities can be represented only in an *estranging* form. The world of art is that of another *Reality Principle*, of estrangement – and only as estrangement does art fulfill a *cognitive* function: it communicates truths not communicable in any other language; it *contradicts*.

However, the strong affirmative tendencies toward reconciliation with the established reality coexist with the rebellious ones. I shall try to show that they are not due to the specific class determination of art but rather to the redeeming character of the *catharsis*. The catharsis itself is grounded in the power of aesthetic form to call fate by its name, to demystify its force, to give the word to the victims – the power of recognition which gives the individual a modicum of freedom and fulfillment in the realm of unfreedom. The interplay between the affirmation and the indictment of that which is, between ideology and truth, pertains to the very structure of art.[3] But in the authentic works, the affirmation does not cancel the indictment: reconciliation and hope still preserve the memory of things past.

The affirmative character of art has yet another source: it is in the commitment of art to Eros, the deep affirmation of the Life Instincts in their fight

against instinctual and social oppression. The permanence of art, its historical immortality throughout the millenia of destruction, bears witness to this
commitment.

Art stands under the law of the given, while transgressing this law. The
concept of art as an essentially autonomous and negating productive force contradicts the notion which sees art as performing an essentially dependent
affirmative-ideological function, that is to say, glorifying and absolving the
existing society.[4] Even the militant bourgeois literature of the eighteenth century remains ideological: the struggle of the ascending class with the nobility
is primarily over issues of bourgeois morality. The lower classes play only a
marginal role, if any. With a few notable exceptions, this literature is not one
of class struggle. According to this point of view, the ideological character of
art can be remedied today only by grounding art in revolutionary praxis and
in the *Weltanschauung* of the proletariat. . . .

The fact that a work truly represents the interests or the outlook of the
proletariat or of the bourgeoisie does not yet make it an authentic work of art.
This "material" quality may facilitate its reception, may lend it greater concreteness, but it is in no way constitutive. The universality of art cannot be
grounded in the world and world outlook of a particular class, for art envisions
a concrete universal, humanity (*Menschlichkeit*), which no particular class can
incorporate, not even the proletariat, Marx's "universal class." The inexorable
entanglement of joy and sorrow, celebration and despair, Eros and Thanatos
cannot be dissolved into problems of class struggle. History is also grounded
in nature. And Marxist theory has the least justification to ignore the metabo-
lism between the human being and nature, and to denounce the insistence on
this natural soil of society as a regressive ideological conception.

The emergence of human beings as "species beings" – men and women
capable of living in that community of freedom which is the potential of the
species – this is the subjective basis of a classless society. Its realization presupposes a radical transformation of the drives and needs of the individuals:
an organic development within the socio-historical. Solidarity would be on
weak grounds were it not rooted in the instinctual structure of individuals. In
this dimension, men and women are confronted with psycho-physical forces
which they have to make their own without being able to overcome the natu-
ralness of these forces. This is the domain of the primary derives: of libidinal
and destructive energy. Solidarity and community have their basis in the subordination of destructive and aggressive energy to the social emancipation of
the life instincts.

Marxism has too long neglected the radical political potential of this
dimension, though the revolutionizing of the instinctual structure is a prerequisite for a change in the system of needs, the mark of a socialist society as

qualitative difference. Class society knows only the appearance, the image of the qualitative difference; this image, divorced from praxis, has been preserved in the realm of art. In the aesthetic form, the autonomy of art constitutes itself. It was forced upon art through the separation of mental and material labor, as a result of the prevailing relations of domination. Dissociation from the process of production became a refuge and a vantage point from which to denounce the reality established through domination.

Nevertheless society remains present in the autonomous realm of art in several ways: first of all as the "stuff" for the aesthetic representation which, past and present, is transformed in this representation. This is the historicity of the conceptual, linguistic, and imaginable material which the tradition transmits to the artists and with or against which they have to work; secondly, as the scope of the actually available possibilities of struggle and liberation; thirdly as the specific position of art in the social division of labor, especially in the separation of intellectual and manual labor through which artistic activity, and to a great extent also its reception, become the privilege of an "elite" removed from the material process of production.

Notes

1   See my *Counterrevolution and Revolt* (Boston: Beacon Press, 1972), p. 81.

2   Ernst Fischer in *Auf den Spuren den Wirklichkeit; sechs Essays* (Reinbek: Rowohlt, 1968) recognizes in the "will to form" (*Wille zur Gestalt*) the will to transcend the actual: negation of that which is, and presentiment (*Ahnung*) of a freer and purer existence. In this sense, art is the "irreconcilable, the resistance of the human being to its vanishing in the [established] order and systems" (p. 67).

3   "Two antagonistic attitudes toward the powers that be are prevalent in literature: *resistance* and *submission*. Literature is certainly not mere ideology and does not merely express a social consciousness that invokes the illusion of harmony, assuring the individuals that everything is as it ought to be, and that nobody has the right to expect fate to give him more than he receives. To be sure, literature has time and again justified established social relationships; nevertheless, it has always kept alive that human yearning which cannot find gratification in the existing society. Grief and sorrow are essential elements of bourgeois literature" (Leo Lowenthal, *Das Bild des Menschen in der Literatur* [Neuwied: Luchterhand, 1966] pp. 14f.). (Published in English as *Literature and the Image of Man* [Boston: Beacon Press 1957].)

4   See my essay "The Affirmative Character of Culture" in *Negations* (Boston: Beacon Press, 1968).

Theodor W. Adorno

(1903–1969)

Adorno's name and career are justly intertwined with the Frankfurt School's Institute for Social Research. He attached himself to the Frankfurt School in the late 1920s and assumed leadership of it in 1958. Helmut Dubiel (*Theory and Politics: Studies in the Development of Critical Theory*) has characterized the Frankfurt School as a foundational site for contemporary "critical theory", fostering research, as it did, within the disciplines of literature, philosophy, and social theory. Critical theory, according to the scholars affiliated with the institute in the 1940s and 1950s (Walter Benjamin, Max Horkheimer, Herbert Marcuse, among others), is a "research program" rooted in the conviction that culture is a proper object of scientific study. The methodology of the Frankfurt School was interdisciplinary, dialectical in a Hegelian vein, and inspired by Marx's critique of capitalism. Adorno's activities as a "researcher" for and as director of the School, focused on better understanding the place of the artwork in social life. His thinking is infused with a zealous belief in the critical purposes that are served by modern art.

It can be fairly stated that Adorno's work as a critical theorist culminates in the *Aesthetic Theory*, despite the fact that it is an incomplete and posthumous text. Edited and assembled by Adorno's wife Gretel and his student Rolf Teidemann, the text still awaited a final "organizational" revision at the time of Adorno's death. *Aesthetic Theory* appeared in 1970, the first of twenty-three volumes of Adorno's *Gesammelte Schriften*. In it can be found all of the burning issues of Adorno's personal career and most of the long-standing problems that have occupied theorists of art since Plato. While the text is typically a montage of short, almost epigrammatic argumentative skirmishes, it reflects the full scope of our experience with works of art in so far as they challenge our most skeptical philosophical ambitions to foster beneficent change in the nature of social life.

In the early pages of Adorno's "Draft Introduction" (not excerpted here), he announces the important thematic and methodological principle that art, as a form of knowledge, derives "from the realm of the particular . . . the particular being more than a mere specimen of the universal." Adorno declares the "obsolescence of traditional aesthetics," with its tendency to fetishize totality, and its bid for abstract universality. For Adorno both are evasions of the realm of material practice. By the same token, Adorno resists the fetishization of form and the reification of craft. Instead, his ambition is to foster an aesthetics "that will provide the capacity for reflection which art on its own is hardly able to achieve" (p. 341). Adorno does not give up on the "truth content" of art. But he would disabuse us of the attitude that equates the truth of the artwork with the mere manifestation of its material form or with whatever philosophical content can be "pumped into" it by its creator or by an avid theorist. "Second reflection," as Adorno likes to call the operative cognition of the aesthetic theorist, is a thought process that neither succumbs to alienation from the object nor dwells hermetically in its formal features. On the contrary: "The more art . . . is driven to reflect on its own presuppositions and when possible to absorb into its own form such reflection as if it were counterpoison, the more skeptical it becomes toward the presupposition of having self-consciousness imposed on it externally" (p. 339). Adorno's vehemence on behalf of critical reflection is meant as a check against the insufficiently dialectical temptation to indulge concreteness or abstraction as mutually exclusive registers of the artwork.

Adorno's campaign against the tyrannies of categorical taste and judgment, his willingness to see art as belonging to a larger "context of problems" (*Problemzusammenhang*), and his conviction about the historical efficacy of aesthetic theory, constitute an important and compelling counterpoint to contemporary curricula within literary study: cultural studies, popular culture, gender studies. From an Adornian point of view, these have, somewhat perversely, sought to make aesthetic value subordinate to the social, material cultural, or political features of literary texts.

Note: Pages cited are from the edition from which the excerpts are taken, details of which are given in the footnote.

Suggested reading

Gillian Rose, *The Melancholy Science: An Introduction to the Thought of Theodor W. Adorno*, New York: Columbia University Press, 1979.

Draft Introduction

The dilemma of aesthetics appears immanently in the fact that it can be constituted neither from above nor from below, neither from concepts nor from aconceptual experience. The only possibility for aesthetics beyond this

Reprinted from: Theodor Adorno, *Aesthetic Theory*, edited by Gretel Adorno and Rolf Tiedemann, translated by Robert Hullot-Kentor, Minneapolis: University of Minnesota Press, 1997, pp. 343, 345–8.

miserable alternative is the philosophical insight that fact and concept are not polar opposites but mediated reciprocally in one another. This must be appropriated by aesthetics for art again stands in need of aesthetics now that criticism has shown itself to be so disoriented by false and arbitrary judgments that it fails *vis-à-vis* art. Yet if aesthetics is to amount neither to art-alien prescriptions nor to the inconsequential classification of what it happens upon, then it is only conceivable as dialectical aesthetics; dialectical method is not unsuitably defined as the refusal to rest content with the diremption of the deductive and inductive that dominates rigid, indurative thought, and this is expressly rejected by the earliest formulations of dialectics in German idealism, those of Fichte. Aesthetics must no more lag behind art than behind philosophy. . . .

Aesthetic theory, wary of a priori construction and cautious of an increasing abstractness, has as its arena the experience of the aesthetic object. The artwork is not to be known simply externally but demands of theory that, at whatever level of abstraction, it be understood. Philosophically the concept of understanding and categories such as empathy have been compromised by Dilthey and his followers. If one sets aside such theorems and insists on an understanding of artworks that would be knowledge determined strictly through their objectivity, difficulties amass. In advance it must be admitted that, if knowledge is anywhere achieved in layers, this is so in aesthetics. Any fixation of the starting point of this layering in experience would be arbitrary. It reaches back far behind aesthetic sublimation, where it is indivisible from lived perception. Experience remains related to such perception, while at the same time it only becomes what it is by distancing itself from immediacy, into which it stands permanently in danger of sinking back, as happens to those excluded from education who use the present rather than the past tense when narrating the events of a film or play; yet, without any trace of such immediacy, artistic experience is no less in vain than when it capitulates to immediacy. In Alexandrian fashion it circumvents the claim to an immediacy of existence that is registered by every artwork, whether it wants to or not. Preartistic experience of the aesthetic is indeed false, in that it identifies and counteridentifies with artworks as in empirical life and, if possible, even to a heightened degree, and thus precisely by way of a comportment that subjectivism holds to be the instrument of aesthetic experience. By approaching the artwork aconceptually, this comportment remains trapped within the radius of taste, and its relation to the work is no less oblique than if it misused art to illustrate philosophical positions. The malleable, readily identifying sensibility collapses when faced with the severity of the artwork; yet obdurate thought cheats itself of the element of receptivity, without which it is no longer thought. Preartistic experience requires projection[17] yet aesthetic experience

– precisely by virtue of the a priori primacy of subjectivity in it – is a coun-
termovement to the subject. It demands something on the order of the self-
denial of the observer, his capacity to address or recognize what aesthetic
objects themselves enunciate and what they conceal. Aesthetic experience first
of all places the observer at a distance from the object. This resonates in the
idea of disinterested observation. Philistines are those whose relation to artworks is ruled by whether and to what degree they can, for example, put themselves in the place of the actors as they come forth; this is what all parts of the
culture industry are based on and they foster it insistently in their customers.
The more artistic experience possesses its objects and the closer it approaches
them in a certain sense, the farther it is at the same time shifted away from
them; artistic enthusiasm is art-alien. It is thus that aesthetic experience, as
Schopenhauer knew, breaks through the spell of obstinate self-preservation; it
is the model of a stage of consciousness in which the I no longer has its happiness in its interests, or, ultimately, in its reproduction. – That, however, to
follow the course of action in a novel or a drama and note the various motivations, or adequately to recognize the thematic content of a painting, does not
amount to understanding the works is as obvious as that they cannot be understood apart from such aspects. There are exact scholarly descriptions of artworks, even analyses – thematic analyses of music, for example – that miss
everything essential. A second layer of understanding is that of the intention
of the work, that which the work itself states and what traditional aesthetics
calls its idea, an example of which would be the guiltiness of subjective morality in Ibsen's *Wild Duck*. The intention of the work is, however, not equivalent
with its content, and thus its understanding remains provisional. The question
remains at this level of understanding whether the intention is realized in the
structure of the work; whether the form carries out the play of forces, the
antagonisms, that objectively govern the work over and beyond its intention.
Moreover, the understanding of the intention does not yet grasp the truth
content of the work. For this reason the understanding of works is essentially
a process, one apart from all biographical accidentalness and in no way comparable to that ominous lived experience [*Erlebnis*] that is supposed to deliver
up all secrets with a wave of the magic wand and indeed provide a doorway
into the object. Understanding has as its idea that one become conscious of the
artwork's content by way of the full experience [*Erfahrung*] of it. This concerns the work's relation to its material, to its appearance and intention, as
much as it concerns its own truth or falseness in terms of the artworks' specific logic, which instructs as to the differentiation between what is true and
false in them. Artworks are understood only when their experience is brought
to the level of distinguishing between true and not true or, as a preliminary

stage, between correct and incorrect. Critique is not externally added into aesthetic experience but, rather, is immanent to it. The comprehension of an artwork as a complexion of truth brings the work into relation with its untruth, for there is no artwork that does not participate in the untruth external to it, that of the historical moment. Aesthetics that does not move within the perspective of truth fails its task; usually it is culinary. Because the element of truth is essential to artworks, they participate in knowledge, and this defines the only legitimate relation to them. Consigning them to irrationality profanes what is important in them under the pretext of what is putatively ultimate. The knowledge of artworks is guided by their own cognitive constitution: They are the form of knowledge that is not knowledge of an object. This paradox is also the paradox of artistic experience. Its medium is the obviousness of the incomprehensible. This is the comportment of artists; it is the objective reason back of their often apocryphal and helpless theories. The task of a philosophy of art is not so much to explain away the element of incomprehensibility, which speculative philosophy has almost invariably sought to do, but rather to understand the incomprehensibility itself. This incomprehensibility persists as the character of art, and it alone protects the philosophy of art from doing violence to art. The question of comprehensibility becomes urgent to the extreme in the face of the contemporary production of art. For the category of comprehensibility, if it is not to be situated in the subject and thus condemned to relativity, postulates something objectively comprehensible in the artwork. If the artwork assumes the expression of incomprehensibility and in its name destroys its own internal comprehensibility, the traditional hierarchy of comprehension collapses. Its place is taken by reflection on art's enigmatic character. Yet, it is precisely the so-called literature of the absurd – a pastiche concept tacked onto such heterogeneous material that it now serves only the misunderstanding of facile agreement – that proves that understanding, meaning, and content are not equivalents. The absence of meaning becomes intention, though not always with the same consequence. A play like Ionesco's *Rhinoceros*, for instance, though it insists that common sense accede in the metamorphosis of people into rhinos, permits the clear inference of what used to be called the idea of an artwork in its internal opposition to sheepish, standardized consciousness, to which the well-functioning I is more successfully adapted than one who has not completely kept up with dominant instrumental rationality. The intention of radical absurdity may have originated in art's need to translate the condition of metaphysical meaninglessness into a language of art that would cast meaning aside; thus it was, perhaps, a polemical act against Sartre, whose works firmly and subjectively posit this metaphysical experience. In Beckett the negative metaphysical content affects the content along with the form. The work does not, however, thereby become something simply incomprehensible; the well-founded refusal of its author to offer explanations for so-called symbols is faithful to an aesthetic tradition that has elsewhere been dismissed. A relation, not identity, operates between the negativity of the metaphysical content and the eclipsing of the aesthetic content. The metaphysical negation no longer permits an aesthetic form that would itself produce metaphysical affirmation; and yet this negation is nevertheless able to become aesthetic content and determine the form.

Hans-Georg Gadamer
(1900–)

A student of Martin Heidegger and steeped in the German hermeneutical tradition, Gadamer takes a stance toward the aesthetic that is best characterized as phenomenological. Like Heidegger and Merleau-Ponty, Gadamer sees the philosopher's engagement with the formal dimensions of art works – paintings, sculptures, poems, novels – as a legitimate arena within which to pose philosophical questions. He therefore commits himself to answering the question, What effect does the work of art have on human consciousness? Gadamer believes that Plato mistrusted the artist because he mistook the moral consequences of mimetic art for a fault intrinsic to art itself. Gadamer argues that art does not necessarily lead to a retreat from reality and to self-alienation as Plato believed. On the contrary, art draws us into collective experience, on the model of the hymns of praise sung by the ancient Greeks to their gods. Instead of banishing the poets from his Republic, Plato should have seen the potential of art to elucidate our understanding of what it means to be a part of living culture and thus to make us better participants in the life of the community.

In his major work, *Truth and Method* (1960), Gadamer explains how the Platonist disenfranchisement of art was paradoxically furthered by the evolution of aesthetic consciousness through the seminal works of Kant (*Critique of Judgment*) and Schiller (*Letters on the Aesthetic Education of Mankind*). Gadamer descries the ascension of the concept of genius over the practice of the judgment of taste. This had the consequence of sequestering art from practical life. Genius, as epitomized in the egotism of romantic poetry, and abetted by the institution of the museum which divorces works from the context of their production, becomes a motive for precisely the introspective turn away from social commitments that prompted Plato's injunction against the poets. Quite to the contrary, Gadamer sees the artwork as a site where we are self-consciously bound to other people. Gadamer also blames eighteenth-century philosophical aesthetics for promoting a standard of disinterestedness in aesthetic judgment. This principle removes the work from the intersubjective conditions under which it is available to us: social ritual, religious belief, political conflict. Gadamer reminds us that art goes far back in our history, well beyond the eighteenth century. Indeed, Gadamer believes that what unites ancient art and modern art is the common anthropological basis of our *experience* of art.

Accordingly, Gadamer's discussion of the scope of artistic activity breaks down into three aspects of cultural existence: play, symbol, and festival. Play is an elemental function of human life. It denotes a non-purposive activity in which we employ our rationality but without subordinating it to one reason or a single ideological purpose: "play is thus the self-representation of its own movement." In play one's identity is realized as a communicative activity. This, for Gadamer, is the basis of festival in social life. In festival the separation between one individual and another is cancelled by a participatory ethos in which ordinary temporal experience, the time that needs to be filled by work, is negated.

Gadamer's discussion of symbol in the excerpt from "The Relevance of the Beautiful," cited below, provides a link between play and festival. The term has significance for him by reference to the Greek *tessera hospitalis*, a token of remembrance presented by a host to a guest. When it is ritually broken each party takes half. When they meet again after an interval of time the halves, fitted together, become a token of mutual and reciprocal recognition. In art, therefore, the symbol should not be confused with the simple bearer of meaning, but "rests upon an intricate interplay of showing and concealing." Its meaning is the act of its presentation. It does not re-present a prior experience. On this basis, Gadamer argues the irreplaceability of the work of art. Its value inheres in a sensuous particularity that cannot be surpassed by conceptual understanding. The ultimate meaning of the artwork is therefore registered in its power to transform the life of the one who embraces it: "The experience of art . . . does not leave him who has it unchanged."

Suggested reading

David Couzzens Hoy, *The Critical Circle: Literature and History in Contemporary Hermeneutics*, New York: Columbia University Press, 1978.

The Relevance of the Beautiful

What does the word "*symbol*" mean? Originally it was a technical term in Greek for a token of remembrance. The host presented his guest with the so-called *tessera hospitalis* by breaking some object in two. He kept one half for himself and gave the other half to his guest. If in thirty or fifty years' time a descen-

Reprinted from: Hans-Georg Gadamer, *The Relevance of the Beautiful and Other Essays*, translated by Nicholas Walker, edited by Robert Bernasconi, Cambridge: Cambridge University Press, 1986, pp. 31–2, 36–9.

dant of the guest should ever enter his house, the two pieces could be fitted together again to form a whole in an act of recognition. In its original technical sense, the symbol represented something like a sort of pass used in the ancient world: something in and through which we recognize someone already known to us.

In Plato's *Symposium* there is a beautiful story which I think gives an even more profound indication of the sort of significance that art has for us. In this dialogue, Aristophanes relates a story about the nature of love that has continued to fascinate up to the present day. He tells us that originally all human beings were spherical creatures. But later, on account of their misbehavior, the gods cut them in two. Thereafter, each of the halves, which originally belonged to one complete living being, seeks to be made whole once again. Thus every individual is a fragment or a *symbolon tou anthropou* [*Symposium*, 191d]. This expectation that there is another half that can complete us and make us whole once more is fulfilled in the experience of love. This profound image for elective affinity and the marriage of minds can be transferred to our experience of the beautiful in art. Clearly it is also the case here that the significance that attaches to the beautiful work of art refers to something that does not simply lie in what we immediately see and understand before us as such. But what sort of reference is this? The proper function of reference is to direct our view toward something else that can be experienced or possessed in an immediate way. If the symbol were referential in this sense, then it would be what has come to be called allegory, at least in the classical use of the term. On this view, "allegory" means that what we actually say is different from what we mean, although we can also say what we mean in an immediate way. As a result of the classicist conception of the symbol, which does not refer to something other than itself in this way, allegory has unfairly come to be regarded as something cold and unartistic. In the case of allegory, the reference must be known in advance. In the case of the symbol, on the other hand, and for our experience of the symbolic in general, the particular represents itself as a fragment of being that promises to complete and make whole whatever corresponds to it. Or, indeed, the symbol is that other fragment that has always been sought in order to complete and make whole our own fragmentary life. The "meaning" of art in this sense does not seem to me to be tied to special social conditions as was the meaning given to art in the later bourgeois religion of culture. On the contrary, the experience of the beautiful, and particularly the beautiful in art, is the invocation of a potentially whole and holy order of things, wherever it may be found. . . .

What is this additional something still present in the work of art that distinguishes it from an article that can be indefinitely reproduced at will?

Antiquity gave an answer to this question, and it only needs to be understood once again in its proper meaning. In every work of art we encounter something like mimesis or *imitatio*. Naturally mimesis here has nothing to do with the mere imitation of something that is already familiar to us. Rather, it implies that something is represented in such a way that it is actually present in sensuous abundance. In its original Greek sense, the *mimesis* is derived from the star-dance of the heavens. The stars represent the pure mathematical regularities and proportions that constitute the heavenly order. In this sense I believe the tradition is justified in saying that "art is always mimesis," that is, it represents something. When we say this, however, we must avoid being misunderstood. Whatever comes to speak to us through representation cannot be grasped or even come to be "there" for us in any other way. This is why I consider the debate about objective versus nonobjective painting to be nothing but a spurious and short-sighted dispute within the politics of art. For we must admit that there are very many forms of artistic production in which something is represented in the concentrated form of a particular and unique creation. However different from our everyday experience it may be, this creation presents itself as a pledge of order. The symbolic representation accomplished in art does not have to depend directly on what is already given. On the contrary, it is characteristic of art that what is represented, whether it is rich or poor in connotations or has none whatsoever, calls us to dwell upon it and give our assent in an act of recognition. We shall have to show how this characteristic defines the task that the art of past and present lays upon each of us. And this means learning how to listen to what art has to say. We shall have to acknowledge that learning to listen means rising above the universal leveling process in which we cease to notice anything – a process encouraged by a civilization that dispenses increasingly powerful stimuli.

We have asked what is communicated in the experience of the beautiful and, in particular, in the experience of art. The decisive and indispensable insight that we gained was that one cannot talk about a simple transference or mediation of meaning there. For this would already be to assimilate the experience of art to the universal anticipation of meaning that is characteristic of theoretical reason. As we have seen, Hegel and the idealists defined the beautiful in art as the sensuous appearance of the Idea, a bold revival of Plato's insight into the unity of the good and the beautiful. However, to go along with this is to presuppose that truth as it appears in art can be transcended by a philosophy that conceives the Idea as the highest and most appropriate form for grasping truth. The weakness of idealist aesthetics lay in its failure to appreciate that we typically encounter art as a unique manifestation of truth whose particularity cannot be surpassed. The significance of the symbol and the symbolic lay in this paradoxical kind of reference that embodies and even vouchsafes its meaning. Art is only encountered in a form that resists pure conceptualization. Great art shakes us because we are always unprepared and defenseless when exposed to the overpowering impact of a compelling work. Thus the essence of the symbolic lies precisely in the fact that it is not related to an ultimate meaning that could be recuperated in intellectual terms. The symbol preserves its meaning within itself.

Thus our exposition of the symbolic character of art returns to our original considerations concerning play. There too we noticed that play is always a kind of self-representation. This fact finds expression in art through the specific nature of *repraesentatio*, that increase in being that something acquires by being represented. If we wish to grasp this aspect of the experience of art in a more appropriate fashion, then I think that idealist aesthetics must be revised accordingly. We have already prepared the ground for the general conclusion to be drawn from this: all art of whatever kind, whether the art of a substantial tradition with which we are familiar or the contemporary art that is unfamiliar because it has no tradition, always demands constructive activity on our part.

I should now like to draw a further conclusion from this which will supply us with a truly comprehensive and universally acceptable structure of art. In the representation that constitutes the work of art, there is no question of the work representing something that it is not, that is, it is not allegory in the sense that it says one thing and gives us to understand something else. On the contrary, what the work has to say can only be found within itself. This is a universal claim and not simply a necessary condition of what we call modernity. It is an objectivist prejudice of astonishing naiveté for our first question to be, "What does this picture represent?" Of course, that is a part of our understanding of a picture. Insofar as we are able to recognize what is represented, that recognition is a moment of our perception of it. Yet we clearly do not regard this as the real goal of our experience of the work. To convince ourselves of this, we only have to consider so-called absolute music, for that is a form of nonobjective art. Here it is quite senseless to expect to find a specific meaning or points of reference, even though the attempt to do so is occasionally made. We need only think of the hybrid, secondary forms of program music, opera, and music drama, which precisely as secondary forms imply the existence of absolute music, that great achievement of musical abstraction in Western culture which reached a peak of development in imperial Austria with the classical Viennese school. Absolute music provides a particularly good illustration of the question that has concerned us all along: What is it about a piece of music that allows us to say that it is rather shallow or, in the case of a late

Beethoven quartet, that it is truly great and profound? What is the basis for this? What accounts for the sense of quality here? Not a determinate relation to anything that we could identify in terms of meaning. Nor, as the information theory of aesthetics would have us believe, is it a question of a specific quantity of information. Is it not precisely the difference in quality that is crucial here? How is it possible to transform a dance-song into a chorale in a Passion? Is there some obscure relationship with language at work here? This may well be so, for interpreters of music have often felt the need to discover such points of reference and something like traces of conceptual meaning. It is also the case that when we look at nonobjective art, we can never escape from the fact that in our everyday experience of the world, our vision is oriented toward recognizing objects. We also hear the concentrated expression of music with the same ear with which we otherwise try to understand language. There remains an ineliminable connection between what we like to call the wordless language of music and the verbal language of normal linguistic communication. Perhaps there is also a similar connection between the objective vision with which we orient ourselves in the world, and the claim that art makes upon us both to construct new compositions directly from the elements of the objective visible world and to participate in the profound tensions that they set up.

These extreme cases help to illuminate how art unites us in its communicative dimension. At the very start I pointed out how the so-called modern age, at least since the beginning of the nineteenth century, had emancipated itself from the shared self-understanding of the humanist–Christian tradition. I also pointed out that the subjects that previously appeared self-evident and binding can now no longer be captured in an artistic form that would allow everyone to recognize them as the familiar language within which new statements are made. This is precisely the new situation as I described it. The artist no longer speaks for the community, but forms his own community insofar as he expresses himself.

Louis Althusser

(1918–1990)

Louis Althusser, most famous as the neo-Marxist theorist of ideology, took up the long unrealized ambition of Marxist aesthetics: to explain the production of the artwork in relation to the production of scientific, which is to say, non-ideological, knowledge. The theory of ideology is pertinent to Althusser's understanding of the artwork in so far as the artwork is produced by the human subject. For Althusser the formation of the human subject is a consequence of mirror relations that play between the desiring self and the surrounding world. Althusser is inspired by Lacan's theory of the "mirror stage," in which it is proposed that the coherence of the self derives from a mirror identification with others. Correlatively, Althusser equates the birth of the subject with a capacity to "insert" itself into sets of social practices. One's assimilation of concrete social practices paradoxically secures recognition of one's identity. Althusser's term for this practice, whereby one can represent oneself to the world, is "interpellation." The term alludes to the experience of being "hailed" or recognized by an "other" on the street. Interpellation is invoked deliberately to emphasize the relative passivity by which one realizes one's subjective existence: we know ourselves first in being hailed by others. It is in this way that Althusser understands the subject to be *inescapably* ideological. The subject is caught in the contradiction of willing itself to inhabit social practices which others will recognize as the token of personal identity. Thus one's cultural currency depends upon an expenditure of the self-alienating energies of social conformism.

For Althusser the work of art is likewise implicated in the representational matrix of ideology. But, while the work of art is inexorably "of" ideology, Althusser demurs from counting it among the ideologies that oppress subjectivity. While art is cut from the fabric of our cultural representations, Althusser believes it possesses the capacity to expose the internal contradictions of ideological practice. In that way it might help to pave the road toward a scientific critique of ideology and the advent of a human knowledge that surpasses ideological subjectivity.

In "A Letter on Art" (1966) excerpted below, and in the related essay "Cremonini, Painter of the Abstract" (1966), we have Althusser's pithiest formulations of the specificity of aesthetic experience. These texts also provide us with some of the most direct reflections upon the nature of the artwork by any Marxist critic. Artworks gives us a "view" of ideology, to which they allude but from which they are distinguished, by presupposing "an *internal distantiation*." They make us "'perceive' (but not know) in some sense *from the inside*, by an *internal distance*, the very ideology in which they are held." By proposing this "distantiation" as a break with ideology *per se*, Althusser stipulates that art does not give us knowledge. Rather it gives us a relation to knowledge. So art conceivably transcends the realm of ideological appearances from within which we are nonetheless bound to contemplate it. We are correlatively bound to see the necessity of producing a knowledge of the "aesthetic effect" in non-aesthetic terms.

Despite his belief in the importance of art, Althusser just as staunchly maintains the distinction between what art can do for us and what we must wait for science to accomplish. Art makes us see things about which we do not yet have a conceptual understanding. Correspondingly the burden of science, according to Althusser, is to produce a conceptual understanding of those "things" in terms that art cannot articulate. Because these "new concepts" are made possible by the "aesthetic effect" of art – though they cannot be represented within its repertoire of practices – Althusser imagines that the history of aesthetics will entail something like a Hegelian surpassing of art by scientific truth. Unfortunately this process remains one of the most vaguely articulated aspects of Althusser's project: "The real difference between art and science lies in the *specific form* in which they give us the same object in quite different ways." While he goes on to specify that art is a form of seeing and perceiving, while science is a form of knowledge, he fails to provide a lucid and historically attuned account of how we know which is occurring. A precise understanding of what it would mean to produce a "knowledge of art" remains an unfinished agenda of Althusser's work.

Suggested reading

Alex Callinicos, *Althusser's Marxism*, London: Pluto Press, 1976.

A Letter on Art in Reply to André Daspre

Art (I mean authentic art, not works of an average or mediocre level) does not give us a *knowledge* in the *strict sense*, it therefore does not replace knowledge (in the modern sense: scientific knowledge), but what it gives us does

Reprinted from: Louis Althusser, *Lenin and Philosophy and Other Essays*, translated by Ben Brewster, New York: Monthly Review Press, 1971, pp. 222–7.

nevertheless maintain a certain *specific relationship* with knowledge. This relationship is not one of identity but one of difference. Let me explain. I believe that the peculiarity of art is to 'make us see' (*nous donner à voir*), 'make us perceive', 'make us feel' something which *alludes* to reality. If we take the case of the novel, Balzac or Solzhenitsyn, as you refer to them, they make us *see*, *perceive* (but not *know*) something which *alludes* to reality.

It is essential to take the words which make up this first provisional definition literally if we are to avoid lapsing into an identification of what art gives us and what science gives us. What art makes us *see*, and therefore gives to us in the form of '*seeing*', '*perceiving*' and '*feeling*' (which is not the form of *knowing*), is the *ideology* from which it is born, in which it bathes, from which it detaches itself as art, and to which it *alludes*. Macherey has shown this very clearly in the case of Tolstoy, by extending Lenin's analyses. Balzac and Solzhenitsyn give us a 'view' of the ideology to which their work alludes and with which it is constantly fed, a view which presupposes a *retreat*, an *internal distantiation* from the very ideology from which their novels emerged. They make us 'perceive' (but not know) in some sense *from the inside*, by an *internal distance*, the very ideology in which they are held.

These distinctions, which are not just shades of meaning but specific differences, should *in principle* enable us to resolve a number of problems.

First the problem of the 'relations' between art and science. Neither Balzac nor Solzhenitsyn gives us any *knowledge* of the world they describe, they only make us 'see', 'perceive' or 'feel' the reality of the ideology of that world. When we speak of ideology we should know that ideology slides into all human activity, that it is identical with the 'lived' experience of human existence itself: that is why the form in which we are 'made to see' ideology in great novels has as its content the 'lived' experience of individuals. This 'lived' experience is not a *given*, given by a pure 'reality', but the spontaneous 'lived experience' of ideology in its peculiar relationship to the real. This is an important comment, for it enables us to understand that art does not deal with a reality *peculiar to itself*, with a *peculiar domain* of reality in which it has a monopoly (as you tend to imply when you write that 'with art, knowledge becomes human', that the object of art is 'the individual'), whereas science deals with a *different domain* of reality (say, in opposition to 'lived experience' and the 'individual', the abstraction of structures). Ideology is also an object of science, the 'lived experience' is also an object of science, the 'individual' is also an object of science. The real difference between art and science lies in the *specific form* in which they give us the same object in quite different ways: art in the form of 'seeing' and 'perceiving' or 'feeling', science in the form of *knowledge* (in the strict sense, by concepts).

The same thing can be said in other terms. If Solzhenitsyn does 'make us see' the 'lived experience' (in the sense defined earlier) of the 'cult of personality' and its effects, in no way does he give us a *knowledge* of them: this knowledge is the conceptual knowledge of the complex mechanisms which eventually produce the 'lived experience' that Solzhenitsyn's novel discusses. If I wanted to use Spinoza's language again here, I could say that art makes us 'see' 'conclusions without premises', whereas knowledge makes us penetrate into the mechanism which produces the 'conclusions' out of the 'premises'. This is an important distinction, for it enables us to understand that a novel on the 'cult', however profound, may draw attention to its 'lived' effects, but *cannot give an understanding of it*; it may put the question of the 'cult' on the agenda, but it cannot *define the means* which will make it possible to remedy these effects.

In the same way, these few elementary principles perhaps enable us to point the direction from which we can hope for an answer to another question you pose: how is it that Balzac, despite his personal political options, 'makes us see' the 'lived experience' of capitalist society in a critical form? I do not believe one can say, as you do, that he '*was forced by the logic of his art to abandon certain of his political conceptions in his work as a novelist*'. On the contrary, we know that Balzac *never abandoned* his political positions. We know even more: his peculiar, reactionary political positions played a decisive part in the production of the content of his work. This is certainly a paradox, but it is the case, and history provides us with a number of examples to which Marx drew our attention (on Balzac, I refer you to the article by R. Fayolle in the special 1965 number of *Europe*). These are examples of a deformation of sense very commonly found in the dialectic of ideologies. See what Lenin says about Tolstoy (cf. Macherey's article): Tolstoy's personal ideological position is one component of the deep-lying causes of the *content* of his work. The fact that the content of the work of Balzac and Tolstoy is 'detached' from their political ideology and in some way makes us 'see' it from the *outside*, makes us 'perceive' it by a distantiation inside that ideology, *presupposes that ideology itself*. It is certainly possible to say that it is an 'effect' of *their art* as novelists that it produces this distance inside their ideology, which makes us 'perceive' it, but it is not possible to say, as you do, that art '*has its own logic*' which '*made Balzac abandon his political conceptions*'. On the contrary, *only because he retained them could he produce his work*, only because he stuck to his political ideology could he produce *in it* this internal 'distance' which gives us a critical 'view' of it.

As you see, in order to answer most of the questions posed for us by the existence and specific nature of art, we are forced to produce an adequate (scientific) *knowledge* of the processes which produce the 'aesthetic effect' of a

work of art. In other words, in order to answer the question of the relationship between art and knowledge we must produce a *knowledge of art*.

. . . Since art in fact provides us with *something else* other than science, there
is not an opposition between them, but a difference. On the contrary, if it is a
matter of *knowing* art, it is absolutely essential to begin with '*rigorous reflection
on the basic concepts of Marxism*': there is no other way. And when I say, '*it is
essential to begin . . .*', it is not enough to *say* it, it is essential to *do* it. If not,
it is easy to extricate oneself with a passing acknowledgement, like '*Althusser
proposes to return to a rigorous study of Marxist theory. I agree that this is
indispensable. But I do not believe that it is enough.*' My response to this is the
only real criticism: there is a way of declaring an exigency 'indispensable'
which consists precisely of *dispensing with it*, dispensing with a careful consideration of all its implications and consequences – by the acknowledgement
accorded it in order to move quickly on to 'something else'. Now I believe that
the only way we can hope to reach a real knowledge of art, to go deeper into
the specificity of the work of art, to know the mechanisms which produce the
'aesthetic effect', is precisely to spend a long time and pay the greatest attention to the '*basic principles of Marxism*' and not to be in a hurry to 'move on to
something else', for if we move on too quickly to 'something else' we shall
arrive not at a *knowledge* of art, but at an *ideology* of art: e.g., at the latent
humanist ideology which may be induced by what you say about the relations
between art and the 'human', and about artistic 'creation', etc.

If we must turn (and this demands slow and arduous work) to the 'basic
principles of Marxism' in order to be able to pose correctly, in concepts which
are not the *ideological* concepts of aesthetic spontaneity, but *scientific* concepts
adequate to their object, and thus necessarily *new* concepts, it is not in order
to pass art silently by or to sacrifice it to science: it is quite simply in order to
know it, and to give it its due.

Fredric Jameson

(1934–)

Fredric Jameson is one of the most important and influential contemporary Marxist critics. His work is based on a theory of literary and cultural interpretation which he has developed and refined since the early 1970s and includes wide-ranging analyses of various aspects of contemporary culture such as art, architecture, the media, and politics, as well as literary criticism. Jameson has been influenced most profoundly by western rather than Soviet Marxism, but part of his success as a critic derives from his ability to combine and synthesize various different and sometimes hostile traditions of Marxist cultural interpretation. Indeed, he is often described as a consummate dialectical thinker who, in the tradition of Marx and Hegel, is able to combine antithetical arguments or perspectives in order to create a more inclusive point of view.

Jameson's commitment to dialectical thinking is well illustrated by the way in which he describes the relationship between content and form in literature. In *Marxism and Form*, his first major work, he argues that the style in which a work of literature is written reflects not the personality or genius of the writer or even the writer's thematic interests but, rather, the social and political pressures which shaped the moment in which the text was created. This means that it is wrong to think of the style and content of a literary work as somehow opposed to one another, since style is a form of literary content and not just a vehicle for its expression. Jameson demonstrates the way in which style reflects its historical moment in a reading of Ernest Hemingway's fiction. Here he argues that "it is a mistake to think, for instance, that the books of Hemingway deal essentially with such things as courage, love, and death; in reality, their deepest subject is simply the writing of a certain type of sentence" (1972: 409). What Hemingway has done, Jameson claims, is turn literary writing into the kind of skill that is particularly useful in the society in which he lives: like the Hemingway cult of *machismo*, this concentration on style as technique "satisfies the Protestant work ethic at the same time that it glorifies leisure" (1972: 412).

Jameson has also shown dialectical skill in incorporating the work of non-Marxist thinkers in his literary criticism. Most notably, he has made extensive use of the structuralist linguistic analysis of A. J. Greimas, and the poststructuralist psychoanalysis of Jacques Lacan. Despite his willingness to use the insights of these and other contemporary continental thinkers, however, Jameson carefully distinguishes his Marxism from either structuralism or poststructuralism. As he explains in *The Prison-House of Language*, the structuralists assume that culture is shaped by language rather than, as the Marxists would have it, by the class struggle created by specific economic conditions. For similar reasons, Jameson rejects poststructuralism, which he sees more as a symptom of cultural fragmentation than as the basis for an effective critique of culture.

The *Political Unconscious*, Jameson's most ambitious and influential work, further develops his theory of the ways in which literary form reflects the historical moment in which a work was written. Here Jameson argues that all legitimate literary theory must accept a Marxist notion of history as an all-inclusive framework for interpretation. Jameson insists that all narratives, progressive and conservative alike, are attempts to overcome historical conflicts and reconcile, harmonize, and integrate human society. Often, however, narratives propose false or ideological solutions to the problems which they describe, and Jameson labels these false solutions "strategies of containment." In analyzing Joseph Conrad's *Lord Jim*, for instance, Jameson suggests that Conrad attempts to contain and manage the social conflicts generated by European economic expansion by translating them into the terms of an adventure set at sea.

The first passage from *The Political Unconscious*, below, argues that literature of the past is a mere curiosity unless it is understood in terms of the larger Marxist narrative of history. The second passage contains Jameson's claim that appeals to individual moral responsibility can function as strategies of containment by blinding people to larger political realities.

Reference

Fredric Jameson, *Marxism and Form*, Princeton, NJ: Princeton University Press, 1972.

Suggested reading

William C. Dowling, *Jameson, Althusser, Marx: An Introduction to the Political Unconscious*, Ithaca, NY: Cornell University Press, 1989.

On Interpretation

My position here is that only Marxism offers a philosophically coherent and ideologically compelling resolution to the dilemma of historicism evoked

Reprinted from: Fredric Jameson, *The Political Unconscious: Narrative as a Socially Symbolic Act*, Ithaca, NY: Cornell University Press, 1981, pp. 19–21, 210–11.

above. Only Marxism can give us an adequate account of the essential *mystery* of the cultural past, which, like Tiresias drinking the blood, is momentarily returned to life and warmth and allowed once more to speak, and to deliver its long-forgotten message in surroundings utterly alien to it. This mystery can be reenacted only if the human adventure is one; only thus – and not through the hobbies of antiquarianism or the projections of the modernists – can we glimpse the vital claims upon us of such long-dead issues as the seasonal alternation of the economy of a primitive tribe, the passionate disputes about the nature of the Trinity, the conflicting models of the *polis* or the universal Empire, or, apparently closer to us in time, the dusty parliamentary and journalistic polemics of the nineteenth-century nation states. These matters can recover their original urgency for us only if they are retold within the unity of a single great collective story; only if, in however disguised and symbolic a form, they are seen as sharing a single fundamental theme – for Marxism, the collective struggle to wrest a realm of Freedom from a realm of Necessity;[1] only if they are grasped as vital episodes in a single vast unfinished plot: "The history of all hitherto existing society is the history of class struggles: freeman and slave, patrician and plebeian, lord and serf, guild master and journeyman – in a word, oppressor and oppressed – stood in constant opposition to one another, carried on an uninterrupted, now hidden, now open fight, a fight that each time ended, either in a revolutionary reconstitution of society at large or in the common ruin of the contending classes."[2] It is in detecting the traces of that uninterrupted narrative, in restoring to the surface of the text the repressed and buried reality of this fundamental history, that the doctrine of a political unconscious finds its function and its necessity.

From this perspective the convenient working distinction between cultural texts that are social and political and those that are not becomes something worse than an error: namely, a symptom and a reinforcement of the reification and privatization of contemporary life. Such a distinction reconfirms that structural, experiential, and conceptual gap between the public and the private, between the social and the psychological, or the political and the poetic, between history or society and the "individual," which – the tendential law of social life under capitalism – maims our existence as individual subjects and paralyzes our thinking about time and change just as surely as it alienates us from our speech itself. To imagine that, sheltered from the omnipresence of history and the implacable influence of the social, there already exists a realm of freedom – whether it be that of the microscopic experience of words in a text or the ecstasies and intensities of the various private religions – is only to strengthen the grip of Necessity over all such blind zones in which the

individual subject seeks refuge, in pursuit of a purely individual, a merely psychological, project of salvation. The only effective liberation from such constraint begins with the recognition that there is nothing that is not social and historical – indeed, that everything is "in the last analysis" political.

The assertion of a political unconscious proposes that we undertake just such a final analysis and explore the multiple paths that lead to the unmasking of cultural artifacts as socially symbolic acts. It projects a rival hermeneutic to those already enumerated; but it does so, as we shall see, not so much by repudiating their findings as by arguing its ultimate philosophical and methodological priority over more specialized interpretive codes whose insights are strategically limited as much by their own situational origins as by the narrow or local ways in which they construe or construct their objects of study.

Still, to describe the readings and analyses contained in the present work as so many *interpretations*, to present them as so many exhibits in the construction of a new *hermeneutic*, is already to announce a whole polemic program, which must necessarily come to terms with a critical and theoretical climate variously hostile to these slogans. It is, for instance, increasingly clear that hermeneutic or interpretive activity has become one of the basic polemic targets of contemporary post-structuralism in France, which – powerfully buttressed by the authority of Nietzsche – has tended to identify such operations with historicism, and in particular with the dialectic and its valorization of absence and the negative, its assertion of the necessity and priority of totalizing thought. I will agree with this identification, with this description of the ideological affinities and implications of the ideal of the interpretive or hermeneutic act; but I will argue that the critique is misplaced.

Romance and Reification

The privileged place of the strategy of containment in Conrad is the sea; yet the fact of the sea also allows us to weigh and appreciate the relative structural difference between the "nascent modernism" that we will observe in these texts and the more fully achieved and institutionalized modernisms of the canon. For the sea is both a strategy of containment and a place of real business: it is a border and a decorative limit, but it is also a highway, out of the world and in it at once, the repression of work – on the order of the classic English novel of the country-house weekend, in which human relations can be presented in all their ideal formal purity precisely because concrete content is relegated to the rest of the week – as well as the absent work-place itself.

So the sea is the place from which Jim can contemplate that dreary prose of the world which is daily life in the universal factory called capitalism:

> His station was in the fore-top, and often from there he looked down, with the contempt of a man destined to shine in the midst of dangers, at the peaceful multitude of roofs cut in two by the brown tide of the stream, while scattered on the outskirts of the surrounding plain the factory chimneys rose perpendicular against a grimy sky, each slender like a pencil, and belching out smoke like a volcano. (*Lord Jim*, ed. T. Moser (New York: Norton, 1968), p. 5)

Jim's externality to this world, his absolute structural distance from it, can be measured by a process to which we will shortly return, namely the impulse of Conrad's sentences to transform such realities into impressions. These distant factory spires may be considered the equivalent for Jim and, in this novelistic project, for Conrad, of the great Proustian glimpses of the steeples of Martinville (with the one obvious qualification that the latter are already sheer impression and need neither aesthetic transformation, nor the Archimedean point of a structural externality, all the energy of Proustian style now being invested in the meditation on the object itself).

Two comments on this geographical strategy of containment need to be made before we do justice to its historical ambiguity. First of all, in a certain sense Jim tries to reverse one of Marx's classical ideological models (the repetition in pure thought of concrete social situations) and to reenact in reality what his father achieves symbolically, in speech and idea. His father's vocation, as ideologue in the characteristic British class system (he is an Anglican parson), is carefully underscored in the paragraph that precedes the one quoted above:

> Jim's father possessed such certain knowledge of the Unknowable as made for the righteousness of people in cottages without disturbing the case of mind of those whom an unerring Providence enables to live in mansions. (Ibid., p. 4)

From our point of view, and from the logic of its insertion in Conrad's text, this ideological function of religion is also to be grasped in terms of containment and totality; the geographical vision of cottage, mansion, and "little church" (the place of the production of the ideology that harmonizes them) requires that neither class position be able to focus or indeed to see the other. Jim's method for living this geography, harmonized by ideological blindness, is an uncommon one: choosing a vocation such that he can step completely outside all three class terrains and see them all equally, from over a great distance, as so much picturesque landscape.

Notes

1 "The realm of freedom actually begins only where labor which is in fact determined by necessity and mundane considerations ceases; thus in the very nature of things it lies beyond the sphere of actual material production. Just as the savage must wrestle with Nature to satisfy his wants, to maintain and reproduce life, so must civilized man, and he must do so in all social formations and under all possible modes of production. With his development this realm of physical necessity expands as a result of his wants; but, at the same time, the forces of production which satisfy these wants also increase. Freedom in this field can only consist in socialized men, the associated producers, rationally regulating their interchange with Nature, bringing it under their common control, instead of being ruled by it as by the blind forces of Nature; and achieving this with the least expenditure of energy and under conditions most favorable to, and worthy of, their human nature. But it nonetheless still remains a realm of necessity. Beyond it begins that development of human energy which is an end in itself, the true realm of freedom, which, however, can blossom forth only with this realm of necessity as its basis" (Karl Marx, *Capital*, New York: International Publishers, 1977, III, 820).

2 Karl Marx and Friedrich Engels, "The Communist Manifesto," in K. Marx, *On Revolution*, ed. and trans. S. K. Padover (New York: McGraw-Hill, 1971), p. 81.

II
Beauty and Sublimity

Longinus

(first century AD)

Little is known about the author of *On the Sublime*; even his name remains a mystery. The oldest copy of the treatise, the one from which other manuscript copies seem to derive, dates from the tenth century, and about a third of the manuscript is missing. The table of contents of this manuscript is inscribed "of Dionysius or Longinus," while the phrase "of Dionysius Longinus" is included with the title (Russel 1989: 306). Most scholars assume that these names are scribal guesses rather than established fact, but the name "Longinus" is retained for convenience. Evidence indicates that the author was a Greek living in the first century AD, and that he seems to have emigrated to Italy where he may have been employed as the tutor of a young man from a wealthy Roman family. *On the Sublime* is addressed to one Postumius Terentianus, whom Longinus seems to be coaching in oratory. It is written in response to another first-century rhetorician named Cecilius whose work Longinus finds deficient because it presents numerous examples of sublimity without explaining what sublimity is or how it can be achieved.

Longinus presents sublimity or "greatness" as a special kind of eloquence. Most rhetorical strategies, he claims, are designed to persuade an audience by offering arguments. These arguments are designed to help the audience with the process of deliberation. By contrast, sublimity overwhelms its audience; rather than leading them through the steps of an argument toward a desired conclusion, sublime eloquence transports those who hear it, winning them over with its power and grandeur. Longinus describes sublimity as the "echo of a great soul," but this greatness of soul belongs simultaneously to the orator, the orator's subject matter, and the audience. Sublimity flashes "like a thunderbolt," displaying the power of the speaker, Longinus claims, and as a result, the souls of the listeners are uplifted; "we are filled with a proud exaltation and a sense of vaunting joy, just as though we had ourselves produced what we had heard" (ch. 7).

Yet, if sublime speech is the natural result of a great soul, it is not clear that sublimity can be taught at all. Longinus admits that natural talent and inspiration may be prerequisites of sublimity but insists that these natural sources of sublimity can be

nurtured and improved by the study of rhetorical technique. Accordingly, he identifies five sources of sublimity. Great thoughts and grand emotions head the list as the
mental properties which produce sublimity. They are followed by a list of three formal
features of language that are conducive to the sublime; these include appropriate
figures of speech, noble diction, and unity in the composition as a whole. Despite
Longinus' assurance that some aspects of sublimity may be taught, his treatise is in
many ways a caution against a merely mechanical approach to rhetoric. In Longinus'
time there was a disagreement between those orators who favored an attic style
characterized by simplicity, control, and precision and those orators who embraced an
Asiatic style, which was full of elaborate diction and ornate figures of speech.
Longinus argues that without the power of sublimity, both styles can fail. Without
inspiration, the attic style is cold and stiff, and the Asiatic style is bombastic.
   The first edition of On the Sublime was published in Switzerland in 1554, but the
treatise remained little known until it was translated by the influential French critic
Boileau in 1674. After Boileau's translation, sublimity became a popular topic of
discussion, both on the continent and in England. Critics from warring parties used
Longinus to support very different arguments: neoclassical critics turned to Longinus
to support their contention that the literature of the ancients was superior to anything
that modern writers had produced, while those who argued for the superiority of
modern writers claimed that Longinus supported a literature of inspiration and innovation as opposed to one shackled by the rules championed by neoclassical critics.
This notion that sublimity confounds reason, rules, and calculation is reflected in
Edmund Burke's and Immanuel Kant's influential treatments of the subject in the late
eighteenth century. Both of these thinkers draw a sharp distinction between beauty
and sublimity: beauty, they claim, is marked by a perceptible wholeness and harmony,
while sublimity presents the observer with a spectacle of power and complexity that
is beyond human comprehension. Sublimity is inspiring, they argue, because it allows
those who witness it to feel that they possess within themselves a power that defies
human understanding. Postmodern thinkers such as Jean-François Lyotard have
helped revive interest in sublimity among contemporary critics. Like Burke and Kant,
these thinkers claim that sublimity reveals a dimension of experience that modern
scientifically-based schemes of explanation fail to comprehend.

Reference

Donald Russel, "Longinus on Sublimity," in George Kennedy (ed.) *The Cambridge History of Criticism*, vol. 1: *Classical Criticism*, Cambridge: Cambridge University Press, 1989.

Suggested reading

William K. Wimsatt and Cleanth Brooks, *Literary Criticism: A Short History*, vol. 1, London: Rontleddge and Kegan Paul, 1957. See ch. 6: "Roman Classicism: Longinus."

1   First Thoughts on Sublimity

Since you have urged me in my turn to write down my thoughts on the sublime for your gratification, we should consider whether my views contain anything of value to men in public life. And as your nature and your sense of fitness prompt you, my dear friend, you will help me to form the truest possible judgements on the various details; for it was a sound answer that was given by the man who, when asked what we have in common with the gods, replied, "Benevolence and truth."

As I am writing for you, Terentianus, who are a man of some erudition, I almost feel that I can dispense with a long preamble showing that sublimity consists in a certain excellence and distinction in expression, and that it is from this source alone that the greatest poets and historians have acquired their pre-eminence and won for themselves an eternity of fame. For the effect of elevated language is, not to persuade the hearers, but to entrance them; and at all times, and in every way, what transports us with wonder is more telling than what merely persuades or gratifies us. The extent to which we can be persuaded is usually under our own control, but these sublime passages exert an irresistible force and mastery, and get the upper hand with every hearer. Inventive skill and the proper order and disposition of material are not manifested in a good touch here and there, but reveal themselves by slow degrees as they run through the whole texture of the composition; on the other hand, a well-timed stroke of sublimity scatters everything before it like a thunderbolt, and in a flash reveals the full power of the speaker. But I should think, my dear Terentianus, that you could develop these points and others of the same kind from your own experience.

2   Is There an Art of the Sublime?

Before going any farther, I must take up the question whether there is such a thing as an art of sublimity or profundity, for some people think that those who relate matters of this kind to a set of artistic precepts are on a completely wrong track. Genius, they say, is innate; it is not something that can be learnt, and nature is the only art that begets it. Works of natural genius are spoilt, they believe, are indeed utterly debased, when they are reduced to the bare bones

Reprinted from: Longinus, *On the Sublime*, in *Classical Literary Criticism*, translated by T. S. Dorsch, Baltimore: Penguin Books, 1965, pp. 100–1, 107–10.

of rules and systems. However, I suggest that there is a case for the opposite point of view when it is considered that, although nature is in the main subject only to her own laws where sublime feelings are concerned, she is not given to acting at random and wholly without system. Nature is the first cause and the fundamental creative principle in all activities, but the function of a system is to prescribe the degree and the right moment for each, and to lay down the clearest rules for use and practice. Furthermore, sublime impulses are exposed to greater dangers when they are left to themselves without the ballast and stability of knowledge; they need the curb as often as the spur.

7   The True Sublime

It must be understood, my dear friend, that, as in everyday life nothing is great which it is considered great to despise, so is it with the sublime. Thus riches, honours, reputation, sovereignty, and all the other things which possess in marked degree the external trappings of a showy splendour, would not seem to a sensible man to be great blessings, since contempt for them is itself regarded as a considerable virtue; and indeed people admire those who possess them less than those who could have them but are high-minded enough to despise them. In the same way we must consider, with regard to the grand style in poetry and literature generally, whether certain passages do not simply give an impression of grandeur by means of much adornment indiscriminately applied, being shown up as mere bombast when these are stripped away – passages which it would be more noble to despise than to admire. For by some innate power the true sublime uplifts our souls; we are filled with a proud exaltation and a sense of vaunting joy, just as though we had ourselves produced what we had heard.

If an intelligent and well-read man can hear a passage several times, and it does not either touch his spirit with a sense of grandeur or leave more food for reflection in his mind than the mere words convey, but with long and careful examination loses more and more of its effectiveness, then it cannot be an example of true sublimity – certainly not unless it can outlive a single hearing. For a piece is truly great only if it can stand up to repeated examination, and if it is difficult, or, rather, impossible to resist its appeal, and it remains firmly and ineffaceably in the memory. As a generalization, you may take it that sublimity in all its truth and beauty exists in such works as please all men at all times. For when men who differ in their pursuits, their ways of life, their ambitions, their ages, and their languages all think in one and the same way about the same works, then the unanimous judgement, as it were, of men who have so little in common induces a strong and unshakeable faith in the object of admiration.

8 Five Sources of Sublimity

It may be said that there are five particularly fruitful sources of the grand style, and beneath these five there lies as a common foundation the command of language, without which nothing worth while can be done. The first and most important is the ability to form grand conceptions, as I have explained in my commentary on Xenophon. Second comes the stimulus of powerful and inspired emotion. These two elements of the sublime are very largely innate, while the remainder are the product of art – that is, the proper formation of the two types of figure, figures of thought and figures of speech, together with the creation of a noble diction, which in its turn may be resolved into the choice of words, the use of imagery, and the elaboration of the style. The fifth source of grandeur, which embraces all those I have already mentioned, is the total effect resulting from dignity and elevation.

We must consider, then, what is involved under each of these heads, with a preliminary reminder that Cecilius has left out of account some of the five divisions, one of them obviously being that which relates to emotion. Now if he thought that these two things, sublimity and emotion, were the same thing, and that they were essentially bound up with each other, he is mistaken. For some emotions can be found that are mean and not in the least sublime, such as pity, grief, and fear; and on the other hand many sublime passages convey no emotion, such as, among countless examples, the poet's daring lines about the Aloadae:

Keenly they strove to set Ossa upon Olympus, and upon Ossa the forest-clad Pelion, that they might mount up to heaven;

and the still greater conception that follows:

And this would they have accomplished.[1]

With the orators, again, their eulogies, ceremonial addresses, and occasional speeches contain touches of majesty and grandeur at every point, but as a rule lack emotion; thus emotional speakers are the least effective eulogists, while, on the other hand, those who excel as panegyrists avoid emotionalism. But if Cecilius believed that emotion contributes nothing at all to the sublime, and

for this reason considered it not worth mentioning, once again he was making
a very serious mistake; for I would confidently maintain that nothing contributes so decisively to the grand style as a noble emotion in the right setting,
when it forces its way to the surface in a gust of frenzy, and breathes a kind of
divine inspiration into the speaker's words.

9   Nobility of Soul

Now since the first of these factors, that is to say, nobility of soul,[2] plays the
most important part of them all, here too, even though it is a gift rather than
an acquired characteristic, we should do all we can to train our minds towards
the production of grand ideas, perpetually impregnating them, so to speak,
with a noble inspiration. By what means, you will ask, is this to be done? Well,
I have written elsewhere to this effect: "Sublimity is the echo of a noble mind."
Thus, even without being spoken, a simple idea will sometimes of its own
accord excite admiration by reason of the greatness of mind that it expresses;
for example, the silence of Ajax in 'The calling up of the spirits'[3] is grand,
more sublime than any words.

First, then, it is absolutely necessary to indicate the source of this power,
and to show that the truly eloquent man must have a mind that is not mean or
ignoble. For it is not possible that those who throughout their lives have feeble
and servile thoughts and aims should strike out anything that is remarkable,
anything that is worthy of an immortality of fame; no, greatness of speech is
the province of those whose thoughts are deep, and stately expressions come
naturally to the most high-minded of men.

Notes

1   *Odyssey* XI, 315–16; 317.
2   The first of the five sources of sublimity, listed in the previous chapter as "the
    ability to form grand conceptions."
3   *Odyssey* XI, 543ff.

Plotinus

(204–270)

The most influential Neoplatonist thinker of the ancient world, Plotinus was a Hellenized Egyptian. He conducted a school of philosophy in Rome. His works come down to us from his pupil Porphyry, who arranged them according to content in six sections called enneads (each ennead is a book of nine chapters).

Plato's importance as an aesthetic theorist inhered in his negative characterization of the artist's work as imitation: the imitator is three times removed from the truth, after the user and the maker. By contrast, Plotinus' significance derives from his characterization of the artwork as integral to the contemplation of beauty. It is consequently independent of imitative practice. Plotinus does not discuss literary art directly but sets the terms of discussion that will make the attribution of beauty to literary artifacts an important precedent for formalist aesthetics.

Although it is Platonist in origin, Plotinus' thinking about the beautiful posits form as existing in a productive tension with natural material. All formed matter is understood in relation to a Platonist principle of unity. Contrary to Plato's teaching however, Plotinus does not claim to know the forms of the material world as imperfect images of an Ideal Form. Rather they are to be known as emanations from or *effulgurations* of the ultimately unknowable "One." The sensuous particulars of the material world are therefore not impediments to knowledge. They are proper media of communion with the "One." Though Plotinus countenances a hierarchy of levels and distinct modes of attention by which the mind approaches the One – i.e. from soul to intellect to the One – his doctrine of emanation brooks no analytical dissociation of the Being of the One from the existents embodied in sense experience.

By virtue of this understanding of the One as becoming manifest through successive emanations, Plotinus eludes the dualist tendencies of Platonism. Sense can serve the mind because it is a means of mental activity. But, by the same token, art "creating in the image of its own nature . . . and working by the Idea or Reason-Principle of the beautiful object it is to produce" transcends any particularized manifestation of formed matter. This is the case inasmuch as its formal aspect is a function of the irresistible predisposition of Intellect toward the apprehension of Beauty. Shaftesbury will call this the "forming form," so as to distinguish it from the purely material armature upon which beautiful form is apprehended as such.

Plotinus' ability to address the artwork directly as an artifact of human creativity is hampered by the realization that any apprehension of beauty based on sensory effects forces us to consider the possibility of a unity that would be apprehensible through partial aspects. Indeed, a notion of artistic creativity would be precluded in Plotinus' view because it imposes the necessity to think the parts of an aesthetic unity as prior to that unity. This idea is anathema to Plotinus' postulate of our communion with the One, which we experience ineluctably in the apprehension of the beautiful. Rather than posit a synthetic principle which would establish a ground of sense particularity prior to the unity through which it is manifested, Plotinus has recourse to a standard of harmoniousness. Harmoniousness does not accommodate any intuition of the parts as differentiable from their sum: "Beauty enthrones itself, giving itself to the parts as to the sum: when it lights on some natural unity, a thing of like parts, then it gives itself to that whole." This idea is resonantly echoed in Coleridge's definition of a poem in the *Biographia Literaria* as a composition that proposes "to itself such delight from the whole, as is compatible with a distinct gratification of each component part."

For his own part, Plotinus strives toward even "loftier beauties" which escape sense-bound existence, since Soul "taking no help from organs, sees and proclaims them." But his nascent *beauty theory* sets the pattern for romantic aesthetic theories that privilege the formative freedom of genius and the virtually unfettered power of imagination.

Suggested reading

Emile Bréhier, *The Philosophy of Plotinus*, trans. Joseph Thomas, Chicago: University of Chicago Press, 1984.

On the Intellectual Beauty

1   It is a principle with us that one who has attained to the vision of the Intellectual Cosmos and grasped the beauty of the Authentic Intellect will be able also to come to understand the Father and Transcendent of that Divine Being. It concerns us, then, to try to see and say, for ourselves and as far as such matters may be told, how the Beauty of the divine Intellect and of the Intellectual Cosmos may be revealed to contemplation.

Reprinted from: Plotinus, *The Enneads*, translated by Stephen MacKenna, 3rd edn. revised by B. S. Page, New York: Pantheon Books, 1992, Eighth Tractate, paras. 1, 2, 3, 8, 13.

Let us go to the realm of magnitudes: suppose two blocks of stone lying side by side: one is unpatterned, quite untouched by art; the other has been minutely wrought by the craftsman's hands into some statue of god or man, a Grace or a Muse, or if a human being, not a portrait but a creation in which the sculptor's art has concentrated all loveliness.

Now it must be seen that the stone thus brought under the artist's hand to the beauty of form is beautiful not as stone – for so the crude block would be as pleasant – but in virtue of the Form or Idea introduced by the art. This form is not in the material; it is in the designer before ever it enters the stone; and the artificer holds it not by his equipment of eyes and hands but by his participation in his art. The beauty, therefore, exists in a far higher state in the art; for it does not come over integrally into the work; that original beauty is not transferred; what comes over is a derivative and a minor: and even that shows itself upon the statue not integrally and with entire realization of intention but only in so far as it has subdued the resistance of the material.

Art, then, creating in the image of its own nature and content, and working by the Idea or Reason-Principle of the beautiful object it is to produce, must itself be beautiful in a far higher and purer degree since it is the seat and source of that beauty, indwelling in the art, which must naturally be more complete than any comeliness of the external. In the degree in which the beauty is diffused by entering into matter, it is so much the weaker than that concentrated in unity; everything that reaches outwards is the less for it, strength less strong, heat less hot, every power less potent, and so beauty less beautiful.

Then again every prime cause must be, within itself, more powerful than its effect can be: the musical does not derive from an unmusical source but from music; and so the art exhibited in the material work derives from an art yet higher.

Still the arts are not to be slighted on the ground that they create by imitation of natural objects; for, to begin with, these natural objects are themselves imitations; then, we must recognize that they give no bare reproduction of the thing seen but go back to the Reason-Principles from which Nature itself derives, and, furthermore, that much of their work is all their own; they are holders of beauty and add where nature is lacking. Thus Pheidias wrought the Zeus upon no model among things of sense but by apprehending what form Zeus must take if he chose to become manifest to sight. (and bk he doesn't he is the more powerful for it)

2   But let us leave the arts and consider those works produced by nature and admitted to be naturally beautiful which the creations of art are charged with imitating, all reasoning life and unreasoning things alike, but especially the consummate among them, where the moulder and maker has subdued the

material and given the form he desired. Now what is the beauty here? It has nothing to do with the blood or the menstrual process: either there is also a colour and form apart from all this or there is nothing unless sheer ugliness or (at best) a bare recipient, as it were the mere Matter of beauty.

Whence shone forth the beauty of Helen, battle-sought; or of all those women like in loveliness to Aphrodite; or of Aphrodite herself; or of any human being that has been perfect in beauty; or of any of these gods manifest to sight, or unseen but carrying what would be beauty if we saw?

In all these is it not the Idea, something of that realm but communicated to the produced from within the producer, just as in works of art, we held, it is communicated from the arts to their creations? Now we can surely not believe that, while the made thing and the Idea thus impressed upon Matter are beautiful, yet the Idea not so alloyed but resting still with the creator – the Idea primal, immaterial, firmly a unity – is not Beauty.

If material extension were in itself the ground of beauty, then the creating principle, being without extension, could not be beautiful: but beauty cannot be made to depend upon magnitude since, whether in a large object or a small, the one Idea equally moves and forms the mind by its inherent power. A further indication is that as long as the object remains outside us we know nothing of it; it affects us by entry; but only as an Idea can it enter through the eyes which are not of scope to take an extended mass: we are, no doubt, simultaneously possessed of the magnitude which, however, we take in not as mass but by an elaboration upon the presented form.

Then again the principle producing the beauty must be, itself, ugly, neutral, or beautiful: ugly, it could not produce the opposite; neutral, why should its product be the one rather than the other? The Nature, then, which creates things so lovely must be itself of a far earlier beauty; we, undisciplined in discernment of the inward, knowing nothing of it, run after the outer, never understanding that it is the inner which stirs us; we are in the case of one who sees his own reflection but not realizing whence it comes goes in pursuit of it.

But that the thing we are pursuing is something different and that the beauty is not in the concrete object is manifest from the beauty there is in matters of study, in conduct and custom; briefly, in soul or mind. And it is precisely here that the greater beauty lies, perceived whenever you look to the wisdom in a man and delight in it, not wasting attention on the face, which may be hideous, but passing all appearance by and catching only at the inner comeliness, the truly personal; if you are still unmoved and cannot acknowledge beauty under such conditions, then looking to your own inner being you will find no beauty to delight you and it will be futile in that state to seek the greater vision, for you will be questing it through the ugly and impure.

This is why such matters are not spoken of to everyone; you, if you are conscious of beauty within, remember. *what?*

3   Thus there is in the Nature-Principle itself an Ideal archetype of the beauty that is found in material forms and, of that archetype again, the still more beautiful archetype in Soul, source of that in Nature. In the proficient soul this is brighter and of more advanced loveliness: adorning the soul and bringing to it a light from that greater light which is Beauty primally, its immediate presence sets the soul reflecting upon the quality of this prior, the archetype which has no such entries, and is present nowhere but remains in itself alone, and thus is not even to be called a Reason-Principle but is the creative source of the very first Reason-Principle which is the Beauty to which Soul serves as Matter.

This prior, then, is the Intellectual-Principle, the veritable, abiding and not fluctuant since not taking intellectual quality from outside itself. By what image, thus, can we represent it? We have nowhere to go but to what is less. Only from itself can we take an image of it; that is, there can be no representation of it, except in the sense that we represent gold by some portion of gold – purified, either actually or mentally, if it be impure – insisting at the same time that this is not the total thing gold, but merely the particular gold of a particular parcel. In the same way we learn in this matter from the purified Intellect in ourselves or, if you like, from the gods and the glory of the Intellect in them.

the limits of representation

For assuredly all the gods are august and beautiful in a beauty beyond our speech. And what makes them so? Intellect; and especially Intellect operating within them (the divine sun and stars) to visibility. It is not through the loveliness of their corporeal forms: even those that have body are not gods by that beauty; it is in virtue of Intellect that they, too, are gods, and as gods beautiful. They do not veer between wisdom and folly: in the immunity of Intellect unmoving and pure, they are wise always, all-knowing, taking cognizance not of the human but of their own being and of all that lies within the contemplation of Intellect. Those of them whose dwelling is in the heavens are ever in this meditation – what task prevents them? – and from afar they look, too, into that further heaven by a lifting of the head. The gods belonging to that higher Heaven itself, they whose station is upon it and in it, see and know in virtue of their omnipresence to it. For all There is heaven; earth is heaven, and sea heaven; and animal and plant and man; all is the heavenly content of that heaven: and the gods in it, despising neither men nor anything else that is there where all is of the heavenly order, traverse all that country and all space in peace.

8   This then is Beauty primally: it is entire and omnipresent as an entirety; and therefore in none of its parts or members lacking in beauty; beautiful thus beyond denial. Certainly it cannot be anything (be, for example, Beauty) without being wholly that thing; it can be nothing which it is to possess partially or in which it utterly fails (and therefore it must entirely be Beauty entire).

If this principle were not beautiful, what other could be? Its prior does not deign to be beautiful; that which is the first to manifest itself – Form and object of vision to the intellect – cannot but be lovely to see. It is to indicate this that Plato, drawing on something well within our observation, represents the Creator as approving the work he has achieved: the intention is to make us feel the lovable beauty of the archetype and of the Divine Idea; for to admire a representation is to admire the original upon which it was made.

It is not surprising if we fail to recognize what is passing within us lovers, and those in general that admire beauty here, do not stay to reflect that it is to be traced, as of course it must be, to the Beauty There. That the admiration of the Demiurge is to be referred to the Ideal Exemplar is deliberately made evident by the rest of the passage: 'He admired; and determined to bring the work into still closer likeness with the Exemplar': he makes us feel the magnificent beauty of the Exemplar by telling us that the Beauty sprung from this world is, itself, a copy from That.

And indeed if the divine did not exist, the transcendently beautiful, in a beauty beyond all thought, what could be lovelier than the things we see? Certainly no reproach can rightly be brought against this world save only that it is not That.

13   The God fettered (as in the Kronos Myth) to an unchanging identity leaves the ordering of this universe to his son (to Zeus), for it could not be in his character to neglect his rule within the divine sphere, and, as though sated with the Authentic-Beauty, seek a lordship too recent and too poor for his might. Ignoring this lower world, Kronos (Intellectual-Principle) claims for himself his own father (Ouranos, the Absolute, or One) with all the upward-tending between them: and he counts all that tends to the inferior, beginning from his son (Zeus, the All-Soul), as ranking beneath him. Thus he holds a mid-position determined on the one side by the differentiation implied in the severance from the very highest and, on the other, by that which keeps him apart from the link between himself and the lower: he stands between a greater father and an inferior son. But since that father is too lofty to be thought of under the name of Beauty, the second God remains the primally beautiful.

Soul also has beauty, but is less beautiful than Intellect as being its image
and therefore, though beautiful in nature, taking increase of beauty by looking
to that original. Since then the All-Soul – to use the more familiar term – since
Aphrodite herself is so beautiful, what name can we give to that other? If Soul
is so lovely in its own right, of what quality must that prior be? And since its
being is derived, what must that power be from which the Soul takes the double
beauty, the borrowed and the inherent?

We ourselves possess beauty when we are true to our own being; our ugliness is in going over to another order; our self-knowledge, that is to say, is our
beauty; in self-ignorance we are ugly.

Thus beauty is of the Divine and comes Thence only.

Do these considerations suffice to a clear understanding of the Intellectual
Sphere or must we make yet another attempt by another road?

Interesting end, way to end, b/c it admits that its formulations are just one among many possible ones.

David Hume

(1711–1776)

Like Shaftesbury and Hutcheson, Hume argues that we perceive beauty because we possess a special mental faculty that is sensitive to aesthetic experience. He goes further than his predecessors, however, in separating this faculty of aesthetic perception from the faculty of judgment or reflection. Hume's aesthetic philosophy thus resembles his moral philosophy in insisting that the beautiful, like the good, is confirmed by our emotions of spontaneous approval rather than our judgments according to abstract principles. In aesthetics as in morality, Hume thinks that reason is and should be the "slave of the passions," to quote his famous phrase. Also like Hutcheson, Hume insists that the aesthetic faculty responds not to objects themselves, but to a special relationship between the mind and the world.

In developing his aesthetic theory, Hume leans heavily on the analogy between aesthetic taste and the literal faculty of taste that allows a person to experience the flavors of food and drink. The human palate naturally finds certain flavors pleasant and others repulsive, Hume reasons, and those whose taste departs dramatically from this norm must be presumed to be suffering from some imperfection in the sense organs, because of a temporary illness or some more permanent condition. Likewise, if the vast majority of people find a particular work of art beautiful while a small minority of people are indifferent to it or actually find it ugly, then, according to Hume's logic, one is justified in assuming that the minority are suffering from some kind of impairment in their aesthetic faculty. This seems to be the basis for Hume's argument that we should trust the judgment of history. When we do so, he claims, we will see that judgments of aesthetic value have been more consistent than judgments of scientific or religious truth. As he puts it in "Of the Standard of Taste," "The same Homer that pleased at Athens and Rome two thousand years ago, is still admired at Paris and at London."

According to Hume, not all departures from the norm are mistaken, however. Just as some gourmets have such sensitive palates that they are able to detect flavors that others cannot taste, so, Hume contends, some critics have the ability to detect and enjoy aesthetic qualities that others have overlooked. When they first appear, these particularly gifted critics may be difficult to distinguish from all the other critics who forcefully assert their opinions, Hume admits, but he confidently asserts that the judgments of the best critics, like the art that they champion, will prevail over time. At this point, however, Hume's argument is difficult to follow. If my ability to recognize and respond to beauty is the result of an innate capacity, then education and expertise will be of little use in bringing about agreement. That is, if my capacity to recognize beauty is like my capacity to recognize blue and to distinguish it from black, then I will either have aesthetic sensitivity or I will not; no amount of education will help the "beauty blind" person, any more than it will help the color-blind person. On the other hand, if there are rules or techniques that I can employ to make my sensitivity to beauty greater, then it seems that the relationship between aesthetic sensitivity and rational and practical judgment might be more complex than some of Hume's pronouncements imply.

Because of Hume's emphasis on the role that tradition and expert authority play in shaping aesthetic judgment, his description of the social function of the aesthetic differs significantly from the description of the social function of beauty found in Shaftesbury and Hutcheson. Shaftesbury and Hutcheson describe aesthetic agreement as evidence of a collective sensibility that is freely expressed, while Hume emphasizes the role that tradition and authority play in shaping agreement.

In the following excerpt Hume explains why there are differences of opinion about matters of beauty, despite the fact that all or more people share the same aesthetic faculty. He then suggests how tradition and expertise can help produce consensus.

Suggested reading

Mary Mothersill, *Beauty Restored*, Oxford: Clarendon Press, 1984.

Of the Standard of Taste

But though all the general rules of art are founded only on experience and on the observation of the common sentiments of human nature, we must not imagine, that, on every occasion, the feelings of men will be conformable to these rules. Those finer emotions of the mind are of a very tender and delicate nature, and require the concurrence of many favourable circumstances to make them play with facility and exactness, according to their general and established principles. The least exterior hindrance to such small springs, or

Reprinted from: David Hume, *Essays Moral, Political, and Literary*, edited by Eugene F. Miller, rev. edn., Indianapolis: Liberty Classics, 1985, pp. 232–4, 241.

the least internal disorder, disturbs their motion, and confounds the operation
of the whole machine. When we would make an experiment of this nature, and
would try the force of any beauty or deformity, we must choose with care a
proper time and place, and bring the fancy to a suitable situation and disposition. A perfect serenity of mind, a recollection of thought, a due attention to
the object; if any of these circumstances be wanting, our experiment will be
fallacious, and we shall be unable to judge of the catholic and universal beauty.
The relation, which nature has placed between the form and the sentiment,
will at least be more obscure; and it will require greater accuracy to trace and
discern it. We shall be able to ascertain its influence not so much from the operation of each particular beauty, as from the durable admiration, which attends
those works, that have survived all the caprices of mode and fashion, all the
mistakes of ignorance and envy.

The same HOMER, who pleased at ATHENS and ROME two thousand years
ago, is still admired at PARIS and at LONDON. All the changes of climate, government, religion, and language, have not been able to obscure his glory.
Authority or prejudice may give a temporary vogue to a bad poet or orator; but
his reputation will never be durable or general. When his compositions are
examined by posterity or by foreigners, the enchantment is dissipated, and his
faults appear in their true colours. On the contrary, a real genius, the longer
his works endure, and the more wide they are spread, the more sincere is the
admiration which he meets with. Envy and jealousy have too much place in a
narrow circle; and even familiar acquaintance with his person may diminish
the applause due to his performances: But when these obstructions are
removed, the beauties, which are naturally fitted to excite agreeable sentiments,
immediately display their energy; and while the world endures, they maintain
their authority over the minds of men.

It appears then, that, amidst all the variety and caprice of taste, there are
certain general principles of approbation or blame, whose influence a careful
eye may trace in all operations of the mind. Some particular forms or qualities, from the original structure of the internal fabric, are calculated to please,
and others to displease; and if they fail of their effect in any particular instance,
it is from some apparent defect or imperfection in the organ. A man in a fever
would not insist on his palate as able to decide concerning flavours; nor would
one, affected with the jaundice, pretend to give a verdict with regard to colours.
In each creature, there is a sound and a defective state; and the former alone
can be supposed to afford us a true standard of taste and sentiment. If, in the
sound state of the organ, there be an entire or a considerable uniformity of
sentiment among men, we may thence derive an idea of the perfect beauty; in
like manner as the appearance of objects in day-light, to the eye of a man in

health, is denominated their true and real colour, even while colour is allowed to be merely a phantasm of the senses.

Many and frequent are the defects in the internal organs, which prevent or weaken the influence of those general principles, on which depends our sentiment of beauty or deformity. Though some objects, by the structure of the mind, be naturally calculated to give pleasure, it is not to be expected, that in every individual the pleasure will be equally felt. Particular incidents and situations occur, which either throw a false light on the objects, or hinder the true from conveying to the imagination the proper sentiment and perception. . . .

Thus, though the principles of taste be universal, and nearly, if not entirely the same in all men; yet few are qualified to give judgment on any work of art, or establish their own sentiment as the standard of beauty. The organs of internal sensation are seldom so perfect as to allow the general principles their full play, and produce a feeling correspondent to those principles. They either labour under some defect, or are vitiated by some disorder; and by that means, excite a sentiment, which may be pronounced erroneous. When the critic has no delicacy, he judges without any distinction, and is only affected by the grosser and more palpable qualities of the object: The finer touches pass unnoticed and disregarded. Where he is not aided by practice, his verdict is attended with confusion and hesitation. Where no comparison has been employed, the most frivolous beauties, such as rather merit the name of defects, are the object of his admiration. Where he lies under the influence of prejudice, all his natural sentiments are perverted. Where good sense is wanting, he is not qualified to discern the beauties of design and reasoning, which are the highest and most excellent. Under some or other of these imperfections, the generality of men labour; and hence a true judge in the finer arts is observed, even during the most polished ages, to be so rare a character: Strong sense, united to delicate sentiment, improved by practice, perfected by comparison, and cleared of all prejudice, can alone entitle critics to this valuable character; and the joint verdict of such, wherever they are to be found, is the true standard of taste and beauty.

Edmund Burke

(1729–1797)

In a manner similar to Hutcheson and Hume, Burke constructs an aesthetic theory based upon the principles of Locke's psychology, but he dramatically revises many of the assumptions found in these philosophers. Beauty, for Burke, is not the basis for an ever-expanding awareness of human sociability, as it is in the work of Shaftesbury and Hutcheson, nor does he share Shaftesbury's conviction that the aesthetic sense may provide support for a more democratic form of government. Rather, Burke describes the human response to beauty as a pre-reflective impulse which has the practical effect of making people more tractable and cooperative, but which by itself will produce only a form of social stagnation. That is, the aesthetic sensitivity to beauty that Shaftesbury and Hutcheson had hoped would bind people with a love for all humanity is reduced by Burke to a kind of thoughtless herd instinct. As the natural antithesis to this herd instinct, Burke introduces his notion of the sublime. Here he revises the work of earlier theorists such as John Dennis, who had assumed that beauty and sublimity were complementary rather than contrasting forms of aesthetic value. For Burke, sublimity is based on the instinct of self-preservation, and so it works to reaffirm the boundaries that separate individuals one from another and ultimately to support various forms of social hierarchy.

Burke's account of aesthetic taste manages to be both complex and inclusive, as well as reductive. He claims that what is called taste is in fact an aggregation of sensation, imagination, and judgment. Unlike Hutcheson and Hume, he believes there is no special faculty or sense that makes people sensitive to aesthetic experience, but unlike the skeptical Hume, he is confident that we can discover the rules which govern such experience. Thus Burke concludes "that beauty is, for the greater part some quality in bodies, acting mechanically upon the human mind by the intervention of the senses" (p. 112). The essence of beauty is not to be found in such abstract qualities at all, Burke insists, but rather it is to be identified with such physical properties as smoothness and smallness, just as sublimity is associated with magnitude. Likewise, Burke claims that the difference between beauty and sublimity is related to the two distinct types of sensation which they produce. Beauty is derived from the social passions of lust and love and is the product of a positive pleasure such as results from the satisfaction of basic human desires; sublimity, by contrast, stimulates the instinct for self-preservation and is the feeling produced by "the ceasing or diminution of pain" (p. 35).

As mentioned above, beauty and sublimity provide the foundations for two types of social relationship, both of which will play a role in Burke's social theory. Beauty is the source of a kind of instinctual fellow feeling that draws humanity together in common sympathy, while sublimity is the source of the respect and reverence which Burke thinks is necessary for the maintenance of social order. His glorification of the sublime reflects his conviction that social order depends upon a well-established hierarchy of authority, even within the family, where there is a clear contrast between the love inspired by feminine beauty and the respect instilled by masculine authority.

Burke's elevation of the sublime over the beautiful implies a concomitant elevation of poetic obscurity over poetic clarity, and thus entails a reversal of one of the primary neoclassical aesthetic values. He admits that language that presents clear and accurate pictures of the world can be pleasingly beautiful, but he leaves no doubt that the language of sublimity is more powerful than the language of beauty and that it depends upon obscurity for its effect. Poetry is superior to painting, Burke argues, precisely because it allows the artist to allude to power and magnitude so great that they escape human comprehension.

Note: Pages cited are from the edition from which the following extracts are taken, details of which are given in the footnote.

Suggested reading

Samuel Holt Monk, *The Sublime: A Study of Critical Theories in Eighteenth-Century England*, Ann Arbor, Mich.: University of Michigan Press, 1960.

VII   Of the Sublime

Whatever is fitted in any sort to excite the ideas of pain, and danger, that is to say, whatever is in any sort terrible, or is conversant about terrible objects, or operates in a manner analogous to terror, is a source of the *sublime*; that is, it is productive of the strongest emotion which the mind is capable of feeling.

Reprinted from: Edmund Burke, *A Philosophical Enquiry into the Origin of our Ideas of the Sublime and Beautiful*, edited by J. T. Boulton, London: Routledge & Kegan Paul 1958, pp. 39–40, 42–3, 51–2. For up-to-date copyright information see Acknowledgments.

I say the strongest emotion, because I am satisfied the ideas of pain are much more powerful than those which enter on the part of pleasure. Without all doubt, the torments which we may be made to suffer, are much greater in their effect on the body and mind, than any pleasures which the most learned voluptuary could suggest, or than the liveliest imagination, and the most sound and exquisitely sensible body could enjoy. Nay I am in great doubt, whether any man could be found who would earn a life of the most perfect satisfaction, at the price of ending it in the torments, which justice inflicted in a few hours on the late unfortunate regicide in France. But as pain is stronger in its operation than pleasure, so death is in general a much more affecting idea than pain; because there are very few pains, however exquisite, which are not preferred to death; nay, what generally makes pain itself, if I may say so, more painful, is, that it is considered as an emissary of this king of terrors.⟩ When danger or pain press too nearly, they are incapable of giving any delight, and are simply terrible; but at certain distances, and with certain modifications, they may be, and they are delightful, as we every day experience. The cause of this I shall endeavour to investigate hereafter.

X   Of Beauty

The passion which belongs to generation, merely as such, is lust only; this is evident in brutes, whose passions are more unmixed, and which pursue their purposes more directly than ours. The only distinction they observe with regard to their mates, is that of sex. It is true, that they stick severally to their own species in preference to all others. But this preference, I imagine, does not arise from any sense of beauty which they find in their species, as Mr. Addison supposes, but from a law of some other kind to which they are subject; and this we may fairly conclude, from their apparent want of choice amongst those objects to which the barriers of their species have confined them. But man, who is a creature adapted to a greater variety and intricacy of relation, connects with the general passion, the idea of some *social* qualities, which direct and heighten the appetite which he has in common with all other animals; and as he is not designed like them to live at large, it is fit that he should have something to create a preference, and fix his choice; and this in general should be some sensible quality; as no other can so quickly, so powerfully, or so surely produce its effect. The object therefore of this mixed passion which we call love, is the *beauty* of the *sex*. Men are carried to the sex in general, as it is the sex, and by the common law of nature; but they are attached to particulars by personal *beauty*. I call beauty a social quality; for where women and men, and not only they, but when other animals give us a sense of joy and pleasure in beholding them, (and there are many that do so) they inspire us with sentiments of tenderness and affection towards their persons; we like to have them near us, and we enter willingly into a kind of relation with them, unless we should have strong reasons to the contrary. But to what end, in many cases, this was designed, I am unable to discover; for I see no greater reason for a connection between man and several animals who are attired in so engaging a manner, than between him and some others who entirely want this attraction, or possess it in a far weaker degree. But it is probable, that providence did not make even this distinction, but with a view to some great end, though we cannot perceive distinctly what it is, as his wisdom is not our wisdom, nor our ways his ways.

XVIII   The Recapitulation

To draw the whole of what has been said into a few distinct points. The passions which belong to self-preservation, turn on pain and danger; they are simply painful when their causes immediately affect us; they are delightful when we have an idea of pain and danger, without being actually in such circumstances; this delight I have not called pleasure, because it turns on pain, and because it is different enough from any idea of positive pleasure. Whatever excites this delight, I call *sublime*. The passions belonging to self-preservation are the strongest of all the passions.

The second head to which the passions are referred with relation to their final cause, is society. There are two sorts of societies. The first is, the society of sex. The passion belonging to this is called love, and it contains a mixture of lust; its object is the beauty of women. The other is the great society with man and all other animals. The passion subservient to this is called likewise love, but it has no mixture of lust, and its object is beauty; which is a name I shall apply to all such qualities in things as induce in us a sense of affection and tenderness, or some other passion the most nearly resembling these. The passion of love has its rise in positive pleasure; it is, like all things which grow out of pleasure, capable of being mixed with a mode of uneasiness, that is, when an idea of its object is excited in the mind with an idea at the same time of having irretrievably lost it. This mixed sense of pleasure I have not called *pain*, because it turns upon actual pleasure, and because it is both in its cause and in most of its effects of a nature altogether different.

Next to the general passion we have for society, to a choice in which we are directed by the pleasure we have in the object, the particular passion under

this head called sympathy has the greatest extent. The nature of this passion
is to put us in the place of another in whatever circumstance he is in, and to
affect us in a like manner; so that this passion may, as the occasion requires,
turn either on pain or pleasure; but with the modifications mentioned in
some cases in section II. As to imitation and preference nothing more need
be said.

Immanuel Kant

(1724–1804)

Kant's *Critique of Judgment* (1790) is arguably the text that has most consistently informed and sustained debates about artistic taste and aesthetic value over the last two hundred years. Nevertheless, for Kant himself the more urgent motive of this work was its refinement of the terms of his larger epistemological system. These terms were launched in the *Critique of Pure Reason* (1781) and elaborated in the *Critique of Practical Reason (1790)*. Thus we must accept the fact that aesthetics, or the status of the artwork as a cultural institution, was less important to Kant, as a body of knowledge in itself, than as an elaboration of his understanding of the human faculties, specifically the faculty of judgment. Judgment is distinguished from pure reason and practical reason in so far as it functions in non-teleological ways.

The judgment of taste and the standard of the beautiful complement and supplement Kant's account of the other constitutive faculties of human nature: the Imagination, which presents the sensorium in images to the Understanding, the Understanding which permits us to conceptualize, and the Reason, which endows our consciousness with freedom from natural determination.

The aesthetic judgment, in Kant's exposition, accounts for those features of human experience that would not otherwise be explained in terms of the concepts of understanding or the ideas of reason. Thus it may be said that the significance of aesthetic theory, within a Kantian framework, depends upon its specification of a unique aspect of human experience, which no other terms will comprehend. The urgency of Kant's aesthetic theory owes more to its elucidation of the limits of human nature than to art-historical traditions in any of the recognized genres or media according to which we organize our museums and our canons of taste.

Notwithstanding Kant's willingness to subordinate aesthetics to epistemology, his legacy crosses disciplinary boundaries and exerts a powerful influence over art theories and art practices that we commonly identify with post-Romantic and modernist formalism. Kant's influence is perhaps greatest in the area of literary study. His ideas are have been appropriated by the shaping figures in modern literary theory beginning with Coleridge, Shelley, and Arnold, and continuing under the influence of proponents of the American "New Criticism" movement: I. A. Richards, Wimsatt and Beardsley, and Cleanth Brooks. Neo-Kantianism has seen a resurgence through the influence of contemporary thinkers as diverse as Jacques Derrida, J.-F. Lyotard, and Pierre Bourdieu.

The most influential part of Kant's aesthetic theory, in the context of literary art, derives from his so-called stance of disinterestedness. Kant asserts that in order to find an object beautiful we must refer the object – in our subjective apprehension of it – without any purpose that attaches to the interests of sense or conceptual understanding. Each aesthetic judgment is therefore unique and ungeneralizable. And though Kant strictly proscribes against any articulation of general rules (e.g. a poetics) that might govern the judgment of taste, he contemplates the mind of genius in terms that are startlingly compatible with the methods of modern artistic practice. Kant's discussion of aesthetic attributes and aesthetic ideas in section 49 of the "Analytic of the Sublime" has no doubt served to advance the purposes of art theorists who have sought to rationalize abstraction and anti-mimetic artistic styles. In particular, Kant's explanation of aesthetic ideas as "a presentation of the imagination which prompts much thought, but to which no determinate thought . . . can be adequate" evokes an ideal of the artwork as both autonomous and conceptually indeterminate.

The exploitability of this thinking with respect to justifications of artistic practice is perhaps nowhere more pronounced than in the American New Criticism. Despite the highly un-Kantian presumptions by which this critical school privileged aesthetic forms over the forms of quotidian experience (promoting an "art for art's sake" ethos based on a principle of formal autonomy), the New Criticism disseminated Kant's influence in the discourse of literary criticism more widely than that of almost any other philosophical thinker. Kant remains a key reference point for literary theorists who wish to orient the experience of the artwork to the nature and workings of human mind and to the legacy of Enlightenment idealism.

Suggested reading

T. Cohen and P. Guyer, *Essays in Kant's Aesthetics*, Chicago: University of Chicago Press, 1982.

On the Powers of the Mind which Constitute Genius

Spirit [*Geist*] in an aesthetic sense is the animating principle in the mind. But what this principle uses to animate [or quicken] the soul, the material it employs for this, is what imparts to the mental powers a purposive momen-

Reprinted from: Immanuel Kant, *Critique of Judgment*, translated by Werner S. Pluhar, Indianapolis: Hackett, 1987, pp. 181–6.

tum, i.e., imparts to them a play which is such that it sustains itself on its own and even strengthens the powers for such play.

Now I maintain that this principle is nothing but the ability to exhibit *aesthetic ideas*; and by an aesthetic idea I mean a presentation of the imagination which prompts much thought, but to which no determinate thought whatsoever, i.e., no [determinate] *concept*, can be adequate, so that no language can express it completely and allow us to grasp it. It is easy to see that an aesthetic idea is the counterpart (pendant) of a *rational idea*, which is, conversely, a concept to which no *intuition* (presentation of the imagination) can be adequate.

For the imagination ([in its role] as a productive cognitive power) is very mighty when it creates, as it were, another nature out of the material that actual nature gives it. We use it to entertain ourselves when experience strikes us as overly routine. We may even restructure experience; and though in doing so we continue to follow analogical laws, yet we also follow principles which reside higher up, namely, in reason (and which are just as natural to us as those which the understanding follows in apprehending empirical nature). In this process we feel our freedom from the law of association (which attaches to the empirical use of the imagination); for although it is under that law that nature lends us material, yet we can process that material into something quite different, namely, into something that surpasses nature. *an echo of Sidney here.*

Such presentations of the imagination we may call *ideas*. One reason for this is that they do at least strive toward something that lies beyond the bounds of experience, and hence try to approach an exhibition of rational concepts (intellectual ideas), and thus [these concepts] are given a semblance of objective reality. Another reason, indeed the main reason, for calling those presentations ideas is that they are inner intuitions to which no concept can be completely adequate. A poet ventures to give sensible expression to rational ideas of invisible beings, the realm of the blessed, the realm of hell, eternity, creation, and so on. Or, again, he takes [things] that are indeed exemplified in experience, such as death, envy, and all the other vices, as well as love, fame, and so on; but then, by means of an imagination that emulates the example of reason in reaching [for] a maximum, he ventures to give these sensible expression in a way that goes beyond the limits of experience, namely, with a completeness for which no example can be found in nature. And it is actually in the art of poetry that the power [i.e., faculty] of aesthetic ideas can manifest itself to full extent. Considered by itself, however, this power is actually only a talent (of the imagination). *agree w Shelley here*

Now if a concept is provided with [*unterlegen*] a presentation of the imagination such that, even though this presentation belongs to the exhibition of the concept, yet it prompts, even by itself, so much thought as can never be comprehended within a determinate concept and thereby the presentation aesthetically expands the concept itself in an unlimited way, then the imagination is creative in [all of] this and sets the power of intellectual ideas (i.e., reason) in motion: it makes reason think more, when prompted by a [certain] presentation, than what can be apprehended and made distinct in the presentation (though the thought does pertain to the concept of the object [presented]).

If forms do not constitute the exhibition of a given concept itself, but are only supplementary [*Neben-*] presentations of the imagination, expressing the concept's implications and its kinship with other concepts, then they are called (aesthetic) *attributes* of an object, of an object whose concept is a rational idea and hence cannot be exhibited adequately. Thus Jupiter's eagle with the lightning in its claws is an attribute of the mighty king of heaven, and the peacock is an attribute of heaven's stately queen. [Through] these attributes, unlike [through] *logical attributes*, [we] do not present the content of our concepts of the sublimity and majesty of creation, but present something different, something that prompts the imagination to spread over a multitude of kindred presentations that arouse more thought than can be expressed in a concept determined by words. These aesthetic attributes yield an *aesthetic idea*, which serves the mentioned rational idea as a substitute for a logical exhibition, but its proper function is to quicken [*beleben*] the mind by opening up for it a view into an immense realm of kindred presentations. Fine art does this not only in painting or sculpture (where we usually speak of attributes): but poetry and oratory also take the spirit that animates [*beleben*] their works solely from the aesthetic attributes of the objects, attributes that accompany the logical ones and that give the imagination a momentum which makes it think more in response to these objects [*dabei*], though in an undeveloped way, than can be comprehended within one concept and hence in one determinate linguistic expression. Here are some examples, though for the sake of brevity I must confine myself to only a few.

The great king, in one of his poems, expresses himself thus:

> Let us part from life without grumbling or regrets,
> Leaving the world behind filled with our good deeds.
> Thus the sun, his daily course completed,
> Spreads one more soft light over the sky;
> And the last rays that he sends through the air
> Are the last sighs he gives the world for its well-being.

The king is here animating his rational idea of a cosmopolitan attitude, even at the end of life, by means of an attribute which the imagination (in remembering all the pleasures of a completed beautiful summer day, which a serene evening calls to mind) conjoins with that presentation, and which arouses a multitude of sensations and supplementary presentations for which no expression can be found. On the other hand, even an intellectual concept may serve, conversely, as an attribute of a presentation of sense and thus animate that presentation by the idea of the supersensible; but [we] may use for this only the aesthetic [element] that attaches subjectively to our consciousness of the supersensible. Thus, for example, a certain poet, in describing a beautiful morning, says: "The sun flowed forth, as serenity flows from virtue." The consciousness of virtue, even if we only think of ourselves as in the position of a virtuous person, spreads in the mind a multitude of sublime and calming feelings and a boundless outlook toward a joyful future, such as no expression commensurate with a determinate concept completely attains.

In a word, an aesthetic idea is a presentation of the imagination which is conjoined with a given concept and is connected, when we use imagination in its freedom, with such a multiplicity of partial presentations that no expression that stands for a determinate concept can be found for it. Hence it is a presentation that makes us add to a concept the thoughts of much that is ineffable, but the feeling of which quickens our cognitive powers and connects language, which otherwise would be mere letters, with spirit.

So the mental powers whose combination (in a certain relation) constitutes *genius* are imagination and understanding. One qualification is needed, however. When the imagination is used for cognition, then it is under the constraint of the understanding and is subject to the restriction of adequacy to the understanding's concept. But when the aim is aesthetic, then the imagination is free, so that, over and above that harmony with the concept, it may supply, in an unstudied way, a wealth of undeveloped material for the understanding which the latter disregarded in its concept. But the understanding employs this material not so much objectively, for cognition, as subjectively, namely, to quicken the cognitive powers, though indirectly this does serve cognition too. Hence genius actually consists in the happy relation – one that no science can teach and that cannot be learned by any diligence – allowing us, first, to discover ideas for a given concept and, second, to hit upon a way of *expressing* these ideas that enables us to communicate to others, as accompanying a concept, the mental attunement that those ideas produce. The second talent is properly the one we call spirit. For in order to express what is ineffable in the mental state accompanying a certain presentation and to make it universally communicable – whether the expression consists in language or painting or plastic art – we need an ability [viz., spirit] to apprehend the imagination's rapidly passing play and to unite it in a concept that can be communicated without the constraint of rules (a concept that on that very account is original, while at the same time it reveals a new rule that could not have been inferred from any earlier principles or examples).

Samuel Taylor Coleridge

(1772–1834)

Samuel Taylor Coleridge was an English poet, philosopher, and critic. His polymathic gifts inspired an account of aesthetic experience that integrated aspects of the natural, the social and the personal under the authority of creative imagination. His sprawling speculations on the nature of beauty and its relevance to the composition of the poem are a synthetic and generative reflection upon the German Idealist tradition. His essay "On the Principles of Genial Criticism" (1814) and the compilation of works known as *Biographia Literaria* (1817) are significant for putting the practical concerns of the poet into provocative and productive relation with the most influential texts of eighteenth-century philosophical aesthetics: the works of Kant (*Critique of Judgment*) and Schelling (*System of Transcendental Idealism*), in particular. In this regard Coleridge establishes a precedent for literary criticism that strives to bridge the experiential distance between understanding art and making art. Neither the methodological principles of the New Critics nor the skeptical-rhetorical destabilization of foundationalist methodologies by poststructuralists are conceivable without the precedent of Coleridge's rough and ready marriage of philosophical and artistic thinking.

Influenced by the Greek Neoplatonist Plotinus, Coleridge made organicism his most important theoretical principle. Art, accordingly, does not strive to copy nature (*natura naturata*) in its manifold parts but to comprehend its essence (*natura naturans*) by intuiting the pattern of its unity. As is the case with Kant, the key to this intuition of unity is knowledge of the beautiful. Beauty is defined by Coleridge – who credits the insight to Pythagoras, not Kant – as "multeity in unity." Beauty entails the reduction of the many to one. The beautiful object exhibits a formal complexity whereby the parts are indistinguishable from the whole and the whole is not intuitable except in our accommodation of the harmonious play of the parts: "There is nothing heterogeneous, nothing to abstract from." Drawing upon perceptual experience in nature, Coleridge's application (in *Biographia Literaria*) of the principle of beauty to artistic practice depends on the poet's ability to transcend the abiding prejudice of our dualistic thinking: the western habit of treating the world in terms of the subject–object polarity. The familiar bifurcation of thought and feeling, indulged in much aesthetic theorizing, is a by-product of this dualism. On the contrary, for the Coleridgean imagination the apparent incommensurability of thought and feeling is belied by our understanding that the realm of the object is "unconsciously involved" in the realm of the subject. Under the auspices of what Coleridge calls "the common sense of mankind at large, namely *I am*," the poet participates in this understanding. As with the Kantian judge of the beautiful, the imagination of the Coleridgean poet operates under a constraint of disinterestedness or indifference to what is good for him or what satisfies his immediate appetites. From the point of view of poetry, however, Coleridge makes a significant advance upon the Kantian judgment of taste. Whereas Kant separates imagination from the purposiveness of will, which we commonly assume to be a *sine qua non* of artistic creation, Coleridge divides the imaginative faculty itself into active (primary imagination) and passive (secondary imagination) components. While primary imagination registers and repeats the forms of nature, the secondary imagination "dissolves, diffuses, dissipates, in order to recreate . . . [I]t struggles to . . . unify." This formulation is readily applicable to the understanding of the artwork as something that exhibits beauty according to a principle of formal shaping.

Coleridge's concept of the poem as an art form hinges on the poet's deployment of what he calls the "esemplatic power" of mind, whereby shaping thought is fused with perception in a manner that recalls the vital agency of Vico's "corporeal imagination." The formal composition of the poem can be judged in so far as it exhibits the harmonious coexistence of different elements bound by a combinational principle that defies abstraction from the form of its presentation. Hence the inevitability of Coleridge's definition of the poem as "that species of composition" which proposes to itself "such delight from the *whole*, as is compatible with a distinct gratification of each component *part*."

Suggested reading

Jerome C. Christiansen, *Coleridge's Blessed Machine of Language*, Ithaca, NY: Cornell University Press.

On the Principles of Genial Criticism
Concerning the Fine Arts

. . . And now with silent wishes that these explanatory prenotices may be attributed to their true cause, a sense of respect for the understanding of my

Reprinted from: Samuel Taylor Coleridge, *Selected Poetry and Prose*, edited by Elizabeth Schneider, New York: Holt, Rinehart and Winston, 1966, pp. 372–7.

reflecting readers, I proceed to my promised and more amusing task, that of establishing, illustrating, and exemplifying the distinct powers of the different modes of pleasure excited by the works of nature or of human genius with their exponent and appropriable terms. . . .

AGREEABLE – We use this word in two senses; in the first for whatever agrees with our nature, for that which is congruous with the primary constitution of our senses. Thus green is naturally agreeable to the eye. In this sense the word expresses, at least involves, a pre-established harmony between the organs and their appointed objects. In the second sense, we convey by the word *agreeable*, that the thing has by force of habit (thence called a second nature) been made to agree with us; or that it has become agreeable to us by its recalling to our minds some one or more things that were dear and pleasing to us; or lastly, on account of some after pleasure or advantage, of which it has been the constant cause or occasion. Thus by force of custom men *make* the taste of tobacco, which was at first hateful to the palate, agreeable to them; thus too, as our Shakspeare observes,

> Things base and vile, holding no quality,
> Love can transpose to form and dignity –

the crutch that had supported a revered parent, after the first anguish of regret, becomes agreeable to the affectionate child; and I once knew a very sensible and accomplished Dutch gentleman, who, spite of his own sense of the ludicrous nature of the feeling, was more delighted by the first grand concert of frogs he heard in this country, than he had been by Catalina singing in the compositions of Cimarosa. The last clause needs no illustrations, as it comprises all the objects that are agreeable to us, only because they are the means by which we gratify our smell, touch, palate, and mere bodily feeling.

The BEAUTIFUL, contemplated in its essentials, that is, in *kind* and not in *degree*, is that in which the *many*, still seen as many, becomes one. Take a familiar instance, one of a thousand. The frost on a window-pane has by accident crystallized into a striking resemblance of a tree or a seaweed. With what pleasure we trace the parts, and their relations to each other, and to the whole! Here is the stalk or trunk, and here the branches or sprays – sometimes even the buds or flowers. Nor will our pleasure be less, should the caprice of the crystallization represent some object disagreeable to us, provided only we can see or fancy the component parts each in relation to each, and all forming a whole. A lady would see an admirably painted tiger with pleasure, and at once pronounce it beautiful, – nay, an owl, a frog, or a toad, who would have shrieked or shuddered at the sight of the things themselves. So far is the Beautiful from depending wholly on association, that it is frequently produced by the mere removal of associations. Many a sincere convert to the beauty of various insects, as of the dragon-fly, the fangless snake, &c., has Natural History made, by exploding the terror or aversion that had been connected with them.

The most general definition of beauty, therefore, is – that I may fulfil my threat of plaguing my readers with hard words – Multëity in Unity. Now it will be always found, that whatever is the definition of the *kind*, independent of degree, becomes likewise the definition of the highest degree of that kind. An old coach-wheel lies in the coachmaker's yard, disfigured with tar and dirt (I purposely take the most trivial instances) – if I turn away my attention from these, and regard the *figure* abstractly, "still," I might say to my companion, "there is beauty in that wheel, and you yourself would not only admit, but would feel it, had you never seen a wheel before. See how the rays proceed from the centre to the circumferences, and how many different images are distinctly comprehended at one glance, as forming one whole, and each part in some harmonious relation to each and to all." But imagine the polished golden wheel of the chariot of the Sun, as the poets have described it: then the figure, and the real thing so figured, exactly coincide. There is nothing heterogeneous, nothing to abstract from: by its perfect smoothness and circularity in width, each part is (if I may borrow a metaphor from a sister sense) as perfect a melody, as the whole is a complete harmony. This, we should say, is beautiful throughout. Of all "the many," which I actually see, each and all are really reconciled into unity: while the effulgence from the whole coincides with, and seems to represent, the effluence of delight from my own mind in the intuition of it.

It seems evident then, first, that beauty is harmony, and subsists only in composition, and secondly, that the first species of the Agreeable can alone be a component part of the beautiful, that namely which is naturally consonant with our senses by the preestablished harmony between nature and the human mind; and thirdly, that even of this species, those objects only can be admitted (according to rule the first) which belong to the eye and ear, because they alone are susceptible of distinction of parts. Should an Englishman gazing on a mass of cloud rich with the rays of the rising sun exclaim, even without distinction of, or reference to its form, or its relation to other objects, how beautiful! I should have no quarrel with him. First, because by the law of association there is in all visual beholdings at least an indistinct subsumption of form and relation: and, secondly, because even in the coincidence between the sight and the object there is an approximation to the reduction of the many into one. But who, that heard a Frenchman call the flavor of a leg of mutton a beautiful taste, would not immediately recognize him for a Frenchman, even though there should be neither grimace or characteristic nasal twang? The result, then, of the whole is that the shapely (i.e. *formosus*) joined with the naturally agreeable, constitutes what, speaking accurately, we mean by the world beautiful (i.e. *pulcher*).

But we are conscious of faculties far superior to the highest impressions of sense; we have life and free-will. – What then will be the result, when the Beautiful, arising from regular form, is so modified by the perception of life and spontaneous action, as that the latter only shall be the object of our conscious *perception*, while the former merely acts, and yet does effectively act, on our feelings? With pride and pleasure I reply by referring my reader to the group in Mr. Allston's grand picture of the "Dead Man reviving from the touch of the bones of the Prophet Elisha," beginning with the slave at the head of the reviving body, then proceeding to the daughter clasping her swooning mother; to the mother, the wife of the reviving man; then to the soldier behind who supports her; to the two figures eagerly conversing: and lastly, to the exquisitely graceful girl who is bending downward, and whose hand nearly touches the thumb of the slave! You will find, what you had not suspected, that you have here before you a circular group. But by what variety of life, motion, and passion is all the stiffness, that would result from an obvious regular figure, swallowed up, and the figure of the group as much concealed by the action and passion, as the skeleton, which gives the form of the human body, is hidden by the flesh and its endless outlines!

In Raphael's admirable Galatea (the print of which is doubtless familiar to most of my readers) the circle is perceived at first sight; but with what multiplicity of rays and chords within the area of the circular group, with what elevations and depressions of the circumference, with what an endless variety and sportive wildness in the component figure, and in the junctions of the figures, is the balance, the perfect reconciliation, effected between these two conflicting principles of the FREE LIFE, and of the confining FORM! How entirely is the stiffness that would have resulted from the obvious regularity of the latter, *fused* and (if I may hazard so bold a metaphor) almost *volatilized* by the interpenetration and electrical flashes of the former.

But I shall recur to this consummate work for more specific illustrations hereafter: and have indeed in some measure offended already against the laws of method, by anticipating materials which rather belong to a more advanced stage of the disquisition. It is time to recapitulate, as briefly as possible, the arguments already advanced, and having summed up the result, to leave behind me this, the only portion of these essays, which, as far as the subject itself is concerned, will demand any *effort* of attention from a reflecting and intelligent reader. And let me be permitted to remind him, that the distinctions, which it is my object to prove and elucidate, have not merely a foundation in nature and the noblest faculties of the human mind, but are likewise the very ground-work, nay, an indispensable condition, of all *rational* enquiry concerning the Arts. For it is self-evident, that whatever may be judged of differently by different persons, in the very same degree of moral and intellectual cultivation, extolled by one and condemned by another, without any error being assignable to either, can never be an object of general principles: and *vice versa*, that whatever can be brought to the test of general principles presupposes a distinct origin from these pleasures and tastes, which, for the wisest purposes, are made to depend on local and transitory fashions, accidental associations, and the peculiarities of individual temperament: to all which the philosopher, equally with the well-bred man of the world, applies the old adage, *de gustibus non est disputandum*. Be it, however, observed that "de gustibus" is by no means the same as "de gustu," nor will it escape the scholar's recollection, that taste, in its metaphorical use, was first adopted by the Romans, and unknown to the less luxurious Greeks, who designated this faculty, sometimes by the word αἴσθησις, and sometimes by φιλοκαλία – "ἀνδρῶν τῶν καθ᾽ ἡμᾶς φιλοκαλώτατος γεγονώς – i.e. endowed by nature with the most exquisite taste of any man of our age," says Porphyry of his friend, Castricius. Still, this metaphor, borrowed from the pregustatores of the old Roman Banquets, is singularly happy and appropriate. In the palate, the perception of the object and its qualities is involved in the *sensation*, in the mental taste it is involved in the *sense*. We have a *sensation* of sweetness, in a healthy palate, from honey; a *sense* of beauty, in an uncorrupted taste, from the view of the rising or setting sun.

Definitions of a Poem and Poetry

My own conclusions on the nature of poetry, in the strictest use of the word, have been in part anticipated in the preceding disquisition on the fancy and imagination. What is poetry? is so nearly the same question with, what is a poet? that the answer to the one is involved in the solution of the other. For it is a distinction resulting from the poetic genius itself, which sustains and modifies the images, thoughts, and emotions of the poet's own mind. The poet,

Reprinted from: Samuel Taylor Coleridge, *Biographia Literaria*, edited by James Engell and W. Jackson Bate, Princeton, NJ: Princeton University Press, 1984, pp. 15–17.

described in *ideal* perfection, brings the whole soul of man into activity, with the subordination of its faculties to each other, according to their relative worth and dignity. He diffuses a tone, and spirit of unity, that blends, and (as it were) *fuses*, each into each, by that synthetic and magical power, to which we have exclusively appropriated the name of imagination. This power, first put in action by the will and understanding, and retained under their irremissive, though gentle and unnoticed, controul (*laxis effertur habenis*) reveals itself in the balance or reconciliation of opposite or discordant qualities: of sameness, with difference; of the general, with the concrete; the idea, with the image; the individual, with the representative; the sense of novelty and freshness, with old and familiar objects; a more than usual state of emotion, with more than usual order; judgement ever awake and steady self-possession, with enthusiasm and feeling profound or vehement; and while it blends and harmonizes the natural and the artificial, still subordinates art to nature; the manner to the matter; and our admiration of the poet to our sympathy with the poetry.

Walter Pater

(1839–1894)

Walter Pater promotes a phenomenological pleasure aesthetic. He values the sensuous intensity of highly particularized experience as a purifying cauldron of human self-understanding. Pater's theory is seminal for a host of current literary and critical conceits which privilege the particular moment or image in which a multiplicity of otherwise discordant events and meanings are convergent. Not surprisingly, Pater favored an aesthetic of portraiture wherein the multiplicity of experiences in a life crystallize into a single sensuous presentation. Pater's emphasis on the unity, intensity, and autonomy of the ideal artwork put his aesthetic theorizing in a lineage with exponents of high romanticism such as Coleridge. Pater's aesthetic furthermore anticipates the formalist program of the New Criticism, with its faith in the power of the literary artwork to confer an organic wholeness upon human experience.

Ultimately however, Pater's name and reputation is most frequently connected with the rubric of "aestheticism." "Aestheticism" speaks for Pater's belief that we need to renounce rational understanding, and the pretense of objective knowledge that goes with it, if we want to grasp what is most valuable in human experience. And so it is no accident that Pater's view of the proper aim of aesthetic study is "To define beauty, not in the most abstract but in the most concrete terms possible" (*The Renaissance*). Pater accepts the time-honored charge to "see the object as in itself it really is" but he pre-empts the objectivist premise of that ambition with the assumption that each of us only has our own impressions to go by. What is required, then, is a refined capacity for using one's faculties, the tools of "taste." The relevant questions about what effects the artwork produces can be answered by each of us only by recourse to our experience of it.

The "downside" of Pater's privileging the individuality of experience – no less individuated than the work of art itself – is his apparent concession to a certain solipsism of experience. As he says in the conclusion to *The Renaissance* (1873), "Experience . . . is ringed round for each one of us by that thick wall of personality through which no real voice has ever pierced on its way to us." Virtue for Pater is the pleasure the individuated moment gives. But, to offset the isolating effect of enjoying this pleasure, Pater challenges the "aesthetic critic" to distinguish, analyze, and understand the relation of the parts of an artwork, such that they produce the impression of beauty or the pleasurable feeling for another. The responsible critic asks two essential questions: (1) What is the source of that impression? (2) What are the conditions under which it is known? In this way, Pater obligates the critic to meet a standard of publicity by which our otherwise private experience might become shareable.

Despite the social motivation Pater gives to the role of the critic, however, he maintains that the critic ultimately defers to "genius" for the production and authentication of aesthetic value. In other words, by his deference to the "heat" of genius, Pater is content to mystify the sources of artistic creation. Consequently, the critic assumes the secondary role of discerning the effects of genius, which in itself is deemed to be "incommunicable."

Pater locates the practical resolution of these theoretical contradictions in the historical past. Fifteenth-century Italy, the subject of Pater's The Renaissance, epitomizes for him an age and a place wherein a rare communicability reigned among artists and philosophers. The divisions between sensibilities and minds were supplanted in the Renaissance by a unity of spirit that eluded Pater in the experience of his own cultural moment. This no doubt accounts in part for Pater's persisting vacillation between celebrating the private ecstasy of artistic appreciation and lamenting the isolation of its joys.

The excerpts printed below from The Renaissance display the alternating optimism and pessimism of Pater's aesthetic purview. In this way, they intimate the deeply founded cultural anxieties that were to beset aesthetic theorizing in the following century.

Suggested reading

Ruth C. Child, *The Aesthetic of Walter Pater*, New York: Macmillan, 1940.

Preface

Many attempts have been made by writers on art and poetry to define beauty in the abstract, to express it in the most general terms, to find some universal formula for it. The value of these attempts has most often been in the suggestive and penetrating things said by the way. Such discussions help us very little to enjoy what has been well done in art or poetry, to discriminate between what is more and what is less excellent in them, or to use words like beauty,

Reprinted from: Walter Pater, The Renaissance, New York: The Modern Library, n.d., pp. xxv–xxviii, 194–6.

excellence, art, poetry, with a more precise meaning than they would otherwise have. Beauty, like all other qualities presented to human experience, is relative; and the definition of it becomes unmeaning and useless in proportion to its abstractness. To define beauty, not in the most abstract but in the most concrete terms possible, to find not its universal formula, but the formula which expresses most adequately this or that special manifestation of it, is the aim of the true student of aesthetics.

"To see the object as in itself it really is," has been justly said to be the aim of all true criticism whatever; and in aesthetic criticism the first step towards seeing one's object as it really is, is to know one's own impression as it really is, to discriminate it, to realise it distinctly. The objects with which aesthetic criticism deals – music, poetry, artistic and accomplished forms of human life – are indeed receptacles of so many powers or forces: they possess, like the products of nature, so many virtues or qualities. What is this song or picture, this engaging personality presented in life or in a book, to *me*? What effect does it really produce on me? Does it give me pleasure? and if so, what sort or degree of pleasure? How is my nature modified by its presence, and under its influence? The answers to these questions are the original facts with which the aesthetic critic has to do; and, as in the study of light, of morals, of number, one must realise such primary data for one's self, or not at all. And he who experiences these impressions strongly, and drives directly at the discrimination and analysis of them, has no need to trouble himself with the abstract question what beauty is in itself, or what its exact relation to truth or experience – metaphysical questions, as unprofitable as metaphysical questions elsewhere. He may pass them all by as being, answerable or not, of no interest to him.

The aesthetic critic, then, regards all the objects with which he has to do, all works of art, and the fairer forms of nature and human life, as powers or forces producing pleasurable sensations, each of a more or less peculiar or unique kind. This influence he feels, and wishes to explain, by analysing and reducing it to its elements. To him, the picture, the landscape, the engaging personality in life or in a book, *La Gioconda*, the hills of Carrara, Pico of Mirandola, are valuable for their virtues, as we say, in speaking of a herb, a wine, a gem; for the property each has of affecting one with a special, a unique, impression of pleasure. Our education becomes complete in proportion as our susceptibility to these impressions increases in depth and variety. And the function of the aesthetic critic is to distinguish, to analyse, and separate from its adjuncts, the virtue by which a picture, a landscape, a fair personality in life or in a book, produces this special impression of beauty or pleasure, to indicate what the source of that impression is, and under what conditions it is experienced. His end is reached when he has disengaged that virtue, and noted it, as a chemist notes some natural element, for himself and others; and the rule for those who would reach this end is stated with great exactness in the words of a recent critic of Sainte-Beuve: "De se borner à connaître de près les belles choses, et à s'en nourrir en exquis amateurs, en humanistes accomplis."

What is important, then, is not that the critic should possess a correct abstract definition of beauty for the intellect, but a certain kind of temperament, the power of being deeply moved by the presence of beautiful objects. He will remember always that beauty exists in many forms. To him all periods, types, schools of taste, are in themselves equal. In all ages there have been some excellent workmen, and some excellent work done. The question he asks is always: In whom did the stir, the genius, the sentiment of the period find itself? Where was the receptacle of its refinement, its elevation, its taste? "The ages are all equal," says William Blake, "but genius is always above its age."

Often it will require great nicety to disengage this virtue from the commoner elements with which it may be found in combination. Few artists, not Goethe or Byron even, work quite cleanly, casting off all *débris*, and leaving us only what the heat of their imagination has wholly fused and transformed. Take, for instance, the writings of Wordsworth. The heat of his genius, entering into the substance of his work, has crystallised a part, but only a part, of it; and in that great mass of verse there is much which might well be forgotten. But scattered up and down it, sometimes fusing and transforming entire compositions, like the Stanzas on *Resolution and Independence*, or the *Ode on the Recollections of Childhood*, sometimes, as if at random, depositing a fine crystal here or there, in a matter it does not wholly search through and transmute, we trace the action of his unique, incommunicable faculty, that strange, mystical sense of a life in natural things, and of man's life as a part of nature, drawing strength and color and character from local influences, from the hills and streams, and from natural sights and sounds. Well! that is the *virtue*, the active principle in Wordsworth's poetry; and then the function of the critic of Wordsworth is to follow up that active principle, to disengage it, to mark the degree in which it penetrates his verse.

Conclusion

Δέγει που Ἡράκλειτος ὅτι πάντα χωρεῖ καὶ οὐδὲν μένει

To regard all things and principles of things as inconstant modes or fashions has more and more become the tendency of modern thought. Let us begin with that which is without – our physical life. Fix upon it in one of its more exquisite intervals, the moment, for instance, of delicious recoil from the flood of water in summer heat. What is the whole physical life in that moment but a combination of natural elements to which science gives their names? But those elements, phosphorus and lime and delicate fibres, are present not in the human body alone: we detect them in places most remote from it. Our physical life is a perpetual motion of them – the passage of the blood, the waste and repairing of the lenses of the eye, the modification of the tissues of the brain under every ray of light and sound – processes which science reduces to simpler and more elementary forces. Like the elements of which we are composed, the action of these forces extends beyond us: it rusts iron and ripens corn. Far out on every side of us those elements are broadcast, driven in many currents; and birth and gesture and death and the springing of violets from the grave are but a few out of ten thousand resultant combinations. That clear, perpetual outline of face and limb is but an image of ours, under which we group them – a design in a web, the actual threads of which pass out beyond it. This at least of flame-like our life has, that it is but the concurrence, renewed from moment to moment, of forces parting sooner or later on their ways.

Or, if we begin with the inward world of thought and feeling, the whirlpool is still more rapid, the flame more eager and devouring. There it is no longer the gradual darkening of the eye, the gradual fading of colour from the wall – movements of the shore-side, where the water flows down indeed, though in apparent rest – but the race of the mid-stream, a drift of momentary acts of sight and passion and thought. At first sight experience seems to bury us under a flood of external objects, pressing upon us with a sharp and importunate reality, calling us out of ourselves in a thousand forms of action. But when reflexion begins to play upon those objects they are dissipated under its influence; the cohesive force seems suspended like some trick of magic; each object is loosed into a group of impressions – colour, odour, texture – in the mind of the observer. And if we continue to dwell in thought on this world, not of objects in the solidity with which language invests them, but of impressions, unstable, flickering, inconsistent, which burn and are extinguished with our consciousness of them, it contracts still further: the whole scope of observation is dwarfed into the narrow chamber of the individual mind. Experience, already reduced to a group of impressions, is ringed round for each one of us by that thick wall of personality through which no real voice has ever pierced on its way to us, or from us to that which we can only conjecture to be without. Every one of those impressions is the impression of the individual in his isolation, each mind keeping as a solitary prisoner its own dream of a world. Analysis goes a step farther still, and assures us that those impressions of the individual mind to which, for each one of us, experience dwindles down, are in perpetual flight; that each of them is limited by time, and that as time is infinitely divisible, each of them is infinitely divisible also; all that is actual in it being a single moment, gone while we try to apprehend it, of which it may ever be more truly said that it has ceased to be than that it is. To such a tremulous wisp constantly re-forming itself on the stream, to a single sharp impression, with a sense in it, a relic more or less fleeting, of such moments gone by, what is real in our life fines itself down. It is with this movement, with the passage and dissolution of impressions, images, sensations, that analysis leaves off – that continual vanishing away, that strange, perpetual weaving and unweaving of ourselves.

Martin Heidegger

(1889–1976)

Martin Heidegger was one of the most controversial philosophers of the twentieth century. While his work has often been attacked or ignored by Anglo-American philosophers, it has had a lasting influence on the Continent. At mid-century, Heidegger's work provided much of the philosophical foundation for existentialism (although this is a term that Heidegger rejected), and more recently his influence has been apparent in the poststructuralist writings of thinkers such as Jacques Derrida. Heidegger's work is controversial not only because he employs an unconventional writing style and argues against many of the assumptions of mainstream philosophers but also because he joined the Nazi Party in the early 1930s and claimed that his own philosophy showed the necessity of the Nazi cause. While Heidegger later resigned from the party and while many of his followers have been staunchly anti-fascist, some of his opponents claim that his work still bears the imprint of the kind of nationalism upon which National Socialism depended.

In the first phase of his career, Heidegger both extends and critiques the work of his mentor Edmund Husserl. Husserl hoped to show that it is futile to attempt to understand either the mind or the world in isolation from one another. He developed what he called a phenomenological method in order to describe the interdependent relationship between the two, a relationship in which mental states are defined by the objects of experience and the objects of experience are shaped by mental states. Heidegger radicalizes this project by insisting that neither the world nor the human beings have determinate identities apart from the ways in which they are situated in time and history. He refers to human beings as *Dasein*, German for "being there," to indicate the way in which humanity is situated in a web of relationships that include and define it, and he argues that the world of everyday objects are not the ultimate expressions of reality but only possible forms of experience that might be configured in different ways. Heidegger designates the objects of everyday reality as beings and distinguishes them from Being (with a capital B) on the grounds that Being is the primordial ground of all possible beings. Particular beings (lower case b) emerge from Being through a process of becoming, and both this process and Being itself are inexhaustible. That is, Being is glimpsed in beings and the process of their becoming, but it is never fully revealed.

According to Heidegger, western philosophy has consistently misrepresented the world by reducing it to an assortment of static objects or beings and by ignoring the temporal process by which Being reveals itself. Science and technology have helped perpetuate this distorted view of the world by transforming the world into so many objects to be manipulated and consumed. In a similar way, Heidegger feels, *Dasein* has been led to misrecognize its own nature. Human beings, he argues, tend to think of themselves as gods who are somehow independent of history and of the culture that shapes them; above all, they tend to forget or suppress the knowledge of their own mortality.

Authentic *Dasein*, Heidegger argues, acknowledges its mortality and its situation in time and history; authentic *Dasein* is sensitive to the process of becoming through which Being reveals itself. In the first part of his career, Heidegger presented his vision of authentic *Dasein* in philosophical arguments, the most developed forms of which are found in his monumental *Being and Time*, published in 1929. After the war and his involvement with Nazism, however, Heidegger turned increasingly to discussions of art and especially to readings of poetry in order to combat what he saw as the negative effects of modern western culture. Heidegger argues that the process of artistic creation differs dramatically from the processes by which other types of objects are created or manufactured. Whereas manufactured goods are simply stamped out so that they reflect human intentions, works of art reflect the ways in which human intentions interact with the non-human world. As Heidegger puts it, "Self-willing man everywhere reckons with things and men as objects. What is so reckoned becomes merchandise" (p. 135).

By contrast, he claims, the artist is able to move beyond such self-willing to construct a view of the world that is open to the full potential of Being. Heidegger designates this view "the Open." In the Open, things appear in their "unifying oneness," and "that oneness as the integral globe of Being, encircles all pure forces of what is" (p. 136). In "The Origin of the Work of Art," Heidegger illustrates this Openness with a description of a Greek temple which provides a space where earthly, human, and divine forces interact. Heidegger goes on to point out that language properly understood is like the temple; that is, it is not an instrument for manipulating the world but an Opening where the world reveals itself. The poet is the person who can call his or her audience's attention to the opening that language specifically and culture more generally provide. For that reason, Heidegger claims, poetry provides the basic model for all artistic endeavors. As he puts it in the passage below, "The nature of art is poetry."

"The Origin of the Work of Art," from whose conclusion the following excerpt is taken, is a treatise that was first delivered as a lecture in 1935, and then published in 1950.

Note: Pages cited are from the edition from which the following extract is taken, details of which are given in the footnote.

Suggested reading

Charles Guignon (ed.) *The Cambridge Companion to Heidegger*, Cambridge: Cambridge University Press, 1993.

The Origin of the Work of Art

Art, as the setting-into-work of truth, is poetry. Not only the creation of the work is poetic, but equally poetic, though in its own way, is the preserving of the work; for a work is in actual effect as a work only when we remove ourselves from our commonplace routine and move into what is disclosed by the work, so as to bring our own nature itself to take a stand in the truth of what is.

The nature of art is poetry. The nature of poetry, in turn, is the founding of truth. We understand founding here in a triple sense: founding as bestowing, founding as grounding, and founding as beginning. Founding, however, is actual only in preserving. Thus to each mode of founding there corresponds a mode of preserving. We can do no more now than to present this structure of the nature of art in a few strokes, and even this only to the extent that the earlier characterization of the nature of the work offers an initial hint.

The setting-into-work of truth thrusts up the unfamiliar and extraordinary and at the same time thrusts down the ordinary and what we believe to be such. The truth that discloses itself in the work can never be proved or derived from what went before. What went before is refuted in its exclusive reality by the work. What art founds can therefore never be compensated and made up for by what is already present and available. Founding is an overflow, an endowing, a bestowal.

The poetic projection of truth that sets itself into work as figure is also never carried out in the direction of an indeterminate void. Rather, in the work, truth is thrown toward the coming preservers, that is, toward an historical group of men. What is thus cast forth is, however, never an arbitrary demand. Genuinely poetic projection is the opening up or disclosure of that into which human being as historical is already cast. This is the earth and, for an historical people, its earth, the self-closing ground on which it rests together with everything

Reprinted from: Martin Heidegger, *Poetry, Language, Thought,* translated by Albert Hofstadter, New York: Harper & Row, 1971, pp. 74–8.

that it already is, though still hidden from itself. It is, however, its world, which prevails in virtue of the relation of human being to the unconcealedness of Being. For this reason, everything with which man is endowed must, in the projection, be drawn up from the closed ground and expressly set upon this ground. In this way the ground is first grounded as the bearing ground.

All creation, because it is such a drawing-up, is a drawing, as of water from a spring. Modern subjectivism, to be sure, immediately misinterprets creation, taking it as the self-sovereign subject's performance of genius. The founding of truth is a founding not only in the sense of free bestowal, but at the same time foundation in the sense of this ground-laying grounding. Poetic projection comes from Nothing in this respect, that it never takes its gift from the ordinary and traditional. But it never comes from Nothing in that what is projected by it is only the withheld vocation of the historical being of man itself.

Bestowing and grounding have in themselves the unmediated character of what we call a beginning. Yet this unmediated character of a beginning, the peculiarity of a leap out of the unmediable, does not exclude but rather includes the fact that the beginning prepares itself for the longest time and wholly inconspicuously. A genuine beginning, as a leap, is always a head start, in which everything to come is already leaped over, even if as something disguised. The beginning already contains the end latent within itself. A genuine beginning, however, has nothing of the neophyte character of the primitive. The primitive, because it lacks the bestowing, grounding leap and head start, is always futureless. It is not capable of releasing anything more from itself because it contains nothing more than that in which it is caught.

A beginning, on the contrary, always contains the undisclosed abundance of the unfamiliar and extraordinary, which means that it also contains strife with the familiar and ordinary. Art as poetry is founding, in the third sense of instigation of the strife of truth: founding as beginning. Always when that which is as a whole demands, as what is, itself, a grounding in openness, art attains to its historical nature as foundation. This foundation happened in the West for the first time in Greece. What was in the future to be called Being was set into work, setting the standard. The realm of beings thus opened up was then transformed into a being in the sense of God's creation. This happened in the Middle Ages. This kind of being was again transformed at the beginning and in the course of the modern age. Beings became objects that could be controlled and seen through by calculation. At each time a new and essential world arose. At each time the openness of what is had to be established in beings themselves, by the fixing in place of truth in figure. At each time there happened unconcealedness of what is. Unconcealedness sets itself into work, a setting which is accomplished by art.

Whenever art happens – that is, whenever there is a beginning – a thrust enters history, history either begins or starts over again. History means here not a sequence in time of events of whatever sort, however important. History is the transporting of a people into its appointed task as entrance into that people's endowment.

Art is the setting-into-work of truth. In this proposition an essential ambiguity is hidden, in which truth is at once the subject and the object of the setting. But subject and object are unsuitable names here. They keep us from thinking precisely this ambiguous nature, a task that no longer belongs to this consideration. Art is historical, and as historical it is the creative preserving of truth in the work. Art happens as poetry. Poetry is founding in the triple sense of bestowing, grounding, and beginning. Art, as founding, is essentially historical. This means not only that art has a history in the external sense that in the course of time it, too, appears along with many other things, and in the process changes and passes away and offers changing aspects for historiology. Art is history in the essential sense that it grounds history.

Art lets truth originate. Art, founding preserving, is the spring that leaps to the truth of what is, in the work. To originate something by a leap, to bring something into being from out of the source of its nature in a founding leap – this is what the word origin (German *Ursprung*, literally, primal leap) means.

The origin of the work of art – that is, the origin of both the creators and the preservers, which is to say of a people's historical existence, is art. This is so because art is by nature an origin: a distinctive way in which truth comes into being, that is, becomes historical.

We inquire into the nature of art. Why do we inquire in this way? We inquire in this way in order to be able to ask more truly whether art is or is not an origin in our historical existence, whether and under what conditions it can and must be an origin.

Such reflection cannot force art and its coming-to-be. But this reflective knowledge is the preliminary and therefore indispensable preparation for the becoming of art. Only such knowledge prepares its space for art, their way for the creators, their location for the preservers.

In such knowledge, which can only grow slowly, the question is decided whether art can be an origin and then must be a head start, or whether it is to remain a mere appendix and then can only be carried along as a routine cultural phenomenon.

Are we in our existence historically at the origin? Do we know, which means do we give heed to, the nature of the origin? Or, in our relation to art, do we still merely make appeal to a cultivated acquaintance with the past?

For this either-or and its decision there is an infallible sign. Hölderlin, the poet – whose work still confronts the Germans as a test to be stood – named it in saying:

Schwer verlässt
was nahe dem Ursprung wohnet, den Ort.

Reluctantly
that which dwells near its origin departs.

("The Journey," verses 18–19)

Maurice Merleau-Ponty

(1908–1961)

Maurice Merleau-Ponty became a key voice in French phenomenology after World War II. In part, the significance of this movement was that it opened the purview of academic philosophy more widely to the experience of everyday life. With the existential philosopher Jean-Paul Sartre, Merleau-Ponty co-founded and edited the influential literary magazine *Les Temps Modernes*. So it is not surprising to note that Merleau-Ponty's writings ranged beyond technical problems in phenomenology to topics in philosophical psychology, language, painting, and political philosophy.

Though none of his writings takes the form of an aesthetic theory *per se*, his striving to know the most "primordial" terms of human experience situates him securely within the realm of the aesthetic. This is most generally so because he takes the situation of the body and its attendant perceptual rapport with the external world to be the significant threshold of philosophical inquiry. Merleau-Ponty posited a fundamental reciprocity between the acquired repertoire of perceptual-motor skills and the things of the world which call them forth in experience. To the extent that Merleau-Ponty thinks of the body as an expressive medium, his commitment to understanding human nature on a threshold of activity links him to other expressive theorists such as Vico, Hegel, Croce, and Dewey. Like these thinkers, Merleau-Ponty rejects the Cartesian view of the world as divided between what one thinks with one's mind and what one does with or within one's body. For Merleau-Ponty, one thinks gesturally, always with respect to the orientation of the body in space. This is a proposition that carries over into the understanding that even words acquire their sense by registering one's place in the world of bodily activity. The meanings of one's words depend, in a significant measure, upon the circumstance in which one is compelled to speak or write them. The rules by which we codify language are a product or an effect – not a cause – of usage.

Art, for Merleau-Ponty, is a further exploration of perceptual experience whereby we come to a finer habitation of what he calls "carnal experience." The embodied nature of experience is best understood by Merleau-Ponty in terms of what he calls *visibilia*: meanings made apparent in perception. They "give[s] visible existence to what profane vision believes to be invisible." By this cryptic formulation, Merleau-Ponty alerts us to the fact that what we see as the visual field is part of a rich and variegated texture of visual being. Discrete perceptual experiences obscure this "invisible" dimension just as the foreground eclipses the background which brings it into view. These relations between what is apparent and its background are the hidden premises of our seeing. Perceptual habit and rational abstraction both make us forgetful of these premises in the course of quotidian existence. Whereas, in ordinary perceptual experience, we relate characteristically though "carnal formulae" ingrained by familiarity, the work of art attunes us to something in the experience that has not yet been grasped in the fluency of habit. In a manner of speaking, the artist's *working* of a medium is, for Merleau-Ponty, an extension of the body's repertoire of "carnal formulae." "Handling" an object with paint instead of one's fingers produces another dimension of familiar experience. It belies our faith that the meaning of a thing could ever inhere independently of our experience of it.

Though painting, especially the work of Cézanne, provided Merleau-Ponty with his most eloquent examples, everything he says about the expressivity of the line, or color value in painting, can be correlated with the representation of the sensuous gestalt in literature: poems and novels. The passage from *The Visible and the Invisible* (1968) cited below, indicates how the novelist's skill at embodying the logic of life taps a meaning that no abstract understanding – acquired through the analytical concepts of science, political analysis, or philosophy – can convey. Merleau-Ponty compares the sensuous presentation of the "world" in a novel, its embodiment in the verbal stylizations of the novelist, to the "invisible" logic of a musical phrase. Proust, he tells us, fixes "the relations between the visible and invisible" by showing us how the ideas that inform our sensuously woven experience in the word are not the antithesis of the sensible but "its lining and depth."

Suggested reading

E. F. Kaelin, *An Existentialist Aesthetic*, Madison, Wis.: University of Wisconsin Press, 1966.

The Visible and the Invisible: Philosophical Interrogation

We touch here the most difficult point, that is, the bond between the flesh and the idea, between the visible and the interior armature which it manifests and which it conceals. No one has gone further than Proust in fixing the relations

Reprinted from: Maurice Merleau-Ponty, *The Visible and the Invisible*, edited by Claude Lefort, translated by Alphonso Lingis, Evanston, Ill.: Northwestern University Press, 1968, pp. 149–53.

between the visible and the invisible, in describing an idea that is not the contrary of the sensible, that is its lining and its depth. For what he says of musical
ideas he says of all cultural beings, such as *The Princess of Clèves* and *René*, and
also of the essence of love which "the little phrase" not only makes present to
Swann, but communicable to all who hear it, even though it is unbeknown to
themselves, and even though later they do not know how to recognize it in the
loves they only witness. He says it in general of many other notions which are,
like music itself "without equivalents," "the notions of light, of sound, of
relief, of physical voluptuousness, which are the rich possessions with which
our inward domain is diversified and adorned."[1] Literature, music, the passions, but also the experience of the visible world are – no less than is the
science of Lavoisier and Ampère – the exploration of an invisible and the disclosure of a universe of ideas.[2] The difference is simply that this invisible, these
ideas, unlike those of that science, cannot be detached from the sensible appearances and be erected into a second positivity. The musical idea, the literary
idea, the dialectic of love, and also the articulations of the light, the modes of
exhibition of sound and of touch speak to us, have their logic, their coherence,
their points of intersection, their concordances, and here also the appearances
are the disguise of unknown "forces" and "laws." But it is as though the secrecy
wherein they lie and whence the literary expression draws them were their
proper mode of existence. For these truths are not only hidden like a physical
reality which we have not been able to discover, invisible in fact but which we
will one day be able to see facing us, which others, better situated, could already
see, provided that the screen that masks it is lifted. Here, on the contrary, there
is no vision without the screen: the ideas we are speaking of would not be better
known to us if we had no body and no sensibility; it is then that they would
be inaccessible to us. The "little phrase," the notion of the light, are not
exhausted by their manifestations, any more than is an "idea of the intelligence"; they could not be given to us *as ideas* except in a carnal experience. It
is not only that we would find in that carnal experience the *occasion* to think
them; it is that they owe their authority, their fascinating, indestructible power,
precisely to the fact that they are in transparency behind the sensible, or in its
heart. Each time we want to get at it[3] immediately, or lay hands on it, or cir-
cumscribe it, or see it unveiled, we do in fact feel that the attempt is miscon-
ceived, that it retreats in the measure that we approach. The explicitation does
not give us the idea itself; it is but a second version of it, a more manageable
derivative. Swann can of course close in the "little phrase" between the marks
of musical notation, ascribe the "withdrawn and chilly tenderness" that makes
up its essence or its sense to the narrow range of the five notes that compose
it and to the constant recurrence of two of them: while he is thinking of these

signs and this sense, he no longer has the "little phrase" itself, he has only "bare values substituted for the mysterious entity he had perceived, for the convenience of his understanding."[4] Thus it is essential to this sort of ideas that they be "veiled with shadows," appear "under a disguise." They give us the assurance that the "great unpenetrated and discouraging night of our soul" is not empty, is not "nothingness"; but these entities, these domains, these worlds that line it, people it, and whose presence it feels like the presence of someone in the dark, have been acquired only through its commerce with the visible, to which they remain attached. As the secret blackness of milk, of which Valéry spoke, is accessible only through its whiteness, the idea of light or the musical idea doubles up the lights and sounds from beneath, is their other side or their depth. Their carnal texture presents to us what is absent from all flesh; it is a furrow that traces itself out magically under our eyes without a tracer, a certain hollow, a certain interior, a certain absence, a negativity that is not nothing, being limited very precisely to *these* five notes between which it is instituted, to that family of sensibles we call lights. We do not see, do not hear the ideas, and not even with the mind's eye or with the third ear: and yet they are there, behind the sounds or between them, behind the lights or between them, recognizable through their always special, always unique manner of entrenching themselves behind them, "perfectly distinct from one another, unequal among themselves in value and in significance."[5]

With the first vision, the first contact, the first pleasure, there is initiation, that is, not the positing of a content, but the opening of a dimension that can never again be closed, the establishment of a level in terms of which every other experience will henceforth be situated. The idea is this level, this dimension. It is therefore not a *de facto* invisible, like an object hidden behind another, and not an absolute invisible, which would have nothing to do with the visible. Rather it is the invisible *of* this world, that which inhabits this world, sustains it, and renders it visible, its own and interior possibility, the Being of this being. At the moment one says "light," at the moment that the musicians reach the "little phrase," there is no lacuna in me; what I live is as "substantial," as "explicit," as a positive thought could be – even more so: a positive thought is what it is, but, precisely, is only what it is and accordingly cannot hold us. Already the mind's volubility takes it elsewhere. We do not possess the musical or sensible ideas, precisely because they are negativity or absence circumscribed; they possess us. The performer is no longer producing or reproducing the sonata: he feels himself, and the others feel him to be at the service of the sonata; the sonata sings through him or cries out so suddenly that he must "dash on his bow" to follow it. And these open vortexes in the sonorous world finally form one sole vortex in which the ideas fit in with one another. "Never was the spoken language so inflexibly necessitated, never did it know to such an extent the pertinence of the questions, the evidence of the responses."[6] The invisible and, as it were, weak being is alone capable of having this close texture. There is a strict ideality in experiences that are experiences of the flesh: the moments of the sonata, the fragments of the luminous field, adhere to one another with a cohesion without concept, which is of the same type as the cohesion of the parts of my body, or the cohesion of my body with the world. Is my body a thing, is it an idea? It is neither, being the measurant of the things. We will therefore have to recognize an ideality that is not alien to the flesh, that gives it its axes, its depth, its dimensions.

But once we have entered into this strange domain, one does not see how there could be any question of *leaving* it. If there is an animation *of* the body; if the vision and the body are tangled up in one another; if, correlatively, the thin pellicle of the *quale*, the surface of the visible, is doubled up over its whole extension with an invisible reserve; and if finally, in our flesh as in the flesh of things, the actual, empirical, ontic visible, by a sort of folding back, invagination, or padding, exhibits a visibility, a possibility that is not the shadow of the actual but is its principle, that is not the proper contribution of a "thought" but is its condition, a style, allusive and elliptical like every style, but like every style inimitable, inalienable, an interior horizon and an exterior horizon between which the actual visible is a provisional partitioning and which, nonetheless, open indefinitely only upon other visibles – then (the immediate and dualist distinction between the visible and the invisible, between extension and thought, being impugned, not that extension be thought or thought extension, but because they are the obverse and the reverse of one another, and the one forever behind the other) there is to be sure a question as to how the "ideas of the intelligence" are initiated over and beyond, how from the ideality of the horizon one passes to the "pure" ideality, and in particular by what miracle a created generality, a culture, a knowledge come to add to and recapture and rectify the natural generality of my body and of the world. But, however we finally have to understand it, the "pure" ideality already streams forth along the articulations of the aesthesiological body, along the contours of the sensible things, and, however new it is, it slips through ways it has not traced, transfigures horizons it did not open, it derives from the fundamental mystery of those notions "without equivalent," as Proust calls them, that lead their shadowy life in the night of the mind only because they have been divined at the junctures of the visible world. It is too soon now to clarify this type of surpassing that does not leave its field of origin. Let us only say that the pure ideality is itself not without flesh nor freed from horizon structures: it lives off them, though they be another flesh and other horizons. It is as though the visibility that animates the sensible world were to emigrate, not outside of every body, but into another less heavy, more transparent body, as though it were to change flesh, abandoning the flesh of the body for that of language, and thereby would be emancipated but not freed from every condition. Why not admit – what Proust knew very well and said in another place – that language as well as music can sustain a sense by virtue of its own arrangement, catch a meaning in its own mesh, that it does so without exception each time it is conquering, active, creative language, each time something is, in the strong sense, said? Why not admit that, just as the musical notation is a *facsimile* made after the event, an abstract portrait of the musical entity, language as a system of explicit relations between signs and signified, sounds and meaning, is a result and a product of the operative language in which sense and sound are in the same relationship as the "little phrase" and the five notes found in it afterwards? This does not mean that musical notation and grammar and linguistics and the "ideas of the intelligence" – which are acquired, available, honorary ideas – are useless, or that, as Leibniz said, the donkey that goes straight to the fodder knows as much about the properties of the straight line as we do; it means that the system of objective relations, the acquired ideas, are themselves caught up in something like a second life and perception, which make the mathematician go straight to entities no one has yet seen, make the *operative* language and algorithm make use of a second visibility, and make ideas be the other side of language and calculus.

Notes

1   *Du côté de chez Swann*, II (Paris, 1926), p. 190. (English translation by C. K. Scott Moncrieff, *Swann's Way* (New York, 1928), p. 503.)
2   Ibid., p. 192. (Eng. trans., p. 505.)
3   Editor: It: that is, the idea.
4   *Du côté de chez Swann*, II, p. 189. (Eng. trans., p. 503.)
5   Ibid.
6   Ibid., p. 192. (Eng. trans., p. 505.)

Jean-François Lyotard
(1924–1998)

Jean-François Lyotard was a French philosopher whose early career was shaped by the intellectual currents of post-World War II France. At this time, Marxism was the most influential political philosophy among French intellectuals, structuralism (the belief that social behavior, like language itself, is governed by a set of unconscious rules) dominated the social sciences, and phenomenology (the attempt to give a philosophically rigorous description of the essential features of different types of experience) and existentialism were the reigning schools of French philosophy. Not surprisingly then, *Phenomenology*, Lyotard's first book, is an attempt to apply the phenomenological method to the problems of analyzing history; he was an important member of "Socialism or Barbarism," a radical political organization that regularly published his articles in its journal, *Worker Power*. Eventually, however, Lyotard became dissatisfied with what he saw as the limitations of theories such as Marxism and structuralism, and this dissatisfaction led him to question the role of theory more generally.

In *Discourse, Figure*, his second book, he argues that there are features of experience that theory cannot capture. The dynamic force of such experience is best represented, he claims, in art because art best reflects the transience, discontinuity, and heterogeneity of the world. Thus the figure to which his title refers represents the multifaceted quality of artistic representation, while the term "discourse" designates the homogeneous and reductive language of philosophy. In *Libidinal Economy*, Lyotard applies this notion to the psychoanalytic theories of Sigmund Freud and Jacques Lacan, whom he claims obscure and repress the dynamic nature of the psyche by representing it in rigid theoretical categories.

Lyotard's mature work remains focused on the limits of philosophical discourse and on the dimensions of experience that philosophy cannot describe. In *The Postmodern Condition* (1979), he speculates that postmodern culture will be characterized by a multiplicity of different systems of meaning, which, following the philosopher Ludwig Wittgenstein, he calls "language games." It will be impossible to incorporate or describe these language games in one unified system (which he terms metanarrative, an all-encompassing story), he argues, because they will each have their own distinct logic and set of values. In similar fashion, in *The Differend* he argues that laws and ethical norms cannot possibly define or elucidate justice, because the injures which each wronged individual suffers is unique and cannot be captured or described by general laws.

As the preceding account of *Discourse, Figure* makes clear, Lyotard's aesthetic theory is based on the notion that art succeeds where philosophy does not because it paradoxically can represent the ways in which experience resists more rigid forms or representation. Lyotard finds precedent for this view in the theories of sublimity that were popular in the eighteenth and nineteenth centuries. According to Kant, the sublime spectacle exceeds human comprehension and threatens to overpower the observer. Lyotard locates the value of art in a similar kind of sublimity. In the following excerpt from *The Postmodern Condition*, Lyotard argues that modern art is defined by its attempt to present the "unrepresentable" and that postmodernity is "that which, in the modern, puts forward the unpresentable in presentation itself."

Suggested reading

Bill Reading, *Introducing Lyotard: Art and Politics*, London and New York: Routledge, 1991.

Answering the Question: What is Postmodernism?

The sublime sentiment, which is also the sentiment of the sublime, is, according to Kant, a strong and equivocal emotion: it carries with it both pleasure and pain. Better still, in it pleasure derives from pain. Within the tradition of the subject, which comes from Augustine and Descartes and which Kant does not radically challenge, this contradiction, which some would call neurosis or masochism, develops as a conflict between the faculties of a subject, the faculty to conceive of something and the faculty to "present" something. Knowledge exists if, first, the statement is intelligible, and second, if "cases" can be derived from the experience which "corresponds" to it. Beauty exists if a certain "case" (the work of art), given first by the sensibility without any conceptual determination, the sentiment of pleasure independent of any interest the work may elicit, appeals to the principle of a universal consensus (which may never be attained).

Reprinted from: Jean-François Lyotard, *The Postmodern Condition: A Report on Knowledge*, this chapter translated by Régis Durand, Minneapolis: University of Minnesota, 1984, pp. 77–81. For further copyright and publication information see Acknowledgments.

Taste, therefore, testifies that between the capacity to conceive and the capacity to present an object corresponding to the concept, an undetermined agreement, without rules, giving rise to a judgment which Kant calls reflective, may be experienced as pleasure. The sublime is a different sentiment. It takes place, on the contrary, when the imagination fails to present an object which might, if only in principle, come to match a concept. We have the Idea of the world (the totality of what is), but we do not have the capacity to show an example of it. We have the Idea of the simple (that which cannot be broken down, decomposed), but we cannot illustrate it with a sensible object which would be a "case" of it. We can conceive the infinitely great, the infinitely powerful, but every presentation of an object destined to "make visible" this absolute greatness or power appears to us painfully inadequate. Those are Ideas of which no presentation is possible. Therefore, they impart no knowledge about reality (experience); they also prevent the free union of the faculties which gives rise to the sentiment of the beautiful; and they prevent the formation and the stabilization of taste. They can be said to be unpresentable.

I shall call modern the art which devotes its "little technical expertise" (*son* "*petit technique*"), as Diderot used to say, to present the fact that the unpresentable exists. To make visible that there is something which can be conceived and which can neither be seen nor made visible: this is what is at stake in modern painting. But how to make visible that there is something which cannot be seen? Kant himself shows the way when he names "formlessness, the absence of form," as a possible index to the unpresentable. He also says of the empty "abstraction" which the imagination experiences when in search for a presentation of the infinite (another unpresentable): this abstraction itself is like a presentation of the infinite, its "negative presentation." He cites the commandment, "Thou shalt not make graven images" (*Exodus*), as the most sublime passage in the Bible in that it forbids all presentation of the Absolute. Little needs to be added to those observations to outline an aesthetic of sublime paintings. As painting, it will of course "present" something though negatively; it will therefore avoid figuration or representation. It will be "white" like one of Malevitch's squares; it will enable us to see only by making it impossible to see; it will please only by causing pain. One recognizes in those instructions the axioms of avant-gardes in painting, inasmuch as they devote themselves to making an allusion to the unpresentable by means of visible presentations. The systems in the name of which, or with which, this task has been able to support or to justify itself deserve the greatest attention; but they can originate only in the vocation of the sublime in order to legitimize it, that is, to conceal it. They remain inexplicable without the incommensurability of reality to concept which is implied in the Kantian philosophy of the sublime.

It is not my intention to analyze here in detail the manner in which the various avant-gardes have, so to speak, humbled and disqualified reality by examining the pictorial techniques which are so many devices to make us believe in it. Local tone, drawing, the mixing of colors, linear perspective, the nature of the support and that of the instrument, the treatment, the display, the museum: the avant-gardes are perpetually flushing out artifices of presentation which make it possible to subordinate thought to the gaze and to turn it away from the unpresentable. If Habermas, like Marcuse, understands this task of derealization as an aspect of the (repressive) "desublimation" which characterizes the avant-garde, it is because he confuses the Kantian sublime with Freudian sublimation, and because aesthetics has remained for him that of the beautiful.

The Postmodern

What, then, is the postmodern? What place does it or does it not occupy in the vertiginous work of the questions hurled at the rules of image and narration? It is undoubtedly a part of the modern. All that has been received, if only yesterday (*modo, modo*, Petronius used to say), must be suspected. What space does Cézanne challenge? The Impressionists'. What object do Picasso and Braque attack? Cézanne's. What presupposition does Duchamp break with in 1912? That which says one must make a painting, be it cubist. And Buren questions that other presupposition which he believes had survived untouched by the work of Duchamp: the place of presentation of the work. In an amazing acceleration, the generations precipitate themselves. A work can become modern only if it is first postmodern. Postmodernism thus understood is not modernism at its end but in the nascent state, and this state is constant.

Yet I would like not to remain with this slightly mechanistic meaning of the word. If it is true that modernity takes place in the withdrawal of the real and according to the sublime relation between the presentable and the conceivable, it is possible, within this relation, to distinguish two modes (to use the musician's language). The emphasis can be placed on the powerlessness of the faculty of presentation, on the nostalgia for presence felt by the human subject, on the obscure and futile will which inhabits him in spite of everything. The emphasis can be placed, rather, on the power of the faculty to conceive, on its "inhumanity" so to speak (it was the quality Apollinaire demanded of modern artists), since it is not the business of our understanding whether or not human sensibility or imagination can match what it conceives. The emphasis can also be placed on the increase of being and the jubilation which result from the invention of new rules of the game, be it pictorial, artistic, or any other. What

I have in mind will become clear if we dispose very schematically a few names on the chessboard of the history of avant-gardes: on the side of melancholia, the German Expressionists, and on the side of *novatio*, Braque and Picasso, on the former Malevitch and on the latter Lissitsky, on the one Chirico and on the other Duchamp. The nuance which distinguishes these two modes may be infinitesimal; they often coexist in the same piece, are almost indistinguishable; and yet they testify to a difference (*un différend*) on which the fate of thought depends and will depend for a long time, between regret and assay.

The work of Proust and that of Joyce both allude to something which does not allow itself to be made present. Allusion, to which Paolo Fabbri recently called my attention, is perhaps a form of expression indispensable to the works which belong to an aesthetic of the sublime. In Proust, what is being eluded as the price to pay for this allusion is the identity of consciousness, a victim to the excess of time (*au trop de temps*). But in Joyce, it is the identity of writing which is the victim of an excess of the book (*au trop de livre*) or of literature.

Proust calls forth the unpresentable by means of a language unaltered in its syntax and vocabulary and of a writing which in many of its operators still belongs to the genre of novelistic narration. The literary institution, as Proust inherits it from Balzac and Flaubert, is admittedly subverted in that the hero is no longer a character but the inner consciousness of time, and in that the diegetic diachrony, already damaged by Flaubert, is here put in question because of the narrative voice. Nevertheless, the unity of the book, the odyssey of that consciousness, even if it is deferred from chapter to chapter, is not seriously challenged: the identity of the writing with itself throughout the labyrinth of the interminable narration is enough to connote such unity, which has been compared to that of *The Phenomenology of Mind*.

Joyce allows the unpresentable to become perceptible in his writing itself, in the signifier. The whole range of available narrative and even stylistic operators is put into play without concern for the unity of the whole, and new operators are tried. The grammar and vocabulary of literary language are no longer accepted as given; rather, they appear as academic forms, as rituals originating in piety (as Nietzsche said) which prevent the unpresentable from being put forward.

Here, then, lies the difference: modern aesthetics is an aesthetic of the sublime, though a nostalgic one. It allows the unpresentable to be put forward only as the missing contents; but the form, because of its recognizable consistency, continues to offer to the reader or viewer matter for solace and pleasure. Yet these sentiments do not constitute the real sublime sentiment, which is in an intrinsic combination of pleasure and pain: the pleasure that reason should exceed all presentation, the pain that imagination or sensibility should not be equal to the concept.

The postmodern would be that which, in the modern, puts forward the unpresentable in presentation itself; that which denies itself the solace of good forms, the consensus of a taste which would make it possible to share collectively the nostalgia for the unattainable; that which searches for new presentations, not in order to enjoy them but in order to impart a stronger sense of the unpresentable. A postmodern artist or writer is in the position of a philosopher: the text he writes, the work he produces are not in principle governed by preestablished rules, and they cannot be judged according to a determining judgment, by applying familiar categories to the text or to the work. Those rules and categories are what the work of art itself is looking for. The artist and the writer, then, are working without rules in order to formulate the rules of what *will have been done*. Hence the fact that work and text have the characters of an *event*; hence also, they always come too late for their author, or, what amounts to the same thing, their being put into work, their realization (*mise en oeuvre*) always begin too soon. *Post modern* would have to be understood according to the paradox of the future (*post*) anterior (*modo*).

III
Truth, Value, Ethics

Plato

(427–347 BCE)

It would be difficult to exaggerate Plato's influence on the development of literary aesthetics. His enormous stature as a philosopher gives even his most casual remarks about literature the weight of his philosophical reputation. He is perhaps best known for dismissing poets from his ideal city in Book 10 of *The Republic*, but even this dramatic judgment is provisional: poets are told they must leave *until* they can provide a better defense for their art – and it is in tension with more conciliatory statements, both in *The Republic* and elsewhere, in which poetry, if not traditional poets, are admitted to be useful educational tools. Plato's ban on poets is also somewhat surprising given the fact that his Socrates often professes to be an ardent admirer of poets and their craft.

Any thorough discussion of Plato's attitudes towards literature would need to allow for the possibility that Plato's and Socrates' views may sometimes differ, and that Plato's own views may have changed over time. It would also need carefully to consider the rhetorical contexts in which Plato's arguments develop. Yet, in spite of this, it is possible to identify three general sets of concerns about poetry which remain relatively constant over Plato's career. First, he is concerned about the origins of poetry, the kinds of knowledge which a poet must possess to write good poetry and how far that knowledge extends. Second, he is interested in the kind of knowledge that poetry conveys. He wants to know both whether specific claims that the poets make are accurate and how poetic knowledge generally compares with philosophical knowledge. Finally, he is concerned with poetry's effects on its audience. How trustworthy, he wanders, are the intellectual and emotional responses which poetry inspires.

In each of these three areas Plato's suspicions about poetry are readily apparent. In the early dialogue *Ion*, for instance, Socrates questions Ion, a popular performer of Homer's works, and concludes that poets and their popularizers have neither the local knowledge of artisans like chariot builders nor the general knowledge of philosophers. Rather, he claims, poets must rely on divine inspiration, which he describes as a kind of temporary madness that poets can neither understand nor control. A similar kind of madness grips those who listen to Ion's performance, Socrates asserts; rather than being enabled to make rational decisions, the audience is transported by waves of powerful emotion. These same charges are repeated in later dialogues, and to them Plato adds arguments against the reliability of poetic knowledge itself. These arguments are most fully developed in *The Republic*, where Socrates claims that poets slander the gods by attributing human flaws to them and that they misrepresent death by portraying it as a tragedy to be avoided. Furthermore, the entire mechanism of poetic representation is flawed, Socrates argues, because it is concerned with appearances rather than with philosophical truth.

Despite this sweeping indictment, however, Plato seems to remain convinced that the love of beauty plays an essential role in a philosophical education, and while he insists that the truth and virtue which philosophy reveal are the highest forms of beauty, he nonetheless is sometimes sympathetic to the notion that passions sparked by earthly beauty can help lead the aspiring philosopher to intellectual enlightenment. This notion is given its most famous expression in Socrates' speech in *The Symposium*, which is reproduced below. Here Socrates explains how a slave woman named Diotoma showed him that physical beauty is only an approximation of the beauty of a person's character and the beauty of a person's character is only a reflection of the absolute beauty of virtue itself. This notion that beauty, and by implication, the arts, can serve as a kind of ladder connecting earthly and spiritual realms plays an important role in Neoplatonism and in the Renaissance schools of literary aesthetics which Neoplatonism inspired.

Suggested reading

Gerald Else, *Plato and Aristotle on Poetry*, Chapel Hill, NC: University of North Carolina Press, 1986.

Socrates' Conversation with Diotoma

I said: "O thou stranger woman, thou sayest well, and now, assuming love to be such as you say, what is the use of him?" "That, Socrates," she replied, "I will proceed to unfold: of his nature and birth I have already spoken; and you acknowledge that love is of the beautiful. But some one will say: Of the beautiful in what, Socrates and Diotima – or rather let me put the question more clearly, and ask: When a man loves the beautiful, what does he love?" I

Reprinted from: Plato, *The Republic and Other Works*, translated by B. Jowett, New York: Anchor Books/Doubleday, 1973, pp. 348–50, 354–5. For up-to-date publication information see Acknowledgments.

answered her "That the beautiful may be his." "Still," she said, "the answer suggests a further question, which is this: What is given by the possession of beauty?" "That," I replied, "is a question to which I have no answer ready." "Then," she said, "let me put the word 'good' in the place of the beautiful, and repeat the question: What does he who loves the good desire?" "The possession of the good," I said. "And what does he gain who possesses the good?" "Happiness," I replied; "there is no difficulty in answering that." "Yes," she said, "the happy are made happy by the acquisition of good things. Nor is there any need to ask why a man desires happiness; the answer is already final." "That is true," I said. "And is this wish and this desire common to all? and do all men always desire their own good, or only some men? – what think you?" "All men," I replied; "the desire is common to all." "But all men, Socrates," she rejoined, "are not said to love, but only some of them; and you say that all men are always loving the same things." "I myself wonder," I said, "why that is." "There is nothing to wonder at," she replied; 'the reason is that one part of love is separated off and receives the name of the whole, but the other parts have other names." "Give an example," I said. She answered me as follows: "There is poetry, which, as you know, is complex and manifold. And all creation or passage of non-being into being is poetry or making, and the processes of all art are creative; and the masters of arts are all poets."

"Very true." "Still," she said, "you know that they are not called poets, but have other names; the generic term 'poetry' is confined to that specific art which is separated off from the rest of poetry, and is concerned with music and metre; and this is what is called poetry, and they who possess this kind of poetry are called poets." "Very true," I said. "And the same holds of love. For you may say generally that all desire of good and happiness is due to the great and subtle power of love; but those who, having their affections set upon him, are yet diverted into the paths of money-making or gymnastic philosophy, are not called lovers – the name of the genus is reserved for those whose devotion takes one form only – they alone are said to love, or to be lovers." "In that," I said, "I am of opinion that you are right." "Yes," she said, "and you hear people say that lovers are seeking for the half of themselves; but I say that they are seeking neither for the half, nor for the whole, unless the half or the whole be also a good. And they will cut off their own hands and feet and cast them away, if they are evil; for they love them not because they are their own, but because they are good, and dislike them not because they are another's, but because they are evil. There is nothing which men love but the good. Do you think that there is?" "Indeed," I answered, "I should say not." "Then," she said, "the conclusion of the whole matter is, that men love the good." "Yes," I said. "To which may be added that they love the possession of the good?" "Yes, that may be added." "And not only the possession, but the everlasting possession of the good?" "That may be added too." "Then, love," she said, "may be described generally as the love of the everlasting possession of the good?" "That is most true," I said.

"Then if this be the nature of love, can you tell me further," she said, "what is the manner of the pursuit? what are they doing who show all this eagerness and heat which is called love? Answer me that." "Nay, Diotima," I said, "if I had known I should not have wondered at your wisdom, or have come to you to learn." "Well," she said, "I will teach you; – love is only birth in beauty, whether of body or soul." "The oracle requires an explanation," I said; "I don't understand you." "I will make my meaning clearer," she replied. "I mean to say, that all men are bringing to the birth in their bodies and in their souls. There is a certain age at which human nature is desirous of procreation; and this procreation must be in beauty and not in deformity: and this is the mystery of man and woman, which is a divine thing, for conception and generation are a principle of immortality in the mortal creature. And in the inharmonical they can never be. But the deformed is always inharmonical with the divine, and the beautiful harmonious. Beauty, then, is the destiny or goddess of parturition who presides at birth, and therefore when approaching beauty the conceiving power is propitious, and diffuse, and benign, and begets and bears fruit: on the appearance of foulness she frowns and contracts in pain, and is averted and morose, and shrinks up, and not without a pang refrains from conception. And this is the reason why, when the hour of conception arrives, and the teeming nature is full, there is such a flutter and ecstasy about beauty whose approach is the alleviation of pain. For love, Socrates, is not, as you imagine, the love of the beautiful only." "What then?" "The love of generation and birth in beauty." "Yes," I said. "Yes, indeed," she replied. "But why of birth?" I said. "Because to the mortal, birth is a sort of eternity and immortality," she replied; "and as has been already admitted, all men will necessarily desire immortality together with good, if love is of the everlasting possession of the good." . . .

"For he who has been instructed thus far in the things of love, and who has learned to see the beautiful in due order and succession, when he comes toward the end will suddenly perceive a nature of wondrous beauty – and this, Socrates, is that final cause of all our former toils, which in the first place is everlasting – not growing and decaying, or waxing and waning; in the next place not fair in one point of view and foul in another, or at one time or in one relation or at one place fair, at another time or in another relation or at another place foul, as if fair to some and foul to others, or in the likeness of a face or hands or any other part of the bodily frame, or in any form of speech or knowledge, nor existing in any other being; as for example, an animal, whether in earth or heaven, but beauty only, absolute, separate, simple, and everlasting, which without diminution and without increase, or any change, is imparted to the ever-growing and perishing beauties of all other things. He who under the influence of true love rising upward from these begins to see that beauty is not far from the end. And the true order of going, or being led by another, to the things of love is to use the beauties of earth as steps along which he mounts upwards for the sake of that other beauty, going from one to two, and from two to all fair forms, and from fair forms to fair actions, and from fair actions to fair notions, until from fair notions he arrives at the notion of absolute beauty, and at last knows what the essence of beauty is. This, my dear Socrates," said the stranger of Mantineia, "is that life above all others which man should live, in the contemplation of beauty absolute; a beauty which if you once beheld, you would see not to be after the measure of gold, and garments, and fair boys and youths, which when you now behold you are in fond amazement, and you and many a one are content to live seeing only and conversing with them without meat or drink, if that were possible – you only want to be with them and to look at them. But what if man had eyes to see the true beauty – the divine beauty, I mean, pure and clear and unalloyed, not clogged with the pollutions of mortality, and all the colors and vanities of human life – thither looking, and holding converse with the true beauty divine and simple, and bringing into being and educating true creations of virtue and not idols only? Do you not see that in that communion only, beholding beauty with the eye of the mind, he will be enabled to bring forth, not images of beauty, but realities; for he has hold not of an image but of a reality, and bringing forth and educating true virtue to become the friend of God and be immortal, if mortal man may. Would that be an ignoble life?"

Giambattista Vico

(1668–1744)

Giambattista Vico shows us the degree to which early Enlightenment methodology sustains a strong expressivist bias on behalf of human culture. Culture stands in Vico's mind as a vigorously productive enterprise that supersedes the creativity of any individual personality. Vico's *Principles of New Science . . . concerning the Common Nature of the Nations* (so reads the title page of the posthumous edition, July 1744) purports to formulate a knowledge of human culture which demonstrates the reciprocity that plays between individual human beings and the institutions within which individual identity stakes its claims of authority.

Vico works from the cardinal concept of totality. This concept underwrites both the rationalistic systems of knowledge which we identify with Enlightenment mind, and the notions of cultural identity that are so commonly founded upon them. Vico, however, rearticulates the metaphysical ideal of totality in such a way that active thought about totality is rendered indistinguishable from totality as an existential value. That is to say, for Vico, the whole of the culture is indistinguishable from the formative act by which culture comes into existence. Totality is neither an essence nor a plenitude but an artifact of human making. The credo of this methodological precept is *verum et factum convertuntur*: the true and the made are indistinguishable.

Following Greek etymology, Vico asserts that the prime cultural maker in human history is the poet or *poein*. Vico's recourse here to a creative agency rather than a rational principle, as a point of departure for philosophical inquiry, dramatically distinguishes Vico's "new science" from the comparative "old science" associated with Cartesian method. Descartes's theory of mind seeks a first principle independent of the historical and social contexts of human activity. In response, Vico performs a compelling etymological demystification of philosophical first principles. He points up the genesis of word logic from *logos*. Logos in turn derives from *fabula* or *favella* (speech). Favella derives from the Greek *mytos*, denoting the condition of muteness. The meaning of the term logic is thus construable by Vico as a psychological compensation for an original human *in*capacity of expression. In a manner of speaking, logic is nothing more than a form of human psychological artfulness.

Vico's theory of cultural making, then, gives a decidedly aesthetic ground to knowledge claims. Accordingly, Vico tells us that poetic wisdom, "the perfecter of man" shows us our essential "stupidity," our dependence on sense as a pretext of intellectual exposition. If follows, in this perspective, that representation must be deemed prior to truth or meaning. Intellect (from *intelligere*) interprets sense by giving it causality. Homer, for example, traces the beginning of "wisdom" to the differentiation of good from evil, which is in turn only a premise for the justification of human suffering.

Thus Vico would remind us that everything that is known as a rational idea (an ideal) began quite simply as an experience that needed justification. The faculty of this imaginative enterprise, which Vico posits as the "corporeal imagination," exhibits a principle of *knowing through sensing*. Vico equates it with the productive capacity of the shaping hand. Corporeal imagination gives meaning to an object by forming it to suit a human use or purpose. Likewise, cultural production is understood by Vico on analogy with children when they take inanimate things in their hands and talk to them. Analogy itself becomes the functional principle of Vichean reason. More to the point, the Platonist dichotomy of reason and sense is supplanted by Vico's postulate of a poetic logic, animated in the tropes of metaphor, allegory, metonymy, and synecdoche. Such tropes signify, above all, the "operations of abstract minds" working upon the substances of the material world. Poetic logic corrects the most destructive error of the old science, which was to treat as separate things that are naturally conjoined: sense/intellect, philosophy/poetry. The methodology of Vico's new science grants the potential intelligibility of everything. It posits the intrinsic value of the totality of human experience.

Suggested reading

A. A. Grimaldi, *The Universal Humanity of Giambattista Vico*, New York: S. F. Vaanni, 1958.

Poetic Wisdom

Prolegomena

361   We have said above in the Axioms that all the histories of the gentile nations have had fabulous beginnings [202], that among the Greeks (who have given us all we know of gentile antiquity) the first sages were the theological poets [199], and that the nature of everything born or made betrays the crude-

Reprinted from: Giambattista Vico, *The New Science of Giambattista Vico*, translation of the 3rd edn. of 1744 by Thomas Goddard Bergin and Max Harold Fisch, Ithaca, NY: Cornell University Press, 1991, pp. 109, 116–18, 129–32.

ness of its origin [239ff]. It is thus and not otherwise that we must conceive the origins of poetic wisdom. And as for the great and sovereign esteem in which it has been handed down to us, this has its origin in the two conceits, that of nations [125] and that of scholars [127], and it springs even more from the latter than from the former. For just as Manetho, the Egyptian high priest, translated all the fabulous history of Egypt into a sublime natural theology [222], so the Greek philosophers translated theirs into philosophy. And they did so not merely for the reason that the histories as they had come down to both alike were most unseemly [221], but for the following five reasons as well.

362   The first was reverence for religion, for the gentile nations were everywhere founded by fables on religion. The second was the grand effect thence derived, namely this civil world, so wisely ordered that it could only be the effect of a superhuman wisdom. The third was the occasions which, as we shall see, these tables, assisted by the veneration of religion and the credit of such great wisdom, gave the philosophers for instituting research and for meditating lofty things in philosophy. The fourth was the ease with which they were thus enabled, as we shall also show farther on, to explain their sublime philosophical meditations by means of the expressions happily left them by the poets. The fifth and last, which is the sum of them all, is the confirmation of their own meditations which the philosophers derived from the authority of religion and the wisdom of the poets.

Poetic Metaphysics

375   Hence poetic wisdom, the first wisdom of the gentile world, must have begun with a metaphysics not rational and abstract like that of learned men now, but felt and imagined as that of these first men must have been, who, without power of ratiocination, were all robust sense and vigorous imagination [185]. This metaphysics was their poetry, a faculty born with them (for they were furnished by nature with these senses and imaginations); born of their ignorance of causes, for ignorance, the mother of wonder, made everything wonderful to men who were ignorant of everything [184]. Their poetry was at first divine, because, as we saw in the passage from Lactantius, they imagined the causes of the things they felt and wondered at to be gods [188]. (This is now confirmed by the American Indians, who call gods all the things that surpass their small understanding. We may add the ancient Germans dwelling about the Arctic Ocean, of whom Tacitus [G. 45] tells that they spoke of hearing the sun pass at night from west to east through the sea, and affirmed that they saw the gods. These very rude and simple nations help us to a much

better understanding of the founders of the gentile world with whom we are now concerned.) At the same time they gave the things they wondered at substantial being after their own ideas, just as children do, whom we see take inanimate things in their hands and play with them and talk to them as though they were living persons [186].

378   But the nature of our civilized minds is so detached from the senses, even in the vulgar, by abstractions corresponding to all the abstract terms our languages abound in, and so refined by the art of writing, and as it were spiritualized by the use of numbers, because even the vulgar know how to count and reckon, that it is naturally beyond our power to form the vast image of this mistress called "Sympathetic Nature." Men shape the phrase with their lips but have nothing in their minds; for what they have in mind is falsehood, which is nothing; and their imagination no longer avails to form a vast false image. It is equally beyond our power to enter into the vast imagination of those first men, whose minds were not in the least abstract, refined, or spiritualized, because they were entirely immersed in the senses, buffeted by the passions, buried in the body. That is why we said above [338] that we can scarcely understand, still less imagine, how those first men thought who founded gentile humanity.

404   All the first tropes are corollaries of this poetic logic. The most luminous and therefore the most necessary and frequent is metaphor. It is most praised when it gives sense and passion to insensate things, in accordance with the metaphysics above discussed [402], by which the first poets attributed to bodies the being of animate substances, with capacities measured by their own, namely sense and passion, and in this way made fables of them. Thus every metaphor so formed is a fable in brief. This gives a basis for judging the time when metaphors made their appearance in the languages. All the metaphors conveyed by likenesses taken from bodies to signify the operations of abstract minds must date from times when philosophies were taking shape. The proof of this is that in every language the terms needed for the refined arts and recondite sciences are of rustic origin [240].

405   It is noteworthy that in all languages the greater part of the expressions relating to inanimate things are formed by metaphor from the human body and its parts and from the human senses and passions. Thus, head for top or beginning; the brow and shoulders of a hill; the eyes of needles and of potatoes; mouth for any opening; the lip of a cup or pitcher; the teeth of a rake, a saw, a comb; the beard of wheat; the tongue of a shoe; the gorge of a river; a neck

of land; an arm of the sea; the hands of a clock; heart for center (the Latins used *umbilicus*, navel, in this sense); the belly of a sail; foot for end or bottom; the flesh of fruits; a vein of rock or mineral; the blood of grapes for wine; the bowels of the earth.[1] Heaven or the sea smiles; the wind whistles; the waves murmur; a body groans under a great weight. The farmers of Latium used to say the fields were thirsty, bore fruit, were swollen with grain; and our rustics speak of plants making love, vines going mad, resinous trees weeping. Innumerable other examples could be collected from all languages. All of which is a consequence of our axiom [120] that man in his ignorance makes himself the rule of the universe, for in the examples cited he has made of himself an entire world. So that, as rational metaphysics teaches that man becomes all things by understanding them (*homo intelligendo fit omnia*), this imaginative metaphysics shows that man becomes all things by *not* understanding them (*homo non intelligendo fit omnia*); and perhaps the latter proposition is truer than the former, for when man understands he extends his mind and takes in the things, but when he does not understand he makes the things out of himself and becomes them by transforming himself into them.

406   In such a logic, sprung from such a metaphysics, the first poets had to give names to things from the most particular and the most sensible ideas. Such ideas are the sources, respectively, of synecdoche and metonymy. Metonymy of agent for act resulted from the fact that names for agents were commoner than names for acts. Metonymy of subject for form and accident was due to inability to abstract forms and qualities from subjects [209]. Certainly metonymy of cause for effect produced in each case a little fable, in which the cause was imagined as a woman clothed with her effects [402]: ugly Poverty, sad Old Age, pale Death.

410   Poetic monsters and metamorphoses arose from a necessity of this first human nature, its inability to abstract forms or properties from subjects [209]. By their logic they had to put subjects together in order to put their forms together, or to destroy a subject in order to separate its primary form from the contrary form which had been imposed upon it. Such a putting together of ideas created the poetic monsters. In Roman law, as Antoine Favre observes in his *Iurisprudentiae papinianeae scientia*, children born of prostitutes are called monsters because they have the nature of men together with the bestial characteristic of having been born of vagabond or uncertain unions [688]. And it was as being monsters of this sort, we shall find, that children born of noble women without benefit of solemn nuptials were commanded by the Law of the Twelve Tables to be thrown into the Tiber [566].

411   The distinguishing of ideas produced metamorphoses. Among other examples preserved by ancient jurisprudence is the heroic Latin phrase *fundum fieri*, to become ground of, used in place of *auctorem fieri*, to become author of, to authorize, to ratify; the explanation being that, as the ground supports the farm or soil and that which is sown, planted, or built thereon, so the ratifier supports an act which without his ratification would fail; and he does this by quitting the form of a being moving at will, which he is, and taking on the contrary form of a stable thing [353, 491].

Note

1   Several of Vico's examples for which there are no common English parallels are here omitted, and substitutions are made for several others.

Alexander Gottlieb Baumgarten

(1714–1762)

Alexander Baumgarten inaugurated the modern usage of the term "aesthetic." Kant, who considered Baumgarten one of the great metaphysicians of his time, showed him the deference of incorporating "the aesthetic" into his own epistemology, making it a key term of the *Critique of Judgment*.

Baumgarten's seminal texts on the aesthetic span his career: *Reflections on Poetry* (1735) written when he was barely 20 years old and *Aesthetica* (1750), a product of his maturity. In these texts he is attempting to work out "some view of poetic cognition," thus to establish a legitimate place for the arts in cognitive experience. He wanted to make artistic knowledge complementary to rather than mutually exclusive of the projects of philosophy and science. Formerly the arts, and the standard of the beautiful by which they could be judged, were subordinated to the so-called "lower faculties" of perception and feeling. The higher faculties of reason and cognition took precedence in the enterprise of human knowledge. Baumgarten, reacting to the rationalist belittling of the aesthetic as a weakly impressionistic register of experience, sought to balance the epistemological picture by reconciling the aesthetic with the methods of rational understanding. He conceded that appreciation of beauty denotes a "lower faculty," but one that is nonetheless cognitive and functions in a manner analogous to reason. Baumgarten explained that both reason and aesthetics aspire to clarity of knowledge. For Baumgarten clarity denoted the capacity of mind to organize its experience of the world according to unifying principles. While the "higher" cognitive faculty penetrates into an object, rendering its nature *intensively* clear in a philosophical idea, the aesthetic purveys a clarity that is *extensive*, available in the manifold of sense particulars that make up the object of perception. While the clarity of reason yields representations that are "distinct," aesthetic representations must be called "confused." This means, however, that aesthetic representations are *fused together*. They are not invidiously irrational or stupid. Just as the clarity of a philosophical idea depends on the unity of thought, so the clarity of the aesthetic artifact is keyed to the unity of perception. The more complexly articulated (i.e. the more *confused* the sensuous particulars that make up the artistic whole), the more aesthetic perfection is embodied in the aesthetic object. The perfection of the aesthetic object might therefore be understood as the subordination of sense particulars to a principle of thematic interconnectedness, which could nevertheless not be reduced to an abstract concept.

Baumgarten extrapolated from this logic to the formal composition of the poem. According to Baumgarten, the verbal construction that presents the most formally complex array of sensuous impressions or images – such that they nonetheless constitute an indistinguishable whole – constitutes the most perfect aesthetic form. *Confused clarity* does not pre-empt or preclude the intensive clarity of the "higher faculty," it merely applies in a different register of experience: sensuous representation. The advantage of poetic clarity is its manifest "extension" of the register of sensuous apprehension. It endows a concreteness and vividness that complements the conceptual or ideational clarity which otherwise remains abstract from sense experience.

The privilege which Baumgarten grants to complexity as an "objective" standard of aesthetic value reappears in later formalist paradigms of critico-aesthetic knowledge: Coleridgean romanticism, Warren and Brooks's version of New Critical organicism and Monroe Beardsley's modernist thesis of the "aesthetic attitude."

Suggested reading

L. Wessel, "Alexander Baumgarten's contribution to the development of aesthetics," *Journal of Aesethetics and Art Criticism*, 30 (1972).

Reflections on Poetry (1735)

§11   By poetic we shall mean whatever can contribute to the perfection of a poem.

§12   Sensate representations are parts of the poem, §10, and hence poetic, §11, §7, but since sensate representations may be either obscure or clear, §3, poetic representations are either obscure or clear.   *subjective dimension of perception / reception.*

Of course, representations of an identical thing can be to one person obscure, to another clear, to a third even distinct. But seeing that the discussion concerns the representations intended to be designated in discourse, we mean those representations which the speaker intends to communicate. Thus *B. resolves the problem by using notion of intention.* we investigate here those representations which the poet intends to designate in the poem.

Reprinted from: A. G. Baumgarten, *Reflections on Poetry*, translated by Karl Aschenbrenner and William Holther, Berkeley: University of California Press, 1954, pp. 40–50, 52–3.

(cf. Kant)

§13   In obscure representations there are not contained as many representations of characteristic traits as would suffice for recognizing them and for distinguishing them from others, and as, in fact, are contained in clear representations (by definition). Therefore, more elements will contribute to the communication of sensate representations if these are clear than if they are obscure. A poem, therefore, whose representations are clear is more perfect than one whose representations are obscure, and clear representations are more poetic than obscure ones, §11.

This should take care of those who wrongly suppose that the more obscure and intricate their effusions the more "poetic" their diction. We certainly do not want to go over to the opinion of those who reject the finest poets, no matter who, because they decide that in them they see, with their rheumy eyes, pure darkness and thick night. For example, Persius says,

> If, overcautious, you pound down the well cap with many a plank, you will have given
> the people thirsty ears in vain.

Only someone ignorant of Neronian history will be so rash as to brand this as Cimmerian darkness. Whoever consults that history will either arrive at the sense and experience sufficiently clear representations, or he knows no Latin.

§14   Distinct representations, complete, adequate, profound through every degree, are not sensate, and, therefore, not poetic, §11.

The truth of this will become evident *a posteriori* by an experiment. Suppose we read to a man trained in philosophy and at the same time not entirely a stranger to poetry little verses overladen with distinct representations, for example:

> Refutation is the proof that others err.
> No one refutes unless he proves thereby
> Another's fallacy. But if you want to prove
> Such things, it's clear you have to study logic.
> When you refute, you're sure to get it wrong
> If you are no logician – by verse one.

He will scarcely let the verses go unchallenged though they are prefect in versification. Perhaps he himself will not know for what reason they seem worthless to him, as there is nothing to criticize either in form or in content. This is the principal reason why philosophy and poetry are scarcely ever thought able to perform the same office, since philosophy pursues <u>conceptual distinctness</u> above everything else, while poetry does not strive to attain this, as falling outside its province. If a man excels in each part of the faculty of understanding and can employ each at will in its proper sphere, he will certainly apply himself to the exercise of the one without detriment to the other. He

[left margin handwritten note: more or less congruent w what Kant says abt. the beautiful being 'that which, apart fr. a concept, is cognized as object of a necessary delight.' (85)]

will see that Aristotle and Leibniz and hundreds of others who added the mantle of the sage to the laurel of the poet were prodigies, not freaks.

§15   Since poetic representations are clear representations, §13, and since they will be either distinct or confused, and since they are not distinct, §14, therefore, they are confused.

§16   When in representation A more is represented than in B, C, D, and so on, but all are confused, A will be said to be extensively clearer than the rest.
We have had to add this restriction so that we may distinguish these degrees of clarity from those, already sufficiently understood, which, through a discrimination of characteristics, plumb the depths of cognition and render one representation *intensively clearer* than another.

§17   In extensively very clear representations more is represented in a sensate way than in those less clear, §16; therefore, they contribute more to the perfection of a poem, §7. For this reason extensively clearer representations are especially poetic, §11.

§18   The more determinate things are, the more their representations embrace. In fact, the more that is gathered together in a confused representation, the more extensive clarity the representation has, §16, and the more poetic it is, §17. Therefore, for things to be determined as far as possible when they are to be represented in a poem is poetic, §11.

§19   Individuals are determined in every respect. Therefore, particular representations are in the highest degree poetic, §18.
Our tyro poets, far from observing this nicety of a poem, turn up their noses at Homer, who tells in *Iliad* II of the
   Leaders and chieftains, commanders of ships, and all the fleet.
In VII he tells the stories of all those who crossed Hector's path. In the Hymn to Apollo he lists the many places sacred to the god. Likewise, in Virgil's *Aeneid*, anyone who reads through book VII following will have many opportunities to observe the same thing. We may also cite, in the *Metamorphoses* of Ovid, the enumeration of the dogs who rend their master to shreds. I do not think anybody can suppose that those things which would be very difficult for us to imitate come into being without study and effort.

§21   By "example" we mean a representation of something more determined which is supplied to clarify the representation of something less determined.

Since I have not seen this definition elsewhere, in order to show that it accords perfectly with accepted usage I may refer to the arithmetician who asserts that equal quantities added to equal produce an equal aggregate, or, if A = Z, B = Y, then A + B = Z + Y. If he substitutes the determinate number 4 in the place of the undetermined number A; in place of Z, 2 + 2; in place of B, 6; in place of Y, 3 + 3; and asserts that 4 + 6 = 2 + 2 + 3 + 3, everyone will say that he has given an example for his axiom, because the substitution was made for the purpose of showing more clearly what he intended by the letters. Suppose a philosopher wants to demonstrate that nonproper locutions ought to be expelled from a definition. If with Campanella he defines "fever" as "the war instigated against disease by the powerful force of the spirit" or as "the spontaneous extraordinary agitation and inflammation of the spirit for giving battle to the irritant cause of the sickness," it is evident that the philosopher has provided an example of a nonproper definition, so that by it we can see more deeply into the nature of such definitions. In place of a definition of "nonproper definitions" in general he has offered an individual case, and in place of a general concept of nonproper locutions he has offered representations of war, agitation of spirit, and inflammation, and so on, concepts in which more has been determined than that they are merely arrived at through a nonproper term, which, moreover, is merely added to this concept for expressing and manifesting it. That person will find our definition [of "example"] productive who attempts to solve the problem of how a teacher furnishes an example for showing the way to others, or who has meditated on the profound words of the pious Spener where he says, "Mathematics, through the certainty and safety of its demonstrations, provides an example for all sciences, which we emulate as far as we can." Cf. §107.

§22   Example confusedly represented are representations that are extensively clearer than those for whose clarification they are offered, §21; hence they are more poetic, §18; and among them individual examples are, of course, the best, §19.

The illustrious Leibniz sees this in that excellent book in which he undertakes to justify the ways of God, where he says, "The chief object of history, as well as of poetry, should be to teach prudence and virtue through examples." When we look for an example of an example, we are confronted, rather like Tantalus, with such swimming abundance that we scarcely know which draught to take. Let us race off to the sea of the unhappy Ovid: the less determined representation –

Often when one god oppresses, another god brings help –

has scarcely escaped from his mouth, which drips with salty streams of tears and sea water, when, behold! the poet suddenly justifies himself, to the extent of six verses, with a gathering flood of examples:

Vulcan stood against Troy, for Troy Apollo . . . , etc.

§23 Concept A, which, independent of the characteristic traits of concept B, is represented along with concept B, is said to "adhere" to it. That concept to which another adheres is called a "complex concept," as opposed to a "simple concept" to which no other adheres. Since a complex concept represents more than a simple one, confused complex concepts are extensively clearer, §16, and hence more poetic than simple concepts, §17.

§24 By "sense representations" we mean representations of present changes in that which is to be represented, and these are sensate, §3, and thus far poetic, §12.

§25 Since affects are rather marked degrees of pleasure or pain, their sense representations are given in the representing of something to oneself confusedly as good or bad. Therefore, they determine poetic representations, §24; and therefore, to arouse affects is poetic, §11.

§26 The same can be demonstrated by this reasoning also: we represent more in those things which we represent as good or bad for us than if we do not so represent them; therefore, representations of things which are confusedly exhibited as good or bad for us are extensively clearer than if they were not so displayed, §16. Hence they are also more poetic, §17. Now such representations are rousings of the affects; therefore, to arouse affects is poetic, §11.

§27 Stronger impressions are clearer impressions, thus more poetic than feeble and less clear impressions, §17. Stronger impressions attend an affect more, rather than less, powerful, §25. Therefore, it is highly poetic to excite the most powerful affects. This is evident from the following: that which we confusedly represent as the worst or as the best for us is represented more clearly, extensively, than if we had represented it as less good or less bad, §16; and hence it is more poetic, §17. Now the confused representation of a thing as very bad or very good for us determines the most powerful affects. Therefore, it is more poetic to excite more powerful, rather than less powerful, affects.

§28 Images are sensate representations, §3, and so poetic, §12.

When we call the reproduced representations of the senses "images," we of course follow philosophers in departing from the vague signification of the word, but not from the common usage of language or the rules of grammar: for who would deny that an image is what we have imagined? The faculty of imagining is already described in the lexicon of Suidas as "that which takes from perception the impressions of the things perceived and transforms them within itself." What, then, are images if they are not newly made (reproduced) impressions (representations) received from sense? This is what is intended here under the concept of things sensed.

§29   Images are less clear than sense impressions, therefore, less poetic, §17. Therefore, since aroused affects determine sense impressions, a poem which arouses affects is more perfect than one which is full of dead imagery, §8, §9, and it is more poetic to arouse affects than to produce other images.

> *It is not enough for poems to be beautiful: they must also be charming and lead the mind of the listener where they please.*

Certainly a neat characteristic by which we can separate Homer from

> *Jackdaw poets and magpie poetesses,*

and from all those who, beginning with much promise,

> *Tack on a purple patch or two, to make a splurge.*

So Horace does not wholly condemn images. Let us see just which images these may be of whose cautious employment the poet, our touchstone, speaks.

> *So we are regaled with Diana's grove and altar* [images 1 and 2], *or the river Rhine* [image 3], *or a rainbow* [image 4], *but this was not the place for them.*

According to §22, when the poet performs, we develop a more universal notion from these specific instances and sharp determinations, as it were from examples. Certainly no other notion will be found under which these things can be classified except that of imaged concepts. Not every place is suitable for an image; the reason is supplied by the foregoing proposition. If I may agree with Horace, the humblest craftsman who "depicts claws and imitates soft hair in bronze" (aptly representing certain images in verse)

> *Fails in the consummation of the work because he does not know how to grasp the whole figure. Now if I cared to indulge in composition, I should no more want to be like that than to live with a crooked nose while admired for my dark hair and eyes.*

§30   When a partial image has been represented, the image of the object recurs as a whole and so far constitutes a complex concept of it, which, if it is confused, will be more poetic than if it is simple, §23. Therefore, to represent the whole with a partial image, and that extensively more clear, is poetic, §17.

metonymy

§31 That which, in respect to place and time, is coexistent with a partial image belongs with it to the same whole. Therefore, to represent extensively clear images along with something to be partially represented is poetic, §30.

The descriptions that poets use most are those of time, for example, of night, of noon, and of evening in Virgil. The four seasons of the year are depicted by Seneca in one passage; descriptions of dawn, of autumn, winter, springtime, and so on, are also found in Virgil; and to rival these, any bad poet you please can produce other specimens. Regarding these, however, the scholium to §28 is especially to be noted.

§38 The more clearly images are represented, the more they will be similar to sense impressions, so that they are often equivalent to rather weak sensations. Now to represent images as clearly as possible is poetic, §17. Therefore, it is poetic to make them very similar to sensations.

§39 It is the function of a picture to represent a composite, and that is poetic, §24; the representation of a picture is very similar to the sense idea to be depicted, and this is poetic, §38. Therefore, a poem and a picture are similar, §30.

Poetry is like a picture.

For in this place the necessities of exegesis require one to concede that the grouping of poetry, meaning by this the poem, with painting, is to be understood in terms not of the art involved but of the effect achieved. Nor for this reason is there to be any argument about the genuine notion of poetry, correctly settled and established in §9, for in such confusion of practically synonymous terms both our poet and others

Have always had an equal right to hazard what they please.

§40 Since a picture represents an image only on a surface, it is not for the picture to represent every aspect, or any motion at all; yet it is poetic to do so, because when these things are also represented, then more things are represented in the object than when they are not, and hence the representing is extensively clearer, §16. Therefore, in poetic images more things tend toward unity than in pictures. Hence a poem is more perfect than a picture.

§41 Although images by way of words and discourse are clearer than those of visible things, nevertheless we are not trying to affirm a prerogative of a poem over a picture, since the *intensive* clarity which, through words, is granted to symbolic cognition beyond the intuitive, contributes nothing to *extensive* clarity, the only clarity that is poetic, §17, §14.

This is true both by experience and as a consequence of §29.

Less vividly is the mind stirred by what finds entrance through the ear, than by what can be seen through one's own trusty eyes – what one can see for oneself.

Johann Georg Hamann

(1730–1788)

J. G. Hamann is commonly referred to as one of the inspirational figures in the German romantic literary movement called *Sturm und Drang* (storm and stress). *Sturm und Drang* is typified by a passionate will to self-abandonment and spontaneous emotion. It stands for a rejection of rule-governed behavior or thought and a privileging of artistic genius over and against ordinary sensibility. These are equally the attitudes expressed in Hamann's own philosophical-cum-theological project of human understanding.

Hamann was a fervent enemy of Enlightenment rationality. He objected to its discounting of spiritual knowledge of the world since he held that such knowledge was ordained by God, who speaks to humanity directly and literally in sacred scriptures. With this belief, Hamann was a passionate antagonist of Baumgarten and Kant. So it comes as no surprise that – contra Baumgarten and Kant – Hamann's writings on the aesthetic presuppose an idea of God as an artist whose manifold purposes are infinitely extensible in the natural world. On this analogy, we are meant to understand art, in its myriad forms, as a medium of divine revelation which therefore cannot be held accountable to an abstract system of rules or principles like those of Baumgarten's "confused clarity" or Kant's "disinterested" judgment of taste.

Correlatively, Hamann sees "mystical rationality" as trivializing the senses and the passions with which divine will has endowed human nature. Hamann believes that the philosopher's displacement of Nature with the authority of abstract theorem threatens to alienate us from God's creations. By "maiming" the human faculties – the passions, the senses, all the sensuous registers of immediate experience – the counter-aesthetic will of the Enlightenment rationalist makes itself the enemy of both man and God.

In *Aesthetica in Nuce* (1762) Hamann sought to reclaim the realm of the aesthetic for the pietist purposes of his Christian humanism. Though this text was nominally a polemic against naturalistic readings of the Bible, it became the staging ground for a revolution in aesthetic theory that freed artistic creativity from all norms of critical judgment. Hamann challenged the classicist teachings of Boileau, Batteau,

Gottsched, Lessing, and Baumgarten, who made the integrity of the work of art depend on upon rational pretexts external to the work itself. Likewise he invoked artistic genius as a counterpart to divine creation. Genius, because it brooks no rules, asserts the unanlyzable unity and metaphysical truthfulness of the artwork, thus putting it beyond the powers of rational inquiry.

And yet while Hamann's first priority was certainly to assert the metaphysical significance of the artwork, the real thrust of his argument is to make the formal elements of artistic expression an irreducible threshold of their appreciation: "Just try to read the *Iliad* after excising, by abstraction, the vowels alpha and omega, and then tell me what you think of the poet's understanding and harmonies."

For Hamann art is in a position to give us immediate knowledge expressly because it is a non-conceptual medium. Rather than dissecting reality into lifeless parts, as does the analytical philosopher or scientist, the artist, who trades primarily in images, directly reproduces the wholeness and richness of experience as God confers it in our experience of the natural world. Hamann does believe that art communicates by imitating nature, but not according to norms of representational practice. Rather, the work of art is, like nature itself, a translation of divine being into a habitable environment for humanity. Just as God found expression of his own Nature in the forms of the natural world, the genius-artist, by following only the "rule" of his own nature, represents the divine truth. Thus the artist's own nature becomes a medium for human faithfulness to God's plan. Thus the work of art must be reverenced as an insight into reality whose truthfulness cannot be questioned by any method beyond the means of its own execution.

Suggested reading

Isaiah Berlin, *The Magus of the North: J. G. Hamann and the Origins of Modern Irrationalism*, London: John Murray, 1993.

Aesthetica in Nuce

Not lyre or paint-brush, but a corn-shovel for my muse, to sweep the barn of holy literature! Hail to the archangel over the relics of the language of Canaan! On fair asses he is victorious in the race; but the wise fool of Greece borrows Euthyphron's proud stallions for the philological exchange of words.

Poetry is the mother-tongue of the human race, as the garden is older than the field, painting than writing, song than declamation, parables than infer-

Reprinted from: J. G. Hamann, "Aesthetica in Nuce," in Ronald Gregor Smith (ed. and trans.) *J. G. Hamann, 1730–1788: A Study in Christian Existence*, London: Collins, 1960, pp. 196–200.

ences, barter than commerce. The rest of our earliest forebears was a deeper sleep; and their movement was a tumultuous dance. Seven days they sat in the silence of reflection or astonishment; and opened their mouths to utter winged words. Senses and passions speak and understand nothing but images. The whole treasure of human knowledge and happiness consists of nothing but images. The first outburst of creation, and the first impression of its historian, the first appearance and the first enjoyment of nature, are united in the words, Let there be light. Herewith begins the experience of the presence of things.

Finally God crowned the revelation of his glory to the senses by the master-work of man. He created man in divine form – in the image of God he created him. This decree of the creator loosens the most complicated knots of human nature and its destiny. Blind heathens have recognised the invisible nature which men have in common with God. The veiled figure of the body, the countenance of the head, and the extremities of the arms are the visible scheme in which we move; yet they are really nothing but a pointer to the hidden man within us.

Exemplumque Dei quisque est in imagine parva.

The earliest nourishment came from the plant realm; the milk of the ancients was wine; the oldest poetic art was called botanic by its learned scholiast (according to the fable of Jotham and Joash); and man's first clothing was a rhapsody of fig-leaves . . .

Speak that I may see thee! This wish was fulfilled in the creation, which is a speaking to the creature through the creature; for day unto day uttereth speech, and night unto night sheweth knowledge. Their line is gone out through all the earth to the end of the world, and there is no speech or language, where their voice is not heard. No matter where the fault is (outside us or within us), in nature we have nothing but a confusion of verses and *disiecti membra poetæ* left for our use. To collect them is for the scholar; to expound them, for the philosopher; to imitate them or even more audaciously to bring them into order is the poet's modest part.

Speech is translation – from the language of angels into a language of men, that is, thoughts into words, things into names, images into signs, which can be poetical or kyriological, historical or symbolical or hieroglyphical, philosophical or characteristic. This kind of translation (that is, speech) is, more than any other, like the underside of a carpet,

And shews the stuff, but not the workman's skill;

or like an eclipse of the sun, which can be seen in a bowl of water . . .

The book of creation contains examples of general ideas, which God desired to reveal to the creature by means of the creature; the books of the covenant contain examples of secret articles which God desired to reveal to man by means of man. The unity of the author is reflected in the very dialect of his works – in them all there is a single accent of immeasurable height and depth! A proof of the most glorious majesty and completest emptying! A miracle of such infinite calm making God to be like nothing, that one must in conscience deny his existence or be a beast; but at the same time of such infinite power, filling all in all, that one does not know where to turn from the intensity of his activity towards us . . .

All the colours of the fairest world fade, as soon as you extinguish that light, the first-born of creation. If your stomach is your god, the very hairs of your head are in his guardianship. Every creature is in turn your sacrifice and your idol. Subject against its will – but still hoping – it sighs in its servitude or over your vanity. It does its best to escape your tyranny and, amid the most passionate embraces, longs for that freedom with which the beasts paid homage to Adam, when God brought them to the man to see what he would call them. For whatever he called them, that was their name.

This analogy of man to the Creator gives to all creatures their content and their character, from which depend loyalty and faith in the whole of nature. The livelier this idea, the image of the invisible God in our heart, the more capable we are of seeing and tasting, looking at and grasping with our hands, the loving-kindness of God in the creatures. Every impression of nature in man is not only a memento but also a pledge of the basic truth – who the Lord is. Every reaction of man towards the creature is a letter and a seal of our share in the divine nature, and that we are of his race.

O for a muse like a refiner's fire, and like fullers' soap! She will dare to purify the natural use of the senses from the unnatural use of abstractions, which mutilate our ideas of things as badly as they suppress and blaspheme the name of the Creator. I speak with you, O Greeks, because you think yourselves wiser than the chamberlains with the gnostic key; just try to read the *Iliad* after excising, by abstraction, the vowels alpha and omega, and then tell me what you think of the poet's understanding and harmonies.

Apostille

As the oldest reader of this rhapsody in cabbalistic prose I consider myself bound by the right of the first-born to leave for my younger brothers, who will come after me, the following merciful judgment:

Everything in this æsthetic nut tastes of vanity – of vanity. The rhapsodist has read, observed, reflected, he has sought and found pleasant words, faithfully quoted them, like a merchant ship he has fetched his provisions from afar.

He has added sentence to sentence, as one counts the arrows on a battle-field; and has measured off his figures of speech like the pegs of a tent . . .

Let us hear the sum of his latest æsthetic, which is also the oldest of all:

Fear God and give him the honour, for the time of his judgment is come, and pray to him who has made heaven and earth and sea and wells of water!

Johann Gottfried Herder

(1744–1803)

Herder's role in the history of aesthetic theorizing aligns with the careers of Vico, Baumgarten, and Hamann. Though his early training was influenced by his acquaintance with Immanuel Kant, Herder became an energetic and at times passionate antagonist of Enlightenment precepts that dictated knowledge of human nature and experience in terms of a priori faculties and abstract legislative principles. The prevailing "faculty psychology" of the Enlightenment era (deriving from the premier rationalistic philosophy of Christian Wolff) purveyed a picture of the human mind as split into compartments (e.g. Kant's reason, understanding, judgment). Each faculty was deemed to exercise separate jurisdiction over the diverse range of human experiences. Such thinking had the effect of absolutizing and universalizing standards of human conduct.

Quite to the contrary, Herder saw the discipline of philosophical judgment (specifically judgements between true and false, the good and the beautiful, the beautiful and the ugly) as anthropologically grounded in the activities of human culture. As Herder saw it, self-cultivation ought to be the proper end of philosophical reflection. Herder recognized a precursor of this stance in A. G. Baumgarten's aesthetic theory. Baumgarten allowed that poetry and philosophy constituted two different modes of human reflection. But he insisted that they were united in the reflective imperative which was an underpinning of both. Against the Enlightenment pundits who maintained a strict partition between philosophy proper and the standards of taste, Herder's anthropological position presupposed that the philosophical consciousness itself emerges from sensibility. Herder understood sensibility to be the basis upon which reflection served the purpose of self-cultivation. In his influential "Essay on the Origin of Language" (1771) Herder contended that because the reflective activity strictly inheres in linguistic capacity it compels our recognition that the study of language and the study of reason are coterminous.

This had the effect of forcing Herder to rethink the nature of the artwork as something no longer subordinate to abstract philosophical principles, principles that sensuous media can only approximate. Whereas the adherents of Enlightenment faculty psychology were obliged to treat art, taste, and the sense of the beautiful, as his-

torically invariant – in so far as they were derived from abstract principles – Herder
offered an alternative. Like his intellectual ancestor Vico, who identified the source
of knowledge with signifying activity, Herder had a gift for seeing beyond the limits
of paradigmatic thought. He therefore reconceived the idea of aesthetic perfection
upon which beauty theory rested as a dynamic economy of forces. This was opposed
to thinking of it as a static proportion of part and whole. If the unity of part and
whole is ordained by an analytic principle then the experience of the artwork is secondary to the knowledge which it embodies. If the unity is synthetic – in the rela-
tionality of parts – then the knowledge purveyed by the work of art is indivisible
from the formal embodiment. By the same token, Herder reasoned that the standard of taste could no longer be understood as transhistorical. Indeed, history would
be the real determinant of taste. The works of art produced in any historical moment
are expressions of the personality of the time.

Herder's *Plastik* (published 1778, composed in the 1760s) gives us his most fully
articulated account of the unique knowledge availed by the artwork. In this still
untranslated text Herder chooses sculpture as his exemplary artform, because the
experience of sculpture ultimately depends on a dynamic tactility which transcends the
more static limits of the visual image. Herder's enthusiasm for the way in which our
experience of sculpture recapitulates the child's imaginative awakening to the reflective capacity of mind – touching, moving around the object, standing back, weighing
it against the hand – is reminiscent of Vico's notion of "corporeal imagination", which
was itself posited as the condition for verbal figuration in literary trope. Like Vico,
Herder was an enemy of scholastic dogmatism. Herder's aesthetic theory makes a significant contribution to the post-romantic consensus which holds that art is instrumental to making culture rather than a mere artifact of pre-fabricated cultural identity.

Suggested reading

R. T. Clark, *Herder: His Life and Thought*, Berkeley: University of California Press, 1955.

Extract from a Correspondence on Ossian and the Songs of Ancient Peoples

My friend,[1] I share your delight at the translation of Ossian[2] for our language
and our nation; it has pleased me as much as an original epic. A poet so full of

Reprinted from: Johann Gottfried Herder, "Extract from a Correspondence on Ossian and the Songs
of Ancient Peoples" [1773] (trans. Joyce P. Crick, with modifications by the editor; German text in
Sämtliche Werke, ed. Suphan (1877–1913), v, 159–207), in H. B. Nisbet (ed.) *German Aesthetic and
Literary Criticism: Winckelmann, Lessing, Hammann, Herder, Schiller, Goethe*, Cambridge: Cambridge University Press, 1985, pp. 154–61.

the grandeur, innocence, simplicity, activity, and bliss of human life must assuredly make an impact – if we do not *in faece Romuli*[3] entirely despair of the effectiveness of good books – and move all those hearts which likewise would dwell in a poor Highland cottage and consecrate their houses to a cottage celebration. And Denis's translation shows such taste, such industry, partly a happy liveliness in the images, partly the vigour of the German language, that I too promptly ranged it among the favourite books in my library, and congratulated Germany on a bard of its own who has but been awakened by the Scottish bard. You used to be so obstinately sceptical of the Scottish Ossian's authenticity,[4] but listen to me now, who once defended him, not obstinately doubting, but nevertheless maintaining that despite all the taste and industry and liveliness and vigour of the German translation, our Ossian is assuredly not the true Ossian any more. I have not enough space to prove it here, so I can only offer my assertion as the Turkish Mufti utters his dictum, and here the name of the Mufti . . .[5]

My arguments against the German Ossian are not, as you kindly imagine, merely a general animus against the German hexameter; for what kind of feeling, of tone or harmony of soul do you credit me with, if I were to have no feeling for Ewald von Kleist's use of the hexameter, for example, or Klopstock's?[6]

Know then, that the more barbarous a people is – that is, the more alive, the more freely acting (for that is what the word means) – the more barbarous, that is, the more alive, the more free, the closer to the senses, the more lyrically dynamic its songs will be, if songs it has. The more remote a people is from an artificial, scientific manner of thinking, speaking, and writing, the less its songs are made for paper and print, the less its verses are written for the dead letter. The purpose, the nature, the miraculous power of these songs as the delight, the driving-force, the traditional chant and everlasting joy of the people – all this depends on the lyrical, living, dance-like quality of the song, on the living presence of the images, and the coherence and, as it were, compulsion of the content, the feelings; on the symmetry of the words and syllables, and sometimes even of the letters, on the flow of the melody, and on a hundred other things which belong to the living world, to the gnomic song of the nation, and vanish with it. These are the arrows of this barbarous Apollo with which he pierces our hearts and transfixes soul and memory. The longer the song is to last, the stronger and more attached to the senses these arousers of the soul must be to defy the power of time and the changes of the centuries – so which way does my argument turn now? . . .

. . . You mock my enthusiasm for these savages almost as Voltaire scoffed at Rousseau for wanting to go on all fours:[7] but do not think that this makes me despise the advantages of our own morals and manners, whatever they may be. The human race is destined to develop through a series of scenes in culture and customs; alas for the man who mislikes the scene on which he has to make his entrance, do his deeds, and live his life! But alas too for the philosopher of mankind and culture who thinks that his scene is the only one, and misjudges the primal scene to be the worst and the most primitive! If they all belong together as part of the great drama of history, then each one displays a new and remarkable aspect of humanity. . . .

You know from travellers' accounts how vigorously and clearly savages always express themselves. Always with a sharp, vivid eye on the thing they want to say, using their senses, feeling the purpose of their utterance immediately and exactly, not distracted by shadowy concepts, half-ideas, and symbolic letter-understanding (the words of their language are innocent of this, for they have virtually no abstract terms); still less corrupted by artifices, slavish expectations, timid creeping politics, and confusing pre-meditation – blissfully ignorant of all these debilitations of the mind, they comprehend the thought as a whole with the whole word, and the word with the thought. Either they are silent, or they speak at the moment of involvement with an unpremeditated soundness, sureness, and beauty, which learned Europeans of all times could not but admire – and were bound to leave untouched. Our pedants who have to clobber everything together in advance and learn it by rote before they can stammer it out with might and method; our schoolmasters, sextons, apothecaries and all the tribe of the little-learned who raid the scholar's house and come out empty-handed until finally, like Shakespeare's gravediggers, his Lancelot or his Dogberry, they speak in the uncertain inauthentic tones of decline and death – compare these learned fellows with the savages! If you are seeking traces of their firm clarity in our own time, do not go looking for it among the pedants. Unspoiled children, women, folk of a sound natural sense, minds formed less by speculation than by activity – these, if what I have been describing is true eloquence, are the finest, nay the only orators of our time.

But in ancient times, it was the poets, the skalds, the scholars who best knew how to wed this sureness and clarity of expression to dignity, sonority, and beauty. And as they had thus united soul and voice and a firm bond, not to confound each other but to be a support and an helpmeet, thus it was that those (to us) half-miraculous works were composed by the ἀοίδοις,[8] singers, bards, minstrels – for that is what the greatest poets of ancient times were. Homer's rhapsodies and Ossian's songs were as it were impromptus, for at that time oratory was known only in impromptu delivery. Ossian was followed, though faintly and at a distance, by the minstrels, but still they did follow him, until finally Art arrived and extinguished Nature. From our youth we have tormented ourselves learning foreign languages and spelling out the syllabic quantity of their verses, to which our ear and nature can no longer respond; working according to rules virtually none of which a genius would acknowledge as rules of Nature; composing poetry about subject-matter that gives us nothing to think about, still less to *sense*, and even less to imagine; feigning passions we do not feel; imitating faculties of the soul we do not possess – until finally it all turned false, insipid, and artificial. Even the best minds were confounded, and lost their sureness of eye and hand, their certainty of thought and expression and with them their true vitality and truth and urgency – everything was lost. Poetry, which should have been the most passionate, confident daughter of the human soul, became the most insecure, weak and hesitant, and poems turned into schoolboys' exercises for correction. And if that is the way our time thinks, then of course we will admire Art rather than Nature in these ancient poems; we will find too much or too little Art in them, according to our predisposition, and we will rarely have ears to hear the voice that sings in them: the voice of Nature. I am sure that if Homer and Ossian were to come back to earth and hear their works read and praised, they would all too often be astonished at what we add to them and take away from them, at the artifices we apply to them, and at our lack of any immediate feeling for them.

Of course our hearts and minds have been formed differently from theirs by our education from youth and by the long intervening generations. We scarcely see and feel any longer: we only think and brood. Our poetry does not emerge from a living world, nor exist in the storm and confluence of such objects and feelings. Instead we force either our theme or our treatment or both, and we have done so for so long and so often and from our tenderest years that if we attempted any free development, it would scarcely prosper; for how can a cripple get up and walk? That is why so many of our recent poems lack that certainty, that exactness, that full contour which comes only from the first spontaneous draft, not from any elaborate later revisions. Our ridiculous versifying would have appeared to Homer and Ossian as the weak scribbles of an apprentice would have appeared to Raphael, or to Apelles,[9] whose barest sketch revealed his mastery.

. . . What I said recently about the first spontaneous draft of a poem in no way justifies the careless and bungling efforts of our young would-be poets. For what deficiency is more obvious in their work than the very indefiniteness of their thoughts and words? They themselves never know what they want or ought to say. But if someone lacks even that knowledge, how can any corrections ever teach him it? Can anyone make a marble statue of Apollo out of a kitchen skewer?

It seems to me, given the state of our poetry at present, that two main possibilities are open to us. If a poet recognises that the mental faculties which are required partly by his subject and by the poetic genre he has chosen, and which also happen to be predominant within him, are the representational and cognitive faculties – he must reflect thoroughly on the content of his poem, comprehend it, turn it over, and order it clearly and distinctly until every letter is, as it were, engraved upon his soul, and his poem need only reproduce this in a complete and honest manner. But if his poem requires an outpouring of passion and feeling, or if this class of faculties supplies the most active and habitual kind of motivation he needs for his work – then he will abandon himself to the inspiration of the happy hour, and will write and enchant us.[10]

All the songs of these savage peoples move around objects, actions, events, around a living world! How rich and various are the details, incidents, immediate features! And the eye has seen it all, the mind has imagined it all. This implies leaps and gaps and sudden transitions. There is the same connection between the sections of these songs as there is between the trees and bushes of the forest; the same between the cliffs and grottoes of the wilderness as there is between the scenes of the event itself. When the Greenlander tells of the seal-hunt, he does not speak; he paints all the details with words and gestures, for they are all part of the picture in his mind. When he holds a graveside eulogy and sings a funeral dirge for his departed, he does not praise or lament, but paints, and the dead man's life, vividly portrayed with all the sudden leaps of the imagination, cannot but speak and cry.[11]

Look at the overloaded artificial Gothick style of the recent so-called philosophical and pindaric odes by the English poets Gray, Akenside, Mason,[12] etc., which they regard as masterpieces! Does the content or the metre or the wording produce the least effect of an ode? Look at the artificial Horatian style we Germans have fallen into at times – Ossian, the songs of the savage tribes and the old Norse skalds, romances, dialect poems could show us a better path, but only if we are ready to learn more than the form, the wording, or the language. But unfortunately this is only our starting-point, and if we stay there, we will get nowhere. Am I wrong, or is it not true that the most beautiful lyric poems we have now – and long have had – are consonant with this virile, firm, vigorous German tone, or at least approach it – so what can we not hope from the awakening of more of that kind!¹³

Notes

This work was first published in an anonymous collection of five essays, edited by Johann Gottfried Herder, entitled *Von deutscher Art und Kunst. Einige fliegende Blätter (On German Character and Art. A Collection of Broadsheets)* (Hamburg, 1773). Herder's epistolary essay on Ossian was the first item in the collection. . . . The present translation of Herder's essay on Ossian omits the numerous folksongs and ballads from various countries which Herder cites as examples of folk poetry, as well as sections in which he discusses Klopstock and various lesser poets of the time.

1   The correspondent is fictitious. His supposed contempt for folk poetry is a rhetorical device which enables Herder to defend such literature in a direct and vigorous manner.

2   James Macpherson's *The Works of Ossian, the Son of Fingal*, 2 vols. (London, 1765) appeared in the German translation of Michael Denis as *Die Gedichte Ossians, eines alten celtischen Dichters*, 3 vols. (Vienna, 1768–9).

3   'among the dregs of Rome' (Cicero, *Letters to Atticus*, II, 1).

4   Herder dismissed all (justified) suggestions that the poems were largely the work of Macpherson himself, and accepted the latter's claim that he had merely translated authentic poems by the ancient Celtic bard.

5   The break in the text is Herder's. It is designed to preserve the fiction that this is a series of extracts from an actual correspondence.

6   Denis's translation is in German hexameters, a form popularised in Germany by the poets Friedrich Gottlieb Klopstock (1724–1803) and Christian Ewald von Kleist (1715–59).

7   In his letter to Rousseau of 30 August 1755, Voltaire ironically distanced himself in such terms from Rousseau's praise of primitive society in his *Discours sur les origines et les fondements de l'inégalité parmi les hommes*.

8   'poets' or 'singers'.

9   Greek painter of the fourth century BC, renowned for the likelike quality of his work.

10 There follows a discussion (omitted here) of various contemporary German poets, who are classified under the two headings which Herder has just specified. More examples of genuine folksong, including 'Sweet William's Ghost' from Percy's *Reliques*, are then quoted.

11 Herder goes on to quote further examples of the free use of language in popular poetry, and praises Luther's hymns in particular. He again attacks slavish adherents of (neo-classical) poetic rules, and defends Klopstock's odes for their bold inversions and innovative language.

12 Thomas Gray (1716–71), *Odes* ('The Progress of Poesy', 'The Bard') (Strawberry Hill, 1757); Mark Akenside (1721–70), author of *The Pleasures of the Imagination*

(1744) and of various odes which appeared in his collected poems in 1772; William Mason (1725–97), a friend of Gray and author of *Poems* (London, 1764).

13   The essay concludes with a 'Postscript', in which Herder ecstatically praises Klopstock's newly published *Odes* (1771), and laments the inadequacy of recent musical settings of German poetry.

Friedrich Nietzsche

(1844–1900)

The German philosopher and poet Friedrich Nietzsche has gained popularity in contemporary literary theory (especially among anti-foundationalist critics such as de Man, Hillis-Miller, Derrida, Foucault) for his skeptical retort to the most pompous certitudes of western philosophical wisdom. Nietzsche's aphoristic, passionately argumentative, and anecdotal style of writing is the perfect vehicle for questioning the philosophical assumptions that predicate knowledge on a fixed and systematically ascertainable truth, a truth supposedly transcending the vagaries of ordinary human experience.

Nietzsche's theory of art is given typically unsystematic exposition over a succession of diversely articulated texts that span his career: *The Birth of Tragedy* (1872), *Human, All Too Human* (1878) and *Twilight of the Idols* (1888). These works exemplify Nietzschean skepticism. This is most explicit in their frank chronicle of the author's reversal of his convictions about the relevance of art to the task of cultural production. The Nietzsche of *The Birth of Tragedy* is an aesthetic universalist who sees in the achievements of Greek art a crucial model for the metaphysical ambitions of the artist to transcend the daily horrors of human existence. In Greek tragedy the desirable aesthetic effect is the complementary play which the artwork occasioned between an irrational Dionysian ecstasy and an Apollonian impetus toward rational ordering of experience. The Nietzsche of *Human, All Too Human* and *Twilight of the Idols*, is a more empirically minded, scientifically oriented partisan of the idea that art should subordinate itself to the cognitive purposes of practical living. In abandoning the pessimistic view that art is a necessary escape from the truths of human suffering, and by taking up an enthusiasm for the meaningfulness of human action, Nietzsche appears to obviate the function of art altogether. Certainly any belief in the essentiality of art as a timeless value is sacrificed, in these later works, to more pragmatic stakes of human existence in the world of the here and now.

In the furtherance of such conviction, Nietzsche aggressively undermines faith in what he thinks of as the quasi-religious function of art in bourgeois society. This idea of artistic value he equates with a privileging of feeling at the expense of thought. Whereas Nietzsche had formerly followed the teaching of his mentor Schopenhauer, who believed that the artist needed to maintain a stance of disinterestedness toward the will-enslaved activities of everyday life, Nietzsche now presumes upon the unapologetic interestedness of human will. He thus invites the paradoxical assumption that, if art is to be meaningful, it may have to shed all of the trappings by which we have distinguished it from life: completeness, beauty, harmony, and eternity.

Indeed, the rant against art conducted in *Human, All Too Human* seems to make Nietzsche into an enemy of the aesthetic and the art world. Yet Nietzsche is never simply doctrinaire. While he mightily resists the socially elitist and prejudicial values of nineteenth-century aestheticism, he cannot deny the presence of art in our lives. Just as the emotional intensity cultured by religion continues to exert a beneficent influence on human nature, so, Nietzsche concedes, the "interested and joyful" engagement with forms of life conferred by artistic tradition, persists as an indispensible mainstay of human existence. In this way, he is motivated to argue for an unexpected continuity between art and science. His thinking, in this regard, portends the project of an aesthetic pragmatism: "The scientific man is a further development of the artistic man."

Suggested reading

Julian Young, *Nietzsche's Philosophy of Art*, New York: Cambridge University Press, 1993.

From the Soul of Artists and Writers

145 *Perfection said not to have evolved.* When something is perfect, we tend to neglect to ask about its evolution, delighting rather in what is present, as if it had risen from the ground by magic. In this regard we are probably still under the influence of an ancient mythological sentiment. We still feel (in a Greek temple like the one at Paestum, for example) *almost* as if a god, playing one morning, had built his residence out of these enormous masses; at other times as if a soul had all of a sudden magically entered into a stone and now wished to use it to speak. The artist knows that his work has its full effect only when it arouses belief in an improvisation, in a wondrous instantaneousness of origin; and so he encourages this illusion and introduces into art elements of inspired unrest, of blindly groping disorder, of expectantly attentive dreaming

Reprinted from: Friedrich Nietzsche, *Human, All Too Human*, translated by Marion Faber, with Stephen Lehmann, Lincoln: University of Nebraska Press, 1984, pp. 103–5, 108–10, 122–3, 136–7.

when creation begins, as deceptions that dispose the soul of the viewer or listener to believe in the sudden emergence of perfection.

As is self-evident, the science of art must oppose this illusion most firmly, and point out the false conclusions and self-indulgences of the intellect that drive it into the artist's trap.

146   *The artist's feeling for truth.* When it comes to recognizing truths, the artist has a weaker morality than the thinker; on no account does he want his brilliant, profound interpretations of life to be taken from him, and he defends himself against sober, plain methods and results. Ostensibly, he is fighting for the higher dignity and meaning of man; in truth, he does not want to give up the *most effective* presuppositions for his art, that is the fantastic, the mythic, uncertain, extreme, feeling for the symbolic, over-estimation of the individual, belief in something miraculous about genius: thus he thinks the continuation of his manner of creating is more important than a scientific dedication to truth in every form, however plain it may appear.

150   *Infusion of soul into art.* Art raises its head where religions decline. It takes over a number of feelings and moods produced by religion, clasps them to its heart, and then becomes itself deeper, more soulful, so that it is able to communicate exaltation and enthusiasm, which it could not yet do before. The wealth of religious feeling, swollen to a river, breaks out again and again, and seeks to conquer new realms: but growing enlightenment has shaken the dogmas of religion and generated a thorough mistrust of it; therefore, feeling, forced out of the religious sphere by enlightenment, throws itself into art; in certain instances, into political life, too, indeed even directly into science. Wherever one perceives a loftier, darker coloration to human endeavors, one may assume that the fear of spirits, the smell of incense, and the shadow of churches have remained attached to them.

159   *Art dangerous for the artist.* When art seizes an individual powerfully, it draws him back to the views of those times when art flowered most vigorously; then its effect is to form by retrogression. The artist comes more and more to revere sudden excitements, believes in gods and demons, imbues nature with a soul, hates science, becomes unchangeable in his moods like the men of antiquity, and desires an overthrow of all conditions that are not favorable to art, and this with the vehemence and unreasonableness of a child. Now, the artist in and of himself is already a laggard creature because he still plays a game that belongs to youth and childhood; in addition, he is gradually being formed by retrogression into former times. Thus between him and the other men of

his period who are the same age a vehement antagonism is finally generated, and a sad end – just as, according to the tales of the ancients, both Homer and Aeschylus finally lived and died in melancholy.

160   *Created people.* When one says that the dramatist (and the artist in general) *creates* real characters, this is a beautiful illusion and exaggeration, in whose existence and dissemination art celebrates one of its unintentional, almost superfluous triumphs. In fact, we don't understand much about real, living people, and generalize very superficially when we attribute to them this character or that; the poet is reflecting this, our *very incomplete* view of man, when he turns into people (in this sense "creates") those sketches which are just as superficial as our knowledge of people. There is much deception in these characters created by artists; they are by no means examples of nature incarnate, but rather, like painted people, rather too thin; they cannot stand up to close examination. Moreover, it is quite false to say that whereas the character of the average living man often contradicts itself, that created by a dramatist is the original model which nature had in mind. A real man is something completely *necessary* (even in those so-called contradictions), but we do not always recognize this necessity. The invented man, the phantasm, claims to signify something necessary, but only for those who would also understand a real person only in terms of a rough, unnatural simplification, so that a few prominent, often recurring traits, with a great deal of light on them and a great deal of shadow and semidarkness about, completely satisfy their demands. They are ready to treat the phantasm as a real, necessary person, because in the case of a real person they are accustomed to taking a phantasm, a silhouette, a deliberate abbreviation as the whole.

That the painter and sculptor express at all the "idea" of man is nothing but a vain fantasy and deception of the senses; one is being tyrannized by the eye when one says such a thing, since, of the human body itself, the eye sees only the surface, the skin; the inner body, however, is as much part of the idea. Plastic art wants to make characters visible on the skin; the spoken arts use the word for the same purpose, portraying character in sound. Art proceeds from man's natural *ignorance* about his interior (in body and character): it is not for physicists and philosophers.

199   *Incompleteness as an artistic stimulation.* Incompleteness is often more effective than completeness, especially in eulogies. For such purposes, one needs precisely a stimulating incompleteness as an irrational element that simulates a sea for the listener's imagination, and, like fog, hides its opposite shore, that is, the limitation of the subject being praised. If one mentions the

well-known merits of a man, and is exhaustive and expansive in doing so, it always gives rise to the suspicion that these are his only merits. He who praises completely places himself above the man being praised; he seems to *take him in at a glance*. For that reason, completeness has a weakening effect.

222 *What remains of art*. It is true that with certain metaphysical assumptions, art has a much greater value – if it is believed, for example, that one's character is unchangeable and that the essence of the world is continually expressed in all characters and actions. Then the artist's work becomes the image of what *endures eternally*. In our way of thinking, however, the artist can give his image validity only for a time, because man as a whole has evolved and is changeable, and not even an individual is fixed or enduring.

The same is true of another metaphysical assumption: were our visible world only appearance, as metaphysicians assume, then art would come rather close to the real world; for there would be much similarity between the world of appearance and the artist's world of dream images; the remaining difference would actually enhance the meaning of art rather than the meaning of nature, because art would portray the symmetry, the types and models of nature.

But such assumptions are wrong: what place remains for art, then, after this knowledge? Above all, for thousands of years, it has taught us to see every form of life with interest and joy, and to develop our sensibility so that we finally call out, "However it may be, life is good." This teaching of art – to have joy in existence and to regard human life as a part of nature, without being moved too violently, as something that developed through laws – this teaching has taken root in us; it now comes to light again as an all-powerful need for knowledge. We could give art up, but in doing so we would not forfeit what it has taught us to do. Similarly, we have given up religion, but not the emotional intensification and exaltation it led to. As plastic art and music are the standard for the wealth of feeling really earned and won through religion, so the intense and manifold joy in life, which art implants in us, would still demand satisfaction were art to disappear. The scientific man is a further development of the artistic man.

Matthew Arnold

(1822–1888)

Matthew Arnold was one of the most influential literary critics of the nineteenth century; he played a major role in defining the modern literary canon and in shaping literary studies in schools and colleges. Arnold began his writing career as poet, but after his poetry received tepid and sometimes hostile reviews, he put aside poetry for literary and social criticism. Indeed, it is probably unwise to draw too sharp a distinction between Arnold's literary criticism and his work dealing with broader social issues, since in all of his writings his primary concern was with a broadly defined notion of culture as a set of beliefs and practices that give human life meaning and direction. Thus, for Arnold, literature was primarily important for its social function. Like Friedrich Schiller, one of his early influences, Arnold believed that literature can provide the means of overcoming social fragmentation and achieving harmony.

According to Arnold, literature achieves this task by presenting human ideals in their most general and inclusive form. As he emphasizes in the first excerpt below, for example, he feels that while philosophical systems present changing and contradictory truth claims, poetry presents a kind of ideal wisdom which all of philosophy's warring factions might endorse. Similarly and more controversially, he claims that religious dogmas, like philosophical beliefs, will inevitably be subject to change and controversy, and that only poetry can preserve the ideals to which religious doctrine aspires in a form that is equally accessible to all. Thus, in "On Poetry," he claims that "the strongest part of our religion today is its unconscious poetry."

If literature is to fulfill this exalted function, Arnold argues, it, of course, must be of the highest order. In "The Study of Poetry," one of his most popular essays, he describes some of the general properties of great literature: it must have "a higher truth and higher seriousness," as well as a poetic style that is perfectly wedded to poetic contents. Yet Arnold denies that there can be any fully adequate description of what constitutes poetic greatness. Each instance of poetic excellence is unique; we know it when we see it without being able to spell out the standards by which we judge it. Because of this, Arnold claims, the surest method of judging a poem of unknown quality is to compare it with an acknowledged masterpiece.

Since Arnold believes that literature contains the best of what has been thought and said in all places and at all times, he does not think that the study of literature should be confined by national or historical boundaries and he specifically warns against letting personal prejudice and national pride interfere with literary judgment. If the value of literature is its ability to provide ideals to which everyone can and should assent, then literary greatness will not be the exclusive property of a single culture or set of traditions; while Arnold focuses most often on western literature, his critical principles imply urbanity and open-mindedness. Arnold has sometimes been criticized by those who, like T. S. Eliot, feel that literature expresses the personality of a specific culture and this necessarily limits its ability to transcend the boundaries of time and place.

In the first part of the twentieth century, Arnold was also criticized for subordinating the formal and aesthetic dimensions of literature to literature's social function. More recently, however, Arnold has been most frequently criticized by those who are skeptical of his claim that literature can present ideals that rise above partisanship. Arnold's notion of literary excellence, they claim, only masks his prejudices, the prejudices of a white, middle-class male who came of age in nineteenth-century Britain. Whatever the justice of these claims, however, the contemporary demand for an inclusive, multicultural approach to literary studies has once again posed the challenge of imagining a world literature.

The first piece below is an introduction to a book containing descriptions of the lives of a hundred "great men." It describes the role poetry plays in preserving ideals that are general enough to survive the test of time. The second excerpt deals more specifically with the qualities that distinguish great from not so great poetry.

Suggested reading

Joseph Carrol, *The Cultural Theory of Matthew Arnold*, Berkeley: University of California Press, 1982.

On Poetry

The men who are the flower and glory of our race are to pass here before us, the highest manifestations, whether on this line or on that, of the force which stirs in every one of us – the chief poets, artists, religious founders, philosophers, historians, scholars, orators, warriors, statesmen, voyagers, leaders in

Reprinted from: Matthew Arnold, *The Complete Prose Works of Matthew Arnold*, vol. IX, *English Literature and Irish Politics*, edited by R. H. Super, Ann Arbor: University of Michigan Press, 1973, pp. 61–3, 170–1.

mechanical invention and industry, who have appeared amongst mankind. And the poets are to pass first. Why? Because, of the various modes of manifestation through which the human spirit pours its force, theirs is the most adequate and happy.

The fact of this superior adequacy of poetry is very widely felt; and, whether distinctly seized or no, is the root of poetry's boundless popularity and power. The reason for the fact has again and again been made an object of inquiry. Partial explanations of it have been produced. Aristotle declared poetry to be more philosophical and of more serious worth than history, because poetry deals with generals, history with particulars. Aristotle's idea is expanded by Bacon, after his own fashion, who extols poetry as "submitting the shews of things to the desires of the mind," to the desires for "a more ample greatness, a more exact goodness, and a more absolute variety, than can be found in the nature of things." No man, however, can fully draw out the reasons why the human spirit feels itself to attain to a more adequate and satisfying expression in poetry than in any other of its modes of activity. For to draw them out fully we should have to go behind our own nature itself, and that we can none of us do. Portions of them we may seize, but not more; Aristotle and Bacon themselves have not succeeded in seizing more than portions of them. And at one time, probably, and to one set of observers, one ground of the primordial and incontestable fact before us comes clearest into light; at another, and to other observers, another.

For us to-day, what ground for the superiority of poetry is the most evident, the most notable? Surely its solidity. Already we have seen Aristotle prefer it to history on this very ground. Poetry has, says he, a higher wisdom and a more serious worth than history. Compare poetry with other efforts of the human spirit besides history. Compare it with art. It is more intellectual than art, more interpretative. Along with the plastic representation it utters the idea, it thinks. Poetry is often called art, and poets are classed with painters and sculptors as artists. But Goethe has with profound truth insisted on the difference between them. "Poetry is held to be art," he says, "and yet it is not, as art is, mechanism, mechanical. I deny poetry to be an art. Neither is it a science. Poetry is to be called neither art nor science, but genius." Poetry is less artistic than the arts, but in closer correspondence with the intelligential nature of man, who is defined, as we know, to be "a thinking animal;" poetry thinks, and the arts do not.

But it thinks emotionally, and herein it differs from science, and is more of a stay to us. Poetry gives the idea, but it gives it touched with beauty, heightened by emotion. This is what we feel to be interpretative for us, to satisfy us – thought, but thought invested with beauty, with emotion. Science thinks, but not emotionally. It adds thought to thought, accumulates the elements of a synthesis which will never be complete until it is touched with beauty and emotion; and when it is touched with these, it has passed out of the sphere of science, it has felt the fashioning hand of the poet. So true is this, that the more the follower of science is a complete man, the more he will feel the refreshment of poetry as giving him a satisfaction which our nature is always desiring, but to which his science can never bring him. And the more an artist, on the other hand, is a complete man, the higher he will appreciate the reach and effectualness which poetry gains by being, in Goethe's words, not art but genius; by being from its very nature forbidden to limit itself to the sphere of plastic representation, by being forced to talk and to think.

Poetry, then, is more of a stay to us than art or science. It is more explicative than art, and it has the emotion which to science is wanting. But the grand sources of explication and emotion, in the popular opinion, are philosophy and religion. Philosophy – the love of wisdom – is indeed a noble and immortal aspiration in man. But the philosophies, the constructions of systematic thought which have arisen in the endeavour to satisfy this aspiration, are so perishable that to call up the memory of them is to pass in review man's failures. We have mentioned Goethe, the poet of that land of philosophies, Germany. What a series of philosophic systems has Germany seen since the birth of Goethe! and what sort of a stay is any one of them compared with the poetry of Germany's one great poet? So necessary, indeed, and so often shown by experience, is the want of solidity in constructions of this kind, that it argues, one may say, a dash of the pedant in a man to approach them, except perhaps in the ardour of extreme youth, with any confidence. And the one philosopher who has known how to give to such constructions, not indeed solidity, but charm, is Plato, the poet among philosophers, who produces his abstractions like the rest, but produces them more than half in play and with a smile.

And religion? The reign of religion as morality touched with emotion is indeed indestructible. But religion as men commonly conceive it – religion depending on the historicalness of certain supposed facts, on the authority of certain received traditions, on the validity of certain accredited dogmas – how much of this religion can be deemed unalterably secure? Not a dogma that does not threaten to dissolve, not a tradition that is not shaken, not a fact which has its historical character free from question. Compare the stability of Shakspeare with the stability of the Thirty-Nine Articles! Our religion has materialised itself in the fact – the supposed fact; it has attached its emotion to the fact. For poetry the idea is everything; the rest is its world of illusion, of divine illusion; it attaches its emotion to the idea, the idea *is* the fact. The strongest part of our religion to-day is its unconscious poetry. The future of poetry is immense, because in conscious poetry, where it is worthy of its high destinies, our race, as time goes on, will find an ever surer and surer stay. . . .

The Study of Poetry

Critics give themselves great labour to draw out what in the abstract consti-tutes the characters of a high quality of poetry. It is much better simply to have recourse to concrete examples; – to take specimens of poetry of the high, the very highest quality, and to say: The characters of a high quality of poetry are what is expressed *there*. They are far better recognised by being felt in the verse of the master, than by being perused in the prose of the critic. Nevertheless if we are urgently pressed to give some critical account of them, we may safely, perhaps, venture on laying down, not indeed how and why the characters arise, but where and in what they arise. They are in the matter and substance of the poetry, and they are in its manner and style. Both of these, the substance and matter on the one hand, the style and manner on the other, have a mark, an accent, of high beauty, worth, and power. But if we are asked to define this mark and accent in the abstract, our answer must be: No, for we should thereby be darkening the question, not clearing it. The mark and accent are as given by the substance and matter of that poetry, by the style and manner of that poetry, and of all other poetry which is akin to it in quality.

Only one thing we may add as to the substance and matter of poetry, guiding ourselves by Aristotle's profound observation that the superiority of poetry over history consists in its possessing a higher truth and a higher seriousness (φιλοσοφώτερον καὶ σπουδαιότερον). Let us add, therefore, to what we have said, this: that the substance and matter of the best poetry acquire their special character from possessing, in an eminent degree, truth and seriousness. We may add yet further, what is in itself evident, that to the style and manner of the best poetry their special character, their accent, is given by their diction, and, even yet more, by their movement. And though we distinguish between the two characters, the two accents, of superiority, yet they are nevertheless vitally connected one with the other. The superior character of truth and seri-ousness, in the matter and substance of the best poetry, is inseparable from the superiority of diction and movement marking its style and manner. The two superiorities are closely related, and are in steadfast proportion one to the other. So far as high poetic truth and seriousness are wanting to a poet's matter and substance, so far also, we may be sure, will a high poetic stamp of diction and movement be wanting to his style and manner. In proportion as this high stamp of diction and movement, again, is absent from a poet's style and manner, we shall find, also, that high poetic truth and seriousness are absent from his substance and matter.

Jacques Lacan
(1901–1981)

Jacques Lacan was a French psychoanalyst whose revisions of Freud's theories have influenced both psychoanalytic practice and those humanities disciplines such as literary criticism that have used psychoanalytic theories in order to interpret human behavior. Lacan was largely responsible for the renewed interest in psychoanalytic criticism in the last part of the twentieth century. He received his doctorate in psychiatry in 1932 and shortly thereafter began his training as an analyst. His methods of treatment were unorthodox, however, and he broke with the International Psychoanalytic Association in 1953 and founded his own school, L'École Freudienne de Paris, which remained in existence until he dissolved it shortly before his death. Most of Lacan's publications originated as oral presentations. This is true of *Écrits* and *The Seminars of Jacques Lacan* (published in several volumes) which contain his most important work.

Lacan was keenly interested in the intellectual developments of his time, and many of his most important insights resulted from the fusion of traditional Freudian theories with ideas derived from post-war philosophy and social theory. This is particularly true of Lacan's notions of human identity. In traditional Freudian psychology, the ego is the foundation of individual identity, governed by a rational self-interest that allows it to balance the demands of the instincts (what in Freud's later work is called the id) against the demands of society. Many of Freud's followers assume that a strong ego is a prerequisite of mental health, but Lacan vigorously contests this assumption. He views the ego as an illusory structure which, rather than regulating instincts, seeks only to perpetuate its own power. Lacan's theory of the ego was strongly influenced by Alexandre Kojève's reading of Hegel, the nineteenth-century German philosopher. Kojève, a contemporary of Lacan, argued that Hegel revealed that all human identity is a struggle for recognition. This means that the true object of human desire is not to be found in the physical world. Rather, all desire is the desire to be desired by other people. If I desire my neighbor's goods, her expensive house, or fancy car, for instance, it is because I know that she desires these things and that I would be viewed as more desirable myself if I possessed them.

Lacan agrees with this description of human desire, and argues further that ultimately it is not just desires for certain objects that are copied or borrowed from others; the very structure of a person's ego is borrowed from others in a formative moment, which Lacan designates the mirror stage. Prior to the mirror stage, according to Lacan, an infant experiences his or her body as a chaos of competing impulses, but in the mirror stage the infant escapes this chaos by identifying with an idealized image, whether that image be found in a mirror or in the body of another person. Thus the infant creates the ego, the ideal of a unified self that is consistent over time, by unconsciously identifying with another person. Hence, the self is really an "other." It is the product of what Lacan calls *méconnaissance* (misrecognition), and is therefore vulnerable to alienation and prone to narcissistic aggression. The mirror phase produces what Lacan calls an imaginary relationship between infant and mother, a relationship in which the mother's gaze confirms the infant's egoistic fantasies. But when the infant acquires language and discovers that, through such laws as the incest taboo, society places strict limits on the intimacy of mother and child, the he or she must look to language in order to find the kind of support that the mother once provided. At this moment, according to Lacan, the infant enters the domain of symbolic experience. Lacan's analysis of this symbolic order depends heavily on the assumptions of French structuralism, especially on the notion that human beings are the effects rather than the causes of language. Desire, Lacan claims, is built into language, and the unconscious, as he insists in one of his most famous pronouncements, is structured like a language and is, in fact, everywhere present in language. According to Lacan's description, desire is generated by a series of figures of speech called metonymies in which one thing is invoked by something to which it is closely related. Each frustrated love affair, for instance, is a metonymic fragment of the perfect relationship for which a person is searching. For Lacan, desire is always driven by the ego's need for wholeness and affirmation, a need that can never be fully met. This generates inevitable frustration which is expressed in psychological symptoms that function as metaphors, representing the ego's repressed fantasies of omnipotence. Both the imaginary and the symbolic dimensions of experience offer support for the ego and its fantasies of power, but to these Lacan adds a third register of experience, which he calls the Real. The Real is experience primarily in moments of trauma; it is experience that does not support the illusions of the imaginary or the symbolic.

Like many other psychoanalysts, Lacan was fond of using literature to illustrate his theories. Unlike earlier psychoanalytic criticism, however, his readings of texts do not attempt to discover the ways in which authors or characters betray symptoms of repressed desires. He is more concerned with the ways in which texts frustrate or confirm the fantasies of the ego, including the ego of the reader. As the following excerpt *The Ethics of Psychoanalysis* show, Lacan defines beauty as that which reveals the limits of the fantasy which drives desire. Beauty exposes the way in which each individual's existence is dependent upon language and thus forces us to confront our relationships to our own deaths.

Suggested reading

Mikkel Borch-Jakobson, *Lacan: The Absolute Master*, Stanford, Calif.: Stanford University Press, 1991.

The Demand for Happiness and the Promise of Analysis

In daring to formulate a satisfaction that isn't rewarded with a repression, the theme that is central or preeminent is, What is desire? And in this connection I can only remind you of what I have articulated in the past: realizing one's desire is necessarily always raised from the point of view of an absolute condition. It is precisely to the extent that the demand always under- or overshoots itself that, because it articulates itself through the signifier, it always demands something else; that in every satisfaction of a need, it insists on something else; that the satisfaction formulated spreads out and conforms to this gap; that desire is formed as something supporting this metonymy, namely, as something the demand means beyond whatever it is able to formulate. And that is why the question of the realization of desire is necessarily formulated from the point of view of a Last Judgment.

Try to imagine what "to have realized one's desire" might mean, if it is not to have realized it, so to speak, in the end. It is this trespassing of death on life that gives its dynamism to any question that attempts to find a formulation for the subject of the realization of desire. To illustrate what I am saying, if we pose directly the question of desire on the basis of that Parminedean absolutism, which eliminates everything that is not being, then we will say, nothing is from that which is not born, and all that exists lives only in the lack of being.

Does life have anything to do with death? Can one say that the relationship to death supports or subtends, as the string does the bow, the curve of the rise and fall of life? It is enough for us to take up again the question that Freud himself thought he could raise on the basis of his experience – everything points to the fact that it is effectively raised by our experience.

Reprinted from: Jacques Lacan, *The Seminar of Jacques Lacan*, Book VII, *The Ethics of Psychoanalysis 1959–1960*, edited by Jacques-Alain Miller, translated by Dennis Porter, New York: W. W. Norton and Routledge, 1992, pp. 294–5, 297–8.

In what I was saying a moment ago, I wasn't talking about that death. I am interested in the second death, the one that you can still set your sights on once death has occurred, as I showed you with concrete examples in Sade's texts.

After all, the human tradition has never ceased to keep this second death in mind by locating the end of our sufferings there; in the same way it has never ceased to imagine a second form of suffering, a suffering beyond death that is indefinitely sustained by the impossibility of crossing the limit of the second death. And that is why the tradition of hell in different forms has always remained alive, and it is still present in Sade in the idea he has of making the sufferings inflicted on a victim go on indefinitely. This refinement is attributed to one of the heroes of his novels, a Sadist who tries to assure himself of the damnation of the person he sends out of life into death.

Whatever the significance of the metapsychological imagining of Freud's that is the death instinct, whether or not he was justified in forging it, the question it raises is articulated in the following form by virtue of the mere fact that it has been raised: How can man, that is to say a living being, have access to knowledge of the death instinct, to his own relationship to death?

The answer is, by virtue of the signifier in its most radical form. It is in the signifier and insofar as the subject articulates a signifying chain that he comes up against the fact that he may disappear from the chain of what he is.

In truth, it's as dumb as can be. Not to recognize it, not to promote it as the essential articulation of non-knowledge as a dynamic value, not to recognize that the discovery of the unconscious is literally there in the form of this last word, simply means that they don't know what they are doing. Not remembering this fundamental principle causes the proliferation that one can observe in analytical theory, a whole jungle, a veritable downpour of references – "It's coming down in handfuls," as they say in Charente – and one cannot help noticing the note of disorientation with which it resonates.

I read no doubt a little hastily the translation of Bergler's last work. He always has something scathing and interesting to say, except that one has the impression of a wild stream of unmastered notions.

I wanted to show you how the function of the signifier in permitting the subject's access to his relationship to death might be made more concrete than is possible through a connotation. That is why I have tried to have you recognize it in our recent meetings in an aesthetic form, namely, that of the beautiful – it being precisely the function of the beautiful to reveal to us the site of man's relationship to his own death, and to reveal it to us only in a blinding flash.

. . . What I am, in effect, attempting to show here is that the beautiful has nothing to do with what is called ideal beauty. It is only on the basis of the apprehension of the beautiful at the very point of the transition between life and death that we can try to reinstate ideal beauty or, in other words, the function of that which sometimes reveals itself to us as the ideal form of beauty, and in the first place the famous human form.

If you read that work of Lessing's which is so rich in all kinds of insights, the *Laocoon*, you will find that he is absorbed from the beginning in the conception of the dignity of the object. Not that it is as the result of historical progress that the dignity of the object has finally been abandoned, thank God, since everything seems to indicate that it always was. Greek artists didn't restrict themselves to producing images of the gods; as we learn from Aristophanes's writings, paintings of onions cost a lot of money. It is thus not just with the Dutch painters that people began to realize that any object may be the signifier by means of which that reflection, mirage, or more or less unbearable brilliance we call the beautiful starts to vibrate.

But since I have just referred to the Dutch, take the example of the still life. You will find there moving in the opposite direction from that of the clodhoppers discussed above, as they began to bud, the same crossing of the line. As Claudel showed so admirably in his study of Dutch painting, it is to the extent that the still life both reveals and hides that within it which constitutes a threat, denouement, unfolding, or decomposition, that it manifests the beautiful for us as a function of a temporal relation.

Moreover, insofar as it engages the ideal, the question of the beautiful can only be found at this level as operating at the limit. Even in Kant's time it is the form of the human body that is presented to us as the limit of the possibilities of the beautiful, as ideal *Erscheinen*. It once was, though it no longer is, a divine form. It is the cloak of all possible fantasms of human desire. The flowers of desire are contained in this vase whose contours we attempt to define.

And it is this that leads me to posit the form of the body, and especially its image, as I have previously articulated it in the function of narcissism, as that which from a certain point of view represents the relationship of man to his second death, the signifier of his desire, his visible desire.

The central mirage is to be found in "Ἵμερος ἐναργής [Desire embodied. AD], which both indicates the site of desire insofar as it is desire of nothing, the relationship of man to his lack of being, and prevents that site from being seen.

René Girard

(1923–)

René Girard is a literary critic and social theorist who is best known for his theory of human desire. Desire, he claims, does not arise spontaneously within individuals but, rather, is acquired through an unconscious process of imitation so that one person's desire is always an imitation of other people's desires. Girard was born in France, where he attended the École Nationale des Chartres in order to study archival sciences. After the Second World War he attended Indiana University, where he received a doctorate degree for his work in medieval French culture, and his later work in other historical periods continues to reflect the broad-based interdisciplinary approach to culture which is characteristic of medieval studies. Since receiving his degree, Girard has taught at a number of universities, including Stanford and Johns Hopkins.

In his first major book, *Deceit, Desire, and the Novel* (1961), Girard develops the theory of "mimetic desire" that is the foundation for the work which follows. Whether we seek wealth, fame, or love, Girard argues, we do so because we believe that other people find these things desirable. That is, desire is mimetic because it mimes or imitates the desires of others. Girard calls attention to the ways in which his mimetic theory contrasts with more conventional romantic notions of desire. Romantic theories assume that desire is inspired by the unique qualities of the object or person and that it expresses wishes that reflect the unique qualities of a person's character; romantic lovers know that they are unique, that they are made for one another. The truth, Girard insists, is that adults are like children on a playground; when one child picks up a toy, all the others discover that they suddenly desire it, and conflict ensues.

As this example makes clear, mimetic desire makes conflict inevitable, since it ensures that different individuals will all struggle to possess the same things. For this reason, Girard views culture primarily as a mechanism for regulating the conflict generated by mimetic desire. In *Violence and the Sacred* (1972), he theorizes that mimetic violence is controlled by the "scapegoat mechanism," in which the ritualistic murder of an innocent victim allows society to dramatize the dangers of violence and to establish the authority of a sacred order (which usually includes the scapegoat), an order that forbids or otherwise controls violence. In *Things Hidden since the Beginning of the World* (1978), Girard admits that in modern times the scapegoat mechanism has lost much of its power to restrain violence, since many people are aware of the way in which it works and hence skeptical of its power to confer sacred authority. Girard argues that Christian myth offers a way out of this dilemma because it is based on a notion of love that does not derive from sacrifice. However, few people who were not already Christians have found this solution satisfying.

Not surprisingly, Girard feels that much of the power of great literature derives from its ability to expose the unconscious workings of mimetic desire and the dangers that it poses. Girard, for instance, frequently praises nineteenth-century fiction for its ability to expose and debunk romantic myths of desire. In the following passage Girard explains why the social sciences need "the great literary masterpieces".

Suggested reading

Eugene Webb, *Philosophers of Consciousness*, Seattle: University of Washington Press, 1988.

"To Double Business Bound"

The enormous emphasis on mimesis throughout the entire history of Western literature cannot be a mere mistake; there must be some deep-seated reason for it that has never been explained. I personally believe that the great masterpieces of our literature, primarily the dramas and novels, really are "more mimetic" in the sense that they portray human relations and desire as mimetic, and implicitly at least – sometimes even explicitly, as in Shakespeare's *Troilus and Cressida* – they reintroduce into their so-called fictions the conflictual dimension always eliminated from the theoretical definitions of this "faculty."

The great masterpieces are "more mimetic" than other works in a sense richer and more problematic than the mutilated definition inherited from Aristotle. Literary critics have never been able to challenge this definition, but they have continued to use the word *mimesis*; until recently at least they remained fascinated by it, as if they sensed its unexplored potential. And the truth is that in all its successive versions, impoverished as they were in regard to desire, the word nevertheless always tangentially referred to an objective

Reprinted from: René Girard, *"To Double Business Bound": Essays on Literature, Mimesis, and Anthropology*, Baltimore: Johns Hopkins University Press, 1978, pp. ix–xii.

element in the superiority of the works to which it was applied, works, in fact, of mimetic revelation.

Being more mimetic in the richer but still undefined sense of mimetic desire, these works are also more mimetic, as a consequence, in all traditional uses of the word. For instance, it is true that, whether or not they consciously imitate them, these works always somewhat resemble the most perfect of the ancient writers, being related to them by the common nature of their mimetic revelation. It is also true that the writers of these works are "more mimetic" or more "realistic" than other writers: human desire really *is* mimetic, and the texts that portray it as such cannot fail to be more "true-to-life" than other texts; the superiority of these texts is undeniable, but our reluctance to acknowledge its source has deeper roots than our respect for Aristotle and Plato. Or, rather, our respect for Aristotle and Plato and, most important, the seminal failure of these philosophers to encompass the entire range of imitative behavior cannot be unrelated to the dearest of all our illusions, the intimate conviction that our desires are really our own, that they are truly original and spontaneous. Far from combating such an illusion, Freud flattered it enormously when he wrote that the relationship of a person to his desires is really the same as his relationship to his mother.

If we are blind to mimetic desire, we will also be blind to the experience of "disillusionment" that makes its revelation possible and to the unmistakable traces left by that experience, not necessarily in all works of mimetic revelation but primarily in those transitional works that accomplish the passage from mimetic reflection to mimetic revelation. For the writer himself, this passage necessarily means the shattering of a mimetic reflection that complacently mirrors itself as pure originality and spontaneity.

How could critical methodologies, traditional and avant-garde, reach a real understanding of these masterpieces, since they themselves remain faithful to the impoverished version of mimesis secretly challenged and rejected by the mimetic revelation. Even though Freud in many respects represents an advance and even though he focused upon significant patterns of dramatic relationships – the "triangular" pattern of erotic entanglements, for instance – he also represents a great stumbling block because the solutions he propounds falsify, once more, the true mimetic nature of desire. These solutions nevertheless exert a powerful influence because for a long time they were the only theoretical solutions available and because they have become almost a second nature to us. As in a Pavlovian experiment, they immediately come to mind when we identify those triangular relationships that the writer himself, we assume, would have interpreted as "oedipal" had he come up to the level of intuition we can all reach now without difficulty, thanks to Freud.

As a result, we never realize that the greatest works have their own version of these triangular relationships, more economical, really, and more efficient than that of Freud. The progress psychoanalysis has achieved by focusing on the more significant relationships and by providing the only technical vocabulary we have for discussing them has been bought at a very dear price; it has made more obscure than ever before the original solution of at least some writers to the problems envisaged by Freud. Even those critics who reject psychoanalysis have become incapable of thinking about desire except in psychoanalytic terms.

There is a quasitheoretical voice in the writers of mimetic desire, and it has always been silenced: first by the conception of art as pure entertainment, then by art for art's sake, and now by critical methodologies that more than ever deny any real investigative power to a literary work. We must unravel the paradoxical but logical network of mimetic entanglements spun by the great literary works. We must elaborate a language more faithful to the intuitions of the authors themselves.

Instead of interpreting the great masterpieces in the light of modern theories, we must criticize modern theories in the light of these masterpieces, once their theoretical voice has become explicit. Our relationship with the works of mimetic revelation cannot be defined as "critical" in the usual sense. We have more to learn from them than they have to learn from us; we must be students in the most literal sense of the word. Our conceptual tools do not come up to their level; instead of "applying" to them our ever changing methodologies, we should try to divest ourselves of our misconceptions in order to reach the superior perspective they embody.

This view should not be confused with some transcendental Romanticism or with the tendency to turn literature into an absolute. During much of this century, literary criticism has been divided between the "reductionists" and the "worshipers of beauty." Behind the opposition of the two schools lies a common belief in the ultimately inconsequential nature of all works of art as far as real knowledge is concerned. The worshipers of beauty have tacitly surrendered to their adversaries a major part of their inheritance, the treatment of human relations. At bottom, they too are awed by the generally spurious claims of contemporary social sciences. They are secretly convinced that these would-be sciences are infinitely wiser and more powerful than even the greatest literary works. They feel that the work must be kept under wraps. Being men of little faith, really, they want to protect that supposedly fragile and evanescent object from the superior insights of the Freudians, the Marxists, the behaviorists, the structuralists, etc. Like the reductionists, therefore, the esthetes put literary works behind bars. The only difference is that the bars of the latter critics are supposed to be protective. However, both groups believe that the type of thinking embodied in literary works is outmoded and irrelevant; it belongs to the concentration camp or the Indian reservation.

The truth, I believe, is that the social sciences, always trapped in a phenomenological or empirical impasse, are impotent. They need the great literary masterpieces to evolve; they need insights into mimetic desire and rivalries. The so-called incompatibility between the humanities and the sciences, at least in the case of the social sciences, is a meaningless academic ritual. Only with close collaboration can real progress become possible once more, both in the social sciences and in literary criticism.

A literary cult that recognizes only dead works, unable to play a vital role in today's world, is really a dead cult. In Europe at least, contemporary criticism has come to resemble a funeral procession more and more. The reductionists and the antireductionists are now marching together behind the hearse, and they confirm by their structuralist and poststructuralist association the vanity of their former opposition. Their common bond lies in the concepts of the inability of language to deal with anything but itself and the absolute irrelevance of all literary works. Concurrently, this criticism has become the last inheritor of "literary life" as a central point of mimetic fascination. Its increasing vulnerability to the most hysterical fads and fashions involuntarily testifies to the more and more tyrannical grip upon it of a still unacknowledged mimetic desire.

The historical mutilation of mimesis, the suppression of its conflictual dimension, was no mere oversight, no fortuitous "error." Real awareness of mimetic desire threatens the flattering delusion we entertain not only about ourselves as individuals but also about the nature and origin of that collective self we call our society. If mimesis, like all primitive gods, has two "sides," one that disrupts the community and another one that holds it together, how do the two sides relate to each other? How can the conflictual and destructive mimesis turn into the nonconflictual mimesis of training and learning, indispensable to the elaboration and perpetuation of human societies? If mimetic desire and rivalries are more or less normal human phenomena, how can societal orders keep back this force of disorder, or, if they are overwhelmed by it, how can a new order be reborn of such disorder? The very existence of human society becomes problematic.

Jacques Derrida

(1930–)

Derrida's significance to contemporary literary criticism stems in large part from his skill at exposing the rhetorical nature of philosophical arguments. By drawing out the paradoxical effects of a text's linguistic structure, Derrida's so called "deconstructive" method points up the figurational ground of writing. This is alternative to presupposing transcendental or metaphysical foundations for textual meaning. By asserting the rhetorical instability of writing in relation to the meanings it "intends," Derrida's deconstructive practice precludes the critic's traditional faith that a transparent meaning is achievable in a systematic interpretation of the text. On this basis Derrida posits an affinity between deconstructive writing and the traditional stakes we hold in aesthetic value. He asks us to consider how the concepts of taste, beauty, and the sublime have all been used to foster belief in a meaning that transcends quotidian experience. The quotidian is ruled by the rigid finitude of truth and fact. In other words, Derrida wants us to see that the key concepts of aesthetic theory, like the practices of deconstruction, seek to expand the limits of discursive intelligibility in the name of freedom, rather than to police those limits in the name of truth.

It is therefore not surprising to find Derrida coming to characteristically slippery terms with the realm of the aesthetic in *The Truth in Painting* (1987). Here Derrida is specifically addressing the Kantian proposal that the judgment of taste does not apply to circumstances in which aesthetic pleasure derives from the sensuous presentation of an object that can be framed conceptually. In his most influential meditations on the nature of written text, *Structure, Sign, and Play in the Human Sciences*, and *Différance*, Derrida argued that meaning in texts must be pursued differentially. Interpretation must respect the internal contradictions of writing. It must always move beyond the framing expectations of semantic and syntactical norms, principles of narrative coherence and conceptual truth. Thus his understanding of text in general seems to harmonize with the Kantian standard of beauty: a conceptually indeterminate presentation of sensuous particulars. In chapter 13 of the "Analytic of the Beautiful" (the first book of his third critique) Kant makes an invidious distinction between the beautiful and "what we call 'ornaments' [*parerga*], i.e.

those things which do not belong to the complete representation of the object internally as elements." *Parerga*, such as a "golden frame" around a painting, might be
used to recommend a beautiful object. But it would in the process "injure" the
beauty it contains. It would contaminate aesthetic form with conceptually purposive
understanding. In other words the frame is what marks off the aesthetic object from
the non-aesthetic. Seeking to disclose an internal contradiction in Kant's aesthetic
theory, Derrida shows that even the distinction between the beautiful and the
parerga, by virtue of its dependency on the conceptual framing of distinction, undoes
the "understanding" of the beautiful it seeks to comprehend.

Derrida's chapter "Parergon," from *The Truth in Painting*, alleges the impossibility
of making our rapport with the aesthetic depend on any framing (conceptual) apparatus, even one as philosophically focused on the aesthetic as Kant's third critique.
Accordingly, Derrida's own text is typographically advanced by a succession of *broken
frames*. They both illustrate the paradox he wishes to reveal and demonstrate the
impossibility of asking the question "What is art?" Asking the question imposes the
frame of one's good faith that some such definable entity exists in the first place.
Anxious not to fall foul of the trap in which Kant has snared himself, Derrida declares:
"When a philosopher repeats this question ["What is art?"] without transforming it,
without destroying it in its form . . . he has already subjected the whole of *space* to the
discursive arts, to voice and the *logos*." The Greek word *logos* is for Derrida a touchstone for the conceptual prejudice we too thoughtlessly impose upon intellectual
inquiry. When Derrida deploys the term here the expectations of truth harbored in
logos, and the adherence to law that the pursuit of such truth depends upon, are
meant to sound an alarm. Derrida wants us to see how the truth- and law-seeking
question "What is art?" is already pre-empting art with expectations that violate – by
framing – its supposedly indeterminate nature. In this way Derrida is able to write a discourse of the aesthetic that is not, strictly speaking, about the aesthetic. He entertains
a rapport with the aesthetic without pre-empting it in a claim to knowledge.

Suggested reading

Rodophe Gasche, *The Tain of the Mirror: Derrida and the Philosophy of Reflection*, Cambridge,
    Mass.: Harvard University Press, 1986.

Parergon

what is a title?

And what if *parergon* were the title?

Reprinted from: Jacques Derrida, *The Truth in Painting*, translated by Geoff Bennington and Ian
McLeod, Chicago: University of Chicago Press, 1987, pp. 18–23.

Here the false title is art. A seminar would treat *of art*. Of art and the fine arts. It would thus answer to a program and to one of its great questions. These questions are all taken from a determinate set. Determined according to history and system. The history would be that of philosophy within which the history of the philosophy of art would be marked off, insofar as it treats of art and of the history of art: its models, its concepts, its problems have not fallen from the skies, they have been constituted according to determinate modes at determinate moments. This set forms a system, a greater logic and an encyclopedia within which the fine arts would stand out as a particular region. The *Agrégation de philosophie* also forms a history and a system

how a question of this type – art – becomes inscribed in a program. We must not only turn to the history of philosophy, for example to the Greater Logic or the Encyclopedia of Hegel, to his *Lectures on Aesthetics* which sketch out, precisely, one part of the encyclopedia, system of training for teaching and cycle of knowledge. We must take account of certain specific relays, for example those of so-called philosophy teaching in France, in the institution of its programs, its forms of examinations and competitions, its scenes and its rhetoric. Whoever undertook such an inquiry – and I do no more here than point out its stakes and its necessity – would no doubt have to direct herself, via a very over-determined political history, toward the network indicated by the proper name of Victor Cousin, that very French philosopher and politican who thought himself very Hegelian and never stopped wanting to *transplant* (that is just about his word for it) Hegel into France, after having insistently asked him, in writing at least, to impregnate him, Cousin, and through him French philosophy (letters quoted in *Glas*, pp. 207ff.) Strengthened, among other things, by this more or less hysterical pregnancy, he played a determinant role, or at least represented one, in the construction of the French University and its philosophical institution – all the teaching structures that we still inhabit. Here I do no more than name, with a proper name as one of the guiding threads, the necessity of a deconstruction. Following the consistency of its logic, it attacks not only the internal edifice, both semantic and formal, of philosophemes, but also what one would be wrong to assign to it as its external housing, its extrinsic conditions of practice: the historical forms of its pedagogy, the social, economic or political structures of this pedagogical institution. It is because deconstruction interferes with solid structures, "material" institutions, and not only with discourses or signifying representations, that it is always distinct from an analysis or a "critique." And in order to be pertinent, deconstruction works as strictly as possible in that place where the supposedly "internal" order of the philosophical is articulated by (internal *and* external) necessity with the institutional conditions and forms of teaching. To the point where the concept of institution itself would be subjected to the same deconstructive treatment. But I am already leading into next year's seminar (1974–5)

to delimit now a narrower entry into what I shall try to expound this year in the course. Traditionally, a course begins by the semantic analysis of its title, of the word or concept which entitles it and which can legitimate its discourse only by receiving its own legitimation from that discourse. Thus one would begin by asking oneself: What is *art*. Then: Where does it come from? What is the origin of art? This assumes that we reach agreement about what we understand by the word *art*? Hence: What is the origin of the *meaning* of "art"? For these questions, the *guiding thread* (but it is precisely toward the notion of the *thread* and the *interlacing* that I should like to lead you, from afar) will *always* have been the existence of "works," of "works of art." Hegel says so at the beginning of the *Lectures on Aesthetics*: we have before us but a single representation, namely, that there are works of art. This representation can furnish us with an appropriate point of departure. So the question then becomes: What is "the origin of the work of art"? And it is not without significance that this question gives its title to one of the last great discourses on art, that of Heidegger.

This protocol of the question installs us in a fundamental presupposition, and massively predetermines the system and combinatory possibilities of answers. What it begins by implying is that art – the word, the concept, the thing – has a unity and, what is more, an originary meaning, an *etymon*, a truth that is *one* and *naked* [*une vérité une et nue*], and that it would be sufficient to unveil it *through* history. It implies first of all that "art" can be reached following the three ways of word, concept, and thing, or again of signifier, signified, and referent, or even by some opposition between presence and representation.

Through history: the crossing can in this case just as well denote historicism, the determining character of the historicity of meaning, as it can denote ahistoricity, history crossed, transfixed in the direction of meaning, in the sense of a meaning [*le sens d'un sens*] in itself ahistorical. The syntagm "through history" could entitle all our questions without constraining them in advance. By pre-supposing the *etymon* – one and naked [*un et nu*] – a presupposition without which one would perhaps never open one's mouth, by beginning with a medi-tation on the apparent polysemy of *tekhnē* in order to lay bare the simple kernel which supposedly lies hidden behind the multiplicity, one gives oneself to thinking that *art* has a meaning, one meaning. Better, that its history is *not* a history or that it is *one* history only in that it is governed by this one and naked meaning, under the regime of its internal meaning, as history of the meaning of art. If one were to consider the *physis/tekhnē* opposition to be irreducible, if one were to accredit so hastily its translation as *nature/art* or *nature/tech-nique*, one would easily commit oneself to thinking that art, being no longer nature, is history. The opposition nature/history would be the analogical relay of *physis/tekhnē*. One can thus already say: as for history, we shall have to deal with the contradiction or the oscillation between two apparently incompatible motifs. They both ultimately come under one and the same logical formality: namely, that if the philosophy of art always has the greatest difficulty in domi-nating the history of art, a certain concept of the historicity of art, this is, para-doxically, because it too easily thinks of art as historical. What I am putting forward here obviously assumes the transformation of the concept of history, from one statement to the other. That will be the work of this seminar

If, therefore, one were to broach lessons on art or aesthetics by a ques-tion of this type ("What is art?" "What is the origin of art or of works of art?" "What is the meaning of art?" "What does art mean?" etc.), the form of the question would already provide an answer. Art would be predetermined or pre-comprehended in it. A conceptual opposition which has traditionally served to comprehend art would already, always, be at work there: for example the oppo-sition between meaning, as inner content, and form. Under the apparent diver-sity of the historical forms of art, the concepts of art or the words which seem to translate "art" in Greek, Latin, the Germanic languages, etc. (but the closure of this list is already problematic), one would be seeking a one-and-naked meaning [*un sens un et nu*] which would inform from the inside, like a content, while distinguishing itself from the forms which it informs. In order to think art in general, one thus accredits a series of oppositions (meaning/form, inside/outside, content/container, signified/signifier, represented/representer, etc.) which, precisely, structure the traditional interpretation of works of art. One makes of art in general an object in which one claims to distinguish an inner meaning, the invariant, and a multiplicity of external variations *through* which, as through so many veils, one would try to see or restore the true, full, originary meaning: one, naked. Or again, in an analogous gesture, by asking what art *means* (to say), one submits the mark "art" to a very determined regime of interpretation which has supervened in history: it consists, in its *tautology* without reserve, in interrogating the *vouloir-dire* of every work of so-called art, even if its form is not that of saying. In this way one wonders what a plastic or musical work means (to say), submitting all productions to the authority of speech and the "discursive" arts

  the philosophical encloses art in its circle but its discourse on art is at once, by the same token, caught in a circle.

Like the figure of the third term, the figure of the circle asserts itself at the beginning of the *Lectures on Aesthetics* and the *Origin of the Work of Art*. So very different in their aim, their procedure, their style, these two discourses have in common, as a common interest, that they exclude – (that) which then comes to form, close and bound them from inside and outside alike.

And if it were a frame

IV
Literary Formalism

Aristotle

(384–322 BC)

Although Aristotle's *Poetics* is well known as the first primer on poetry in the western world, and though it is often studied as a mechanics of tragedy based on taxonomic principles, it is perhaps most usefully seen as a meditation on the mimetic impulse. Indeed the relevance of *Poetics* to literary aesthetics depends pre-eminently on its articulating a knowledge of the constraints imposed upon human action and the consequences flowing from it. The text is only secondarily a blueprint for the production of tragic dramas. Aristotle gives an account of the literary artwork (at least in the genres of poetry and tragic drama) that privileges the experience of the reversal of fortune (*peripeteia*) and the recognition (*anagnorisis*) of one's fate in that reversal. In these terms the stakes of mimetic art have to do less with reproducing Nature than with *producing* knowledge. Consequently Aristotle is more interested in the made thing than in the artistic maker. Though he credits artistic genius as a unique freedom of mind, especially in the making of metaphors, he reminds us that the rewards of genius are eminently available to mere spectators, that is, to readers in their appreciation of a work's formal perfection. In his foregrounding of the formality of the artwork, Aristotle inaugurates the modern attitude that makes critical analysis of the artwork an enterprise that might be put on a par with artistic creation.

Most importantly, Aristotle disagrees with his teacher Plato in characterizing the literary plot as akin to human action rather than as a mere imitation of appearances. In fact Aristotle presents a startling challenge to the Platonic faith in changeless "Ideas." Instead he makes the success of dramatic emplotment depend upon its comprehension of the changeability of experience. For this reason, Aristotle tell us that the artist's ability to represent the world depends on the degree to which the form of the work exhibits the features of reality embodied universally in human action. The reality to which the work of art alludes is therefore not an abstract ideal of truth or beauty but a concordance of creative mind with a process that is roughly equivalent to biological gestation. Indeed Aristotle believed that the structure of dramatic plot determines our grasp of reality in the way that the biological structure of the human body determines life. Furthermore, in *Poetics* emplotment is an exercise of mind that gains authority only to the degree that it exhibits specific formal features. For example, the poet makes his representation of the world meaningful in so far as he can produce a *katharsis*. *Katharsis* is a purgation of the disorderly emotions of pity and fear that disrupt the rational progress of action toward its proper end. The tragic artist must carry a protagonist through a course of action which conjoins the moments of reversal and recognition in order to produce *katharsis*.

In a reversal of fate the knowledge that accrues to the protagonist, as well as and even more significantly to the audience, gives the drama an ethical purpose. By coming to understand the ends of actions, the spectator of tragic drama acquires a template for ordering his or her own life. Because, in Aristotelian plot, *who* a character is depends on *what* a character does, we are invited to equate the truth of personhood with something that we pursue in contemplating the actions of tragic protagonists. The ethical purport of this proposition is that such contemplation preserves *us* from the error of *their* ways. The rationalistic ideals of Aristotelian formalism flourish in almost every period of artistic expression and critical formulation. But the watermark of Aristotelian thought is most notable in the literary aesthetics of Sir Philip Sidney, Samuel Taylor Coleridge, Matthew Arnold, Monroe Beardsley, and R. S. Crane.

Suggested reading

A. O. Rorty (ed.) *Essays on Aristotle's Poetics*, Princeton, NJ: Princeton University Press, 1992.

The General and Comparative View of Poetry and its Principal Species

V Poetry in general seems to have derived its origin from two causes, each of them natural.

To *imitate* is instinctive in man from his infancy. By this he is distinguished from other animals, that he is, of all, the most imitative, and through this instinct receives his earliest education. All men, likewise, naturally receive pleasure from imitation. This is evident from what we experience in viewing the works of imitative art; for in them we contemplate with pleasure, and with the more pleasure the more exactly they are imitated, such objects as, if real, we could not see without pain; as the figures of the meanest and most disgusting animals, dead bodies, and the like. And the reason of this is, that to learn is a

Reprinted from: *Aristotle's Politics and Poetics*, translated by Benjamin Jowett and Thomas Twining, New York: Viking Press, 1966, pp. 226, 230–1, 234–7.

natural pleasure, not confined to philosophers, but common to all men; with this difference only, that the multitude partake of it in a more transient and compendious manner. Hence the pleasure they receive from a picture: in viewing it they learn, they infer, they discover what every object is; that this, for instance, is such a particular man, etc. For if we suppose the object represented to be something which the spectator had never seen, his pleasure, in that case, will not arise from the imitation, but from the workmanship, the colours, or some such cause. . . .

Of Tragedy

II   Now as tragedy imitates by acting, the decoration, in the first place, must necessarily be one of its parts: then the *melopoeia* (or music) and the diction; for these last include the means of tragic imitation. By diction I mean the metrical composition. The meaning of *melopoeia* is obvious to every one.

Again, tragedy being an imitation of an action, and the persons employed in that action being necessarily characterized by their manners and their sentiments, since it is from these that actions themselves derive their character, it follows that there must also be manners and sentiments as the two causes of actions, and, consequently, of the happiness or unhappiness of all men. The imitation of the action is the fable: for by fable I now mean the contexture of incidents, or the plot. By manners, I mean whatever marks the characters of the persons; by sentiments, whatever they say, whether proving anything, or delivering a general sentiment, etc.

Hence all tragedy must necessarily contain six parts, which together constitute its peculiar character or quality: fable, manners, diction, sentiments, decoration, and music. Of these parts, two relate to the means, one to the manner, and three to the object of imitation. And these are all. These specific parts, if we may so call them, have been employed by most poets, and are all to be found in almost every tragedy.

III   But of all these parts the most important is the combination of incidents or the fable. Because tragedy is an imitation, not of men, but of actions – of life, of happiness and unhappiness; for happiness consists in action, and the supreme good itself, the very end of life, is action of a certain kind – not quality. Now the manners of men constitute only their quality or characters; but it is by their actions that they are happy, or the contrary. Tragedy therefore, does not imitate action for the sake of imitating manners, but in the imitation of action that of manners is of course involved. So that the action and the fable are the end of tragedy; and in everything the end is of principal importance.

Again, tragedy cannot subsist without action; without manners it may. The tragedies of most modern poets have this defect; a defect common, indeed, among poets in general. As among painters also, this is the case with Zeuxis, compared with Polygnotus: the latter excels in the expression of the manners; there is no such expression in the pictures of Zeuxis.

Further, suppose any one to string together a number of speeches in which the manners are strongly marked, the language and the sentiments well turned; this will not be sufficient to produce the proper effect of tragedy: that end will much rather be answered by a piece, defective in each of those particulars, but furnished with a proper fable and contexture of incidents. Just as in painting, the most brilliant colours, spread at random and without design, will give far less pleasure than the simplest outline of a figure.

Add to this, that those parts of tragedy by means of which it becomes most interesting and affecting are parts of the fable; I mean revolutions and discoveries.

As a further proof, adventures in tragic writing are sooner able to arrive at excellence in the language and the manners than in the construction of a plot; as appears from almost all our earlier poets.

The fable, then, is the principal part – the soul, as it were – of tragedy, and the manners are next in rank; tragedy being an imitation of an action, and through that principally of the agents. . . .

VI It appears, further, from what has been said, that it is not the poet's province to relate such things as have actually happened, but such as might have happened – such as are possible, according either to probable or necessary consequence.

For it is not by writing in verse or prose that the historian and the poet are distinguished: the work of Herodotus might be versified, but it would still be a species of history, no less with metre than without. They are distinguished by this, that the one relates what has been, the other what might be. On this account poetry is a more philosophical and a more excellent thing than history: for poetry is chiefly conversant about general truth, history about particular. In what manner, for example, any person of a certain character would speak or act, probably or necessarily – this is general; and this is the object of poetry, even while it makes use of particular names. But what Alcibiades did, or what happened to him – this is particular truth.

With respect to comedy this is now become obvious; for here the poet, when he has formed his plot of probable incidents, gives to his characters whatever names he pleases; and is not, like the iambic poets, particular and personal.

Tragedy, indeed, retains the use of real names; and the reason is that what we are disposed to believe, we must think possible. Now, what has never actually happened we are not apt to regard as possible; but what has been is unquestionably so, or it could not have been at all. There are, however, some tragedies in which one or two of the names are historical, and the rest feigned: there are even some in which none of the names are historical; such is Agathon's tragedy called *The Flower*; for in that all is invention, both incidents and names; and yet it pleases. It is by no means, therefore, essential that a poet should confine himself to the known and established subjects of tragedy. Such a restraint would, indeed, be ridiculous; since even those subjects that are known are known comparatively but to few, and yet are interesting to all.

From all this it is manifest that a poet should be a poet or maker of fables, rather than of verses; since it is imitation that constitutes the poet, and of this imitation actions are the object: nor is he the less a poet, though the incidents of his fable should chance to be such as have actually happened; for nothing hinders, but that some true events may possess that probability, the invention of which entitles him to the name of poet.

VII   Of simple fables or actions, the episodic are the worst. I call that an episodic fable, the episodes of which follow each other without any probable or necessary connection; a fault into which bad poets are betrayed by their want of skill, and good poets by the players: for in order to accommodate their pieces to the purposes of rival performers in the dramatic contests, they spin out the action beyond their powers, and are thus frequently forced to break the connection and continuity of its parts.

But tragedy is an imitation, not only of a complete action, but also of an action exciting terror and pity. Now that purpose is best answered by such events as are not only unexpected, but unexpected consequences of each other: for, by this means, they will have more of the wonderful than if they appeared to be the effects of chance; since we find that, among events merely casual, those are the most wonderful and striking which seem to imply design: as when, for instance, the statue of Mitys at Argos killed the very man who had murdered Mitys, by falling down upon him as he was surveying it; events of this kind not having the appearance of accident. It follows, then, that such fables as are formed on these principles must be the best.

VIII   Fables are of two sorts, simple and complicated; for so also are the actions themselves of which they are imitations. An action (having the conti-

nuity and unity prescribed) I call simple, when its catastrophe is produced
without either revolution or discovery; complicated when with one or both.
And these should arise from the structure of the fable itself, so as to be the
natural consequences, necessary or probable, of what has preceded in the
action. For there is a wide difference between incidents that follow from, and
incidents that follow only after, each other.

IX A revolution is a change (such as has already been mentioned) into the
reverse of what is expected from the circumstances of the action; and that
produced, as we have said, by probable or necessary consequence.

Thus, in the *Oedipus*, the messenger, meaning to make Oedipus happy, and
to relieve him from the dread he was under with respect to his mother, by
making known to him his real birth, produces an effect directly contrary to his
intention. Thus also in the tragedy of *Lynceus*, Lynceus is led to suffer death,
Danaus follows to inflict it; but the event, resulting from the course of the
incidents, is that Danaus is killed and Lynceus saved.

A discovery – as, indeed, the word implies – is a change from unknown to
known, happening between those characters whose happiness or unhappiness
forms the catastrophe of the drama, and terminating in friendship or enmity.

The best sort of discovery is that which is accompanied by a revolution as
in the *Oedipus*.

There are also other discoveries; for inanimate things of any kind may be
recognized in the same manner, and we may discover whether such a particular thing was, or was not, done by such a person. But the discovery most appropriated to the fable and the action is that above defined; because such
discoveries and revolutions must excite either pity or terror, and tragedy we
have defined to be an imitation of pitiable and terrible actions: and because,
also, by them the event, happy or unhappy, is produced.

Now discoveries, being relative things, are sometimes of one of the persons
only, the other being already known; and sometimes they are reciprocal: thus,
Iphigenia is discovered to Orestes by the letter which she charges him to
deliver, and Orestes is obliged, by other means, to make himself known to her.

These, then, are two parts of the fable – revolution and discovery. There is
a third, which we denominate disasters. The two former have been explained.
Disasters comprehend all painful or destructive actions: the exhibition of
death, bodily anguish, wounds, and everything of that kind.

Monroe C. Beardsley

(1915–1985)

After John Dewey, Monroe Beardsley, was the most influential English-speaking aesthetic theorist of the twentieth century. Though trained as a philosopher, Beardsley's work had perhaps its greatest influence and widest dissemination in the field of literary criticism. Indeed Beardsley's intent was to provide a more secure philosophical grounding for the practices of the American New Criticism. The "aesthetic dimension" which Beardsley ascribed to the literary work authorized the well-known New Critical presumption that we ought to treat literature as an experience that can be competently evaluated only by comprehending how the formal features of a work interact in their dynamic complexity.

Complexity, along with *intensity* and *unity* were key terms in Beardsley's critical vocabulary. They were touchstones for his belief that any moral or cognitive dimensions of an artwork must be distinguished from and subordinated to the aesthetic experience of the artwork *per se*. A work is *complex* if it brings a manifold of different elements under a dominant aspect. *Intensity* denotes the concentration of emotional energies focused through a narrow field of reference. *Unity* denotes principles of coherence and completeness in the formal composition without which complexity and intensity would not be appreciable. Accordingly, Beardsley judged that the moral and cognitive elements in the artwork cannot in themselves produce aesthetic experience. Rather, they are artifacts of and refer to the "outside" world, *against which* aesthetic value must be appreciated if it is to be properly known. By contrast with aesthetic experience, Beardsley deemed ordinary experience to be diffuse and open-ended.

Furthermore, for Beardsley, the task of isolating and describing the aesthetic experience, or the aesthetic dimension opened up by the artwork, depended upon discerning the counterparts of the work's complexity, intensity and unity in the subjectivity of the perceiving aesthete. The aesthetic object was judged to be knowable in so far as it promoted an aesthetic attitude. From Beardsley's perspective, "nothing is aesthetic or non-aesthetic in itself." Ultimately, we know the authenticity of the aesthetic experience by the detachment from quotidian life which it imposes upon us.

All of this makes up what Beardsley characterized as an "instrumentalist theory" of aesthetic value. Instrumentalist theory is proposed as an alternative to beauty theory and other equally subjectivist definitions of aesthetic value that base aesthetic experience on internal variables of taste or feeling (see Hutcheson, Shaftesbury). Instead Beardsley assumes that "General judgments of critical praise can be cast in the form: 'This is a good aesthetic object.'" Beardsley wants to make it possible for the critic to demonstrate, by deductive methods, what assumptions make such a designation possible, and to show that it is objectively "true." Beardsley furthermore established that the art object proper has integrity as a phenomenal field within which aesthetic experience is anchored to perceptible form. Consequently, Beardsley proscribed the critic from referring to the intentions of the author, or to the affective states of the reader, as bases of aesthetic appreciation or judgment. Beardsley's famous collaboration with the literary critique W. K. Wimsatt (*The Verbal Icon*, 1954), anatomizing the "intentional fallacy" and the "affective fallacy" respectively, promoted a methodological prohibition against biographical and impressionistic criticism. Beardsley's mark on literary criticism was most emphatic in establishing the still prevalent presumption that only the work itself, in its language and its structure, constitutes the legitimate ground of literary study. While Beardsley accepted that the artwork reflected causal and contextual conditions, he warned against making its intelligibility dependent on free-standing institutions of the culture. In that way one would risk obscuring the human need for a distinctly aesthetic experience.

Suggested reading

Richard Rorty, *Contingency, Irony, and Solidarity*, Cambridge: Cambridge University Press, 1989.

Aesthetic Experience

The problem is whether we can isolate, and describe in general terms, certain features of experience that are peculiarly characteristic of our intercourse with aesthetic objects. Of course, listening to music is a very different experience in some ways from looking through a cathedral or watching a motion picture. Reading literature certainly does something to us, and probably *for* us, that listening to music cannot do, and vice versa. A full account of our experience of aesthetic objects would have to deal carefully with these matters. But is there something that all these experiences have in common – something that can be

Reprinted from: Monroe C. Beardsley, *Aesthetics: Problems in the Philosophy of Criticism*, New York: Harcourt, Brace & World, 1958, pp. 527–30. For up-to-date copyright and publication information see Acknowledgments.

usefully distinguished? This is at least an empirical question, open to inquiry. And some inquiry has been made, though many mysteries remain. However, we can be reasonably confident of certain generalizations, which some writers have obtained by acute introspection, and which each of us can test in his own experience.

These are the points on which, I take it, nearly everyone will agree:

First, an aesthetic experience is one in which attention is firmly fixed upon heterogeneous but interrelated components of a phenomenally objective field – visual or auditory patterns, or the characters and events in literature. Some writers have suggested that in such an experience, as when we are deeply absorbed in the tension of a visual design or in the developing design of music, the distinction between phenomenal objectivity and phenomenal subjectivity itself tends to disappear. This may be overstated, but in any case the experience differs from the loose play of fancy in daydreaming by having a central focus; the eye is kept on the object, and the object controls the experience. It is all right, I think, to speak of the object as *causing* the experience, but of course the connection is more intimate, for the object, which is a perceptual object, also appears in the experience as its phenomenally objective field.

Second, it is an experience of some intensity. Some writers have said that it is an experience pervasively dominated by intense feeling or emotion, but these terms still occupy a dubious position in psychological theory; what we call the emotion in an aesthetic experience may be simply the intensity of the experience itself. In any case, the emotion is characteristically bound to its object, the phenomenal field itself – we feel sad *about* the characters, or uncertain *about* the results of an unexpected modulation. Aesthetic objects give us a concentration of experience. The drama presents only, so to speak, a segment of human life, that part of it that is noteworthy and significant, and fixes our minds on that part; the painting and the music invite us to do what we would seldom do in ordinary life – pay attention *only* to what we are seeing or hearing, and ignore everything else. They summon up our energies for an unusually narrow field of concern. Large-scale novels may do more; they are in fact always in danger of dissipating attention by spreading it out into our usual diffuse awareness of the environment.

This is why the expression "feeling no pain" is particularly apt to aesthetic experience. The pleasure is not often comparable in intensity to the pleasures of satisfying the ordinary appetites. But the concentration of the experience can shut out all the negative responses – the trivial distracting noises, organic disturbances, thoughts of unpaid bills and unwritten letters and unpurged embarrassments – that so often clutter up our pleasures. It does what whiskey does, only not by dulling sensitivity and clouding the awareness, but by marshalling the attention for a time into free and unobstructed channels of experience.

But this discussion already anticipates the two other features of aesthetic experience, which may both be subsumed under *unity*. For, third, it is an experience that hangs together, or is coherent, to an unusually high degree. One thing leads to another; continuity of development, without gaps or dead spaces, a sense of overall providential pattern of guidance, an orderly cumulation of energy toward a climax, are present to an unusual degree. Even when the experience is temporarily broken off, as when we lay down the novel to water the lawn or eat dinner, it can retain a remarkable degree of coherence. Pick up the novel and you are immediately back in the world of the work, almost as if there had been no interruption. Stop the music because of a mechanical problem, or the ringing of a phone, but when it is started again, two bars may be enough to establish the connection with what went before, and you are clearly in the *same* experience again.

Fourth, it is an experience that is unusually complete in itself. The impulses and expectations aroused by elements within the experience are felt to be counterbalanced or resolved by other elements within the experience, so that some degree of equilibrium or finality is achieved and enjoyed. The experience detaches itself, and even insulates itself, from the intrusion of alien elements. Of course, it cannot survive all emergencies. I have heard the last movement of Beethoven's "Waldstein" Sonata (Op. 53) interrupted by a fire chief who suddenly appeared on stage to clear the aisles of standees; and even though the pianist, Paul Badura-Skoda, started off again at the beginning of the movement, he could not, of course, recapture the peculiar quality of that beginning, which moves without pause from the slow section of the sonata. But because of the highly concentrated, or localized, attention characteristic of aesthetic experience, it tends to mark itself out from the general stream of experience, and stand in memory as a single experience.

Aesthetic objects have a peculiar, but I think important, aspect: they are all, so to speak, objects *manqués*. There is something lacking in them that keeps them from being quite real, from achieving the full status of things – or, better, that prevents the question of reality from arising. They are complexes of qualities, surfaces. The characters of the novel or lyric have truncated histories, they are no more than they show. The music is movement without anything solid that moves; the object in the painting is not a material object, but only the appearance of one. Even the lifelike statue, though it gives us the shape and gesture and life of a living thing, is clearly not one itself. And the dancer gives us the abstractions of human action – the gestures and movements of joy and sorrow, of love and fear – but not the actions (killing or dying) themselves. This is one sense of "make-believe" in which aesthetic objects are make-believe objects; and upon this depends their capacity to call forth from us the kind of admiring contemplation, without any necessary commitment to practical action, that is characteristic of aesthetic experience.

One aesthetic experience may differ from another in any or all of three connected but independent respects: (1) it may be more *unified*, that is, more coherent and/or complete, than the other; (2) its dominant quality, or pervasive feeling-tone, may be more *intense* than that of the other; (3) the range or diversity of distinct elements that it brings together into its unity, and under its dominant quality, may be more *complex* than that of the other. It will be convenient to have a general term to cover all three characteristics. I propose to say that one aesthetic experience has a greater *magnitude* – that is, it is more of an aesthetic experience – than another; and that its magnitude is a function of at least these three variables. For the more unified the experience, the more of a whole the experience is, and the more concentratedly the self is engaged; the more intense the experience, the more deeply the self is engaged; the more complex the experience, the more of the self is engaged, that is, the more wide-ranging are its responses, perhaps over a longer time.

I do not think of magnitude here as implying measurement – it is merely a collective term for how much is happening, intensively or extensively, in the experience. It may be too vague a concept to be useful. That remains to be seen, but there are two sources of legitimate uneasiness about it that should be frankly faced at once. First, note that I am now applying the terms "unity," "complexity," and "intensity" more broadly than before – not only to the phenomenally objective presentations in the experience, but to the whole experience, which includes affective and cognitive elements as well. The terms are still understandable, even in this extended use, I judge, but of course less capable of sure and exact application. Second, though I claim that these three characteristics all have a bearing upon magnitude, and that the magnitude of the experience is a resultant of them, I am not yet raising certain questions – which will shortly come to our attention – concerning the comparability of magnitudes. Evidently it will be possible to say that of two experiences approximately equal in unity and complexity, the one having a greater intensity will have the greater magnitude. But what if they are equal in one respect, and differ in opposite ways in the other two? This question is still open.

The traits of aesthetic experience are to be found individually in a great many other experiences, of course, but not in the same combination, I think. Play, in the sense in which we play games, involves the enjoyment of activity that has no practical purpose. But though the psychology of play has not yielded up all its secrets to psychological inquiry, it seems not necessarily to be an experience of a high degree of unity. Watching a baseball or football game is also generally lacking in a dominant pattern and consummation, though sometimes it has these characteristics to a high degree and is an aesthetic experience. Carrying through a triumphant scientific investigation or the solution of a mathematical problem may have the clear dramatic pattern and consummatory conclusion of an aesthetic experience, but it is not itself aesthetic experience unless the movement of thought is tied closely to sensuous presentations, or at least a phenomenally objective field of perceptual objects.

Such distinctions are vague and tentative; they are some of the problems that most need to be studied at the present time. In any case, we can identify aesthetic experience as a kind of experience, though it is unique only in its combination of traits, rather than in any specific one. And we can say that aesthetic objects, generally speaking, have the function of producing such experiences, even though quite often aesthetic experiences of some degree of magnitude are obtained in the regular course of life from other things than aesthetic objects. This is their special use, what they are good for. On the whole, it is what they do best; they do it most dependably, and they alone do it in the highest magnitude.

Benedetto Croce

(1866–1952)

Croce's article "Aesthetics," printed in the fourteenth edition of the *Encyclopedia Britannica*, was a distillation of the compendious view of expression he presented in his *Aesthetics as Science of Expression and Linguistics* (*Esthetica come scienza dell'espressione e linguistica generale*, originally published in 1902). The credo of this title, that aesthetics is a general science of language, indicates the degree to which Croce's aesthetic theory was attuned to the needs of literary critics and the practitioners of verbal art. For Croce, expression in literary art, poetry in particular, reveals how a logically universal medium like language gains authority through its embodiments in uniquely individual entities.

Croce's stake in expression as a defining feature of human nature puts him in a long line of expressivist theorists of the aesthetic including Vico, Schiller, Hegel, and Dewey. All are thinkers for whom the artwork is deeply implicated in human activity, and by that route assimilable to the texture of everyday life. Because art manifests what Croce calls "Spirit," it is integral to a profound idealism about human creativity. Croce's reliance on the term Spirit – a measure of his indebtedness to Hegel – gives him a means to characterize art as non-conceptual yet cognitive. The root of this non-conceptual knowledge is intuition. Intuition is a particular image held in consciousness: for example, an "objectified" impression of a river, a brook, a glass of water. While all percepts are intuitions, not all intuitions are percepts, however. This is because intuition is only accessible in expression when an image is united with a feeling. Expression gives an external form to the intuition in the mind of the artist.

Nevertheless, in one of the most controversial qualifications of his theory of expression, Croce insists that the artwork remains secondary, even inferior to the intuition in consciousness. This way of explaining things serves Croce's belief that theoretical activity must have its end in practical activity, but cannot be instrumentalized in the finitude of concrete forms.

Croce's lifelong involvement with poetry led him to elaborate his understanding of the innate lyricism of intuition. "Lyrical intuition" is a quality exhibited in poetry whereby the contextual autonomy of the work defies any attempt to distinguish between the historical/natural raw materials and the abstract concepts which are wedded indissolubly in the artwork itself. Croce doesn't privilege lyric intuition to the exclusion of other kinds of knowledge and practice – for example painting as a mechanics of line and plane – but he does insist upon maintaining a distinction between them.

Croce's emphasis on lyric intuition does mean that his ideas could be confused with romanticism. But on the contrary, "lyric intuition" was his way of navigating between the intellectual or taxonomic aridity of classical aesthetic theory (with its baggage of rules and genres) and the emotional sentimentalism of the Romantics, which like all excess of feeling, has little cognitive bearing on the facts of human existence. For Croce, lyrical intuition was by contrast "cosmic." He judged that the particulars presented in a poem, because they were free of existential constraints, attained to a universality that nonetheless did not court abstraction.

Suggested reading

Angelo De Gennaro, *The Philosophy of Benedetto Croce: An Introduction*, New York: Citadel Press, 1961.

Aesthetics

If we examine a poem in order to determine what it is that makes us feel it to be a poem, we at once find two constant and necessary elements: a complex of *images*, and a *feeling* that animates them. Let us, for instance, recall a passage learnt at school: Virgil's lines (Aeneid, iii, 294, sqq.), in which Aeneas describes how on hearing that in the country to whose shores he had come the Trojan Helenus was reigning, with Andromache, now his wife, he was overcome with amazement and a great desire to see this surviving son of Priam and to hear of his strange adventures. Andromache, whom he meets outside the walls of the city, by the waters of a river renamed Simois, celebrating funeral rites before a cenotaph of green turf and two altars to Hector and Astyanax; her astonishment on seeing him, her hesitation, the halting words in which she questions him, uncertain whether he is a man or a ghost; Aeneas's no less agitated replies and interrogations, and the pain and confusion with which she recalls the past – how she lived through scenes of blood and shame, how she

Reprinted from: Benedetto Croce, "Aesthetics," from *Encyclopaedia Britannica*, 14th edn., reprinted in Albert Hofstadter and Richard Kuhns (eds.) *Philosophies of Art and Beauty*, Chicago: University of Chicago Press, 1964, pp. 556–8, 565–6, 574–6.

was assigned by lot as slave and concubine to Pyrrhus, abandoned by him and united to Helenus, another of his slaves, how Pyrrhus fell by the hand of Orestes and Helenus became a free man and a king; the entry of Aeneas and his men into the city, and their reception by the son of Priam in this little Troy, this mimic Pergamon with its new Xanthus, and its Scaean Gate whose threshold Aeneas greets with a kiss – all these details, and others here omitted, are images of persons, things, attitudes, gestures, sayings, joy and sorrow; mere images, not history or historical criticism, for which they are neither given nor taken. But through them all there runs a feeling, a feeling which is our own no less than the poet's, a human feeling of bitter memories, of shuddering horror, of melancholy, of homesickness, of tenderness, of a kind of childish *pietas* that could prompt this vain revival of things perished, these playthings fashioned by a religious devotion, the *parva Troia*, the *Pergama simulata magnis*, the *arentem Xanthi cognomine rivum*: something inexpressible in logical terms, which only poetry can express in full. Moreover, these two elements may appear as two in a first abstract analysis, but they cannot be regarded as two distinct threads, however intertwined; for, in effect, the feeling is altogether converted into images, into this complex of images, and is thus a feeling that is contemplated and therefore resolved and transcended. Hence poetry must be called neither feeling, nor image, nor yet the sum of the two, but "contemplation of feeling" or "lyrical intuition" or (which is the same thing) "pure intuition" – pure, that is, of all historical and critical reference to the reality or unreality of the images of which it is woven, and apprehending the pure throb of life in its ideality. Doubtless, other things may be found in poetry besides these two elements or moments and the synthesis of the two; but these other things are either present as extraneous elements in a compound (reflections, exhortations, polemics, allegories, etc.), or else they are just these image-feelings themselves taken in abstraction from their context as so much material, restored to the condition in which it was before the act of poetic creation. In the former case, they are non-poetic elements merely interpolated into or attached to the poem; in the latter, they are divested of poetry, rendered unpoetical by a reader either unpoetical or not at the moment poetical, who has dispelled the poetry, either because he cannot live in its ideal realm, or for the legitimate ends of historical inquiry or other practical purposes which involve the degradation – or rather, the conversion – of the poem into a document or an instrument. . . .

Intuition and expression: One of the first problems to arise, when the work or art is defined as "lyrical image," concerns the relation of "intuition" to "expression" and the manner of the transition from the one to the other. At bottom this is the same problem which arises in other parts of philosophy: the problem of inner and outer, of mind and matter, of soul and body, and, in ethics, of intention and will, will and action, and so forth. Thus stated, the problem is insoluble; for once we have divided the inner from the outer, body from mind, will from action, or intuition from expression, there is no way of passing from one to the other or of reuniting them, unless we appeal for their reunion to a third term, variously represented as God or the Unknowable. Dualism leads necessarily either to transcendence or to agnosticism. But when a problem is found to be insoluble in the terms in which it is stated the only course open is to criticize these terms themselves, to inquire how they have been arrived at, and whether their genesis was logically sound. In this case, such inquiry leads to the conclusion that the terms depend not upon a philosophical principle, but upon an empirical and naturalistic classification, which has created two groups of facts called internal and external respectively (as if internal facts were not also external, and as if an external fact could exist without being also internal), or souls and bodies, or images and expressions; and everyone knows that it is hopeless to try to find a dialectical unity between terms that have been distinguished not philosophically or formally but only empirically and materially. The soul is only a soul in so far as it is a body; the will is only a will in so far as it moves arms and legs, or is action; intuition is only intuition in so far as it is, in that very act, expression. An image that does not express, that is not speech, song, drawing, painting, sculpture or architecture – speech at least murmured to oneself, song at least echoing within one's own breast, line and colour seen in imagination and colouring with its own tint the whole soul and organism – is an image that does not exist. We may assert its existence, but we cannot support our assertion; for the only thing we could adduce in support of it would be the fact that the image was embodied or expressed. This profound philosophical doctrine, the *identity of intuition and expression* is, moreover, a principle of ordinary common sense, which laughs at people who claim to have thoughts they cannot express or to have imagined a great picture which they cannot paint. *Rem tene, verba sequentur*; if there are no *verba*, there is no *res*. This identity, which applies to every sphere of the mind, has in the sphere of art a clearness and self-evidence lacking, perhaps, elsewhere. In the creation of a work of poetry, we are present, as it were, at the mystery of the creation of the world; hence the value of the contribution made by aesthetics to philosophy as a whole, or the conception of the One that is All. Aesthetics, by denying in the life of art an abstract spiritualism and the resulting dualism, prepares the way and leads the mind towards idealism or absolute spiritualism. . . .

The criticism and history of art and literature: Another group of questions raised in works on aesthetics, though not unsuitable to such works, properly belongs to logic and the theory of historical thought. These concern the aesthetic judgment and the history of poetry and the arts. By showing that the aesthetic activity (or art) is one of the forms of mind, a value, a category, or whatever we choose to call it, and not (as philosophers of various schools have thought) an empirical concept referable to certain orders of utilitarian or mixed facts, by establishing the *autonomy of aesthetic value*, aesthetics has also shown that it is the predicate of a special judgment, the *aesthetic judgment*, and the subject-matter of history, of a special history, the history of poetry and the arts, *artistic and literary history*.

The questions that have been raised concerning the aesthetic judgment and artistic and literary history are making allowance for the peculiar character of art, identical with the methodological questions that arise in every field of historical study. It has been asked whether the aesthetic judgment is *absolute* or *relative*; but every historical judgment (and the aesthetic judgment affirming the reality and quality of aesthetic facts is an historical judgment) is always both absolute and relative at once: absolute, in so far as the category involved in the construction possesses universal truth; relative, in so far as the object constructed by that category is historically conditioned: hence in the historical judgment the category is individualized and the individual becomes absolute. Those who in the past have denied the absoluteness of the aesthetic judgment (sensationalistic, hedonistic or utilitarian aestheticians) denied in effect the quality, reality and autonomy of art. It has been asked whether a knowledge of the history of the time – the whole history of the time in question – is necessary for the aesthetic judgment of the art of that time; it certainly is, because, as we know, poetic creation presupposes all the rest of the mind which it is converting into lyrical imagery, and the one aesthetic creation presupposes all the other creations (passions, feelings, customs, etc.) of the given historical moment. Hence may be seen the error both of those who advocate a merely historical judgment upon art (historical critics) and of those who advocate a merely aesthetic (aesthetic critics). The former would find in art all the rest of history (social conditions, biography of the artist, etc.), but would omit that part which is proper to art; the latter would judge the work of art in abstraction from history, depriving it of its real meaning and giving it an imaginary meaning or testing it by arbitrary standards. Lastly, there has appeared a kind of scepticism or pessimism as to the possibility of understanding the art of the past; a scepticism or pessimism which in that case ought to extend to every part of history (history of thought, politics, religion and morality), and refutes itself by a *reductio ad absurdum*, since what we call contemporary art and history really belong to the past as much as those of more distant ages, and must, like them, be re-created in the present, in the mind that feels them and the intellect that understands them. There are artistic works and periods that remain to us unintelligible; but this only means that we are not now in a position to enter again into their life and to understand them, and the same is true of the ideas and customs and actions of many peoples and ages. Humanity, like the individual, remembers some things and forgets many others; but it may yet, in the course of its mental development, reach a point where its memory of them revives.

A final question concerns the form proper to artistic and literary history, which, in the form that arose in the romantic period, and still prevails to-day, expounds the history of works of art as a function of the concepts and social needs of its various periods, regarding them as aesthetic expressions of these things and connecting them closely with civil history. This tends to obscure and almost to render invisible the peculiar character of the individual work of art, the character which makes it impossible to confuse one work of art with any other, and results in treating them as documents of social life. In practice no doubt this method is tempered by what may be called the "individualizing" method, which emphasizes the individual character of the works; but the mixture has the defects of all eclecticism. To escape this, there is nothing to do but consistently to develop individualizing history, and to treat works of art not in relation to social history but as each a world in itself, into which from time to time the whole of history is concentrated, transfigured and imaginatively transcended in the individuality of the poetic work, which is a creation, not a reflection, a monument, not a document. Dante is not simply a document of the middle ages, nor Shakespeare of the English Renaissance; as such, they have many equals or superiors among bad poets and non-poets. It has been objected that this method imposed on artistic and literary history the form of a series of disconnected essays or monographs; but, obviously, the connection is provided by human history as a whole, of which the personalities of poets constitute a part, and a somewhat conspicuous part (Shakespearian poetry is an event no less important than the Reformation or the French Revolution), and, precisely because they are a part of it, they ought not to be submerged and lost in it, that is, in its other parts, but ought to retain their proper proportions and their original character.

Victor Shklovsky

(1893–1984)

Though Victor Shklovsky was only one of the charter members of the school of Russian formalist criticism, he was a leading activist in the cause of making the literary artwork into an autonomous object of study. Shklovsky insisted that the work of art be treated as independent of the social and historical forces that otherwise govern the diverse meaningfulness of cultural experience and held that the formal properties of the artwork are the most legitimate basis of critical inquiry. His forcefully articulated defense of these notions crystallized the message of what was otherwise a set of rather loosely affiliated doctrines espoused by the Russian formalists. Shklovsky's formalist theorizing furthermore gave impetus to the widely popularized late-twentieth-century aesthetic dictum that says a poem should not "mean" but "be."

Russian formalism emerged out of the work of two research groups: the Moscow Linguistic Circle founded by Roman Jakobson in 1915 and the Petersburg OPOIaZ, or Society for Study of Poetic Language formed the following year. Shklovsky was officially affiliated with the latter. Both groups challenged the psychologism and biographism that had prevailed in literary studies within Russian universities since the eighteenth century. The efforts of these self-proclaimed "modern" research groups, however, had a precedent in the work of the literary theorist Aleksander Potebnya (1835–81). Potebnya promoted an aesthetic based on the assertion that literature represented a unique modality of "thinking in images," which warranted study exclusively in those formal terms. Shklovsky's critical identity was forged in his decision to challenge Potebnya's terms as inadequate to the specifically linguistic complexities of literary expression.

Shklovsky saw the necessity to develop a critical language that would be more responsive to those aspects of literary meaning that transcended visualization. For example, quoting lines from Wordsworth – "The world is too much with us; late and soon|Getting and spending, we lay waste our powers" – Shklovsky observed that, what we would want to call their uniquely poetic meaning, could not be said to depend on the discernment of even latent imagery. For in these lines the visual register does not conspicuously organize the perceptual experience purveyed. Rather, he attributes the power of this verse to a *defamiliarization* (in Russian *ostraneniye*, which means "making strange") of language. With this term Shklovsky supplied Russian formalism with a convincing technical basis for distinguishing literary from non-literary, or poetic from prosaic modes of expression. *Defamiliarization* grounded the aesthetic dimension of literature in a perceptual field that tapped all of the specifically linguistic resources of literary form – meter, rhythm, rhyme – as well as the more generalized features of voice and concept.

Shklovsky's commitment to defamiliarization as a creative/critical practice furthermore imputed to literature an ethical purpose. Shklovsky pointed out that familiarity, all that is automatic in our ways of processing language (as well as the experiences that language conveys), had the undesirable effect of deadening our sensibilities in automatic responses to the world. The work of art, in its defamiliarizing technique, impedes familiarity. In doing so it opens up an otherwise unapproachable horizon of perceptual experience that gives added weight and depth to human experience. This stance established a critical pretext for privileging formalist experimentation, wordplay, rhythmic irregularities, and eclectic diction. The formalist critic, by definition, is thereby a patron of innovation.

Shklovsky is often accused of divorcing literary art from social and historical reality. It ought to be noted in his defense, however, that by rooting aesthetic experience in perceptual experience, he guaranteed that the work of art would be addressed as rigorously, in its object-like dimensionality, as any other item of "objective reality." If only by virtue of this quasi-scientific rigor, Shklovsky's standard of "literariness" put the literary artwork squarely in the realm of real-world concerns.

Suggested reading

Peter Steiner, *Russian Formalism: A Metapoetics*, Ithaca, NY: Cornell University Press, 1984.

Art as Technique

We must, then, speak about the laws of expenditure and economy in poetic language not on the basis of an analogy with prose, but on the basis of the laws of poetic language.

If we start to examine the general laws of perception, we see that as perception becomes habitual, it becomes automatic. Thus, for example, all of our habits retreat into the area of the unconsciously automatic; if one remembers

Reprinted from: Victor Shklovsky, "Art as Technique," in *Russian Formalist Criticism: Four Essays*, translated by Lee T. Lemon and Marion J. Reis, Lincoln: University of Nebraska Press, 1933, pp. 11–13, 18, 22–4.

the sensations of holding a pen or of speaking in a foreign language for the first time and compares that with his feeling at performing the action for the ten thousandth time, he will agree with us. Such habituation explains the principles by which, in ordinary speech, we leave phrases unfinished and words half expressed. In this process, ideally realized in algebra, things are replaced by symbols. Complete words are not expressed in rapid speech; their initial sounds are barely perceived. Alexander Pogodin offers the example of a boy considering the sentence "The Swiss mountains are beautiful" in the form of a series of letters: *T, S, m, a, b*.[1]

This characteristic of thought not only suggests the method of algebra, but even prompts the choice of symbols (letters, especially initial letters). By this "algebraic" method of thought we apprehend objects only as shapes with imprecise extensions; we do not see them in their entirety but rather recognize them by their main characteristics. We see the object as though it were enveloped in a sack. We know what it is by its configuration, but we see only its silhouette. The object, perceived thus in the manner of prose perception, fades and does not leave even a first impression; ultimately even the essence of what it was is forgotten. Such perception explains why we fail to hear the prose word in its entirety . . . and, hence, why (along with other slips of the tongue) we fail to pronounce it. The process of "algebrization," the over-automatization of an object, permits the greatest economy of perceptive effort. Either objects are assigned only one proper feature – a number, for example – or else they function as though by formula and do not even appear in cognition:

> I was cleaning a room and, meandering about, approached the divan and couldn't remember whether or not I had dusted it. Since these movements are habitual and unconscious, I could not remember and felt that it was impossible to remember – so that if I had dusted it and forgot – that is, had acted unconsciously, then it was the same as if I had not. If some conscious person had been watching, then the fact could be established. If, however, no one was looking, or looking on unconsciously, if the whole complex lives of many people go on unconsciously, then such lives are as if they had never been.[2]

And so life is reckoned as nothing. Habitualization devours works, clothes, furniture, one's wife, and the fear of war. "If the whole complex lives of many people go on unconsciously, then such lives are as if they had never been." And art exists that one may recover the sensation of life; it exists to make one feel things, to make the stone *stony*. The purpose of art is to impart the sensation of things as they are perceived and not as they are known. The technique of art is to make objects "unfamiliar," to make forms difficult, to increase the difficulty and length of perception because the process of perception is an aesthetic end in itself and must be prolonged. *Art is a way of experiencing the artfulness of an object; the object is not important.*

The range of poetic (artistic) work extends from the sensory to the cognitive, from poetry to prose, from the concrete to the abstract: from Cervantes' Don Quixote – scholastic and poor nobleman, half consciously bearing his humiliation in the court of the duke – to the broad but empty Don Quixote of Turgenev; from Charlemagne to the name "king" [in Russian "Charles" and "king" obviously derive from the same root, *korol*]. The meaning of a work broadens to the extent that artfulness and artistry diminish; thus a fable symbolizes more than a poem, and a proverb more than a fable. Consequently, the least self-contradictory part of Potebnya's theory is his treatment of the fable, which, from his point of view, he investigated thoroughly. But since his theory did not provide for "expressive" works of art, he could not finish his book. As we know, *Notes on the Theory of Literature* was published in 1905, thirteen years after Potebnya's death. Potebnya himself completed only the section on the fable.[3]

After we see an object several times, we begin to recognize it. The object is in front of us and we know about it, but we do not see it – hence we cannot say anything significant about it. Art removes objects from the automatism of perception in several ways. Here I want to illustrate a way used repeatedly by Leo Tolstoy, that writer who, for Merezhkovsky at least, seems to present things as if he himself saw them, saw them in their entirety, and did not alter them.

Tolstoy makes the familiar seem strange by not naming the familiar object. He describes an object as if he were seeing it for the first time, an event as if it were happening for the first time. In describing something he avoids the accepted names of its parts and instead names corresponding parts of other objects. For example, in "Shame" Tolstoy "defamiliarizes" the idea of flogging in this way: "to strip people who have broken the law, to hurl them to the floor, and to rap on their bottoms with switches," and, after a few lines, "to lash about on the naked buttocks." Then he remarks:

> Just why precisely this stupid, savage means of causing pain and not any other – why not prick the shoulders or any part of the body with needles, squeeze the hands or the feet in a vise, or anything like that?

I apologize for this harsh example, but it is typical of Tolstoy's way of pricking the conscience. The familiar act of flogging is made unfamiliar both by the description and by the proposal to change its form without changing its nature. Tolstoy uses this technique of "defamiliarization" constantly. . . .

The technique of defamiliarization is not Tolstoy's alone. I cited Tolstoy because his work is generally known.

Now, having explained the nature of this technique, let us try to determine the approximate limits of its application. I personally feel that defamiliarization is found almost everywhere form is found. In other words, the difference between Potebnya's point of view and ours is this: An image is not a permanent referent for those mutable complexities of life which are revealed through it; its purpose is not to make us perceive meaning, but to create a special perception of the object – *it creates a "vision" of the object instead of serving as a means for knowing it*. . . .

. . . The usual poetic language for Pushkin's contemporaries was the elegant style of Derzhavin; but Pushkin's style, because it seemed trivial then, was unexpectedly difficult for them. We should remember the consternation of Pushkin's contemporaries over the vulgarity of his expressions. He used the popular language as a special device for prolonging attention, just as his contemporaries generally used Russian words in their usually French speech (see Tolstoy's examples in *War and Peace*).

Just now a still more characteristic phenomenon is under way. Russian literary language, which was originally foreign to Russia, has so permeated the language of the people that it has blended with their conversation. On the other hand, literature has now begun to show a tendency towards the use of dialects (Remizov, Klyuyev, Essenin, and others,[4] so unequal in talent and so alike in language, are intentionally provincial) and of barbarisms (which gave rise to the Severyanin group[5]). And currently Maxim Gorky is changing his diction from the old literary language to the new literary colloquialism of Leskov.[6] Ordinary speech and literary language have thereby changed places (see the work of Vyacheslav Ivanov and many others). And finally, a strong tendency, led by Khlebnikov, to create a new and properly poetic language has emerged. In the light of these developments we can define poetry as *attenuated, tortuous* speech. Poetic speech is *formed speech*. Prose is ordinary speech – economical, easy, proper, the goddess of prose [*dea prosae*] is a goddess of the accurate, facile type, of the "direct" expression of a child. I shall discuss roughened form and retardation as the general *law* of art at greater length in an article on plot construction.[7]

Nevertheless, the position of those who urge the idea of the economy of artistic energy as something which exists in and even distinguishes poetic language seems, at first glance, tenable for the problem of rhythm. Spencer's description of rhythm would seem to be absolutely incontestable:

Just as the body in receiving a series of varying concussions, must keep the muscles ready to meet the most violent of them, as not knowing when such may

come: so, the mind in receiving unarranged articulations, must keep its perspectives active enough to recognize the least easily caught sounds. And as, if the
concussions recur in definite order, the body may husband its forces by adjust-
ing the resistance needful for each concussion; so, if the syllables be rhythmi-
cally arranged, the mind may economize its energies by anticipating the attention
required for each syllable.[8]

This apparently conclusive observation suffers from the common fallacy, the
confusion of the laws of poetic and prosaic language. In *The Philosophy of Style*
Spencer failed utterly to distinguish between them. But rhythm may have two
functions. The rhythm of prose, or of a work song like "Dubinushka," permits
the members of the work crew to do their necessary "groaning together" and
also eases the work by making it automatic. And, in fact, it is easier to march
with music than without it, and to march during an animated conversation is
even easier, for the walking is done unconsciously. Thus the rhythm of prose
is an important automatizing element; the rhythm of poetry is not. There is
"order" in art, yet not a single column of a Greek temple stands exactly in its
proper order; poetic rhythm is similarly disordered rhythm. Attempts to
systematize the irregularities have been made, and such attempts are part
of the current problem in the theory of rhythm. It is obvious that
the systematization will not work, for in reality the problem is not one of
complicating the rhythm but of disordering the rhythm – a disordering
which cannot be predicted. Should the disordering of rhythm become a convention, it would be ineffective as a device for the roughening of language.
But I will not discuss rhythm in more detail since I intend to write a book
about it.[9]

Notes

1 Alexander Pogodin, *Yazyk, kak tvorchestvo* [*Language as Art*] (Kharkov, 1913), p.
   42. [The original sentence was in French, "*Les montaignes de la Suisse sont belles,*"
   with the appropriate initials.]
2 Leo Tolstoy's *Diary*, entry dated February 29, 1897. [The date is transcribed
   incorrectly; it should read March 1, 1897.]
3 Alexander Potebnya, *Iz lektsy po teorii slovesnosti* [*Lectures on the Theory of
   Language*] (Kharkov, 1914).
4 Alexy Remizov (1877–1957) is best known as a novelist and satirist; Nicholas
   Klyuyev (1885–1937) and Sergey Essenin (1895–1925) were "peasant poets." All
   three were noted for their faithful reproduction of Russian dialects and colloquial
   language [Ed.].
5 A group noted for its opulent and sensuous verse style [Ed.].

6   Nicholas Leskov (1831–1895), novelist and short story writer, helped popularize
    the *skaz*, or yarn, and hence, because of the part dialect peculiarities play in the
    skaz, also altered Russian literary language [Ed.].
7   Shklovsky is probably referring to his *Razvyortyvaniye syuzheta* [*Plot Development*]
    (Petrograd, 1921) [Ed.].
8   Spencer, p. 169. Again the Russian text is shortened from Spencer's original.
9   We have been unable to discover the book Shklovsky promised [Ed.].

T. S. Eliot

(1888–1965)

Thomas Stearns Eliot is, of course, most famous as one of the leading poets of Anglo-American modernism, but throughout his long and distinguished career, he also exerted considerable influence as a literary critic. Eliot was born in St. Louis and received his Ph.D. in philosophy from Harvard. While he was completing his dissertation, he moved to England· where he fell in with Ezra Pound and other poets of the nascent modernist movement. After arriving in England, Eliot worked first in banking and then in publishing, while at the same time producing some of his most important poetry and criticism. In 1927 Eliot became a British citizen and converted to Anglo-Catholicism, after which time he took pains to make it clear that he saw his literary work as ultimately devoted to religious ends.

Like other modernists, Eliot felt it necessary to break with the aesthetic doctrines of romanticism. In "Tradition and the Individual Talent" (1919), he attacks the romantic notion that a poem is the expression of the poet's soul and that the value of poetry is to be found in its originality. Rather, Eliot argues, a poem achieves value only as it responds to and is incorporated within a vast literary tradition. Its meaning can only be determined in relationship to that tradition; its worth can be measured only by its contribution to that tradition. The modern poet who writes a love poem, for example, is not primarily expressing a strongly felt emotion but making use of poetic images and ideas that have been passed down through the ages. This means, Eliot insists, that poet must know "the mind of Europe – the mind of his own country – a mind which he learns in time to be much more important than his own private mind" (1950: 6). Therefore, "the progress of an artist is a continual self-sacrifice, a continual extinction of personality," rather than a developing project of self-expression (p. 7). To illustrate this point, Eliot introduces a famous analogy: just as a catalyst in an explosive chemical reaction causes chemicals to combine in a new configuration without itself being affected by the reaction, so the poet's mind facilitates the combination of the "feelings, phrases, and images" that comprise the poem, but the poem itself neither expresses nor includes the poet (p. 8). If the poem is successful, its "feelings, phrases, and images" will combine in a unified and harmonious structure, and it is on the basis of its formal structure that it will earn its place in the tradition. Eliot develops this idea that poetry needs to be judged on the basis of its objective structure in his essay "Hamlet and his Problems" (1919). *Hamlet* fails, he argues, because the play does not present its characters' emotions in an objective form – that is, the play lacks what he calls an "objective correlative" for the feelings that it explores.

Despite their anti-romantic rhetoric, however, modernists retained many of the attitudes and assumptions of their Romantic predecessors, and Eliot was no exception to this generalization. In particular, Eliot's account of the history of poetry is based upon the romantic narrative of loss and recovery. Like Friedrich Schiller, he believed that pre-modern poetry and culture possessed a wholeness and harmony that was lost in the process of modernization. In the essay "The Metaphysical Poets," Eliot describes this loss of unity as "the dissociation of sensibility" and claims that it occurred sometime in the seventeenth century. As a result of this dissociation of sensibility, poets of later centuries such as Tennyson and Browning cannot effectively combine and unify the abstract and concrete dimensions of their experience; "they do not feel their thought as immediately as the odour of a rose". For earlier poets like John Donne, however, this was not a problem: "A thought to Donne was an experience; it modified his sensibility" (1950: 247). It is the responsibility of twentieth-century poets. Eliot argues, to recover the unifying vision found in pre-seventeenth-century poets. This will allow them to take the disparate experiences of everyday life and form them into "new wholes" and thus help to unify a fragmented culture.

Not surprisingly, Eliot's critical perspective changed after his conversion to Anglo-Catholicism. As the critic René Wellek observes, he never held literary criticism in very high esteem. Early in his career, Eliot claims that only practicing poets should write criticism and then only as a means of helping other poets write better poetry. Even after he modified this view, however, he continued to emphasize that even the best criticism can never be fully adequate to its object.

In the following excerpt from "The Social function of Poetry," Eliot describes the poet's responsibilities to her or his local culture. This contrasts with the account of the poet that he presents in "Tradition and the Individual Talent," where he claims that the individual poet embodies "the mind of Europe."

Reference

T. S. Eliot, *Selected Essays: New Edition*, New York: Harcourt, Brace, and Co., 1950.

Suggested reading

Louis Menand, *Discovering Modernism: T. S. Eliot and his Context*, New York: Oxford University Press, 1987.

The Social Function of Poetry

Now if we are to find the essential social function of poetry we must look first at its more obvious functions, those which it must perform if it is to perform any. The first, I think, that we can be sure about is that poetry has to give pleasure. If you ask what kind of pleasure then I can only answer, the kind of pleasure that poetry gives: simply because any other answer would take us far afield into aesthetics, and the general question of the nature of art.

I suppose it will be agreed that every good poet, whether he be a great poet or not, has something to give us besides pleasure: for if it were only pleasure, the pleasure itself could not be of the highest kind. Beyond any specific intention which poetry may have, such as I have already instanced in the various kinds of poetry, there is always the communication of some new experience, or some fresh understanding of the familiar, or the expression of something we have experienced but have no words for, which enlarges our consciousness or refines our sensibility. But it is not with such individual benefit from poetry, any more than it is with the quality of individual pleasure, that this paper is concerned. We all understand, I think, both the kind of pleasure which poetry can give, and the kind of difference, beyond the pleasure, which it makes to our lives. Without producing these two effects it simply is not poetry. We may acknowledge this, but at the same time overlook something which it does for us collectively, as a society. And I mean that in the widest sense. For I think it is important that every people should have its own poetry, not simply for those who enjoy poetry – such people could always learn other languages and enjoy their poetry – but because it actually makes a difference to the society as a whole, and that means to people who do not enjoy poetry. I include even those who do not know the names of their own national poets. That is the real subject of this paper.

We observe that poetry differs from every other art in having a value for the people of the poet's race and language, which it can have for no other. It is true that even music and painting have a local and racial character: but certainly the difficulties of appreciation in these arts, for a foreigner, are much less. It is true on the other hand that prose writings have significance in their own language which is lost in translation; but we all feel that we lose much less in reading a novel in translation than in reading a poem; and in a translation of some kinds of scientific work the loss may be virtually nil. That poetry is much more local

Reprinted from: T. S. Eliot, *On Poetry and Poets*, New York: Noonday Press/Farrar, Straus & Giroux, 1957, pp. 6–10. For up-to-date copyright and publication information see Acknowledgments.

than prose can be seen in the history of European languages. Through the Middle Ages to within a few hundred years ago Latin remained the language for philosophy, theology, and science. The impulse towards the literary use of the languages of the peoples began with poetry. And this appears perfectly natural when we realize that poetry has primarily to do with the expression of feeling and emotion; and that feeling and emotion are particular, whereas thought is general. It is easier to think in a foreign language than it is to feel in it. Therefore no art is more stubbornly national than poetry. A people may have its language taken away from it, suppressed, and another language compelled upon the schools; but unless you teach that people to *feel* in a new language, you have not eradicated the old one, and it will reappear in poetry, which is the vehicle of feeling. I have just said 'feel in a new language', and I mean something more than merely 'express their feelings in a new language'. A thought expressed in a different language may be practically the same thought, but a feeling or emotion expressed in a different language is not the same feeling or emotion. One of the reasons for learning at least one foreign language well is that we acquire a kind of supplementary personality; one of the reasons for not acquiring a new language *instead* of our own is that most of us do not want to become a different person. A superior language can seldom be exterminated except by the extermination of the people who speak it. When one language supersedes another it is usually because that language has advantages which commend it, and which offer not merely a difference but a wider and more refined range, not only for thinking but for feeling, than the more primitive language.

Emotion and feeling, then, are best expressed in the common language of the people – that is, in the language common to all classes: the structure, the rhythm, the sound, the idiom of a language, express the personality of the people which speaks it. When I say that it is poetry rather than prose that is concerned with the expression of emotion and feeling, I do not mean that poetry need have no intellectual content or meaning, or that great poetry does not contain more of such meaning than lesser poetry. But to develop this investigation would take me away from my immediate purpose. I will take it as agreed that people find the most conscious expression of their deepest feelings in the poetry of their own language rather than in any other art or in the poetry of other languages. This does not mean, of course, that true poetry is limited to feelings which everyone can recognize and understand; we must not limit poetry to *popular* poetry. It is enough that in a homogeneous people the feelings of the most refined and complex have something in common with those of the most crude and simple, which they have not in common with those of people of their own level speaking another language. And, when a civilization is healthy, the great poet will have something to say to his fellow countrymen at every level of education.

We may say that the duty of the poet, as poet, is only indirectly to his people: his direct duty is to his *language*, first to preserve, and second to extend and improve. In expressing what other people feel he is also changing the feeling by making it more conscious; he is making people more aware of what they feel already, and therefore teaching them something about themselves. But he is not merely a more conscious person than the others; he is also individually different from other people, and from other poets too, and can make his readers share consciously in new feelings which they had not experienced before. That is the difference between the writer who is merely eccentric or mad and the genuine poet. The former may have feelings which are unique but which cannot be shared, and are therefore useless; the latter discovers new variations of sensibility which can be appropriated by others. And in expressing them he is developing and enriching the language which he speaks.

Cleanth Brooks

(1906–1994)

Cleanth Brooks is known primarily as one of the foremost representatives of the New Criticism, although he often disagreed with other New Critics and sometimes advocated rejecting the label entirely. By Brooks's own account, the New Critics believed that the work of literature should be viewed as an organic whole, the value of which lies in its structure and the structure of which is best appreciated by close reading, that is, by a careful analysis of the ways in which a work's verbal parts contribute to the literary whole. The New Critics were united in insisting that the proper object of literary criticism is the literary text and not the author's intentions, the readers' various responses, or the social conditions which helped shape and influence the text's composition. We should evaluate literature, the New Critics insisted, on the basis of how well or poorly it is written and not in response to whether we agree with the ideas that it expresses or sympathize with the characters it presents. Not surprisingly, this claim has made the New Critics the target of frequent criticism from Marxist critics and from others who are committed to analyzing literature in its social contexts.

Throughout his long career, Brooks was an influential spokesman for New Critical principles, and by the mid-twentieth-century, New Criticism had become the dominant form of literary criticism in America. In 1935, he and Robert Penn Warren established *The Southern Review*, a journal that published many of Brooks's fellow New Critics and which reflected the views of the Southern Agrarians, a conservative group who wished to protect traditional cultures such as those found in the South from what they saw as the negative effects of industrialization and modernization. In 1938, Brooks and Warren published *Understanding Poetry*, a very influential anthology, which was designed to facilitate the use of New Critical principles in teaching literature.

The following year, Brooks published *Modern Poetry and Tradition*, his first book of essays. Here he follows T. S. Eliot in suggesting that the best poetry employs dramatic and complex figures of speech, which Eliot and others termed "metaphysical wit." Like Eliot and Matthew Arnold before him, Brooks thinks that the history of

English literature reflects the fragmentation of society. He was particularly critical of the subjectivism of Romantic poetry and feels that the emphasis on poetic form which is found in Modernist poetry provides a necessary corrective to the emotional excesses of romanticism. *The Well Wrought Urn*, Brooks's most influential work of criticism, provides a succinct summary of his critical principles and, as is usual in Brooks's criticism, an application of these principles in numerous exemplary close readings of poems. Brooks argues that poetic structure is predicated upon the dynamic balance of opposing ideas, attitudes, and feelings. As one example, he cites the opening lines of a sonnet by Wordsworth:

> It is a beauteous evening, calm, and free,
> The holy time is quiet as a Nun
> Breathless with adoration . . .

Brooks then notes the tension between Wordsworth's adjectives: beauteous, calm, free, holy, quiet, breathless. "The adjective 'breathless,'" he observes, "suggests tremendous excitement; and yet the evening is not only quiet but *calm*". Brooks labels this verbal tension "paradox" and argues that it is the indispensable foundation of all good poetry. Because of the emphasis that he places on poetic form, Brooks has been accused of reducing poetic language to a fixed or static structure, but this accusation overlooks the dramatic conflict that Brooks sees as the source of paradox. Poetry is more successful than scientific description in capturing the drama of human thought, he argues, precisely because it is able to balance multiple and conflicting points of view. Yet, a question remains as to how Brooks would have us understand the relationship between poetic dramas of thought and those which we experience in everyday life. Can we appreciate the form of a poet's dramatization of a moral conflict, for instance, without judging the contents of her or his arguments? To some extent, we can, Brooks insists, although this claim has been often challenged.

Suggested reading

Lewis P. Simpson (ed.) *The Possibilities of Order: Cleanth Brooks and His Work*, Baton Rouge, La.: Louisiana State University Press, 1976.

The Language of Paradox

Few of us are prepared to accept the statement that the language of poetry is the language of paradox. Paradox is the language of sophistry, hard, bright,

Reprinted from: Cleanth Brooks, *The Well Wrought Urn: Studies in the Structure of Poetry*, New York: Harcourt, Brace & World, 1947, pp. 3–5, 7–10.

witty; it is hardly the language of the soul. We are willing to allow that paradox is a permissible weapon which a Chesterton may on occasion exploit. We may permit it in epigram, a special subvariety of poetry; and in satire, which though useful, we are hardly willing to allow to be poetry at all. Our prejudices force us to regard paradox as intellectual rather than emotional, clever rather than profound, rational rather than divinely irrational.

Yet there is a sense in which paradox is the language appropriate and inevitable to poetry. It is the scientist whose truth requires a language purged of every trace of paradox; apparently the truth which the poet utters can be approached only in terms of paradox. I overstate the case, to be sure; it is possible that the title of this chapter is itself to be treated as merely a paradox. But there are reasons for thinking that the overstatement which I propose may light up some elements in the nature of poetry which tend to be overlooked.

The case of William Wordsworth, for instance, is instructive on this point. His poetry would not appear to promise many examples of the language of paradox. He usually prefers the direct attack. He insists on simplicity; he distrusts whatever seems sophistical. And yet the typical Wordsworth poem is based upon a paradoxical situation. Consider his celebrated

> It is a beauteous evening, calm and free,
> The holy time is quiet as a Nun
> Breathless with adoration . . .

The poet is filled with worship, but the girl who walks beside him is not worshiping. The implication is that she should respond to the holy time, and become like the evening itself, nunlike; but she seems less worshipful than inanimate nature itself. Yet

> If thou appear untouched by solemn thought,
> Thy nature is not therefore less divine:
> Thou liest in Abraham's bosom all the year;
> And worship'st at the Temple's inner shrine,
> God being with thee when we know it not.

The underlying paradox (of which the enthusiastic reader may well be unconscious) is nevertheless thoroughly necessary, even for that reader. Why does the innocent girl worship more deeply than the self-conscious poet who walks beside her? Because she is filled with an unconscious sympathy for *all* of nature, not merely the grandiose and solemn. One remembers the lines from Wordsworth's friend, Coleridge:

> He prayeth best, who loveth best
> All things both great and small.

Her unconscious sympathy is the unconscious worship. She is in communion with nature "all the year," and her devotion is continual whereas that of the poet is sporadic and momentary. But we have not done with the paradox yet. It not only underlies the poem, but something of the paradox informs the poem, though, since this is Wordsworth, rather timidly. The comparison of the evening to the nun actually has more than one dimension. The calm of the evening obviously means "worship," even to the dull-witted and insensitive. It corresponds to the trappings of the nun, visible to everyone. Thus, it suggests not merely holiness, but, in the total poem, even a hint of Pharisaical holiness, with which the girl's careless innocence, itself a symbol of her continual secret worship, stands in contrast. . . .

In his preface to the second edition of the *Lyrical Ballads* Wordsworth stated that his general purpose was "to choose incidents and situations from common life" but so to treat them that "ordinary things should be presented to the mind in an unusual aspect." Coleridge was to state the purpose for him later, in terms which make even more evident Wordsworth's exploitation of the paradoxical: "Mr. Wordsworth . . . was to propose to himself as his object, to give the charm of novelty to things of every day, and to excite a feeling analogous to the supernatural, by awakening the mind's attention from the lethargy of custom, and directing it to the loveliness and the wonders of the world before us . . ." Wordsworth, in short, was consciously attempting to show his audience that the common was really uncommon, the prosaic was really poetic.

Coleridge's terms, "the charm of novelty to things of every day," "awakening the mind," suggest the Romantic preoccupation with wonder – the surprise, the revelation which puts the tarnished familiar world in a new light. This may well be the *raison d'être* of most Romantic paradoxes; and yet the neo-classic poets use paradox for much the same reason. Consider Pope's lines from "The Essay on Man":

> In doubt his Mind or Body to prefer;
> Born but to die, and reas'ning but to err;
> Alike in ignorance, his Reason such,
> Whether he thinks too little, or too much . . .

> Created half to rise, and half to fall;
> Great Lord of all things, yet a Prey to all;
> Sole Judge of Truth, in endless Error hurl'd;
> The Glory, Jest, and Riddle of the world!

Here, it is true, the paradoxes insist on the irony, rather than the wonder. But Pope too might have claimed that he was treating the things of everyday, man himself, and awakening his mind so that he would view himself in a new and blinding light. Thus, there is a certain awed wonder in Pope just as there is a certain trace of irony implicit in the Wordsworth sonnets. There is, of course, no reason why they should not occur together, and they do. Wonder and irony merge in many of the lyrics of Blake; they merge in Coleridge's *Ancient Mariner*. The variations in emphasis are numerous. Gray's "Elegy" uses a typical Wordsworth "situation" with the rural scene and with peasants contemplated in the light of their "betters." But in the "Elegy" the balance is heavily tilted in the direction of irony, the revelation an ironic rather than a startling one:

> Can storied urn or animated bust
> Back to its mansion call the fleeting breath?
> Can Honour's voice provoke the silent dust?
> Or Flatt'ry sooth the dull cold ear of Death?

But I am not here interested in enumerating the possible variations; I am interested rather in our seeing that the paradoxes spring from the very nature of the poet's language: it is a language in which the connotations play as great a part as the denotations. And I do not mean that the connotations are important as supplying some sort of frill or trimming, something external to the real matter in hand. I mean that the poet does not use a notation at all – as the scientist may properly he said to do so. The poet, within limits, has to make up his language as he goes.

T. S. Eliot has commented upon "that perpetual slight alteration of language, words perpetually juxtaposed in new and sudden combinations," which occurs in poetry. It *is* perpetual; it cannot be kept out of the poem; it can only be directed and controlled. The tendency of science is necessarily to stabilize terms, to freeze them into strict denotations; the poet's tendency is by contrast disruptive. The terms are continually modifying each other, and thus violating their dictionary meanings. To take a very simple example, consider the adjectives in the first lines of Wordsworth's evening sonnet: *beauteous, calm, free, holy, quiet, breathless*. The juxtapositions are hardly startling; and yet notice this: the evening is like a nun breathless with adoration. The adjective "breathless" suggests tremendous excitement; and yet the evening is not only quiet but *calm*. There is no final contradiction, to be sure: it is *that* kind of calm and *that* kind of excitement, and the two states may well occur together. But the poet has no one term. Even if he had a polysyllabic technical term, the term would not provide the solution for his problem. He must work by contradiction and qualification.

We may approach the problem in this way: the poet has to work by analogies. All of the subtler states of emotion, as I. A. Richards has pointed out, necessarily demand metaphor for their expression. The poet must work by analogies, but the metaphors do not lie in the same plane or fit neatly edge to edge. There is a continual tilting of the planes; necessary overlappings, discrepancies, contradictions. Even the most direct and simple poet is forced into paradoxes far more often than we think, if we are sufficiently alive to what he is doing.

Roland Barthes

(1915–1980)

Roland Barthes was a French literary and social critic who was educated at the Sorbonne in classics and French literature and taught at the École Practique des Hautes Études from 1960 until his death in 1980. Barthes is known as one of the founders and chief advocates of structuralism, a movement in literary criticism and the social sciences that assumes that literature and other cultural activities such as fashion and dining are governed by unconscious rules in the same way that language is governed by grammatical rules of which most speakers are not conscious. Ironically, Barthes's later work is usually described as poststructuralist and is credited with undermining the same structuralist methodology that he had previously championed. In this work, Barthes argues that the activities by which we make and interpret meanings are too complex and too dependent on variable contexts to be explained by single hierarchically arranged system of codes.

In his first book, *Writing Degree Zero*, Barthes develops a type of argument that will remain important to both his structuralist and poststructuralist work. Here he claims that language is never a simple, neutral channel of communication; rather, it is always shaped and inflected with various styles which reflect the social status of the speaker or writer. According to Barthes, until the mid-nineteenth century, good writing or speaking styles were considered to be merely the most natural forms of expression. That is, these styles were considered good because they were natural. This assumption that society's standards for good writing are a reflection of natural laws is a reflection of bourgeois ideology, Barthes contends, and part of the way in which the bourgeoisie imposes its values on society as a whole. Modern literature, he suggests, calls these assumptions into question. Barthes makes a similar point in *Mythologies*, one of his most popular works. The essays in this volume consider various facets of everyday life, from tourist books, toys, advertisements for soap and clothes, to museum displays and even professional wrestling. In analyzing these various cultural phenomena, Barthes seeks to demonstrate that although they seem to be natural, they in fact contain cultural messages. He notes, for instance, the way in which modern toys "prefigure the world of adult functions" for which children are destined. These toys are complicated objects made out of artificial materials which are not likely to last; "they are," he observes, "meant to produce children who are users, not creators" (1975: 53, 54).

In the 1950s and 1960s, Barthes published several influential accounts of the structuralist method of analyzing and interpreting culture, including works such as *Elements of Semiology* (1964) and "Introduction to the Structuralist Analysis of Narrative" (1966). In his analysis of narrative, for instance, Barthes compares stories to sentences and suggests that critics should break down the narratives they analyze into the actions and descriptions that are its components, and then look for the "grammatical" rules by which these components are combined. However, as was mentioned above, Barthes's own application of this structuralist methodology helped undermine the hope that there would ever be a structuralist science of interpretation. In a ground-breaking book entitled *S/Z* (1966) Barthes analyzes Balzac's short story "Sarrasine" by breaking it into 561 reading "units" and analyzing each of these units according to five different codes. This exhaustive and exhausting reading of the story generates a wealth of possible interpretations but offers little hope for producing a single, unified interpretation of the text. In Barthes's analysis, linguistic and cultural codes create a kaleidoscope of interpretive possibilities rather than one authoritative reading. In *S/Z* he also distinguishes between "readerly" texts, which restrict the reader's interpretive activity, and "writerly" texts, which encourage readers to engage in creative interpretation. But later, in a famous article of 1968 entitled "The Death of the Author", he denies that any form of literary meaning should be stabilized or fixed by assumptions about the author's intentions. "The birth of the reader," he writes, "must be requited by the death of the Author" (1986: 55).

In the excerpt which follows, Barthes describes the role that structuralist analysis should play: it must uncover the implicit ideological rules by which a text is structured while remaining aware that its own critical activity is part of the system that it describes.

References

Roland Barthes, *Mythologies*, 5th edn., New York: Hill and Wang (Farrar, Straus, and Giroux), 1975.
——, "The Death of the Author," in *The Rustle of Language*, New York: Hill and Wang (Farrar, Straus, and Giroux), 1986.

Suggested reading

Rick Rylance, *Roland Barthes*, New York and London: Harvester Wheatsheaf, 1994.

What Is Criticism?

Criticism is more than discourse in the name of "true" principles. It follows that the capital sin in criticism is not ideology but the silence by which it is masked: this guilty silence has a name: *good conscience*, or again, *bad faith*. How could we believe, in fact, that the work is an object exterior to the psyche and history of the man who interrogates it, an object over which the critic would exercise a kind of extraterritorial right? By what miracle would the profound communication which most critics postulate between the work and its author cease in relation to their own enterprise and their own epoch? Are there laws of creation valid for the writer but not for the critic? All criticism must include in its discourse (even if it is in the most indirect and modest manner imaginable) an implicit reflection on itself; every criticism is a criticism of the work *and* a criticism of itself. In other words, criticism is not at all a table of results or a body of judgments, it is essentially an activity, i.e., a series of intellectual acts profoundly committed to the historical and subjective existence (they are the same thing) of the man who performs them. Can an activity be "true"? It answers quite different requirements.

Every novelist, every poet, whatever the detours literary theory may take, is presumed to speak of objects and phenomena, even if they are imaginary, exterior and anterior to language: the world exists and the writer speaks: that is literature. The object of criticism is very different; the object of criticism is not "the world" but a discourse, the discourse of someone else: criticism is discourse upon a discourse; it is a second language, or a *metalanguage* (as the logicians would say), which operates on a first language (or *language object*). It follows that the critical language must deal with two kinds of relations: the relation of the critical language to the language of the author studied, and the relation of this language object to the world. It is the "friction" of these two languages which defines criticism and perhaps gives it a great resemblance to another mental activity, logic, which is also based on the distinction between language object and metalanguage.

For if criticism is only a metalanguage, this means that its task is not at all to discover "truths," but only "validities." In itself, a language is not true or false, it is or is not valid: valid, i.e., constitutes a coherent system of signs. The rules of literary language do not concern the conformity of this language to reality (whatever the claims of the realistic schools), but only its submission to the system of signs the author has established (and we must, of course, give

Reprinted from: Roland Barthes, *Critical Essays*, translated by Richard Howard, Evanston, Ill.: Northwestern University Press, 1972, pp. 257–60.

the word *system* a very strong sense here). Criticism has no responsibility to say whether Proust has spoken "the truth," whether the Baron de Charlus was indeed the Count de Montesquiou, whether Françoise was Céleste, or even, more generally, whether the society Proust described reproduces accurately the historical conditions of the nobility's disappearance at the end of the nineteenth century; its role is solely to elaborate a language whose coherence, logic, in short whose *systematics* can collect or better still can "integrate" (in the mathematical sense of the word) the greatest possible quantity of Proustian language, exactly as a logical equation tests the validity of reasoning without taking sides as to the "truth" of the arguments it mobilizes. One can say that the criticial task (and this is the sole guarantee of its universality) is purely formal: not to "discover" in the work or the author something "hidden," "profound," "secret" which hitherto passed unnoticed (by what miracle? Are we more perspicacious than our predecessors?), but only to adjust the language his period affords him (existentialism, Marxism, psychoanalysis) to the language, i.e., the formal system of logical constraints elaborated by the author according to his own period. The "proof" of a criticism is not of an "alethic" order (it does not proceed from truth), for critical discourse – like logical discourse, moreover – is never anything but tautological: it consists in saying ultimately, though placing its whole being within that delay, what thereby is not insignificant: Racine is Racine, Proust is Proust; critical "proof," if it exists, depends on an aptitude not to *discover* the work in question but on the contrary to *cover* it as completely as possible by its own language.

Thus we are concerned, once again, with an essentially formal activity, not in the esthetic but in the logical sense of the term. We might say that for criticism, the only way of avoiding "good conscience" or "bad faith" is to take as a moral goal not the decipherment of the work's meaning but the reconstruction of the rules and constraints of that meaning's elaboration; provided we admit at once that a literary work is a very special semantic system, whose goal is to put "meaning" in the world, but not "a meaning"; the work, at least the work which ordinarily accedes to critical scrutiny – and this is perhaps a definition of "good" literature – the work is never entirely nonsignifying (mysterious or "inspired"), and never entirely clear; it is, one may say, a *suspended* meaning: it offers itself to the reader as an avowed signifying system yet withholds itself from him as a signified object. This disappointment of meaning explains on the one hand why the literary work has so much power to ask the world questions (undermining the assured meanings which ideologies, beliefs, and common sense seem to possess), yet without ever answering them (there is no great work which is "dogmatic"), and on the other hand why it offers itself to endless decipherment, since there is no reason for us ever to stop speaking of Racine or Shakespeare (unless by a disaffection which will itself be a language): simultaneously an insistent proposition of meaning and a stubbornly fugitive meaning, literature is indeed only a *language*, i.e., a system of signs; its being is not in its message but in this "system." And thereby the critic is not responsible for reconstructing the work's message but only its system, just as the linguist is not responsible for deciphering the sentence's meaning but for establishing the formal structure which permits this meaning to be transmitted.

It is by acknowledging itself as no more than a language (or more precisely, a metalanguage) that criticism can be – paradoxically but authentically – both objective and subjective, historical and existential, totalitarian and liberal. For on the one hand, the language each critic chooses to speak does not come down to him from Heaven; it is one of the various languages his age affords him, it is objectively the end product of a certain historical ripening of knowledge, ideas, intellectual passions – it is a *necessity*; and on the other hand, this necessary language is chosen by each critic as a consequence of a certain existential organization, as the exercise of an intellectual function which belongs to him in his own right, an exercise in which he puts all his "profundity," i.e., his choices, his pleasures, his resistances, his obsessions. Thus begins, at the heart of the critical work, the dialogue of two histories and two subjectivities, the author's and the critic's. But this dialogue is egoistically shifted toward the present: criticism is not an "homage" to the truth of the past or to the truth of "others" – it is a construction of the intelligibility of our own time.

Gérard Genette

(1930–)

A French critic and rhetorician who has published essays most influentially in the field of narratology, Gérard Genette came to the attention of American literary critics with the translation of his internationally heralded volume *Narrative Discourse: An Essay in Method* (1972). This work articulated a systematic narrative theory based on the writings of Marcel Proust. Genette's method respected the French structuralist distinction between story and discourse, whereby the intersecting axes of lived time (story) and structured time (discourse) were deemed to be the essential coordinates on which narratives yielded up their meanings. An underlying assumption is that knowledge of the universal structures of emplotment determines the possibilities of narrative experience. Genette helped to establish temporality as an inescapable register of intelligibility in literary texts. Along with Roland Barthes and Tzvetan Todorov, and in contrast with structuralist narratologists who stressed the static and paradigmatic aspects of narrative structure, Genette emphasized the intrinsic dynamism of the temporal axes upon which narrative structure is plotted.

Recently Genette has turned his attention from systems of time relations in narrative works of art to the question, What is the nature of the general category of experience designated by the word "art"? *The Work of Art: Immanence and Transcendence*, projected to be a two-volume work, attempts to anatomize the "modes of existence of artworks," with the understanding that there are two controlling categories by which we grapple with aesthetic experience: immanence and transcendence. Genette's thinking here draws candidly on the work of the American nominalist philosopher, Nelson Goodman. Goodman divides artworks into the realms of the autographic, which manifests itself directly (hence a counter for immanence), and the allographic, which manifests itself indirectly (hence a counter for transcendence). For Genette immanence designates the proposition that the significance of the artwork "consists in" its objecthood. Transcendence designates the competing idealist proposition that material art works are mere embodiments of an "idea" that has substantial existence only in the creative mind of the artist. Immanent work, of painting or sculpture for example, is authenticated by its presence and is degraded when it is reproduced or translated by other communicative media. Transcendent work, of literature or music for example, is authenticated in its absence. Transcendent work, in other words, is dependent upon "translating" media such as performance or reproduction.

While Genette's ambitious study begins by anatomizing the regimes of the immanent-autographic and the transcendent-allographic in their own terms, he concludes by admitting that the distinction between them is not clear-cut. In a way that is reminiscent of his earlier narratological work, with its emphasis upon the dynamic relational play between the axes of story and discourse, Genette stresses the reciprocity that inevitably plays between the realms of the autographic and the allographic. Thus his inquiry intimates the intrinsic plurality of the artwork, the postulate of a "plural work." Consequently, when he turns to the examination of specific works of art Genette is led to deal with (a) *mixed cases*, such as concrete poems, which confuse the ideality of a text with the materiality of writing (b) *intermediate cases*, autographic works that exist as multiple copies, and (c) *ambiguous cases*, such as instances of performance art where the performance is uniquely itself and at the same time a version of what it performs.

In the concluding passage of volume 1 of *The Work of Art* (cited below), Genette reflects generally on the consequences of surpassing the dualism of immanence and transcendence. Arriving at what he calls a "functional definition of the work of art," Genette looks toward the possibility of our making the work of art an ever more integral aspect of practical life. For Genette, our practicality in life and art is determined by our self-consciousness with respect to the objects we are inspired to make use of.

Suggested reading

Jonathan Culller, *Structuralist Poetics: Structuralism, Linguistics, and the Study of Literature*, Ithaca, NY: Cornell University Press, 1975.

Plural Receptions

We will conclude, then, with a consideration of the functional (attentional, receptional) plurality of works – or, to put it more simply, the fact that a work (independently of the physical modifications that only autographic works inevitably undergo in the course of time) never produces exactly the same effect twice; in other words – but this amounts to the same thing – is never invested with exactly the same meaning. I use the word *meaning* in its broadest sense,

Reprinted from: Gérard Genette, *The Work of Art: Immanence and Transcendence*, translated by G. M. Goshgarian, Ithaca, NY: Cornell University Press, 1997, pp. 237–8, 254–7.

which covers not only the denotational values characteristic of the "representational" works of literature, painting, or sculpture, but also the exemplificational and expressive values (Goodman) characteristic of the merely "presentative" (Souriau) works of music, architecture, or abstract painting, which, if they do not (as a rule) denote anything, nonetheless do have meaning.

I will take as my starting point an elementary, well-known example, Jastrow's duck-rabbit,[1] already referred to. In question here, we remember, is an ambiguous figure, which can be read either as the head of a rabbit facing right, or the head of a duck facing left. We have only one (physical) line, but two (functional) drawings;[2] if a purely "syntactical" description is unambigu-

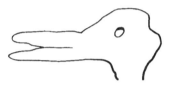

ous, a semantic description is necessarily equivocal, or, more precisely, two such descriptions are possible, unless we choose between the two readings on the basis of the author's declared intention ("I meant to represent a rabbit, and nothing else"). Such a choice is not, however, always possible or even relevant – if, for example, what is at issue is a randomly drawn line, or if the question posed is, "What does this drawing represent *for you*?", or a fortiori, if the line is purposely ambiguous, as in the present case. . . .

The simplest (albeit paradoxical) formulation of this state of affairs seems to me to be the following: "A book changes by virtue of the fact that it does not change, while the world does."[3] As we know, texts, by virtue of their ideal character, are the only objects of immanence which "do not change," in the strict sense, though, in many respects, all works "change" unceasingly, each in its own way. But the change we are concerned with here is of a different kind, and does not spare the most inalterable works – spares *them*, perhaps, even less than the others. In establishing our relation to the works of the past or to works come from elsewhere, our sole choice is between, on the one hand, the spontaneous anachronism (or "anatopianism") which induces us to receive ancient works, or works of remote cultures, in the light and from the standpoint of our time and place, and, on the other, an effort at adjustment and restitution that consists in recovering and respecting their original value – in seeking out, as Malraux would say, "what they *once* said" behind "what they say to *us*." But, as everyone knows, this effort can in its turn be dated and situated:

seventeenth-century historians (and painters) made no effort to correct their anachronisms; as Caillois more or less says, not all cultures have their ethnographers. Be that as it may, neither a naively anachronistic attitude nor an attempt at adjustment place us, *vis-à-vis* these works, in the situation of their producers and contemporaneous public. There is an effect of cultural parallax that one cannot adjust for without first being aware of it; but this awareness produces another such effect. In any event, the work is "brought back to life" or lives on in a "world of art" different from its own. Wölfflin's famous remark to the effect that not every art would have been possible in every period[4] holds not only for the creation, but also for the reception of works. In question here is not impossibility in the physical sense (Poussin or Hokusai *could* have painted *Guernica*), but cultural signification: the function of an act changes when it is taken out of context, and the truth of the matter is that, in art, not everything has the same *meaning* in every period and culture. "There are beautiful things still waiting to be composed in C major," Schönberg liked to say; but, to the best of my knowledge, he did not compose them, and, in any case, the key word in this sentence (as in many others) is plainly the word "still."

For several pages now, I have had the disagreeable impression that I am merely rehashing what have been truisms, not merely since Malraux and Borges, but since Benjamin, or, in a more ponderous, backward-looking mode, the Heidegger of "The Origin of the Work of Art" ("the Aegina sculptures in the Munich collection, Sophocles' Antigone in the best critical edition, are, as the works they are, torn out of their own native sphere . . . World-withdrawal and world-decay can never be undone. The works are no longer the same as they once were," etc.); or even since Hegel's *Aesthetics*, in which the "death of art" means, among other things, that "art, considered in its highest vocation, is and remains for us a thing of the past. Thereby it has lost for us genuine truth and life, and has rather been transferred into our ideas, instead of maintaining its earlier necessity in reality and occupying its higher place," etc.[5] It is perhaps to leap from truism to hyperbole to speak of *operal plurality* in connection with these matters of functional variation – which are in themselves obvious, though we are not obliged to interpret them in unrelievedly apocalyptic fashion. It nevertheless seems to me impossible to define a work without including functional traits in the definition. A work is an object of immanence *plus* a certain, potentially infinite, number of functions. Every time the actual set of these functions is modified – even if the object itself "does not change," or changes in some other way – the resulting work is modified. Whether one conceives it (first mode of transcendence) as something operating through several different objects, or (second mode) as something operating through a lacunary, indirect manifestation, or (third mode) as something operating through the same object in diverse ways, depending on the context, the relation of "transcendence" between the work and its object of immanence can in every case be defined in functional terms: the work, as its name partially indicates,[6] is the *action* performed by an object of immanence.

With this, we have crossed the threshold of what will make up the subject-matter of a future volume, which perhaps authorizes me to break off here. Before closing, I should simply like to point out that this functional definition of the work of art, which here seems, by virtue of certain of its consequences, to counterpose Borges, or Collingwood, or Danto, and many others, to Goodman, nevertheless finds its counterpart *in* Goodman, so that the present chapter is also a sort of *Goodman* vs. *Goodman*. For, let us not forget, Borges and Danto are not alone in constructing arguments around pairs of physically indiscernible but functionally distinct objects, like the two *Don Quixotes* or the two series of Brillo boxes. It is, after all, *Languages of Art* which counterposes, functionally, the two indiscernable objects constituted by a scientific diagram, on the one hand, and a drawing by Hokusai on the other. Here the context determines not only the *type* of artistic function, but also the presence or absence of an artistic function. And it is again Goodman who shows us that one and the same object can function as an object of art or not, depending on the symbolic function it fulfils. It is difficult to reconcile propositions of this sort, and a number of others,[7] with the refusal, in evidence elsewhere, to distinguish between, for example, a text as a mere "syntactic" object and the work it constitutes, or does not constitute, or constitutes in some other manner, according to whether its significance changes. That contradiction perhaps rests on (or boils down to) another, between an ontology which considers it a point of honor to be as purely nominalist as possible, and an aesthetics that is basically (and commendably) pragmatist, in which "function may underlie status."[8] You will have understood which choice I believe is dictated by the facts; but I will reserve my treatment of this point until later, along with my supporting argument, if I can make one.

It is, then, less than ever a question of concluding now; at most, it is time to turn the page, or, rather, to notice that the page has begun to turn on its own. In a provisional or preliminary way, when all is said and done, this volume was devoted to the modes of existence of works, with a view to a future examination of their modes of operation. Only this aim justifies the effort spent on the present preliminary study, sometimes arid because of its conceptual abstraction, sometimes ponderously empirical, owing to a welter of examples: if works of art were not what they are – objects of an aesthetic relation – we would not, perhaps, have much cause to study their modes of existence, at least as I see it. I am, then, well aware that I have inflicted too long an approach upon such readers as have, improbably, borne with me, given that the goal is still no more than a promise, and the *raison d'être* no more than a hypothesis. But it seems to me – and I hope I have shown – that of the two modes of existence considered in the preceding pages, the second already had a great deal to do with the modes of action that will soon concern us, time allowing. If immanence, in its two regimes, does indeed belong to the order of being ("what kinds of objects are involved?"), transcendence, in its diverse modes, is more of the order of "doing" or "acting," since it hinges on the variable relation between the object of immanence and the effect it has (or fails to have) on its audience – an effect which, of course, we have yet to describe. If immanence defines, in some sort, the work at rest (or, rather, in suspension), transcendence already shows us, if only on the horizon, the work in action, and art at work.

Notes

1   The drawing may be found in Joseph Jastrow, *Fact and Fable in Psychology* (1901) (rpt. North Stratford, NH: Ayer, 1979), and in Ludwig Wittgenstein, *Philosophical Investigations*, 3d edn., trans. G. E. M. Anscombe (Oxford: Basil Blackwell, 1968), p. 194. See also Ernst Gombrich, *Art and Illusion: A Study in the Psychology of Pictorial Representations*, 5th edn. (Princeton: Princeton University Press, 1977), p. 4. The drawing is doubtless part of a broad graphic folklore that also includes Necker's cube and Roger Price's droodles – for example, the two concentric circles that are supposed to represent, by way of his sombrero, a Mexican viewed from above.
2   See Virgil Aldrich, *Philosophy of Art* (Englewood Cliffs, NJ: Prentice-Hall, 1963). Aldrich, like Wittgenstein, use the term "seeing as" to describe competing interpretations of the same line. See George Dickie, *Aesthetics: An Introduction* (Indianapolis: Bobbs-Merrill, 1971), p. 56.
3   Pierre Bourdieu, citing the Sinologist J. R. Levenson, in Roger Chartier (ed.) *Pratiques de la lecture* (Paris: Rivages, 1985), p. 236.
4   Heinrich Wölfflin, *Principles of Art History: The Problem of the Development of Style in Later Art* (1915), trans. M. D. Hottinger (New York: Dover, 1950), p. 11.
5   Martin Heidegger, "The Origin of the Work of Art." trans. Albert Hofstadter, in David Farrell Krell, *Basic Writings from* Being and Time (*1927*) to the Task of Thinking (*1964*) (New York, 1977), p. 167; G. W. F. Hegel; *Aesthetics: Lectures on Fine Art* (1832), trans. T. H. Knox (Oxford: Clarendon Press, 1975), vol. 1, p. 11. Schaeffer, *L'Art de l'âge moderne*, p. 427. is right to remind us that awareness (here critical) of the effects of the Museum and what would soon be called Elginism goes back at least to Quatremère de Quincy, *Lettres sur le projet d'enlever les monuments de l'Italie* (1796) and *Considérations morales sur la destination des ouvrages de l'art* (1815).
6   And as the adjective I have attributed to it, "operal," plainly shows: something that is *operal* is something that operates.

7   See especially the recent introduction of the notion of implementation*, in Nelson Goodman, *Of Mind and Other Matters* (Cambridge, Mass.: Harvard University Press, 1984), p. 142ff., and in "L'art en action," *Cahiers du Musée national de l'art moderne*, no. 41 (Fall 1992), pp. 7–14, where this notion, defined in 1984 as "all that goes into making a work work," is also christened (this is the more memorable term) *activation*; the notion embraces not only the conservation and recovery of works, but also the means of acting "indirectly" which are provided it by reproductions and even "verbal commentaries." This is, of course, our second mode of transcendence.

8   Goodman, *Of Mind and Other Matters*, p. 145.

V
Agency, Expression

Friedrich Schiller

(1759–1805)

Friedrich Schiller makes some of the boldest claims for the powers of art of any aesthetic theorist. Like Kant, who provides his theoretical starting point, Schiller assigns art a mediating and unifying role. Schiller, however, extends this role beyond what he sees as the formalism of Kantian aesthetics and claims that aesthetics provide the necessary means for unifying the individual psyche and the political state. While Schiller's sweeping claims for the centrality of aesthetics have always been the target of skeptical criticism, his diagnosis of the ills of modernity have been more widely accepted, even by his critics. Thus thinkers as divergent as Matthew Arnold and Karl Marx have attacked the alienation and fragmentation of modern culture in terms similar to those used by Schiller, noting, in particular, the ways in which modern culture tends to pit the individual against the social whole.

Schiller gives his most famous account of the social function of art in a series of letters entitled *On the Aesthetic Education of Man* (or *Aesthetic Education*). These letters were written during the bloody Reign of Terror which followed the French Revolution, and some critics have interpreted them as Schiller's strategic withdrawal from the liberal political commitments of his youth. According to this reading, the letters translate political issues into a language of aesthetic abstraction, abandoning the dangers and promise of real politics for a safe but ineffectual form of political allegory. It is true that Schiller's argument for the political and social importance of the aesthetic proceeds at a high level of abstraction. Yet, as was already mentioned, his letters address social issues of widely recognized importance. Schiller observes that modern societies are organized by divisions of labor and class and that these divisions force people to become specialists and prevent them from developing the full range of their capacities. Furthermore, this division of labor encourages individuals to concern themselves only with their own private welfare and to view the demands of government or community as an infringement on their freedom. In response to this dilemma, Schiller asks two related questions: How can individual freedom be more than the unrestrained expression of selfish appetites, and how can community be more than the tyrannical imposition of alienating law, the kind of law that seems to be imposed from the outside of the individual's life-world?

In *Aesthetic Education* Schiller describes this predicament as the conflict of two competing drives, the formal drive associated with law and reason, and the sensuous drive associated with the personal appetites of individuals. The only way to resolve the conflict between these drives, Schiller argues, is by means of a third drive, the play drive. In play, he says, humans can achieve real freedom, a freedom that reconciles the claims of appetite and law, individual and community, rather than asserting the priority of one over the other. Play manages to bring abstract form to sensuous life, Schiller claims, and the result is beauty, a harmony that he describes as "living form." Thus Schiller feels that the play that art makes possible will provide a means to both psychological and social unity.

It is easy to understand Schiller's claim that both the creation and reception of art provide models of human freedom, but his claims that artistic play is the source of all freedom and that free societies must therefore depend upon the development of an aesthetic sensibility are more difficult to understand and evaluate. Perhaps the gist of Schiller's theory is contained in the notion that in the absence of certain kinds of compulsion, individuals can attend to their lives with the same kind of attention that an artist brings to a work of art and that this kind of individual freedom provides the surest foundation for a free but cohesive society.

Suggested reading

R. D. Miller, *A Study of Schiller's Letters*, "On the Aesthetic Education of Man," Harrogate: Dutchy, 1986.

Sixteenth Letter

1   We have seen how beauty results from the reciprocal action of two opposed drives and from the uniting of two opposed principles. The highest ideal of beauty is, therefore, to be sought in the most perfect possible union and equilibrium of reality and form. This equilibrium, however, remains no more than an idea, which can never be fully realized in actuality. For in actuality we shall always be left with a preponderance of the one element over the other, and the utmost that experience can achieve will consist of an oscillation between the two principles, in which now reality, now form, will predominate. Beauty as

Reprinted from: Friedrich Schiller, *On the Aesthetic Education of Man, in a series of letters*, edited and translated by Elizabeth M. Wilkinson and L. A. Willoughby, Oxford: Clarendon Press, pp. 111–15.

Idea, therefore, can never be other than one and indivisible, since there can never be more than one point of equilibrium; whereas beauty in experience will be eternally twofold, because oscillation can disturb the equilibrium in twofold fashion, inclining it now to the one side, now to the other.

2   I observed in one of the preceding Letters – and it follows with strict necessity from the foregoing argument – that we must expect from beauty at once a releasing and a tensing effect: a releasing effect in order to keep both the sense-drive and the form-drive within proper bounds; a tensing effect, in order to keep both at full strength. Ideally speaking, however, these two effects must be reducible to a single effect. Beauty is to release by tensing both natures uniformly, and to tense by releasing both natures uniformly. This already follows from the concept of a reciprocal action, by virtue of which both factors necessarily condition each other and are at the same time conditioned by each other, and the purest product of which is beauty. But experience offers us no single example of such perfect reciprocal action; for here it will always happen that, to a greater or lesser degree, a preponderance entails a deficiency, and a deficiency a preponderance. What, then, in the case of ideal beauty is but a distinction which is made in the mind, is in the case of actual beauty a difference which exists in fact. Ideal Beauty, though one and indivisible, exhibits under different aspects a melting as well as an energizing attribute; but in experience there actually is a melting and an energizing type of beauty. So it is, and so it always will be, in all those cases where the Absolute is set within the limitations of time, and the ideas of Reason have to be realized in and through human action. Thus man, when he reflects, can conceive of Virtue, Truth, Happiness; but man, when he acts, can only practise virtues, comprehend truths, and enjoy happy hours. To refer these experiences back to those abstractions – to replace morals by Morality, happy events by Happiness, the facts of knowledge by Knowledge itself – that is the business of physical and moral education. To make Beauty out of a multiplicity of beautiful objects is the task of aesthetic education.

3   Energizing beauty can no more preserve man from a certain residue of savagery and hardness than melting beauty can protect him from a certain degree of effeminacy and enervation. For since the effect of the former is to brace his nature, both physical and moral, and to increase its elasticity and power of prompt reaction, it can happen all too easily that the increased resistance of temperament and character will bring about a decrease in receptivity to impressions; that our gentler humanity, too, will suffer the kind of repression which ought only to be directed at our brute nature, and our brute nature profit

from an increase of strength which should only be available to our free Person. That is why in periods of vigour and exuberance we find true grandeur of conception coupled with the gigantic and the extravagant, sublimity of thought with the most frightening explosions of passion; that is why in epochs of discipline and form we find nature as often suppressed as mastered, as often outraged as transcended. And because the effect of melting beauty is to relax our nature, physical and moral, it happens no less easily that energy of feeling is stifled along with violence of appetite, and that character too shares the loss of power which should only overtake passion. That is why in so-called refined epochs, we see gentleness not infrequently degenerating into softness, plainness into platitude, correctness into emptiness, liberality into arbitrariness, lightness of touch into frivolity, calmness into apathy, and the most despicable caricatures in closest proximity to the most splendid specimens of humanity. The man who lives under the constraint of either matter or forms is, therefore, in need of melting beauty; for he is moved by greatness and power long before he begins to be susceptible to harmony and grace. The man who lives under the indulgent sway of taste is in need of energizing beauty; for he is only too ready, once he has reached a state of sophisticated refinement, to trifle away the strength he brought with him from the state of savagery.

4   And now, I think, we have explained and resolved the discrepancy commonly met with in the judgements people make about the influence of beauty, and in the value they attach to aesthetic culture. The discrepancy is explained once we remember that, in experience, there are two types of beauty, and that both parties to the argument tend to make assertions about the whole genus which each of them is only in a position to prove about one particular species of it. And the discrepancy is resolved once we distinguish a twofold need in man to which that twofold beauty corresponds. Both parties will probably turn out to be right if they can only first agree among themselves which kind of beauty and which type of humanity each has in mind.

5   In the rest of my inquiry I shall, therefore, pursue the path which nature herself takes with man in matters aesthetic, and setting out from the two species of beauty move upwards to the generic concept of it. I shall examine the effects of melting beauty on those who are tensed, and the effects of energizing beauty on those who are relaxed, in order finally to dissolve both these contrary modes of beauty in the unity of Ideal Beauty, even as those two opposing types of human being are merged in the unity of Ideal Man.

Georg Wilhelm Friedrich Hegel

(1770–1831)

G. W. F. Hegel was the pre-eminent German philosopher of the early nineteenth century. He is known as the seminal force in phenomenological theories of mind. Hegel's aesthetic theory is an integral part of his phenomenology of mind. This theory holds that expression in art is coherent with those activities of mind which raise it to ultimate self-consciousness. Mind develops through the labors of history toward what Hegel calls the Idea, a modality of "knowing" which is *for itself* and goes beyond the divisions of mind and its objects. Art can further the mind in its articulation of the Idea. But Hegel contends that art is not the highest manifestation of the Idea. Art must ultimately give way to religion and philosophy in the historical progress of subjective consciousness.

Hegel's aesthetic theory appears as a lengthy treatise called *Lectures on Fine Art*, published posthumously and mainly from transcripts prepared by members of the audience. The point of departure for Hegel's "Introduction", excerpted below, is the common assumption that art is antithetical to thought. Hegel wishes to correct the misconception – given currency under the auspices of early nineteenth-century standards of taste, where a Platonic idea of beauty reigned supreme – that art is a realm in which we indulge our freedom from the fetters of abstract rule and regularity. On the contrary, for Hegel thought in art "presents" itself to sense, feeling, perception, and imagination. In other words, in art neither the abstraction of pure thought nor the concretions of sensuous being hold sway.

For this reason, Hegel rejects the idea that art is mimesis. Mere imitation is a parody of life, which he likens to a worm trying to crawl after an elephant. Instead, the work of art is charged with the task of bringing into contact with our sense and feeling all that has a place in the mind of man. Art has no purpose beyond what it presents. And because it "furnishes the empty form for every possible kind of significance and content," art implicates mind in material contradictions that impel a dialectical stance towards experience. Thus we might say that expression in art arises from a rational impulse to transform the outer world into a richer expression of subjective mind. It constitutes a mode of development. It furthermore finds its law within the processes of productive activity – the sensuous shaping of natural matter – in order to give more articulate form to human spirit. This emphasis on productive activity takes a cue from Vico and has consequence in the subsequent expressivist aesthetic theories of Croce, Dewey, and even Gadamer.

Since, from Hegel's perspective, the productive activity of art has no end beyond development, it finds its motive in the ever more fully determined adequation of the Idea to plastic form. Accordingly Hegel is prompted to elaborate an evolutionary typology of art. There are three basic modalities of art upon which the history of artistic production from classical times to Hegel's time can be mapped in terms of the adequation of idea to form.

Symbolic art, identified with Greek culture, exhibits the disproportion in the relationship between the Idea and its formal embodiment. Hegel compares this with our attempt to represent the concept of strength with the figure of the lion. Because, as in literary allegory, the relation between the Idea and its formal embodiment in symbolic art is arbitrary, Hegel considers it to be woefully indeterminate. In other words, there is more to strength than can be expressed in the image of the lion. Classical art corrects this defect by more fully determining the plasticity of form, bringing it into better accord with the Idea. Hegel's example here is the sculptor's realization of the human form in stone. Purified of any external contingencies, as exemplified in Greco-Roman sculpture, classical art presents the adequacy of form to spirit with a high degree of self-containment. Romantic art, the highest form of art, frees the self-containment of the Idea from all formal sense of limitation. Hegel compares the way in which the mind surpasses formal limitation in romantic art to the process of digestion.

Hegel makes architecture the prime example of symbolic art, and sculpture that of classical art. Romantic art is exemplified in painting, music, and poetry. Hegel ranks these in an ascending order, indicating by that hierarchy the Idea's greater and greater freedom from external contingency. In this way, artistic evolution charts a path toward Absolute Mind.

Suggested reading

Stephen Bungay, *Beauty and Truth: A Study of Hegel's Aesthetics*, New York: Oxford University Press, 1984.

Division of the Subject

[cvii] (γ) The romantic form of art destroys the completed union of the Idea and its reality, and recurs, though in a higher phase, to that difference and

Reprinted from: G. W. F. Hegel, *Introductory Lectures on Aesthetics*, translated by Bernard Bosanquet, edited by Michael Inwood, Harmondsworth: Penguin Books, 1993, pp. 85–8, 95–6.

antagonism of two aspects which was left unvanquished by symbolic art. The classical type attained the highest excellence, of which the sensuous embodiment of art is capable; and if it is in any way defective, the defect is in art as a whole, i.e. in the limitation of its sphere. This limitation consists in the fact that art as such takes for its object Mind – the conception of which is *infinite* concrete universality – in the shape *sensuous* concreteness, and in the classical phase sets up the perfect amalgamation of spiritual and sensuous existence as a Conformity of the two. Now, as a matter of fact, in such an amalgamation Mind cannot be represented according to its true notion. For mind is the infinite subjectivity of the Idea, which, as absolute inwardness, is not capable of finding free expansion in its true nature on condition of remaining transposed into a bodily medium as the existence appropriate to it.

As *an escape from such a condition* the romantic form of art in its turn dissolves the inseparable unity of the classical phase, because it has won a significance which goes beyond the classical form of art and its mode of expression. This significance – if we may recall familiar ideas – coincides with what Christianity declares to be true of God as Spirit, in contradistinction to the Greek faith in gods which forms the essential and appropriate content for classical art. In Greek art the concrete import is potentially, but not explicitly, the unity of the human and divine nature; a unity which, just because it is purely *immediate* and *not explicit*, is capable of adequate manifestation in an immediate and sensuous mode. The Greek god is the object of naïve intuition and sensuous imagination. His shape is, therefore, the bodily shape of man. The circle of his power and of his being is individual and individually limited. In relation with the subject, he is, therefore, an essence and a power with which the subject's inner being is merely in latent unity, not itself possessing this unity as inward subjective knowledge. Now the higher stage is the *knowledge* of this *latent* unity, which as latent is the import of the classical form of art, and capable of perfect representation in bodily shape. The elevation of the latent or potential into self-conscious knowledge produces an enormous difference. It is the infinite difference which, e.g., separates man as such from the animals. Man is animal, but even in his animal functions he is not confined within the latent and potential as the animal is, but becomes conscious of them, learns to know them, and raises them – as, for instance, the process of digestion – into self-conscious science. By this means Man breaks the boundary of merely potential and immediate consciousness, so that just for the reason that he knows himself to be animal, he ceases to be animal, and, as *mind*, attains to self-knowledge.

If in the above fashion the unity of the human and divine nature, which in the former phase was potential, is raised from an *immediate* to a *conscious* unity, it follows that the true medium for the reality of this content is no longer the sensuous immediate existence of the spiritual, the human bodily shape, but *self-conscious inward intelligence*. Now, Christianity brings God before our intelligence *as spirit*, or mind – not as particularized individual spirit, but as absolute, in *spirit* and in truth. And for this reason Christianity retires from the sensuousness of imagination into intellectual inwardness, and makes this, not bodily shape, the medium and actual existence of its significance. So, too, the unity of the human and divine nature is a conscious unity, only to be realized by *spiritual* knowledge and in *spirit*. Thus the new content, won by this unity, is not inseparable from sensuous representation, as if that were adequate to it, but is freed from this immediate existence, which has to be posited as negative, absorbed, and reflected into the spiritual unity. In this way romantic art must be considered as art transcending itself, while remaining within the artistic sphere and in artistic form.

Therefore, in short, we may abide by the statement that in this third stage the object (of art) is *free*, concrete intellectual being, which has the function of revealing itself as spiritual existence for the inward world of spirit. In conformity with such an object-matter, art cannot work for sensuous perception. It must address itself to the inward mind, which coalesces with its object simply and as though this were itself, to the subjective inwardness, to the heart, the feeling, which, being spiritual, aspires to freedom within itself, and seeks and finds its reconciliation only in the spirit within. It is this *inner* world that forms the content of the romantic, and must therefore find its representation as such inward feeling, and in the show or presentation of such feeling. The world of inwardness celebrates its triumph over the outer world, and actually in the sphere of the outer and in its medium manifests this its victory, owing to which the sensuous appearance sinks into worthlessness.

But, on the other hand, this type of Art, like every other, needs an external vehicle of expression. Now the spiritual has withdrawn into itself out of the external and its immediate oneness therewith. For this reason, the sensuous externality of concrete form is accepted and represented, as in symbolic art, as something transient and fugitive. And the same measure is dealt to the subjective finite mind and will, even including the peculiarity or caprice of the individual, of character, action, etc., or of incident and plot. The aspect of external existence is committed to contingency, and left at the mercy of freaks of imagination, whose caprice is no more likely to mirror what is given *as* it is given, than to throw the shapes of the outer world into chance medley, or distort them into grotesqueness. For this external element no longer has its notion and significance, as in classical art, in its own sphere, and in its own medium. It has come to find them in the feelings, the display of which is *in themselves* instead of being in the external and *its* form of reality, and which have the power to preserve or to regain their state of reconciliation with themselves, in every accident, in every unessential circumstance that takes independent shape, in all misfortunes and grief, and even in crime.

Owing to this, the characteristics of symbolic art, in difference, discrepancy, and severance of Idea and plastic shape, are here reproduced, but with an essential difference. In the sphere of the romantic, the Idea, whose defectiveness in the case of the symbol produced the defect of external shape, has to reveal itself in the medium of spirit and feelings as perfected in itself. And it is because of this higher perfection that it withdraws itself from any adequate union with the external element, inasmuch as it can seek and achieve its true reality and revelation nowhere but in itself.

This we may take as in the abstract the character of the symbolic, classical, and romantic forms of art, which represent the three relations of the Idea to its embodiment in the sphere of art. They consist in the aspiration after, and the attainment and transcendence of, the Ideal as the true Idea of beauty. . . .

[CXIV] (iii) As regards the *third* and most spiritual mode of representation of the romantic art-type, we must look for it in *poetry*. Its characteristic peculiarity lies in the power with which it subjects to the mind and to its ideas the sensuous element from which music and painting in their degree began to liberate art. For sound, the only external matter which poetry retains, is in it no longer the feeling of the sonorous itself, but is a *sign*, which by itself is void of import. And it is a sign of the idea which has become concrete in itself, and not merely of indefinite feeling and of its nuances and grades. This is how sound develops into the *Word*, as voice articulate in itself, whose import it is to indicate ideas and notions. The merely negative point up to which music had developed now makes its appearance as the completely concrete point, the point which is mind, the self-conscious individual, which, producing out of itself the infinite space of its ideas, unites it with the temporal character of sound. Yet this sensuous element, which in music was still immediately one with inward feeling, is in poetry separated from the content of consciousness. In poetry the mind determines this content for its own sake, and apart from all else, into the shape of ideas, and though it employs sound to express them, yet treats it solely as a symbol without value or import. Thus considered, sound may just as well be reduced to a mere letter, for the audible, like the visible, is thus depressed into a mere indication of mind. For this reason the proper medium of poetical representation is the poetical imagination and intellectual portrayal itself. And as this element is common to all types of art, it follows that poetry runs through them all and develops itself independently in each. Poetry is the universal art of the mind which has become free in its own nature, and which is not tied to find its realization in external sensuous matter, but expatiates exclusively in the inner space and inner time of the ideas and feelings. Yet just in this its highest phase art ends by transcending itself, inasmuch as it abandons the medium of a harmonious embodiment of mind in sensuous form, and passes from the poetry of imagination into the prose of thought.

Friedrich Schlegel

(1772–1829)

Friedrich Schlegel, like his brother August Wilhelm Schlegel, is remembered as one of the founders of the German Romantic Movement. Originally Friedrich's work was overshadowed by his brother's, but today Friedrich is generally considered to have been the most important writer of the two. Together the brothers founded and edited the journal *Athenaeum*, in which most of Friedrich Schlegel's important contributions to romantic literary theory appeared. His ideas were strongly influenced by German idealist philosophy deriving from the work of Immanuel Kant and, especially, by the philosophy of Johann Fichte and Friedrich Hegel. From the work of Fichte and Hegel, Schlegel adopted the notion that the world as we experience it is not a collection of inert objects but is, rather, the product of a human consciousness, which creates the world even as it perceives it. Furthermore, according to these philosophers, in this act of perceiving and creating the world, human consciousness creates and discovers its own identity. In the process of investigating the world, humanity discovers itself. As we shall see, this is a metaphysics that is tailor-made for a romantic poet. In 1808, Schlegel converted to Catholicism and would later revise his earlier writings to make them agree with his new-found faith.

At the heart of Schlegel's aesthetic is the notion that all reality is the product of a dynamic creative process. Like the Neoplatonic philosopher Plotinus, he believed that the cosmos itself is the product of creative energy that somehow manages to express and objectify itself in material form. As mentioned above, he thought that human consciousness is a reflection of this same creative energy and that poetry is an intensified form of the drama found in all acts of perception. "Every good man progressively becomes God," Schlegel announces in one of the aphorisms included below. This is true, he believes, because all human creative activity participates in the divine. Yet creations of human beings always must fall short of human aspirations, Schlegel claims, since human creations are limited finite objects and human aspirations are essentially infinite and know no bounds. The result, Schlegel argues, is irony; there is an ironic discrepancy between the ideal beauty that poets strive to represent and the greater or lesser amounts of real beauty that they manage to create.

Irony, Schlegel observes, is a result of "the insoluble conflict of the absolute and the relative, of the impossibility and necessity of total communication" (in Behler and Struc: 131). The artist who attempts to make her- or himself totally understood is pathetic, but the artist whose work reflects an awareness of art's inevitable imperfection can use irony to her or his advantage. Schlegel's own writing provides many illustrations of this intentional irony. His aphorisms, for instance, give the impression of fragmentary and incomplete glimpses of a deeper truth, a truth that resists presentation in the more orderly and complete essay form that is characteristic of neoclassical aesthetics. Schlegel rejects attempts to create or classify literature according to the laws of genre or literary type. Since it is the duty of literature to capture the spirit in the process of becoming, he feels that fixed forms will inevitably be inadequate.

Like Schiller, Schlegel hoped that poetry could play a role in transforming society. In his "Talk on Mythology" which is included in *Dialogue on Poetry* (1800), he predicts that modern poets will be able to create a new modern mythology that will play the same role in modern society that classical mythology played in classical antiquity. That is, Schlegel hopes that this modern mythology will provide a unifying narrative, which will give individuals a common cultural reference point. Yet, unlike classical myth, the new myth will be recognized as poetic creation rather than as gospel truth. In embracing an artificial myth, Schlegel speculates, humanity will be able to recognize its own powers of self-creation. Later in the century, Matthew Arnold will suggest a similar role for poetry as a substitute for religious dogma.

Reference and suggested reading

Friedrich Schlegel, *Dialogue on Poetry and Literary Aphorisms*, translated and introduced by Ernst Behler and Roman Struc, University Park, Pa. and London: Pennsylvania State University Press, 1968.

From *Dialogue on Poetry*

Poetry befriends and binds with unseverable ties the hearts of all those who love it. Even though in their own lives they may pursue the most diverse ends, may feel contempt for what the other holds most sacred, may fail to appreciate or to communicate with one another, and remain in all other realms strangers forever; in poetry through a higher magic power, they are united and

Reprinted from: Friedrich Schlegel, *Dialogue on Poetry and Literary Aphorisms*, translated by Ernst Behler and Roman Struc, University Park, Pa.: Pennsylvania State University Press, 1968, pp. 53–5, 140–1, 146.

at peace. Each Muse seeks and finds another, and all streams of poetry flow together into the one vast sea.

There is only one reason, and for everyone it remains the same; but just as every man has his own nature and his own love, so does he bear within him his own poetry which must and should remain his own as surely as he is himself, as surely as there is anything original in him. And he must not allow himself to be robbed of his own being, his innermost strength by a criticism that wishes to purge and purify him into a stereotype without spirit and without sense. Fools attempt that who do not know what they are about. But the sublime discipline of genuine criticism should teach the lover of poetry how he ought to form his inner self. Above all it should teach him to grasp every other independent form of poetry in its classical power and abundance, so that the flower and kernel of other minds may become a sustenance and seed for his own imagination.

Never will the mind that knows the orgies of the true Muse journey on this road to the very end, nor will he presume to have reached it; for never will he be able to quench a longing which is eternally regenerated out of the abundance of gratifications. The world of poetry is as infinite and inexhaustible as the riches of animating nature with her plants, animals, and formations of every type, shape, and color. Nor are the artificial or natural products which bear the form and name of poems easily included under the most inclusive term. And what are they, compared with the unformed and unconscious poetry which stirs in the plant and shines in the light, smiles in a child, gleams in the flower of youth, and glows in the loving bosom of women? This, however, is the primeval poetry without which there would be no poetry of words. Indeed, there is and never has been for us humans any other object or source of activity and joy but that one poem of the godhead the earth, of which we, too, are part and flower. We are able to perceive the music of the universe and to understand the beauty of the poem because a part of the poet, a spark of his creative spirit, lives in us and never ceases to glow with secret force deep under the ashes of our self-induced unreason.

It is not necessary for anyone to sustain and propagate poetry through clever speeches and precepts, or, especially, to try to produce it, invent it, establish it, and impose upon it restrictive laws as the theory of poetics would like to. Just as the core of the earth adorned itself with formations and growths, just as life sprang forth of itself from the deep and everything was filled with beings merrily multiplying; even so, poetry bursts forth spontaneously from the invisible primordial power of mankind when the warming ray of the divine sun shines on it and fertilizes it. Only through form and color can man recreate his own creation, and thus one cannot really speak of poetry except in the language of poetry.

Everyone's view of poetry is true and good as far as that view itself is poetry. But since one's poetry is limited, just because it is one's own, so one's view of poetry must of necessity be limited. The mind cannot bear this; no doubt because, without knowing it, it nevertheless does know that no man is merely man, but that at the same time he can and should be genuinely and truly all mankind. Therefore, man, in reaching out time and again beyond himself to seek and find the complement of his innermost being in the depths of another, is certain to return ever to himself. The play of communicating and approaching is the business and the force of life; absolute perfection exists only in death.

Therefore, the poet cannot be satisfied with leaving behind in lasting works the expression of his unique poetry as it was native to him and which he acquired by education. He must strive continually to expand his poetry and his view of poetry, and to approximate the loftiest possibility of it on earth by endeavoring in the most specific way to integrate his part with the entire body of poetry: deadening generalizations result in just the opposite.

He can do this when he has found the center point through communication with those who have found theirs from a different side, in a different way. Love needs a responding love. Indeed, for the true poet communication, even with those who only play on the colorful surface, can be beneficial and instructive. He is a sociable being.

For there has always been a great attraction in speaking about poetry with poets and the poetically-minded. Many such conversations I have never forgotten; in the case of others I do not know exactly what belongs to my imagination and what to my memory; much in them is true, other things are invented. Such, too, is the present dialogue. It is intended to set against one another quite divergent opinions, each of them capable of shedding new light upon the infinite spirit of poetry from an individual standpoint, each of them striving to penetrate from a different angle into the real heart of the matter. It was my interest in this many-sidedness that made me resolve to communicate publicly things that I had observed in a circle of friends and had considered at first only in relation to them – to communicate these things to all those who feel a love in their own hearts and who, by virtue of the fullness of life within them, are disposed to be initiated into the sacred mysteries of nature and poetry.

Selected Aphorisms (1798)

116   Romantic poetry is a progressive universal poetry. Its mission is not merely to reunite all separate genres of poetry and to put poetry in touch with

philosophy and rhetorics. It will, and should, now mingle and now amalgamate poetry and prose, genius and criticism, the poetry of art and the poetry of nature, render poetry living and social, and life and society poetic, poetize wit, fill and saturate the forms of art with solid cultural material of every kind, and inspire them with vibrations of humor. It embraces everything poetic, from the greatest system of art which, in turn, includes many systems, down to the sigh, the kiss, which the musing child breathes forth in artless song. It can lose itself in what it represents to such a degree that one might think its one and only goal were the characterization of poetic individuals of every type; and yet no form has thus far arisen appropriate to expressing the author's mind so perfectly, so that artists who just wanted to write a novel have by coincidence described themselves. Romantic poetry alone can, like the epic, become a mirror of the entire surrounding world, a picture of its age. And yet, it too can soar, free from all real and ideal interests, on the wings of poetic reflection, midway between the work and the artist. It can even exponentiate this reflection and multiply it as in an endless series of mirrors. It is capable of the highest and the most universal education; not only by creating from without, but also from without, since it organizes in similar fashion all parts of what is destined to become a whole; thus, a view is opened to an endlessly developing classicism. Among the arts Romantic poetry is what wit is to philosophy, and what society, association, friendship, and love are in life. Other types of poetry are completed and can now be entirely analyzed. The Romantic type of poetry is still becoming; indeed, its peculiar essence is that it is always becoming and that it can never be completed. It cannot be exhausted by any theory, and only a divinatory criticism might dare to characterize its ideal. It alone is infinite, as it alone is free; and as its first law it recognizes that the arbitrariness of the poet endures no law above him. The Romantic genre of poetry is the only one which is more than a genre, and which is, as it were, poetry itself: for in a certain sense all poetry is or should be Romantic.

262   Every good man progressively becomes God. To become God, to be man, and to educate oneself, are expressions that are synonymous.

Ralph Waldo Emerson

(1803–1882)

Ralph Waldo Emerson was a poet, essayist, and philosopher. Working under the influence of the German Idealist thinking of Samuel Taylor Coleridge and Johan Wolfgang Von Goethe, Ralph Waldo Emerson inflected the romantic imagination with an American ethos. His "transcendentalism" inaugurated a distinctly American penchant for resisting the impulse toward system-building, for rejecting fixed sets of organizing principles or controlling conceits of intellectual will in philosophical thinking. Literary theorists in the pragmatist vein as diverse as Kenneth Burke, Harold Bloom, Stanley Cavell, Richard Rorty, and Cornel West acknowledge Emerson's thought as a catalyst of their own skepticism about ideas that pre-empt lived experience with prejudicial knowledge of what ought to be.

As an aesthetic theorist Emerson follows an expressivist path. His essay "The Poet" (1842–3) sets a pattern for speculative thought about the place of the artist in American culture. The poet serves a social and spiritual function as one who can give voice to human nature beyond the powers of the ordinary man. In this presumption Emerson is acknowledging that there is a common core of human experience, which only the poet possesses the power to articulate, just as only prophets have been privileged to disseminate the truth of a "divine energy." The medium of this dissemination is the word, but this does not presuppose a passive or contemplative relation between the poetic mind and the world.

"Words are also actions, and actions are a kind of words," Emerson avers. This bold credo carries the implication that poetry is an activity in the world. Unfortunately Emerson remains evasive about how the word translates the world into a human deed. The impressionistically conceived image of the poet as a "winged man, who will carry me into the heaven, whirls me into mists, then leaps and frisks about" frustrates our hope that Emerson could clarify the means by which such feats are accomplished. Instead of explaining the means of poetic agency he takes refuge in the symbolism of beauty.

The beauty of natural things expressed in the language of poetry makes them more beautiful because it is the soul of mankind upon which the apprehension of their beauty depends. While every man possesses access to the world through his fluency with symbols – the outer forms of life – only the poet, "by an ulterior intellectual perception," knows that the underlying reality is a human thought. Because habit causes the ordinary man to confuse the symbol with the thought and lose touch with the intellectual process that gives experience its vitality, he depends on the interventions of the poet. In other words, the poet reanimates the world with new meanings. Emerson declares that every word was originally a poem, but became lost to the deadening effects of common usage. In an attitude evocative of Shelley's contemporaneous "A Defense of Poetry" (published 1840), Emerson seems to conceive of the poet's charge as intuiting new relations between the objects of the natural world and the human faculty of observation. In that way the poet posits or presupposes an underlying unity of experience.

So while the pragmatist strain in Emerson's thinking emphasizes the subordination of given expressive forms of language to the "life" of the world in which they can be made use of, his ultimate stance is universalist and holistic. Expression is the touchstone of a divine spiritual essence which the poet can attune us to. Thus the effort towards personal self-realization dovetails with knowledge of the transcendental truths of the creator.

Suggested reading

Stanley Cavell, *Conditions Handsome and Unhandsome: The Constitution of Emersonian Perfectionism*, Chicago: University of Chicago Press, 1990.

The Poet

The Universe is the externization of the soul. Wherever the life is, that bursts into appearance around it. Our science is sensual, and therefore superficial. The earth, and the heavenly bodies, physics, and chemistry, we sensually treat, as if they were self-existent; but these are the retinue of that Being we have. "The mighty heaven," said Proclus, "exhibits, in its transfigurations, clear images of the splendor of intellectual perceptions; being moved in conjunction with the unapparent periods of intellectual natures." Therefore, science always goes abreast with the just elevation of the man, keeping step with religion and metaphysics; or, the state of science is an index of our self-knowledge. Since every thing in nature answers to a moral power, if any phenomenon remains brute and dark, it is that the corresponding faculty in the observer is not yet active.

Reprinted from: *Essays by Ralph Waldo Emerson*, New York: Thomas Y. Crowell, 1926, pp. 270–2, 282–6, 288–90.

No wonder, then, if these waters be so deep, that we hover over them with a religious regard. The beauty of the fable proves the importance of the sense; to the poet, and to all others; or if you please, every man is so far a poet as to be susceptible of these enchantments of nature: for all men have the thoughts whereof the universe is the celebration. I find that the fascination resides in the symbol. Who loves nature? Who does not? Is it only poets, and men of leisure and cultivation, who live with her? No; but also hunters, farmers, grooms, and butchers, though they express their affection in their choice of life, and not in their choice of words. The writer wonders what the coachman or the hunter values in riding, in horses, and dogs. It is not superficial qualities. When you talk with him, he holds these at as slight a rate as you. His worship is sympathetic; he has no definitions, but he is commanded in nature, by the living power which he feels to be there present. No imitation, or playing of these things, would content him; he loves the earnest of the northwind, of rain, of stone, and wood, and iron. A beauty not explicable, is dearer than a beauty which we can see to the end of. It is nature the symbol, nature certifying the supernatural, body overflowed by life, which he worships, with coarse, but sincere rites.

The inwardness and mystery of this attachment, drives men of every class to the use of emblems. The schools of poets, and philosophers, are not more intoxicated with their symbols, than the populace with theirs. In our political parties, compute the power of badges and emblems. See the great ball which they roll from Baltimore to Bunker Hill! In the political processions, Lowell goes in a loom, and Lynn in a shoe, and Salem in a ship. Witness the cider-barrel, the log cabin, the hickory-stick, the palmetto, and all the cognizances of party. See the power of national emblems. Some stars, lilies, leopards, a crescent, a lion, an eagle, or other figure, which came into credit God knows how, on an old rag of bunting, blowing in the wind, on a fort, at the ends of the earth, shall make the blood tingle under the rudest, or the most conventional exterior. The people fancy they hate poetry, and they are all poets and mystics!

. . . Poets are thus liberating gods. Men have really got a new sense, and found within their world, another world or nest of worlds; for the metamorphosis once seen, we divine that it does not stop. I will not now consider how much this makes the charm of algebra and the mathematics, which also have their tropes, but it is felt in every definition; as, when Aristotle defines *space* to be an immovable vessel, in which things are contained; – or, when Plato defines a *line* to be a flowing point; or, *figure* to be a bound of solid; and many the like. What a joyful sense of freedom we have, when Vitruvius announces the old opinion of artists, that no architect can build any house well, who does not know something of anatomy. When Socrates, in Charmides, tells us that the soul is cured of its maladies by certain incantations, and that these incantations are beautiful reasons, from which temperance is generated in souls; when Plato calls the world an animal; and Timæus affirms that the plants also are animals; or affirms a man to be a heavenly tree, growing with his root, which is his head, upward; and, as George Chapman, following him, writes,

> So in our tree of man, whose nervie root
> Springs in his top;

when Orpheus speaks of hoariness as "that white flower which marks extreme old age"; when Proclus calls the universe the statue of the intellect; when Chaucer, in his praise of "Gentilesse," compares good blood in mean condition to fire, which, though carried to the darkest house betwixt this and the mount of Caucasus, will yet hold its natural office, and burn as bright as if twenty thousand men did it behold; when John saw, in the apocalypse, the ruin of the world through evil, and the stars fall from heaven, as the figtree casteth her untimely fruit; when Æsop reports the whole catalogue of common daily relations through the masquerade of birds and beasts; – we take the cheerful hint of the immortality of our essence, and its versatile habit and escapes, as when the gypsies say, "it is vain to hang them, they cannot die."

The poets are thus liberating gods. The ancient British bards had for the title of their order, "Those who are free throughout the world." They are free, and they make free. An imaginative book renders us much more service at first, by stimulating us through its tropes, than afterward, when we arrive at the precise sense of the author. I think nothing is of any value in books, excepting the transcendental and extraordinary. If a man is inflamed and carried away by his thought, to that degree that he forgets the authors and the public, and heeds only this one dream, which holds him like an insanity, let me read his paper, and you may have all the arguments and histories and criticism. All the value which attaches to Pythagoras, Paracelsus, Cornelius Agrippa, Cardan, Kepler, Swedenborg, Schelling, Oken, or any other who introduces questionable facts into his cosmogony, as angels, devils, magic, astrology, palmistry, mesmerism, and so on, is the certificate we have of departure from routine, and that here is a new witness. That also is the best success in conversation, the magic of liberty, which puts the world like a ball, in our hands. How cheap even the liberty then seems; how mean to study, when an emotion communicates to the intellect the power to sap and upheave nature: how great the perspective! nations, times, systems, enter and disappear like threads in tapestry of large figure and many colors; dream delivers us to dream, and, while the drunkenness lasts, we will sell our bed, our philosophy, our religion, in our opulence.

There is good reason why we should prize this liberation. The fate of the poor shepherd, who, blinded and lost in the snow-storm, perishes in a drift within a few feet of his cottage door, is an emblem of the state of man. On the brink of the waters of life and truth, we are miserably dying. The inaccessibleness of every thought but that we are in, is wonderful. What if you come near to it, – you are as remote, when you are nearest, as when you are farthest. Every thought is also a prison; every heaven is also a prison. Therefore we love the poet, the inventor, who in any form, whether in an ode, or in an action, or in looks and behavior, has yielded us a new thought. He unlocks our chains, and admits us to a new scene.

This emancipation is dear to all men, and the power to impart it, as it must come from greater depth and scope of thought, is a measure of intellect. Therefore all books of the imagination endure, all which ascend to that truth, that the writer sees nature beneath him, and uses it as his exponent. Every verse or sentence, possessing this virtue, will take care of its own immortality. The religions of the world are the ejaculations of a few imaginative men.

But the quality of the imagination is to flow, and not to freeze. The poet did not stop at the color, or the form, but read their meaning; neither may he rest in this meaning; but he makes the same objects exponents of his new thought. Here is the difference betwixt the poet and the mystic, that the last nails a symbol to one sense, which was a true sense for a moment, but soon becomes old and false. For all symbols are fluxional; all language is vehicular and transitive, and is good, as ferries and horses are, for conveyance, not as farms and houses are, for homestead. Mysticism consists in the mistake of an accidental and individual symbol for an universal one. The morning-redness happens to be the favorite meteor to the eyes of Jacob Behman, and comes to stand to him for truth and faith; and he believes should stand for the same realities to every reader. But the first reader prefers as naturally the symbol of a mother and child, or a gardener and his bulb, or a jeweller polishing a gem. Either of these, or of a myriad more, are equally good to the person to whom they are significant. Only they must be held lightly, and be very willingly translated into the equivalent terms which others use. And the mystic must be steadily told, – All that you say is just as true without the tedious use of that symbol as with it. Let us have a little algebra, instead of this trite rhetoric, – universal signs, instead of these village symbols, – and we shall both be gainers. The history of hierarchies seems to show, that all religious error consisted in making the symbol too stark and solid, and, at last, nothing but an excess of the organ of language. . . .

Art is the path of the creator to his work. The paths, or methods, are ideal and eternal, though few men ever see them, not the artist himself for years, or for a lifetime, unless he come into the conditions. The painter, the sculptor, the composer, the epic rhapsodist, the orator, all partake one desire, namely, to express themselves symmetrically and abundantly, not dwarfishly and fragmentarily. They found or put themselves in certain conditions, as, the painter and sculptor before some impressive human figures; the orator, into the assembly of the people; and the others, in such scenes as each has found exciting to his intellect; and each presently feels the new desire. He hears a voice, he sees a beckoning. Then he is apprised, with wonder, what herds of dæmons hem him in. He can no more rest; he says, with the old painter, "By God, it is in me, and must go forth of me." He pursues a beauty, half seen, which flies before him. The poet pours out verses in every solitude. Most of the things he says are conventional, no doubt; but by and by he says something which is original and beautiful. That charms him. He would say nothing else but such things. In our way of talking, we say, "That is yours, this is mine"; but the poet knows well that it is not his; that it is as strange and beautiful to him as to you; he would fain hear the like eloquence at length. Once having tasted this immortal ichor, he cannot have enough of it, and, as an admirable creative power exists in these intellections, it is of the last importance that these things get spoken. What a little of all we know is said! What drops of all the sea of our science are baled up! and by what accident it is that these are exposed, when so many secrets sleep in nature! Hence the necessity of speech and song; hence these throbs and heart-beatings in the orator, at the door of the assembly, to the end, namely, that thought may be ejaculated as Logos, or Word.

Doubt not, O poet, but persist. Say, "It is in me, and shall out." Stand there, balked and dumb, stuttering and stammering, hissed and hooted, stand and strive, until, at last, rage draw out of thee that *dream*-power which every night shows thee is thine own; a power transcending all limit and privacy, and by virtue of which a man is the conductor of the whole river of electricity. Nothing walks, or creeps, or grows, or exists, which must not in turn arise and walk before him as exponent of his meaning. Comes he to that power, his genius is no longer exhaustible. All the creatures, by pairs and by tribes, pour into his mind as into a Noah's ark, to come forth again to people a new world. This is like the stock of air for our respiration, or for the combustion of our fireplace, not a measure of gallons, but the entire atmosphere if wanted. And therefore the rich poets, as Homer, Chaucer, Shakspeare, and Raphael, have obviously no limits to their works, except the limits of their lifetime, and resemble a mirror carried through the street, ready to render an image of every created thing.

John Dewey

(1859–1952)

The American pragmatist philosopher John Dewey wrote only one book focused on aesthetics, *Art as Experience* (1934). He nonetheless exerts a powerful secularizing influence upon present-day theories of the artwork, especially the literary work of art which, from Dewey's point of view, had too long been sequestered from the experiential world by the privileges of genius and the purity of form.

As the title of his work indicates, Dewey understands human self-expression to be continuous with experience and likewise reciprocal with the activity of the human organism. The term "experience," according to Dewey's usage, however, has little to do with the external world understood as an impersonal entity. Rather it designates the full range of symbolically mediated human actions. In so far as the symbolic mediation of human actions renders them sharable, it makes them serviceable to the task of discovering our "objective" situation in the world around us. In this way Dewey challenges the attitudes of high modernist formalism which treats art as a refuge from the alienating effects of historical determinism. It is precisely because Dewey sees the work of art as developing the culture, and so as emphatically historical, that he can confidently proclaim art to be "the greatest intellectual achievement in the history of humanity."

For Dewey the work of art is neither instantaneous or timeless. Its integrity depends upon its ability to impose a shaping principle upon the flow of temporality. The cultural significance of the artwork has chiefly to do with its capacity for organizing human experience. In this way the artist's self-expression is understood to be a form of participation in social reality. The artist properly strives toward a "common life," eschewing the romantic privileges of genius and inspiration. Despite his emphasis on the expressiveness of the artist, Dewey needs to be distinguished from expressivist theorists who treat expression strictly as an element of the creative act. Dewey uses the term "expression" to denote a continuous relation between the work of art and the consuming public. The work of art is a function of the interaction of formed material and the appreciative mind or sensibility. This makes it part of the process of ongoing life: "Works of art that are not remote from common life, that are widely enjoyed in a community, are signs of a unified collective life" (p. 80). In this respect, Dewey's sense of the social function of the artwork is complementary to that of Hans-Georg Gadamer.

Indeed, like the phenomenologically oriented aesthetic theories of Heidegger and Gadamer, Dewey's aesthetic privileges the artwork above other philosophies of experience on the basis of its transformative capacity. The artwork does not imitate given experience. For example, while Dewey understands that the work of art may have something to do with morality and emotion, it is never to be understood as a vehicle for representing them. The emotion expressed by the work of art in no way precedes its embodiment in artistic form. Accordingly, Dewey maintains a distinction between the "subject matter" of the work and its "substance." Substance is what is embodied by the work as opposed to its theme. The intelligibility of the work cannot depend on anything that could be discursively isolated from the formal artifact in all its compositional complexity. As Dewey says in "The Act of Expression," "The real work of art is the building up of an integral experience out of the interaction of organic and environmental conditions and energies." Here the emphasis on the experiential underpinning of art presupposes what Dewey calls the co-efficiency of the artist as an agent with "things in the environment that would otherwise be mere smooth channels or else blind obstructions." In the artwork those "things" become "media." Dewey believes that, because art amounts to a "remaking of the material of experience" rather than a reflection of it, the efficacy of the artwork will be a measure of its practical contribution to the life of the culture in which it is produced. By the same token, the strength of the culture can be measured in the integrity of its aesthetic practices.

Suggested reading

Thomas M. Alexander, *John Dewey's Theory of Art, Experience, and Nature: The Horizons of Feeling*, Albany, NY: State University of New York Press, 1993.

The Act of Expression

The transition from an act that is expressive from the standpoint of an outside observer to one intrinsically expressive is readily illustrated by a simple case. At first a baby weeps, just as it turns its head to follow light; there is an inner urge but nothing to express. As the infant matures, he learns that particular acts effect different consequences, that, for example, he gets attention if he

Reprinted from: John Dewey, *Art as Experience*, New York: Perigree Books/G. P. Putnam's Sons, 1980, pp. 62–5, 80–1.

cries, and that smiling induces another definite response from those about him. He thus begins to be aware of the *meaning* of what he does. As he grasps the meaning of an act at first performed from sheer internal pressure, he becomes capable of acts of true expression. The transformation of sounds, babblings, lalling, and so forth, into language is a perfect illustration of the way in which acts of expression are brought into existence and also of the difference between them and mere acts of discharge.

There is suggested, if not exactly exemplified, in such cases the connection of expression with art. The child who has learned the effect his once spontaneous act has upon those around him performs "on purpose" an act that was blind. He begins to manage and order his activities in reference to their consequences. The consequences undergone because of doing are incorporated as the meaning of subsequent doings because the relation between doing and undergoing is perceived. The child may now cry for a purpose, because he wants attention or relief. He may begin to bestow his smiles as inducements or as favors. There is now art in incipiency. An activity that was "natural" – spontaneous and unintended – is transformed because it is undertaken as a means to a consciously entertained consequence. Such transformation marks every deed of art. The result of the transformation may be artful rather than esthetic. The fawning smile and conventional smirk of greeting are artifices. But the genuinely gracious act of welcome contains also a change of an attitude that was once a blind and "natural" manifestation of impulsion into an act of art, something performed in view of its place or relation in the processes of intimate human intercourse.

The difference between the artificial, the artful, and the artistic lies on the surface. In the former there is a split between what is overtly done and what is intended. The appearance is one of cordiality; the intent is that of gaining favor. Wherever this split between what is done and its purpose exists, there is insincerity, a trick, a simulation of an act that intrinsically has another effect. When the natural and the cultivated blend in one, acts of social intercourse are works of art. The animating impulsion of genial friendship and the deed performed completely coincide without intrusion of ulterior purpose. Awkwardness may prevent adequacy of expression. But the skillful counterfeit, however skilled, goes *through* the form of expression; it does not have the form of friendship and abide in it. The substance of friendship is untouched.

An act of discharge or mere exhibition lacks a medium. Instinctive crying and smiling no more require a medium than do sneezing and winking. They occur through some channel, but the means of outlet are not used as immanent means of an end. The act that *expresses* welcome uses the smile, the outreached hand, the lighting up of the face as media, not consciously but because they have become organic means of communicating delight upon meeting a valued friend. Acts that were primitively spontaneous are converted into means that make human intercourse more rich and gracious – just as a painter converts pigment into means of expressing an imaginative experience. Dance and sport are activities in which acts once performed spontaneously in separation are assembled and converted from raw, crude material into works of expressive art. Only where material is employed as media is there expression and art. Savage taboos that look to the outsider like mere prohibitions and inhibitions externally imposed may be to those who experience them media of expressing social status, dignity, and honor. Everything depends upon the way in which material is used when it operates as medium.

The connection between a medium and the act of expression is intrinsic. An act of expression always employs natural material, though it may be natural in the sense of habitual as well as in that of primitive or native. It becomes a medium when it is employed in view of its place and rôle, in its relations, an inclusive situation – as tones become music when ordered in a melody. The same tones might be uttered in connection with an attitude of joy, surprise, or sadness, and be natural outlets of particular feelings. They are *expressive* of one of these emotions when other tones are the medium in which one of them occurs.

Etymologically, an act of expression is a squeezing out, a pressing forth. Juice is expressed when grapes are crushed in the wine press; to use a more prosaic comparison, lard and oil are rendered when certain fats are subjected to heat and pressure. Nothing is pressed forth except from original raw or natural material. But it is equally true that the mere issuing forth or discharge of raw material is not expression. Through interaction with something external to it, the wine press, or the treading foot of man, juice results. Skin and seeds are separated and retained; only when the apparatus is defective are they discharged. Even in the most mechanical modes of expression there is interaction and a consequent transformation of the primitive material which stands as raw material for a product of art, in relation to what is actually pressed out. It takes the wine press as well as grapes to ex-press juice, and it takes environing and resisting objects as well as internal emotion and impulsion to constitute an *expression* of emotion.

Speaking of the production of poetry, Samuel Alexander remarked that "the artist's work proceeds not from a finished imaginative experience to which the work of art corresponds, but from passionate excitement about the subject matter. . . . The poet's poem is wrung from him by the subject which excites him." The passage is a text upon which we may hang four comments. One of these comments may pass for the present as a reënforcement of a point made in previous chapters. The real work of art is the building up of an integral experience out of the interaction of organic and environmental conditions and energies. Nearer to our present theme is the second point: The thing expressed is wrung from the producer by the pressure exercised by objective things upon the natural impulses and tendencies – so far is expression from being the direct and immaculate issue of the latter. The third point follows. The act of expression that constitutes a work of art is a construction in time, not an instantaneous emission. And this statement signifies a great deal more than that it takes time for the painter to transfer his imaginative conception to canvass and for the sculptor to complete his chipping of marble. It means that the expression of the self in and through a medium, constituting the work of art, is *itself* a prolonged interaction of something issuing from the self with objective conditions, a process in which both of them acquire a form and order they did not at first possess. Even the Almighty took seven days to create the heaven and the earth, and, if the record were complete, we should also learn that it was only at the end of that period that he was aware of just what He set out to do with the raw material of chaos that confronted Him. Only an emasculated subjective metaphysics has transformed the eloquent myth of Genesis into the conception of a Creator creating without any unformed matter to work upon. . . .

Finally, what has been said locates, even if it does not solve, the vexed problem of the relation of esthetic or fine art to other modes of production also called art. The difference that exists in fact cannot be leveled, as we have already seen, by defining both in terms of technique and skill. But neither can it be erected into a barrier that is insuperable by referring the creation of fine art to an impulse that is unique, separated from impulsions which work in modes of expression not usually brought under the caption of fine art. Conduct can be sublime and manners gracious. If impulsion toward organization of material so as to present the latter in a form directly fulfilling in experience had no existence outside the arts of painting, poetry, music, and sculpture, it would not exist anywhere; there would be no fine art.

The problem of conferring esthetic quality upon all modes of production is a serious problem. But it is a human problem for human solution; not a problem incapable of solution because it is set by some unpassable gulf in human nature or in the nature of things. In an imperfect society – and no society will ever be perfect – fine art will be to some extent an escape from, or an adventitious decoration of, the main activities of living. But in a better-ordered society than that in which we live, an infinitely greater happiness than is now the case would attend all modes of production. We live in a world in which there is an immense amount of organization, but it is an external organization, not one of the ordering of a growing experience, one that involves, moreover, the whole of the live creature, toward a fulfilling conclusion. Works of art that are not remote from common life, that are widely enjoyed in a community, are signs of a unified collective life. But they are also marvelous aids in the creation of such a life. The remaking of the material of experience in the act of expression is not an isolated event confined to the artist and to a person here and there who happens to enjoy the work. In the degree in which art exercises its office, it is also a remaking of the experience of the community in the direction of greater order and unity.

Ludwig Wittgenstein
(1889–1951)

Wittgenstein is viewed by many as the most important philosopher of the twenti-eth century. His impact on aesthetics, however, has primarily been indirect. Although his work contains scattered speculations about art, literature, and music, and although he lectured on aesthetics at Cambridge, he never produced a systematic study of the subject. Yet the enormous impact of his work has been felt by literary critics as well as those in adjacent fields of the humanities.

Wittgenstein's career is generally divided into two periods, each of which is represented by one of his two major works. The first period begins in 1912 when he abandoned his plans to become an engineer and entered Cambridge to study philosophy with Bertrand Russell, and it culminates in the *Tractatus Logico-philosophicus*, which Wittgenstein wrote when he was a prisoner during the First World War and published in 1921. The *Tractatus* argues that language is a picture of the world. Philosophy, it contends, cannot determine how accurately language represents the world (that role belongs to science), but it can evaluate the logical form of sentences or assertions that employ these representations, and towards this goal Wittgenstein invents truth tables and other methods for determining the logical consistency of statements. Wittgenstein's intention here is to limit severely the scope of philosophy, but in doing so to make it a more rigorous discipline. The *Tractatus* concludes with the argument that certain topics cannot be either represented in lan-guage or evaluated by philosophy; about such topics, Wittgenstein bids his readers remain silent. Unfortunately for those interested in literary aesthetics, these topics include all talk of ethical and aesthetic values. Had Wittgenstein's career concluded at this point, his impact on aesthetic theory would have been largely negative.

With the publication of the *Tractatus*, Wittgenstein thought that he had solved all of the fundamental problems of philosophy, and after the war he withdrew from uni-versity life and became a teacher in an elementary school in Austria. Eventually, however, he was convinced that there was more philosophical work to be done and was persuaded to return to Cambridge, first in 1929 to finish his doctorate, and later, in 1939, to assume a chair in philosophy. The work that Wittgenstein did during this second period did not appear in print during his lifetime, but in 1953, two years after his death, *Philosophical Investigations*, his second great work, was published, and the publication of notebooks, lectures, and other writings followed. In *Philosophical Investigations* Wittgenstein rejects the picture theory of language that he had developed in the *Tractatus*, and in its place he advocates a theory of "language games." According to the *Tractatus*, sentences have meaning because they conform to a system of universal logic. In *Philosophical Investigations*, by contrast, Wittgenstein claims that meaning is produced by local practices or language games. Like other kinds of games, the rules and goals of language games differ; they construct meanings in response to specific situations. In one of the examples that Wittgenstein develops at the beginning of *Philosophical Investigations*, for instance, a builder and his assistant work out a set of terms for various building materials so that when the builder calls for certain materials such as a slab or a beam, the assistant will know what to bring. This language game will be judged successful if it produces practical results, but, of course, other builders and their assistants may invent their own versions of such a game. Wittgenstein's theory does not imply, however, that language games are private or that they can be invented by individuals alone. Indeed, *Philosophical Investigations* presents strong arguments against the possibility of a private language and insists that meaning is not something that exists first in the mind of an individual and then gets put into language. Rather, meaning is created by the language game itself, and as Wittgenstein emphasizes, this argues against expressivist theories of art, which assume that meaning comes from deep in the poet's soul.

As the following excerpts from his lectures on aesthetics (in *Lectures and Conversations*) make clear, Wittgenstein assumes that the various forms of artistic and literary criticism employ different kinds of language games, and while these games might share some family resemblances, it does not follow that critics of different types of art object necessarily share any assumptions about values. The way a critic of sculpture uses the term "beautiful," for instance, may have little to do with the way a literary critic uses the term or with the way the term gets used in everyday conversation. This follows from Wittgenstein's insistence that the meaning of an artistic language game is to be found in the practice itself rather than in a set of timeless essences.

Note: Wittgenstein's *Lectures and Conversations* is a collection of notes taken by his students at Cambridge. The lectures on aesthetics were compiled from the notes of Yorick Smythies, Rush Rhees, and James Taylor, and subsequently edited for publication by Cyril Barrett. These four are the authors of the editorial notes within and at the end of the excerpts below.

Suggested reading

Stanley Cavell, *The Claim of Reason: Wittgenstein, Skepticism, Morality, and Tragedy*, Oxford: Clarendon Press, 1979.

Lectures on Aesthetics

1   The subject (Aesthetics) is very big and entirely misunderstood as far as I can see. The use of such a word as 'beautiful' is even more apt to be misunderstood if you look at the linguistic form of sentences in which it occurs than most other words. 'Beautiful' [and 'good' – R] is an adjective, so you are inclined to say: "This has a certain quality, that of being beautiful."

2   We are going from one subject-matter of philosophy to another, from one group of words to another group of words.

3   An intelligent way of dividing up a book on philosophy would be into parts of speech, kinds of words. Where in fact you would have to distinguish far more parts of speech than an ordinary grammar does. You would talk for hours and hours on the verbs 'seeing', 'feeling', etc., verbs describing personal experience. We get a peculiar kind of confusion or confusions which comes up with all these words.[1] You would have another chapter on numerals – here there would be another kind of confusion: a chapter on 'all', 'any', 'some', etc. – another kind of confusion: a chapter on 'you', 'I', etc. – another kind: a chapter on 'beautiful', 'good' – another kind. We get into a new group of confusions; language plays us entirely new tricks.

4   I have often compared language to a tool chest, containing a hammer, chisel, matches, nails, screws, glue. It is not a chance that all these things have been put together – but there are important differences between the different tools – they are used in a family of ways – though nothing could be more different than glue and a chisel. There is constant surprise at the new tricks language plays on us when we get into a new field.

5   . . . If you ask yourself how a child learns 'beautiful', 'fine', etc., you find it learns them roughly as interjections. ('Beautiful' is an odd word to talk about because it's hardly ever used.) A child generally applies a word like 'good' first to food. One thing that is immensely important in teaching is exaggerated gestures and facial expressions. The word is taught as a substitute for a facial expression or a gesture. The gestures, tones of voice, etc., in this case are expressions of approval. What *makes* the word an interjection of approval?[2] It is the game it appears in, not the form of words. (If I had to say what is the main mistake made by philosophers of the present generation, including Moore, I would say that it is that when language is looked at, what is looked

Reprinted from: Ludwig Wittgenstein, *Lectures and Conversations on Aesthetics, Psychology and Religious Belief*, compiled from notes taken by Yorick Smythies, Rush Rhees and James Taylor, edited by Cyril Barrett, Berkeley: University of California Press, 1972, pp. 1–5, 7–8.

at is a form of words and not the use made of the form of words.) Language is a characteristic part of a large group of activities – talking, writing, travelling on a bus, meeting a man, etc.[3] We are concentrating, not on the words 'good' or 'beautiful', which are entirely uncharacteristic, generally just subject and predicate ('This is beautiful'), but on the occasions on which they are said – on the enormously complicated situation in which the aesthetic expression has a place, in which the expression itself has almost a negligible place.

6 If you came to a foreign tribe, whose language you didn't know at all and you wished to know what words corresponded to 'good', 'fine', etc., what would you look for? You would look for smiles, gestures, food, toys. ([Reply to objection:] If you went to Mars and men were spheres with sticks coming out, you wouldn't know what to look for. Or if you went to a tribe where noises made with the mouth were just breathing or making music, and language was made with the ears. Cf. "When you see trees swaying about they are talking to one another." ("Everything has a soul.") You compare the branches with arms. Certainly we must interpret the gestures of the tribe on the analogy of ours.) How far this takes us from normal aesthetics [and ethics – T]. We don't start from certain words, but from certain occasions or activities.

7 A characteristic thing about our language is that a large number of words used under these circumstances are adjectives – 'fine', 'lovely', etc. But you see that this is by no means necessary. You saw that they were first used as interjections. Would it matter if instead of saying "This is lovely", I just said "Ah!" and smiled, or just rubbed my stomach? As far as these primitive languages go, problems about what these words are about, what their real subject is, [which is called 'beautiful' or 'good'. – R.][4] don't come up at all.

8 It is remarkable that in real life, when aesthetic judgements are made, aesthetic adjectives such as 'beautiful', 'fine', etc., play hardly any role at all. Are aesthetic adjectives used in a musical criticism? You say: "Look at this transition",[5] or [Rhees] "The passage here is incoherent". Or you say, in a poetical criticism, [Taylor]: "His use of images is precise". The words you use are more akin to 'right' and 'correct' (as these words are used in ordinary speech) than to 'beautiful' and 'lovely'.[6]

9 Words such as 'lovely' are first used as interjections. Later they are used on very few occasions. We might say of a piece of music that it is lovely, by this not praising it but giving it a character. (A lot of people, of course, who can't express themselves properly use the word very frequently. As they use it, it is used as an interjection.) I might ask: "For what melody would I most like to use the word 'lovely'?" I might choose between calling a melody 'lovely' and calling it 'youthful'. It is stupid to call a piece of music 'Spring Melody' or

'Spring Symphony'. But the word 'springy' wouldn't be absurd at all, any more than 'stately' or 'pompous'.

12   Take the question: "How should poetry be read? What is the correct way of reading it?" If you are talking about blank verse the right way of reading it might be stressing it correctly – you discuss how far you should stress the rhythm and how far you should hide it. A man says it ought to be read *this* way and reads it out to you. You say: "Oh yes. Now it makes sense." There are cases of poetry which should almost be scanned – where the metre is as clear as crystal – others where the metre is entirely in the background. I had an experience with the 18th century poet Klopstock.[7] I found that the way to read him was to stress his metre abnormally. Klopstock put ˘ – ˘ (etc.) in front of his poems. When I read his poems in this new way, I said: "Ah-ha, now I know why he did this." What had happened? I had read this kind of stuff and had been moderately bored, but when I read it in this particular way, intensely, I smiled, said: "This is *grand*," etc. But I might not have said anything. The important fact was that I read it again and again. When I read these poems I made gestures and facial expressions which were what would be called gestures of approval. But the important thing was that I read the poems entirely differently, more intensely, and said to others: "Look! This is how they should be read." Aesthetic adjectives played hardly any role.

20   It is not only difficult to describe what appreciation consists in, but impossible. To describe what it consists in we would have to describe the whole environment.

23   . . . When we talk of a Symphony of Beethoven we don't talk of correctness. Entirely different things enter. One wouldn't talk of appreciating the *tremendous* things in Art. In certain styles in Architecture a door is correct, and the thing is you appreciate it. But in the case of a Gothic Cathedral what we do is not at all to find it correct – it plays an entirely different role with us.[8] The entire *game* is different. It is as different as to judge a human being and on the one hand to say 'He behaves well' and on the other hand 'He made a great impression on me'.

24   'Correctly', 'charmingly', 'finely', etc. play an entirely different role. Cf. the famous address of Buffon – a terrific man – on style in writing; making ever so many distinctions which I only understand vaguely but which he didn't mean vaguely – all kinds of nuances like 'grand', 'charming', 'nice'.[9]

25   The words we call expressions of aesthetic judgement play a very complicated role, but a very definite role, in what we call a culture of a period. To describe their use or to describe what you mean by a cultured taste, you have

to describe a culture.[10] What we now call a cultured taste perhaps didn't exist in the Middle Ages. An entirely different game is played in different ages.

26   What belongs to a language game is a whole culture. In describing musical taste you have to describe whether children give concerts, whether women do or whether men only give them, etc., etc.[11] In aristocratic circles in Vienna people had [such and such] a taste, then it came into bourgeois circles and women joined choirs, etc. This is an example of tradition in music.

Notes

1   Here we find similarities – we find peculiar sorts of confusion which come up with *all* these words. – R.

2   And not of disapproval or of surprise, for example?
      (The child understands the gestures which you use in teaching him. If he did not, he could understand nothing. – R.)

3   When we build houses, we talk and write. When I take a bus, I say to the conductor: 'Threepenny.' We are concentrating not just on the word or the sentence in which it is used – which is highly uncharacteristic – but on the occasion on which it is said: the framework in which (nota bene) the actual aesthetic judgment is practically nothing at all. – R.

4   What the thing that is really good is – T.

5   'The transition was made in the right way.' – T.

6   It would be better to use 'lovely' descriptively, on a level with 'stately', 'pompous,' etc. – T.

7   Friedrich Gottlieb Klopstock (1724–1803). Wittgenstein is referring to the Odes (*Gesammelte Werke*, Stuttgart, 1886–7). Klopstock believed that poetic diction was distinct from popular language: He rejected rhyme as vulgar and introduced instead the metres of ancient literature. – Ed.

8   Here there is no question of *degree*. – R.

9   *Discours sur le style*: the address on his reception into L'Academie Française. 1753. – Ed.

10   To describe a set of aesthetic rules fully means really to describe the culture of a period. – T.

11   That children are taught by adults who go to concerts, etc., that the schools are like they are, etc. – R.

Kenneth Burke

(1897–1993)

Kenneth Burke liked to position himself as an outsider in his relationship with twentieth-century American literary criticism. Because he was an avowedly eclectic critic, borrowing ideas from such different and incompatible sources as the New Criticism, Marxism, psychoanalysis, and nineteenth- and twentieth-century philosophy, he was a critic who might have claimed affiliations with many groups but membership in none. His career as a literary critic was roughly coterminous with the development of the New Criticism and its eventual domination of American academic literary criticism. Like the New Critics, Burke often employs the technique of close reading, which involves the careful analysis of the verbal structure of a work of literature, and he also shares the New Critics' notion that literature is best understood as a drama of conflicting ideas and attitudes.

Burke dramatically deviates from New Critical doctrine, however, by insisting that literary drama must be understood not only as a work of art but also in terms of the social and psychological contexts that influenced the work's creation. This interest in the contexts of literature led him naturally to the political theories of Karl Marx, the sociology of Herbert Mead, and the psychology of Sigmund Freud. He argues, for instance, that in order to arrive at an adequate understanding of Samuel Taylor Coleridge's poetry, the reader needs to take five different contexts into account, each of which reflects a set of problems or conflicts that Coleridge encountered. Besides looking at the aesthetic or artistic problems faced by Coleridge in writing his poetry, the reader, Burke argues, needs to consider Coleridge's marital problems, his shifting political allegiances, his struggles with religious and philosophical issues, and even his addiction to opium. Burke was interested in the ways in which these various contexts are interrelated, but he did not try to reduce them to a single type of explanation.

At the heart of Burke's dramatistic approach to literary and cultural interpretation is his determination to understand human action. He was particularly interested in the ways in which various kinds of motives, conscious and unconscious, combine with environmental influences to shape human behavior. Toward this goal he wrote

A Grammar of Motives and *A Rhetoric of Motives*, two of his most important works. Burke's grammar of motives provides a systematic way of analyzing the structure of actions using what he calls the dramatistic "pentad," five features that every human action may be presumed to share. These include act, scene, agent, agency, and purpose. Not only do these terms provide the critic with tools for analyzing specific actions, but, more importantly, they provide a way to analyze the language in which an action is described. A sociologist is likely to describe human behavior in terms of different *scenes* or social environments, for example, while a lyric poet is likely to describe behavior in terms of an *agent's* personal motives. Rhetoric, for Burke, is the study of techniques of persuasion, and his rhetoric of motives studies the ways in which groups come to share descriptions of individual and group actions. This is illustrated by a famous reading of Hitler's *Mein Kampf* in which Burke analyzes the way in which Hitler's rhetoric offers the Germans a new and consoling vision of their national identity after their defeat in the First World War. For Burke, rhetoric is ritual, and here he notes the way in which Hitler invokes rituals of scapegoating and rebirth as part of his rhetorical strategy.

The following passage outlines Burke's critical method and situates literature as a part of a larger social drama. As the passage makes clear, the drama to which Burke refers in the opening sentence is nothing less than culture itself. To appreciate this drama and literature's part in it, Burke argues, one must view it in its entirety and from several different perspectives.

Suggested reading

Stephen Bygrave, *Kenneth Burke: Rhetoric and Ideology*, London: Routledge, 1993.

Literary Form

Where does the drama get its materials? From the "unending conversation" that is going on at the point in history when we are born. Imagine that you enter a parlor. You come late. When you arrive, others have long preceded you, and they are engaged in a heated discussion, a discussion too heated for them to pause and tell you exactly what it is about. In fact, the discussion had already begun long before any of them got there, so that no one present is qualified to retrace for you all the steps that had gone before. You listen for a while, until you decide that you have caught the tenor of the argument; then you put in your oar. Someone answers; you answer him; another comes to your defense;

Reprinted from: Kenneth Burke, *The Philosophy of Literary Form: Studies in Symbolic Action*, 3rd edn., Berkeley: University of California Press, 1973, pp. 110–12, 114–17.

another aligns himself against you, to either the embarrassment or gratifica-
tion of your opponent, depending upon the quality of your ally's assistance.
However, the discussion is interminable. The hour grows late, you must depart.
And you do depart, with the discussion still vigorously in progress.

It is from this "unending conversation" (the vision at the basis of Mead's
work) that the materials of your drama arise. Nor is this verbal action all there
is to it. For all these words are grounded in what Malinowski would call "contexts of situation." And very important among these "contexts of situation"
are the kind of factors considered by Bentham, Marx, and Veblen, the material interests (of private or class structure) that you symbolically defend or
symbolically appropriate or symbolically align yourself with in the course of
making your own assertions. These interests do not "cause" your discussion;
its "cause" is in the genius of man himself as *homo loquax*. But they greatly
affect the *idiom* in which you speak, and so the idiom by which you think. Or,
if you would situate the genius of man in a *moral* aptitude, we could say that
this moral aptitude is universally present in all men, to varying degrees, but
that it must express itself through a medium, and this medium is in turn
grounded in material structures. In different property structures, the moral
aptitude has a correspondingly different idiom through which to speak.

By the incorporation of these social idioms we build ourselves, our "personalities," i.e., our *roles* (which brings us again back into the matter of the
drama). The movie version of Shaw's *Pygmalion* shows us the process in an
almost terrifyingly simplified form, as we observe his heroine building herself
a character synthetically, by mastering the insignia, the linguistic and manner-
istic labels of the class among whom she would, by this accomplishment, symbolically enroll herself (with the promise that this symbolic enrollment would
culminate in objective, material fulfillment). In its simplicity, the play comes
close to heresy, as might be revealed by matching it with a counter-heresy:
Joyce's individualistic, absolutist, "dictatorial" establishment of a language
from within. Shaw's heroine, in making herself over by artificially acquiring
an etiquette of speech and manners, is "internalizing the external" (the term
is Mead's). But Joyce is "externalizing the internal." . . .

The broad outlines of our position might be codified thus:

(1)   We have the drama and the scene of the drama. The drama is enacted
against a background.

(2)   The description of the scene is the role of the physical sciences; the
description of the drama is the role of the social sciences.

(3)   The physical sciences are a calculus of events; the social sciences are
a calculus of acts. And human affairs being dramatic, the discussion of human

affairs becomes dramatic criticism, with more to be learned from a study of tropes than from a study of tropisms.

(4)   Criticism, in accordance with its methodological ideal, should attempt to develop rules of thumb that can be adopted and adapted (thereby giving it the maximum possibility of development via the "collective revelation," a development from first approximation to closer approximation, as against the tendency, particularly in impressionistic criticism and its many scientific variants that do not go by this name, to be forever "starting from scratch").

(5)   The error of the social sciences has usually resided in the attempt to appropriate the scenic calculus for a charting of the act.

(6)   However, there is an interaction between scene and role. Hence, dramatic criticism takes us into areas that involve the act as "response" to the scene. Also, although there may theoretically be a common scenic background for all men when considered as a collectivity, the acts of other persons become part of the scenic background for any individual person's act.

(7)   Dramatic criticism, in the idiom of theology, considered the individual's act with relation to God as a personal background. Pantheism proclaimed the impersonality of this divine role. I. e., whereas theology treated the scenic function of Nature as a "representative" of God, pantheism made the natural background identical with God. It narrowed the circumference of the context in which the act would be located. Naturalism pure and simple sought to eliminate the role of divine participation completely, though often with theological vestiges, as with the "God-function" implicit in the idea of "progressive evolution," where God now took on a "historicist" role. History, however, deals with "events," hence the increasing tendency in the social sciences to turn from a calculus of the act to a "pure" calculus of the event. Hence, in the end, the ideal of stimulus-response psychology.

(8)   Whatever may be the character of existence in the physical realm, this realm functions but as scenic background when considered from the standpoint of the human realm. I. e., it functions as "lifeless," as mere "property" for the drama. And an ideal calculus for charting this physical realm must treat it as lifeless (in the idiom of mechanistic determinism). But to adopt such a calculus for the charting of life is to chart by a "planned incongruity" (i. e., a treatment of something in terms of what it is *not*).

(9)   The ideal calculus of dramatic criticism would require, not an incongruity, but an inconsistency. I. e., it would be required to employ the coördinates of *both* determinism *and* free will.

(10)   Being, like biology, in an indeterminate realm between vital assertions and lifeless properties, the realm of the dramatic (hence of dramatic criticism) is neither physicalist nor anti-physicalist, but physicalist-plus.

Narrowing our discussion from consideration of the social drama in general to matters of poetry in particular, we may note that the distinction between the "internalizing of the external" and the "externalizing of the internal" involves two different functions of imagery: imagery as confessional and imagery as incantatory, the two elements that John Crowe Ransom has isolated from Aristotle's *Poetics* in his chapters on "The Cathartic Principle" and "The Mimetic Principle." Imagery, as confessional, contains in itself a kind of "personal irresponsibility," as we may even relieve ourselves of private burdens by befouling the public medium. If our unburdening attains an audience, it has been "socialized" by the act of reception. In its public reception, even the most "excremental" of poetry becomes "exonerated" (hence the extreme anguish of a poet who, writing "with maximum efficiency" under such an aesthetic, does not attain absolution by the suffrage of customers).

But we must consider also the "incantatory" factor in imagery: its function as a device for inviting us to "make ourselves over in the image of the imagery." Seen from this point of view, a thoroughly "confessional" art may enact a kind of "individual salvation at the expense of the group." Quite as the development of the "enlightenment" in the economic sphere was from a collective to an individual emphasis (with "private enterprise" as the benign phase of an attitude which has its malign counterpart in the philosophy of "*sauve qui peut* – and the devil take the hindmost"), so have mass rituals tended to be replaced by individualist revisions, with many discriminations that adjust them with special accuracy to the particular needs of their inventor and "signer"; while this mode in turn attains its logical conclusion or reduction to absurdity in poetry having the maximum degree of confessional efficiency, a kind of literary metabolistic process that may satisfy the vital needs of the poet well enough, but through poetic passages that leave offal in their train. Such puns seem to have been consciously exploited by Joyce when he is discussing his *ars poetica* in *Finnegans Wake*, hence should be considered by any reader looking for the work's motivations (i. e., the center about which its structure revolves, or the law of its development). Freud's "cloacal theory" would offer the simplest explanation as to the ways in which the sexually private and the excrementally private may become psychologically merged, so that this theme could be treated as consubstantial with the theme of incest previously mentioned.

Charles Altieri

(1942–)

Charles Altieri is an American literary theorist and critic whose work draws heavily on recent developments in both continental and Anglo-American philosophy. He believes that literature derives its value from its ability to express and to exemplify various subtle facets of human identity. Literature, he argues, can reveal the complexity, beauty, and pathos of our everyday lives, even when we ourselves are otherwise unaware of these qualities. Altieri's account of literary value reflects his interest in modern and postmodern lyric poetry, a genre dedicated to the exploration of personal experience, identity, and the problems of expression. He received his doctorate from the University of North Carolina at Chapel Hill for his dissertation on Yeats, and since that time he has published several books on twentieth-century poetry, including *Modernism and Painterly Abstraction* and *Self and Sensibility in Contemporary Poetry*.

The theoretical foundations for his criticism are set out in two books on human agency, *Act and Quality* and *Subjective Agency*. In both books Altieri uses the philosophy of Ludwig Wittgenstein to argue that moral and aesthetic values are best understood as the products of community practice. That is, he claims that these values are not merely the expressions of personal preferences on the one hand or determined by absolute objective principles on the other, but rather originate in the complex vocabularies that different communities use to describe the qualities of human action. These vocabularies are usually open-ended and flexible, Altieri observes, and this allows them to be meaningfully contested, but he insists that individuals can reject some of their community's values only by taking other values seriously.

In *Act and Quality*, Altieri argues that literature is best understood as a set of dramatic performances which illustrate the qualities that make individual lives interesting and valuable. In order to illustrate the expressive potential of this kind of literary performance, Altieri offers a reading of William Carlos Williams's poem "This is Just to Say," a poem that takes the form of a note left on an icebox door. In the poem, the poet apologizes for having eaten the plums that his wife was saving for

breakfast ("Forgive me|they were delicious|so sweet|and so cold"). Altieri notes
that the poem can be read as a record of marital conflict and aggression, as a reflection on the grounds of forgiveness and human community, or as a combination of
these two perspectives. Ultimately, Altieri concludes, the poem's simple language
invites the reader to reflect on the minimal conditions that make human understanding and human community possible; the poet's plea for his wife's understanding becomes a model for poetry's plea for a provisional understanding. This miniature
domestic drama, he notes, becomes for Williams "a possible metaphor for an 'identity' that conquers 'partiality' and a condition of 'mutual understanding and toler-
ance' that attends upon imaginative measures of performance" (1981: 175). For
Altieri, this meaning is the product of nothing more than the provisional arrange-
ments that Wittgenstein calls "shared forms of life."

In *Subjective Agency*, Altieri shifts his attention from the qualities that literature
exemplifies to the human agents who express and appreciate those qualities. In
describing human agency, he attempts to avoid two extremes: on the one hand, he
wants to reject romantic notions of expression that assume that human identity is
the product of a soul, a deep and abiding repository of personal essence, while on
the other, he eschews what he sees as the reductive language of science, a language
that systematically collapses the differences between first and third person points of
view. In order to establish a middle ground between these positions, Altieri again
returns to the work of Wittgenstein for an account of language that allows him to
take human identity seriously without locating it in a metaphysical substance.

The following excerpt from *Canons and Consequences* offers an account of the
way in which aesthetics provides the model for an inclusive theory of ethical value.

Reference

Charles Altieri, *Act and Quality*, Amherst, Mass.: University of Massachusetts Press, 1981.

Suggested reading

Charles Altieri, *Canons and Consequences: Reflections on the Ethical Force of Imaginative Ideals*,
    Evanston, Ill.: Northwestern University Press, 1990.

From Expressivist Aesthetics to Expressivist Ethics

Clearly, cultural grammars establish conditions for identity: Telemachus
becomes truly Odysseus's son when he imitates his father's courage and

Reprinted from: Charles Altieri, *Canons and Consequences: Reflections on the Ethical Force of Imaginative Ideals*, Evanston, Ill.: Northwestern University Press, 1990, pp. 248–52.

cunning. But it does not take Lacan to remind us of the price we must pay because we must subsume our desires under the Father's authoritative models: thus *Hamlet* becomes the measure of a world unsatisfied with the ideals Telemachus served. Yet for a culture that had to develop expressivist principles, even these alienated heroics could no longer suffice. We require a model of community responsive to Joyce's transformation of Telemachus and Hamlet into a self-consciously adopted heritage where one's public identity lies precisely in how the agent manipulates complex structures of identity and difference. The character of Stephen Dedalus posits, reveals, and tests something that endures in the examples of Telemachus and Hamlet, while insisting on the need to define one's own difference by pursuing principles abstract enough to make received positive values and actual social affiliations seem mere positivities, the tokens that communities must rely on when they are not fully responsive to the imaginative worlds we can invoke as alternative contexts giving a richer sense of both the content and the possible significance of certain values. . . .

Indeed, for what I have been calling morality there remains a strong need for impersonal, objectively applied standards. But these do not help us appreciate what agents seek in choosing moral stances. The only proposal that will work, I think, requires a simple transformation of Kantian aesthetics. The normative ground for expression is a grammar for valuing action sustained by the specific community from which an agent seeks identity. Agents choose communities, but then they accept as a substitute for universals the principles of judgment that observers construct as plausible within the community. This approach requires constant negotiation, but it satisfies in practice the basic practical concerns that drive Kant to rationalism: determinations of the good must be different from the simple pursuit of preferences because the agent in the former case cannot be the only arbiter. There must be sufficient critical force in one's concept of community to allow it to generate three conditions for ethical actions: goals to pursue, possibilities of distinguishing purely empirical interests from principled actions, and means of standing in judgment on our own behavior as it responds to these goals and possibilities. Communities must be sufficiently determinate to provide standards and criteria, but sufficiently indeterminate to allow agents to criticize their values, form new allegiances, and change the level on which the culture's products are viewed so as to distinguish positivities from principles. By satisfying these conditions, we have a claim to reconcile the Kantian polarities of actuality and ideality.

The major influence of aesthetic theory here is on how we choose to specify what holds a community together so that we internalize its role as a normative ground in our acts of judgment.[1] Obviously, reliance on rules or principles simply recreates the gulf between anyone and someone, while at the other pole definition of communities in terms of beliefs we ground in social practices or responses to questionnaires eliminates the question of second-order ethics entirely, except as itself a specific cultural formation. The "I" begins to look suspiciously like "anyone," on the basis of social rather than rational determinants.

. . . All ethical grounds must provide transitions between the empirical and the ideal. Here that conjunction takes explicit human form, allowing a direct equation between the psychological processes that constitute both ego ideals and ideal egos and the symbolic ones sustained by cultural traditions. And because we base cultural authority on the dual properties of serving as a grammar and serving as an audience, we can understand how ideals can exist on the level of principles rather than of positivities. We use the past to make ourselves intelligible, and we construct from the past an audience capable of judging the modifications we make in the values that audience exemplifies.

We cannot, of course, specify conditions for these judgments, but we can use the context provided by the model of an audience as the basis for communal discussions. Culture as a set of contents becomes culture as a shareable process of identifications and projections. Different people can construct somewhat different versions of Socrates and still use him as an exemplar they hold in common. Or they can negotiate ways of reading the relation between positivities and principles he offers. Or they can use the same readings of characters to explain differences on another level – by developing contrastive stories that use the models or by accounting for a range of their own emotional investments. Conversely, there is strong pressure on us to locate identities capacious enough to allow our different expressions to remain intelligible to one another, even to make demands on one another. We need not have only one fixed canon of saints in order to be able to define how our ideals form overlapping circles.

Instead of the one canon, we need an attitude that acknowledges what Angel Medina calls the reciprocal play of regressive and progressive moments in the process of existential elucidation.[2] The regressive features of identification entail taking responsibility for both a personal past and its relation to the exemplars that make a community articulate about their values. That in turn becomes the basis for making public and testable the projections that construct possible future selves. If one desires these progressive moments to sustain a sense of continuous identities (not necessarily a rigid single self), one could not simply choose any community that comes to hand as a possible source of approval for one's actions. Because the projection of identity looks both backward and forward, it constrains us to be able to explain why we do or do not remain committed to the communities we have invoked on past occasions.

Thus, while one can in principle keep changing one's community, one cannot on this basis seek any of the forms of deep ethical identity that in our culture seem to have made the process worth pursuing in the first place.

Notes

1   Richard Eldridge, "Philosophy and the Achievement of Community: Rorty, Cavell, and Criticism," *Metaphilosophy* 14 (1983): 124–5, is an instructive case, because although he is quite good on the roles examples play as a form of knowledge carried by a culture, he ignores the force of idealization they can project. Conversely, Nozick's model of realization (*Philosophical Explanations*) is very powerful on how individuals can pursue ideal states. But his atomistic sense of society is thin on what it is one can realize. Without a strong notion of communal bonds he is trapped in the vaguest Romantic abstractions about unity and complexity, with each of these predicates filled out largely in terms of perceptions and relations to immediate scenes rather than cultural contexts.
2   Angel Medina, "Edwardian Couples: Aesthetic and Moral Experience in 'The Golden Bowl,'" *New Literary History* 15 (1983): 51–72.

VI
Gender

Aphra Behn

(1640?–1689)

Aphra Behn was one of the first women in Britain to earn her living as a writer. Her career as playwright spanned seventeen years, and she also published poetry and prose fiction. Because she depended upon literature for her livelihood, it is not surprising that most of her literary criticism was written to defend her literary practice; much of it is found in the forewords and prefaces to the printed versions of her plays. Despite her numerous successes as a playwright and the scandal occasioned by the bawdy nature of some of her work, relatively little is known of her life. In *The Secret Life of Aphra Behn*, her biographer, Janet Todd, speculates that she was the daughter of a wet nurse and a barber, both of whom were attached in some way to the Sidney family whose most famous member, Sir Philip Sidney, flourished a couple of generations earlier. In any event, Behn's connections with the Sidney family are well documented, and from them she seems to have adopted a hatred of the Puritans who ruled during Cromwell's Protectorate and a fierce loyalty to the Royalist cause of Charles II. In the early 1660s Behn traveled to Surinam, in South America. Some suspect that she was then working as an agent for the newly restored monarchy, as she certainly was when she undertook a spying mission to Holland during the war between Britain and Holland in 1666.

Like many who espoused the Royalist cause, Behn is fond of pastoral fantasy, with its image of a golden past when human affairs were ordered by a natural harmony. In this world, kings rule their kingdoms as loving fathers care for their families, and there is no dissension among the king's happy subjects. Furthermore, nature is bountiful and supplies all human needs with a minimum of toil or drudgery. We catch glimpses of this golden world in Behn's poetry and also in *Oronooko*, her tragic romance. Yet this yearning for an ideal world is balanced by Behn's keen awareness of the many ways in which the real world falls short of the pastoral ideal, and this awareness fuels her skepticism about the world in which she lives. Like Jonathan Swift and Alexander Pope, she relentlessly attacks the pretense and hypocrisy of those who fail to live up to the values that they profess. Not surprisingly, she finds such moral failings to be most common among the Puritans and Whigs whose politics she abhors.

A similar skepticism colors her literary criticism wherein she sometimes attacks the critical commonplaces of the day. In the excerpt from the preface to the *Dutch Lover*, which is included below, for instance, she rejects the notion that literature serves a moral purpose. At its best, she argues, art provides entertainment, not moral education; it serves the passions, not reason. The most popular characters in drama present not models of virtue but opportunities for vicarious emotional gratification. In a move that her readers may have found equally scandalous, Behn also rejects the authority and the rules of the classically trained academic critics. One does not require a classical education to provide entertainment, she insists, and this means that a woman (who was likely to lack such an education) is at no disadvantage in the theater. The true test of a play is the pleasure it produces, and commoners may judge this as well as those who are classically trained.

In some of her later criticism Behn seems to modify or even reverse her skeptical assessment of classical aesthetics and of the moral claims made for literature. In the dedication to *The Lucky Chance*, for instance, she boldly asserts (quoting Cardinal Richelieu) that theaters are "Schools of Vertue," and she goes on to assert that " 'tis Example alone that inspires Morality, and best establishes Vertue" (Todd 1996: 213). Behind this apparent paradox lies Behn's fervent hope that pleasure need not be sacrificed for virtue nor virtue for pleasure. Certainly, in a golden world there would be a reconciliation of the two, and perhaps, Behn implies in this dedication, art can at least help bring the two closer together.

Reference

Janet Todd (ed.) *The Works of Aphra Behn*, vol. 7, *The Plays*, Columbus: Ohio State University Press, 1996.

Suggested reading

Heidi Hunter (ed.) *Rereading Aphra Behn: History Theory and Criticism*, Charlottesville, Va.: University of Virginia Press, 1993.

An Epistle to the Reader

Good, sweet, honey, sugar-candied reader,

. . . I will have leave to say that in my judgment the increasing number of our latter plays have not done so much more towards the amending of men's

Reprinted from: Aphra Behn, *The Dutch Lover, A Comedy in Five Acts*, in *Selected Writings of the Ingenious Mrs. Aphra Behn*, edited by Robert Phelps, New York: Grove Press, 1950, pp. 119, 121–4.

morals, or their wit, than hath the frequent preaching, which this last age hath been pestered with (indeed without all controversy they have done less harm) nor can I once imagine what temptation anyone can have to expect it from them; for sure I am no play was ever writ with that design. If you consider tragedy, you'll find their best of characters unlikely patterns for a wise man to pursue: for he that is the knight of the play, no sublunary feats must serve his Dulcinea; for if he can't bestride the moon, he'll ne'er make good his business to the end, and if he chance to be offended, he must without considering right or wrong confound all things he meets, and put you half-a-score likely tall fellows into each pocket; and truly if he come not something near this pitch I think the tragedy's not worth a farthing; for plays were certainly intended for the exercising of men's passions not their understandings, and he is infinitely far from wise that will bestow one moment's meditation on such things: And as for comedy, the finest folks you meet with there are still unfitter for your imitation, for though within a leaf or two of the prologue, you are told that they are people of wit, good humor, good manners, and all that: yet if the authors did not kindly add their proper names, you'd never know them by their characters; for whatsoe'er's the matter, it hath happened so spitefully in several plays, which have been pretty well received of late, that even those persons that were meant to be the ingenious censors of the play, have either proved the most debauched, or most unwitty people in the company: nor is this error very lamentable, since as I take it, comedy was never meant, either for a converting or a comforting ordinance: In short, I think a play the best divertisement that wise men have: but I do also think them nothing so who discourse as formally about the rules of it, as if 'twere the grand affair of human life. This being my opinion of plays, I studied only to make this as entertaining as I could, which whether I have been successful in, my gentle reader, you may for your shilling judge. To tell you my thoughts of it were to little purpose, for were they very ill, you may be sure I would not have exposed it; nor did I so till I had first consulted most of those who have a reputation for judgment of this kind; who were at least so civil (if not kind) to it as did encourage me to venture it upon the stage, and in the press: Nor did I take their single word for it, but used their reasons as a confirmation of my own.

Indeed, that day 'twas acted first, there comes me into the pit, a long, lither, phlegmatic, white, ill-favored, wretched fop, an officer in masquerade newly transported with a scarf and feather out of France, a sorry animal that has naught else to shield it from the uttermost contempt of all mankind, but that respect which we afford to rats and toads, which though we do not well allow to live, yet when considered as a part of God's creation, we make honorable mention of them. A thing, reader – but no more of such a smelt: This thing,

I tell ye, opening that which serves it for a mouth, out issued such a noise as this to those that sat about it, that they were to expect a woeful play, God damn him, for it was a woman's.

Now how this came about I am not sure, but I suppose he brought it piping hot from some who had with him the reputation of a villanous wit: for creatures of his size of sense talk without all imagination such scraps as they pick up from other folks. I would not for a world be taken arguing with such a property as this; but if I thought there were a man of any tolerable parts, who could upon mature deliberation distinguish well his right hand from his left, and justly state the difference between the number of sixteen and two, yet had this prejudice upon him; I would take a little pains to make him know how much he errs. For waiving the examination why women having equal education with men, were not as capable of knowledge, of whatsoever sort as well as they: I'll only say as I have touched before, that plays have no great room for that which is men's great advantage over women, that is learning; we all well know that the immortal Shakespeare's plays (who was not guilty of much more of this than often falls to women's share) have better pleased the world than Jonson's works, though by the way 'tis said that Benjamin was no such Rabbi neither, for I am informed that his learning was but grammar high; (sufficient indeed to rob poor Salust of his best orations) and it hath been observed that they are apt to admire him most confoundedly, who have just such a scantling of it as he had. . . .

Then for their musty rules of unity, and God knows what besides, if they meant anything, they are enough intelligible and as practible by a woman; but really methinks that they disturb their heads with any other rule of plays besides the making of them pleasant, and avoiding of scurrility, might much better be employed in studying how to improve men's too imperfect knowledge of that ancient English game which hight long Lawrence:[1] And if comedy should be the picture of ridiculous mankind I wonder anyone should think it such a sturdy task, whilst we are furnished with such precious originals as him I lately told you of; if at least that character do not dwindle into farce, and so become too mean an entertainment for those persons who are used to think.

Note

1   ". . . that ancient English game which hight long Lawrence": *To play at Lawrence* meant to do nothing at all [Ed.].

George Eliot (Mary Ann Evans)

(1819–1880)

Although Marian (also Mary Ann) Evans is best known today as George Eliot, the author of *Middlemarch* and several other major works of fiction, she first came to prominence as a translator, essayist, and editor of the *Westminster Review*, one of the leading journals of progressive thought in nineteenth-century Britain. Indeed, Eliot's fiction is in many ways the natural outgrowth of her early essays on ethics, aesthetics, and politics. She was born into a prosperous family in Warwickshire. Her father was a successful land agent for the local aristocracy and a political and religious conservative. Mary Ann, however, was a precocious student, and her voracious reading and the friendships that she formed with progressive intellectuals in the area led her to reject religion, and to embrace a philosophical materialism that made her skeptical of claims incapable of being supported with scientific evidence.

Throughout her life Evans continued to insist that politics, ethics, and aesthetics should be validated with scientific reason. She did, however, show an increasing appreciation of the role that emotional sympathy plays in inspiring ethical action and cementing social bonds, and she insisted that one of the chief tasks of the novelist is to cultivate the reader's sympathetic appreciation for various cultures and lifestyles. In German literature and philosophy, Evans, like Thomas Carlyle, found a strategy for reconciling a rigorous scientific reason bent on destroying myth and superstition with an appreciation of the kinds of virtue which she felt were evident in all religions, as well as in the everyday practices of people with different cultural backgrounds. The strategy involved interpreting religion as a partial or distorted version of the truth. Ludwig Feuerbach, a German philosopher whose work she both translated and championed, provided Evans with one of its most useful formulations. Feuerbach argued that religion reveals not the attributes of an inhuman god or gods but, rather, the highest moral principles that humanity has succeeded in creating for itself. Thus those attributes usually attributed to a deity should be attributed to an ideal humanity, and human history should be viewed as humanity's quest for self-creation and self-discovery, a quest that is as valuable for the noble struggles which it inspires as for the results that it produces. The epigraph to the *Westminster Review* is a quotation from Goethe that nicely summarizes this attitude: "The wise man looks for good everywhere, and finds it."

Yet if Evans believed that the novel should inspire understanding of and sympathy for the good to be found diverse cultures and lifestyles, she was emphatically opposed to novels that rely upon merely impressionistic descriptions of the world and offer easy moral optimism. She praised John Ruskin's insistence that art should be based upon a painstaking scientific observation and ridiculed the idea that living a virtuous life is simply a matter of conforming to the dictates of a self-evident duty. The world is a complex place, she insisted, and even the most conscientious people must choose between different and sometimes conflicting forms of the good. Thus, in "Silly Novels by Women Novelists," an excerpt of which appears below, Evans attacks a group of authors whom she thinks have given women novelists a bad name. Their novels, she complains, lack accurate observation; they often demonstrate a comic ignorance in their attempts to portray ancient times or distant places, and their accounts of everyday people and events are also often lacking in plausibility. Furthermore, Evans argues, their treatments of human values are even more ridiculous. The characters whom these women portray are either all good or all bad, and whatever problems or conflicts these characters confront are resolved in terms of a romantic fantasy that culminates in a successful marriage. Evans is careful to insist that she is not criticizing all women novelists, and she specifically mentions Currer Bell (Charlotte Brontë) and Elizabeth Gaskell as women authors who are free of the flaws that she describes. Indeed, when the essay was written, she herself was about to launch a successful career as a woman novelist.

What is less clear, however, is the extent to which Evans feels that the work of the woman novelist may or should reflect a feminine sensibility. Elsewhere she argues forcefully that women should have access to all the knowledge that is available to men; healthy relationships between the sexes depend on such equal access to education, she insists. Yet Evans also seems to endorse the conventional notion that women are more naturally sympathetic than men and to leave open the possibility that traditional distinctions between men's and women's roles in society are in some way justified. This tension between a thoroughgoing egalitarianism and a determination to find some good in traditional social roles is characteristic of Evans's work. Most famously, it is evident in the struggles that lead Dorothea to embrace wifely virtues at the end of *Middlemarch* and to renounce any hope of more glamorous achievements. Some critics have pointed to this conflict in Eliot's thought as proof that she would have little sympathy with modern feminism. But this oversimplifies the matter somewhat since even contemporary feminists continue to debate whether at least some of the traditional feminine virtues should be defended as society moves toward gender equality. In any event, this dogged determination to find good everywhere, even in the roles assigned by an imperfect world, is entirely consistent both with Marian Evans's philosophy and with George Eliot's practice as a novelist.

Suggested reading

Valerie A. Dodd, *George Eliot: An Intellectual Life*, Basingstoke: Macmillan, 1990.

Silly Novels by Women Writers

The epithet "silly" may seem impertinent, applied to a novel which indicates so much reading and intellectual activity as "The Enigma"; but we use this epithet advisedly. If, as the world has long agreed, a very great amount of instruction will not make a wise man, still less will a very mediocre amount of instruction make a wise woman. And the most mischievous form of feminine silliness is the literary form, because it tends to confirm the popular prejudice against the more solid education of women. When men see girls wasting their time in consultations about bonnets and ball dresses, and in giggling or sentimental love-confidences, or middle-aged women mismanaging their children, and solacing themselves with acrid gossip, they can hardly help saying, "For Heaven's sake, let girls be better educated; let them have some better objects of thought – some more solid occupations." But after a few hours' conversation with an oracular literary woman, or a few hours' reading of her books, they are likely enough to say, "After all, when a woman gets some knowledge, see what use she makes of it! Her knowledge remains acquisition, instead of passing into culture; instead of being subdued into modesty and simplicity by a larger acquaintance with thought and fact, she has a feverish consciousness of her attainments; she keeps a sort of mental pocket-mirror, and is continually looking in it at her own 'intellectuality'; she spoils the taste of one's muffin by questions of metaphysics; 'puts down' men at a dinner-table with her superior information; and seizes the opportunity of a *soirée* to catechize us on the vital question of the relation between mind and matter. And then, look at her writings! She mistakes vagueness for depth, bombast for eloquence, and affectation for originality; she struts on one page, rolls her eyes on another, grimaces in a third, and is hysterical in a fourth. She may have read many writings of great men, and a few writings of great women; but she is as unable to discern the difference between her own style and theirs as a Yorkshireman is to discern the difference between his own English and a Londoner's: rhodomontade is the native accent of her intellect. No – the average nature of women is too shallow and feeble a soil to bear much tillage; it is only fit for the very lightest crops."

Reprinted from: *George Eliot: Selected Critical Writings*, edited by Rosemary Ashton, Oxford and New York: Oxford University Press, 1992, pp. 311–13, 318–20.

It is true that the men who come to such a decision on such very superficial and imperfect observation may not be among the wisest in the world; but we have not now to contest their opinion – we are only pointing out how it is unconsciously encouraged by many women who have volunteered themselves as representatives of the feminine intellect. We do not believe that a man was ever strengthened in such an opinion by associating with a woman of true culture, whose mind had absorbed her knowledge instead of being absorbed by it. A really cultured woman, like a really cultured man, is all the simpler and the less obtrusive for her knowledge; it has made her see herself and her opinions in something like just proportions; she does not make it a pedestal from which she flatters herself that she commands a complete view of men and things, but makes it a point of observation from which to form a right estimate of herself. She neither spouts poetry nor quotes Cicero on slight provocation; not because she thinks that a sacrifice must be made to the prejudices of men, but because that mode of exhibiting her memory and Latinity does not present itself to her as edifying or graceful. She does not write books to confound philosophers, perhaps because she is able to write books that delight them. In conversation she is the least formidable of women, because she understands you, without wanting to make you aware that you *can't* understand her. She does not give you information, which is the raw material of culture, – she gives you sympathy, which is its subtlest essence. . . .

"Be not a baker if your head be made of butter," says a homely proverb, which, being interpreted, may mean, let no woman rush into print who is not prepared for the consequences. We are aware that our remarks are in a very different tone from that of the reviewers who, with a perennial recurrence of precisely similar emotions, only paralleled, we imagine, in the experience of monthly nurses, tell one lady novelist after another that they "hail" her productions "with delight." We are aware that the ladies at whom our criticism is pointed are accustomed to be told, in the choicest phraseology of puffery, that their pictures of life are brilliant, their characters well-drawn, their style fascinating, and their sentiments lofty. But if they are inclined to resent our plainness of speech, we ask them to reflect for a moment on the chary praise, and often captious blame, which their panegyrists give to writers whose works are on the way to become classics. No sooner does a woman show that she has genius or effective talent, than she receives the tribute of being moderately praised and severely criticized. By a peculiar thermometric adjustment, when a woman's talent is at zero, journalistic approbation is at the boiling pitch; when she attains mediocrity, it is already at no more than summer heat; and if ever she reaches excellence, critical enthusiasm drops to the freezing point. Harriet

Martineau, Currer Bell, and Mrs Gaskell have been treated as cavalierly as if they had been men. And every critic who forms a high estimate of the share women may ultimately take in literature, will, on principle, abstain from any exceptional indulgence towards the productions of literary women. For it must be plain to every one who looks impartially and extensively into feminine literature, that its greatest deficiencies are due hardly more to the want of intellectual power than to the want of those moral qualities that contribute to literary excellence – patient diligence, a sense of the responsibility involved in publication, and an appreciation of the sacredness of the writer's art. In the majority of women's books you see that kind of facility which springs from the absence of any high standard; that fertility in imbecile combination or feeble imitation which a little self-criticism would check and reduce to barrenness; just as with a total want of musical ear people will sing out of tune, while a degree more melodic sensibility would suffice to render them silent. The foolish vanity of wishing to appear in print, instead of being counterbalanced by any consciousness of the intellectual or moral derogation implied in futile authorship, seems to be encouraged by the extremely false impression that to write *at all* is a proof of superiority in a woman. On this ground, we believe that the average intellect of women is unfairly represented by the mass of feminine literature, and that while the few women who write well are very far above the ordinary intellectual level of their sex, the many women who write ill are very far below it. So that, after all, the severer critics are fulfilling a chivalrous duty in depriving the mere fact of feminine authorship of any false prestige which may give it a delusive attraction, and in recommending women of mediocre faculties – as at least a negative service they can render their sex – to abstain from writing.

The standing apology for women who become writers without any special qualification is, that society shuts them out from other spheres of occupation. Society is a very culpable entity, and has to answer for the manufacture of many unwholesome commodities, from bad pickles to bad poetry. But society, like "matter," and Her Majesty's Government, and other lofty abstractions, has its share of excessive blame as well as excessive praise. Where there is one woman who writes from necessity, we believe there are three women who write from vanity; and, besides, there is something so antiseptic in the mere healthy fact of working for one's bread, that the most trashy and rotten kind of feminine literature is not likely to have been produced under such circumstances. "In all labour there is profit"; but ladies' silly novels, we imagine, are less the result of labour than of busy idleness.

Happily, we are not dependent on argument to prove that Fiction is a department of literature in which women can, after their kind, fully equal men.

A cluster of great names, both living and dead, rush to our memories in evidence that women can produce novels not only fine, but among the very finest; – novels, too, that have a precious speciality, lying quite apart from masculine aptitudes and experience. No educational restrictions can shut women out from the materials of fiction, and there is no species of art which is so free from rigid requirements. Like crystalline masses, it may take any form, and yet be beautiful; we have only to pour in the right elements – genuine observation, humour, and passion. But it is precisely this absence of rigid requirement which constitutes the fatal seduction of novel-writing to incompetent women.

Virginia Woolf

(1882–1941)

Virginia Woolf is most famous as the novelist whose fiction is celebrated as one of the high points of British modernism. She was also, however, a very productive and insightful critic who published regularly in such venues as the *Time Literary Supplement* and whose essays provide vigorous defenses of modernist literary practice as well as advocating social and political reform. The growth of feminist literary criticism since the 1970s has brought renewed attention to Woolf's critical work. She was an outspoken advocate of women's rights, an attentive reader of women writers and their literary legacy, and her writing style itself is considered by many to embody a distinctly feminist point of view, a view that works to undermine the settled assumptions of a conventionally masculine viewpoint.

Despite Woolf's staunch feminism, however, the role that gender plays in her literary aesthetic is still hotly debated. Like the work of several other modernist theorists, Woolf's criticism shows a broad affinity with the philosophy of Henri Bergson. That is, Woolf assumes, as does Bergson, that there are two levels of human consciousness, one of which reflects the flux, immediacy, and chaos of experience itself, while the other reflects the more ordered reality of the social world. In many of her most famous statements about fiction, Woolf insists that it is the novelist's responsibility to probe beneath the external reality of habitual, everyday experience and to engage the underlying drama of experience itself. In "Modern Fiction," an essay from *The Common Reader* (1925), for instance, she compares realist writers such as H. G. Wells and Arnold Bennett with modernist writers such as James Joyce. She labels the realists "materialists" and accuses them of paying so much attention to the details of the physical world that they neglect the inner lives of their characters (p. 210). By contrast, she claims, the modernists are "spiritual" and will violate standards of literary propriety in order to bring the reader closer to the inner lives of their characters "Let us," Woolf says, "record the atoms as they fall upon the mind in the order in which they fall, let us trace the pattern, however disconnected and incoherent in appearance, which each sight or incident scores upon the consciousness" (pp. 213–14).

Woolf notes that because they have been traditionally confined to the domestic sphere, women have been well situated for observing this inner dimension of human experience, but it is not clear to what extent she thinks that this sensitivity is the defining feature of a feminine sensibility or of a women's literary tradition. For example, in the essay just mentioned, she attributes this sensitivity to a male writer, and in a famous passage from *A Room of One's Own* (1929), Woolf insists that good novelists should be androgynous, that is, that they should incorporate both masculine and feminine characteristics. Yet, in other places, she speaks as if women writers are best understood in terms of their own distinctive tradition and sensibility. Of course, if gender is the product of social conditioning rather than an inborn essence, these two positions may not be incompatible, and the attitudes and perspectives that traditionally have been supposed to divide the sexes may, in fact, be available to all individuals.

In the following excerpt from "Women and Fiction" (1929), Woolf describes women writers as sharing a unified, although changing, sensibility, a sensibility which is distinct from that of masculine writers; hence, she feels that contemporary women writers must invent new kinds of sentences, since the sentences written by men are too ponderous to convey a woman's thoughts. At the same time, however, Woolf emphasizes the way in which changing social circumstances have altered the nature of feminine identity. She stresses, later in the essay, that "the basis of the poetic attitude is of course largely founded on material things" such as leisure and money.

Reference

Virginia Woolf, *The Common Reader*, New York: Harcourt, Brace, and Co., 1925 (originally published 1919).

Suggested reading

Toril Moi, *Sexual Textual Politics: Feminist Literary Theory*, London: Routledge, 1985.

Women and Fiction

The great change that has crept into women's writing is, it would seem, a change of attitude. The woman writer is no longer bitter. She is no longer angry. She is no longer pleading and protesting as she writes. We are approach-

Reprinted from: Virginia Woolf, *Women and Writing*, edited by Michèle Barrett, New York: Harcourt Brace Jovanovich, 1979, pp. 48–50. For up-to-date copyright and publication information see Acknowledgments.

ing, if we have not yet reached, the time when her writing will have little or no foreign influence to disturb it. She will be able to concentrate upon her vision without distraction from outside. The aloofness that was once within the reach of genius and originality is only now coming within reach of ordinary women. Therefore the average novel by a woman is far more genuine and far more interesting today than it was a hundred or even fifty years ago.

But it is still true that before a woman can write exactly as she wishes to write, she has many difficulties to face. To begin with, there is the technical difficulty – so simple, apparently; in reality, so baffling – that the very form of the sentence does not fit her. It is a sentence made by men; it is too loose, too heavy, too pompous for a woman's use. Yet in a novel, which covers so wide a stretch of ground, an ordinary and usual type of sentence has to be found to carry the reader on easily and naturally from one end of the book to the other. And this a woman must make for herself, altering and adapting the current sentence until she writes one that takes the natural shape of her thought without crushing or distorting it.

But that, after all, is only a means to an end, and the end is still to be reached only when a woman has the courage to surmount opposition and the determination to be true to herself. For a novel, after all, is a statement about a thousand different objects – human, natural, divine; it is an attempt to relate them to each other. In every novel of merit these different elements are held in place by the force of the writer's vision. But they have another order also, which is the order imposed upon them by convention. And as men are the arbiters of that convention, as they have established an order of values in life, so too, since fiction is largely based on life, these values prevail there also to a very great extent.

It is probable, however, that both in life and in art the values of a woman are not the values of a man. Thus, when a woman comes to write a novel, she will find that she is perpetually wishing to alter the established values – to make serious what appears insignificant to a man, and trivial what is to him important. And for that, of course, she will be criticized; for the critic of the opposite sex will be genuinely puzzled and surprised by an attempt to alter the current scale of values, and will see in it not merely a difference of view, but a view that is weak, or trivial, or sentimental, because it differs from his own.

But here, too, women are coming to be more independent of opinion. They are beginning to respect their own sense of values. And for this reason the subject matter of their novels begins to show certain changes. They are less interested, it would seem, in themselves; on the other hand, they are more interested in other women. In the early nineteenth century, women's novels were largely autobiographical. One of the motives that led them to write was the desire to expose their own suffering, to plead their own cause. Now that this desire is no longer so urgent, women are beginning to explore their own sex, to write of women as women have never been written of before; for of course, until very lately, women in literature were the creation of men.

Here again there are difficulties to overcome, for, if one may generalize, not only do women submit less readily to observation than men, but their lives are far less tested and examined by the ordinary processes of life. Often nothing tangible remains of a woman's day. The food that has been cooked is eaten; the children that have been nursed have gone out into the world. Where does the accent fall? What is the salient point for the novelist to seize upon? It is difficult to say. Her life has an anonymous character which is baffling and puzzling in the extreme. For the first time, this dark country is beginning to be explored in fiction; and at the same moment a woman has also to record the changes in women's minds and habits which the opening of the professions has introduced. She has to observe how their lives are ceasing to run underground; she has to discover what new colours and shadows are showing in them now that they are exposed to the outer world.

If, then, one should try to sum up the character of women's fiction at the present moment, one would say that it is courageous; it is sincere; it keeps closely to what women feel. It is not bitter. It does not insist upon its femininity. But at the same time, a woman's book is not written as a man would write it. These qualities are much commoner than they were, and they give even to second- and third-rate work the value of truth and the interest of sincerity.

Julia Kristeva

(1941–)

The Bulgarian-born literary theorist and practicing psychoanalyst, Julia Kristeva, was a student of Roland Barthes and Lucien Goldmann. Kristeva gained prominence as an exponent of semiotic criticism. Her work is especially preoccupied with the signifying properties of the speaking body. Kristeva's emphasis on the materiality of the body challenges the traditional practice of western metaphysics, which subordinates material existence to our ideas about it. She says that "our philosophies of Language, embodiments of the Idea, are nothing more than the thoughts of archivists, archaeologists, and necrophiliacs."

As an alternative to these "necrophiliac" knowledges, Kristeva proposed a method of "semanalysis." In this quasi-scientific pursuit, informed by psychoanalysis as well as semiotics, Kristeva seeks to address that which animates language but which is, nonetheless, heterogeneous to language. Kristeva asserts that the logic of this animating force is built into the materiality of the physical body. In an argument reminiscent of the Freudian discourse of the drives and the discourse of the Lacanian "Real," Kristeva contends that our acquisition of, or submission to language, causes us to suffer a kind of "castration." Following the lesson of Lacan's "mirror stage," Kristeva presupposes that signification in language speaks to a primordial lack, which it can never fill (see introduction to excerpts from Lacan). In order to facilitate access to the underlying drive structure of symbolic language, Kristeva distinguishes between the registers of the symbolic and the semiotic. The semiotic denotes a non-discursive modality of signification, which precedes linguistic communication. It indicates the discharging of the drives in language. The semiotic is available to us in the formal features of rhythm, tone, and vocal gesture. The rule-driven formalities of semantics and syntax are, by contrast, our access to the symbolic. On the threshold of the symbolic, the subject is instantiated as a unified point of view, a centered and centering perspective of knowledge. Semanalysis seeks to deny this point of view its post-Enlightenment imperial authority.

Kristeva's career-long focus on discourses in which signification constitutes a break with identity (poetry, maternity, and psychoanalysis, are three sites of this

break) makes her speculations especially productive for developing the concept of
the aesthetic. In *Revolution in Poetic Language* (1974), from which the following
excerpt is taken, poetry is treated as a process akin to Derridean alterity and the
Kantian judgment of taste, where an indeterminacy principle determines value. Consequently, when Kristeva looks at literary art and the signifying practices associated
with literary criticism, she gives a privileged place to the qualities of polysemy, unde-
cidability, and pleasurable excess. Ironically, these are features of the text which, it
could be said, are already privileged under the formalist tenets of the American New
Criticism. In Kristeva's view, however, the elements of poetic language are leverage
for a cultural innovation rather than the reaffirmation of a dominant culture. In the
conflicts that play between the semiotic and symbolic – a dialectic of identity and
difference, stasis and destabilization – Kristeva marks the emergence of the speaking subject as bound to its pre-symbolic origins, in a way that precludes any resolution of its identity in epistemological, political, or gender terms. For Kristeva the
investigation of literature is a corollary of this knowledge, revealing the vicissitudes
of what has since come to be called "the subject in process." This revelatory power
of the aesthetic, contrary to the revelations of romantic genius, is more conducive
to engaging the intersubjective tensions of the social rather than indulging the
abstract freedom of the deified individual. Kristeva contends that literary and artistic practice in general refigures the relation of the subject to the signifier. In effect,
the refiguration of this relation constitutes a test of the subject's freedom with respect
to the signifier as well as with respect to lived reality. The literary is a "trial" whereby
the subject comes to know its limits and simultaneously intuits the objective possibilities implicit in the displacement of those limits.

Suggested reading

Kelly Oliver, *Unraveling the Double-Bind: Julia Kristeva's Theory of the Subject on Trial*, Bloom-
  ington, Ind.: Indiana University Press, 1993.

The Semiotic *Chora* Ordering the Drives

We understand the term "semiotic" in its Greek sense: $\sigma\eta\mu\varepsilon\tilde{\iota}o\nu$ = distinctive
mark, trace, index, precursory sign, proof, engraved or written sign, imprint,
trace, figuration. . . . Discrete quantities of energy move through the body of
the subject who is not yet constituted as such and, in the course of his development, they are arranged according to the various constraints imposed on this

Reprinted from: Julia Kristeva, *Revolution in Poetic Language*, translated by Margaret Waller, New
York: Columbia University Press, 1984, pp. 25–30.

body – always already involved in a semiotic process – by family and social structures. In this way the drives, which are "energy" charges as well as "psychical" marks, articulate what we call a *chora*: a nonexpressive totality formed by the drives and their stases in a motility that is as full of movement as it is regulated.

We borrow the term *chora* from Plato's T*imaeus* to denote an essentially mobile and extremely provisional articulation constituted by movements and their ephemeral stases. We differentiate this uncertain and indeterminate *articulation* from a *disposition* that already depends on representation, lends itself to phenomenological, spatial intuition, and gives rise to a geometry. Although our theoretical description of the *chora* is itself part of the discourse of representation that offers it as evidence, the *chora*, as rupture and articulations (rhythm), precedes evidence, verisimilitude, spatiality, and temporality. Our discourse – all discourse – moves with and against the *chora* in the sense that it simultaneously depends upon and refuses it. Although the *chora* can be designated and regulated, it can never be definitively posited: as a result, one can situate the *chora* and, if necessary, lend it a topology, but one can never give it axiomatic form.

The *chora* is not yet a position that represents something for someone (i.e., it is not a sign); nor is it a *position* that represents someone for another position (i.e., it is not yet a signifier either); it is, however, generated in order to attain to this signifying position. Neither model nor copy, the *chora* precedes and underlies figuration and thus specularization, and is analogous only to vocal or kinetic rhythm. We must restore this motility's gestural and vocal play (to mention only the aspect relevant to language) on the level of the socialized body in order to remove motility from ontology and amorphousness where Plato confines it in an apparent attempt to conceal it from Democritean rhythm. The theory of the subject proposed by the theory of the unconscious will allow us to read in this rhythmic space, which has no thesis and no position, the process by which significance is constituted. Plato himself leads us to such a process when he calls this receptacle or *chora* nourishing and maternal, not yet unified in an ordered whole because deity is absent from it. Though deprived of unity, identity, or deity, the *chora* is nevertheless subject to a regulating process |*réglementation*|, which is different from that of symbolic law but nevertheless effectuates discontinuities by temporarily articulating them and then starting over, again and again. . . .

Drives involve pre-Oedipal semiotic functions and energy discharges that connect and orient the body to the mother. We must emphasize that "drives" are always already ambiguous, simultaneously assimilating and destructive; this dualism, which has been represented as a tetrad or as a double helix, as in the configuration of the DNA and RNA molecule, makes the semiotized body a place of permanent scission. The oral and anal drives, both of which are oriented and structured around the mother's body, dominate this sensorimotor organization. The mother's body is therefore what mediates the symbolic law organizing social relations and becomes the ordering principle of the semiotic *chora*, which is on the path of destruction, aggressivity, and death. For although drives have been described as disunited or contradictory structures, simultaneously "positive" and "negative," this doubling is said to generate a dominant "destructive wave" that is drive's most characteristic trait: Freud notes that the most instinctual drive is the death drive. In this way, the term "drive" denotes waves of attack against stases, which are themselves constituted by the repetition of these charges; together, charges and stases lead to no identity (not even that of the "body proper") that could be seen as a result of their functioning. This is to say that the semiotic *chora* is no more than the place where the subject is both generated and negated, the place where his unity succumbs before the process of charges and stases that produce him. We shall call this process of charges and stases a *negativity* to distinguish it from negation, which is the act of a judging subject. . . .

Mallarmé calls attention to the semiotic rhythm within language when he speaks of "The Mystery in Literature" ("Le Mystère dans les lettres"). Indifferent to language, enigmatic and feminine, this space underlying the written is rhythmic, unfettered, irreducible to its intelligible verbal translation; it is musical, anterior to judgment, but restrained by a single guarantee: syntax. As evidence, we could cite "The Mystery in Literature" in its entirety. For now, however, we shall quote only those passages that ally the functioning of that "air or song beneath the text" with woman:

> And the instrument of Darkness, whom they have designated, will not set down a word from then on except to deny that she must have been the enigma; lest she settle matters with a wisk of her skirts: "I don't get it!"

> .   .   .

> – They [the critics] play their parts disinterestedly or for a minor gain: leaving our Lady and Patroness exposed to show her dehiscence or lacuna, with respect to certain dreams, as though this were the standard to which everything is reduced.

VII
Aesthetic/Anti-aesthetic:
Contemporary Debates

Paul de Man

(1919–1983)

Paul de Man is usually described as an American deconstructionist, although decon-struction is only one of the many European influences reflected in his work. He was born in Belgium and after the Second World War emigrated to the United States, where he worked at a number of jobs before completing his Ph.D. at Harvard and launching into a distinguished career of teaching and scholarship. For the last eight years of his life he taught at Yale, where he became known as one of the Yale Decon-structionists, a group of influential professors in the Yale English Department who some believed were setting the agenda for literary study in the United States. After de Man's death it came to light that he had written articles for collaborationist news-papers during the Nazi occupation. Many of these endorse a cultural nationalism that remind de Man's opponents of National Socialism, and some of the articles appear to be anti-Semitic, although many of de Man's supporters claim that these articles are, in fact, ironic. The scandal generated a debate about the political impli-cations of de Man's criticism and of deconstruction more broadly.

De Man's criticism centers on the ironies and contradictions of human experi-ence. Human beings, he claims, are perpetually frustrated by the lack of correspon-dence between the world as it is represented in language and thought and the world as it is experienced. Like the Existentialists, whom he sometimes cites in his early work, de Man assumes that the world of brute existence is essentially meaningless and that it becomes meaningful only in so far as human meaning is imposed upon it. In his essay "The Rhetoric of Temporality," for instance, de Man describes irony as the result of the gap between an objectified or empirical self that remains a part of nature and a reflective self that remains aware of the empirical self but can never fully identify with it. De Man illustrates this predicament with an example from Baudelaire: a philosopher who is lost in contemplation falls into a ditch and laughs at himself. The philosopher's laughter, according to de Man, exemplifies the way in which the reflective self asserts its difference from the empirical self. The reflective self can know its difference from and superiority to the empirical self, but it exists only as difference; it has no positive form. This troubling gap between various forms of human identity is not just present in the difference between mind and body, however; it occurs also whenever consciousness objectifies itself. Thus, to cite another one of de Man's examples, the anthropologist who wants to understand foreign cultures must first attempt to understand her position in her own culture, but if the anthropologist is of a philosophical bent, this self that tries to understand itself must also be interrogated and so on in a potentially infinite regression. In each case, the self that attempts to do the understanding is different from the self that is understood.

The primary cause of this fracture in human experience, de Man claims, is language itself; it is language that opens the gap between the empirical self and the self that attempts its own definition. This latter reflective self, he insists, becomes a sign or a symbol of its own mysterious difference from the world in which it is situated. Literature, de Man postulates, is primarily about this slippage between language and the world, between the self as sign and the empirical self. Not only does literature constitute an example of such ironic slippage, but the best literature is aware of its own irony and foregrounds it as part of a self-conscious strategy. In *Blindness and Insight* (1971), de Man argues that when critics accuse literary texts of inconsistency, of ignoring the differences between the world as it is ideally imagined and described and the world as it really is, it is usually the critics themselves who are blind and who fail to see that the literature that they are analyzing is cognizant of its own internal contradictions. Furthermore, de Man asserts, critics themselves are likely to be unaware of the ironic discrepancies between their declared methods and principles and their own critical practice, since literature is more complex and contradictory than most theoretical schemes allow.

In his later work, de Man focuses not so much on the discrepancy between language and reality as he does on the self-contradiction within language itself. He observes that, especially in literary language, there is a tension between the literal or grammatical meaning of words and their figurative implications; even simple acts of reference can be interpreted figuratively, and no figure of speech is without its literal sense. In his reading of Yeats's "Among School Children," for example, de Man notes that the poem's final question – "How can we know the dancer from the dance?" – is usually read as a rhetorical question affirming the unity of the actor and his or her actions. However, de Man argues, "the question could just as well express bewilderment" (1984: 200).

De Man distinguishes sharply between literary criticism that assumes literature can provide models of wholeness, harmony, and reconciliation, and criticism like his own, which demonstrates the impossibility of any reconciliation between literature's fractured perspectives. In *Resistance to Theory* (1986), he identifies the former kind of criticism with literary aesthetics and claims that literary aesthetics ignores or glosses over the social and linguistic contradictions that literature reveals. By contrast, he designates his own critical practice as theory. Theory inspires resistance because it insists on exposing the fundamental contradictions of both literature and social life.

Reference

Paul de Man, *The Rhetoric of Romanticism*, New York: Columbia University Press, 1984.

Suggested reading

Christopher Norris, *Paul de Man: Deconstruction and the Critique of Aesthetic Ideology*, New York: Routledge, 1988.

Resistance to Theory

Literariness, however, is often misunderstood in a way that has provoked much of the confusion which dominates today's polemics. It is frequently assumed, for instance, that literariness is another word for, or another mode of, aesthetic response. The use, in conjunction with literariness, of such terms as style and stylistics, form or even "poetry" (as in "the poetry of grammar"), all of which carry strong aesthetic connotations, helps to foster this confusion, even among those who first put the term in circulation. Roland Barthes, for example, in an essay properly and revealingly dedicated to Roman Jakobson, speaks eloquently of the writer's quest for a perfect coincidence of the phonic properties of a word with its signifying function. . . . Barthes and Jakobson often seem to invite a purely aesthetic reading, yet there is a part of their statement that moves in the opposite direction. For the convergence of sound and meaning celebrated by Barthes . . . is also considered here to be a mere *effect* which language can perfectly well achieve, but which bears no substantial relationship, by analogy or by ontologically grounded imitation, to anything beyond that particular effect. It is a rhetorical rather than an aesthetic function of language, an identifiable trope (paronomasis) that operates on the level of the signifier and contains no responsible pronouncement on the nature of the world – despite its powerful potential to create the opposite illusion. The phenomenality of the signifier, as sound, is unquestionably involved in the correspondence between the name and the thing named, but the link, the relationship between word and thing, is not phenomenal but conventional.

Reprinted from: Paul de Man, *The Resistance to Theory*, Minneapolis: University of Minnesota Press, 1986, pp. 9–12. For up-to-date copyright and publication information see Acknowledgments.

This gives the language considerable freedom from referential restraint, but it makes it epistemologically highly suspect and volatile, since its use can no longer be said to be determined by considerations of truth and falsehood, good and evil, beauty and ugliness, or pleasure and pain. Whenever this autonomous potential of language can be revealed by analysis, we are dealing with literariness and, in fact, with literature as the place where this negative knowledge about the reliability of linguistic utterance is made available. The ensuing foregrounding of material, phenomenal aspects of the signifier creates a strong illusion of aesthetic seduction at the very moment when the actual aesthetic function has been, at the very least, suspended. It is inevitable that semiology or similarly oriented methods be considered formalistic, in the sense of being aesthetically rather than semantically valorized, but the inevitability of such an interpretation does not make it less aberrant. Literature involves the voiding, rather than the affirmation, of aesthetic categories. One of the consequences of this is that, whereas we have traditionally been accustomed to reading literature by analogy with the plastic arts and with music, we now have to recognize the necessity of a non-perceptual, linguistic moment in painting and music, and learn to *read* pictures rather than to *imagine* meaning.

If literariness is not an aesthetic quality, it is also not primarily mimetic. Mimesis becomes one trope among others, language choosing to imitate a non-verbal entity just as paronomasis "imitates" a sound without any claim to identity (or reflection on difference) between the verbal and non-verbal elements. The most misleading representation of literariness, and also the most recurrent objection to contemporary literary theory, considers it as pure verbalism, as a denial of the reality principle in the name of absolute fictions, and for reasons that are said to be ethically and politically shameful. The attack reflects the anxiety of the aggressors rather than the guilt of the accused. By allowing for the necessity of a non-phenomenal linguistics, one frees the discourse on literature from naive oppositions between fiction and reality, which are themselves an offspring of an uncritically mimetic conception of art. In a genuine semiology as well as in other linguistically oriented theories, the referential function of language is not being denied – far from it; what is in question is its authority as a model for natural or phenomenal cognition. Literature is fiction not because it somehow refuses to acknowledge "reality," but because it is not *a priori* certain that language functions according to principles which are those, or which are *like* those, of the phenomenal world. It is therefore not *a priori* certain that literature is a reliable source of information about anything but its own language.

It would be unfortunate, for example, to confuse the materiality of the signifier with the materiality of what it signifies. This may seem obvious enough

What does he have in mind when he speaks of the aesthetic fn.?

on the level of light and sound, but it is less so with regard to the more general phenomenality of space, time or especially of the self; no one in his right mind will try to grow grapes by the luminosity of the word "day," but it is very difficult not to conceive the pattern of one's past and future existence as in accordance with temporal and spatial schemes that belong to fictional narratives and not to the world. This does not mean that fictional narratives are not part of the world and of reality; their impact upon the world may well be all too strong for comfort. What we call ideology is precisely the confusion of linguistic with natural reality, of reference with phenomenalism. It follows that, more than any other mode of inquiry, including economics, the linguistics of literariness is a powerful and indispensable tool in the unmasking of ideological aberrations, as well as a determining factor in accounting for their occurrence. Those who reproach literary theory for being oblivious to social and historical (that is to say ideological) reality are merely stating their fear at having their own ideological mystifications exposed by the tool they are trying to discredit. They are, in short, very poor readers of Marx's *German Ideology*.

In these all too summary evocations of arguments that have been much more extensively and convincingly made by others, we begin to perceive some of the answers to the initial question: what is it about literary theory that is so threatening that it provokes such strong resistances and attacks? It upsets rooted ideologies by revealing the mechanics of their workings; it goes against a powerful philosophical tradition of which aesthetics is a prominent part; it upsets the established canon of literary works and blurs the borderlines between literary and non-literary discourse. By implication, it may also reveal the links between ideologies and philosophy. All this is ample enough reason for suspicion, but not a satisfying answer to the question. For it makes the tension between contemporary literary theory and the tradition of literary studies appear as a mere historical conflict between two modes of thought that happen to hold the stage at the same time. If the conflict is merely historical, in the literal sense, it is of limited theoretical interest, a passing squall in the intellectual weather of the world. As a matter of fact, the arguments in favor of the legitimacy of literary theory are so compelling that it seems useless to concern oneself with the conflict at all. Certainly, none of the objections to theory, presented again and again, always misinformed or based on crude misunderstandings of such terms as mimesis, fiction, reality, ideology, reference and, for that matter, relevance, can be said to be of genuine rhetorical interest.

Arthur C. Danto

(1924–)

Danto's powers as an aesthetic theorist develop from his engagement with the visual arts: painting, and sculpture. Nevertheless his thinking applies just as well to literary works inasmuch as they are also representational endeavors. Danto's arguments are generally directed towards countering Plato's disenfranchisement of art. In one respect he echoes Nietzsche's rebuttal to that "aesthetic socratism" whereby the philosopher makes all the functions of the artist submit to a standard of rational ontology. Danto understands this as a two-stage attack on art. Philosophy produces a straw man for its own critical powers and, in the act of doing so, colonizes the realm of the beautiful with rationalistic principle. Danto promises to re-enfranchise art *vis-à-vis* the authority of philosophical wisdom. Specifically he will justify the artwork in terms of its "aboutness" with respect to the world in which it is produced and appreciated.

Danto does not, however, indulge a conventional mimeticism. Rather, under the influence of Wittgenstein, Danto is interested in investigating the status of the art object in so far as it has a capacity to invoke frames of reference within which its own significance is made apparent. Wittgenstein famously wondered how we should account for differences between indiscernibles. How does one interpret the difference between raising one's right arm and seeing one's arm go up? How does one understand that there are two meanings for the same reality? Danto gave such questioning a very concrete relevance to aesthetics by addressing Marcel Duchamp's practice of trading in ready-mades: exhibiting a prefabricated and mass-marked urinal or a snow shovel in museum space. Danto drew the conclusion that what distinguishes ordinary objects from art objects was the dependency of the latter on interpretive structures. Duchamp's works are specifically dependent upon the interpretative biases latent in the history of art production. More generally, Danto reverses the usual priorities of art criticism and asserts that artistic appreciation always follows interpretation.

In the passage from "Aesthetics and the Work of Art," excerpted below, Danto takes off from a consideration of the paintings of Roy Lichtenstein. Lichtenstein's

signature technique was a hand-painted mimicry of the Ben Day dots, the techno-
logical signature, so to speak, of image reproduction processes. Danto is interested
in the fact that the artist's hand-painted reproduction of the process of mechanical
reproduction graphically reveals how artistic practice is densely theoretical at the
same time that it is vividly presentational. In other words, Lichtenstein's dots are
about the process that they belie. By belying it they transfigure it into something
that has never been apparent in our habituated reception of those dot matrix images,
which come to us from the Sunday comics, the wire services, or the television screen.

Thus Danto asserts that the aesthetic qualities of the artwork are in no way essential to its formal embodiment. But its formal embodiment is essential to the assertion that aesthetic qualities are present as pretexts for interpretive re-framing. In
Danto's words, "the aesthetic qualities of the work are a function of their own historical identity, so that one may have to revise utterly one's assessment of a work
in the light of what one comes to know about it." This observation conveys his conviction that while many forms of representation may depend upon an interpretive
frame of reference – including newspaper articles, biographical narrative, historical
records – the artwork uniquely *transfigures* itself in invoking commentary about what
it represents: the artwork is "a transfigurative representation rather than a representation *tout court*."

Aesthetics and the Work of Art

The first thing we must note about Lichtenstein's paintings is that *they* have
none of the properties associated with what they are of. One would traditionally have expected this as a matter of course, since paintings of landscapes
seldom have the properties of what they show, but it is somewhat remarkable
here through the fact that these are paintings of painting. These, for example,
show brushstrokes but do not consist, in their own right, of brushstrokes, and
for just the reason the spectator must grasp the discrepancies between what is
shown and the way in which it is shown, surface and subject being virtually
antonymic. The brushstrokes are shown in a way that is inconsistent with what
they are in further ways still: they are imprisoned in heavy black outlines, as
in Leger's work or, better, as in a child's coloring book. But the brushstrokes
these paintings are about were not filled into preexisting boundaries; they
were densely swept across the canvas in a single impulsive gesture, defining
their own boundaries. By contrast with the free and liberated spirit with which
those strokes emerged onto their canvases, these strokes are shown almost

Reprinted from: Arthur C. Danto, *The Transfiguration of the Commonplace*, Cambridge, Mass.:
Harvard University Press, 1981, pp. 109–14.

mechanically, almost as though printed onto Lichtenstein's canvases; and indeed Lichtenstein uses the Ben Day dots of mechanical reproduction processes. So the canvases look like mechanical representations of vital gestures.

But there is another level still, which we ascend to when we realize that the dots were not printed but painted in, each one deposited onto the surface by hands: so we have artistic representations of mechanical processes. The monotony of the process of painting these in was somewhat mitigated through the fact that Lichtenstein used a lot of students from his classes at Rutgers, and again, I think, the knowledge of this history has to be taken as a comment upon the ridiculously heroized view of The Artist in the period when brush-strokes meant the opposite of what *this* mode of representing them shows. The interposition of the Ben Day dot has a profound symbolism of its own, inasmuch as it encodes the manner in which we perceive the major events of our time, through the wine-service photograph and the television screen; the depiction of the victims of the Vietnam war takes on an added dimension of horror when the mechanical mode of depiction is incorporated as part of the image, for our experiences are modulated through the medium which has indeed, in MacLuhan's slogan, come to be part, at least, of the message. The brushstrokes of the masters of the 1950s were meant not to represent anything, simply to be: fresh created realities. And Lichtenstein has treated them as artists have always treated reality, namely as something to put into works of art. Thus victimized, these poor deflated swags stand like specimens of something once vital, in *representational* works that belie at every point the intentions of those painters whose life was defined by squeezing paint out like hoses gone mad. These paintings are a minor victory in the battle with reality. If the canvas is indeed the arena in which the battle goes on, it has been lost to representation in the canvases of Lichtenstein.

I have dwelt at such length upon Lichtenstein's paintings in part because they are so rich in their utilization of artistic theory: they are about theories they also reject, and they internalize theories it is required that anyone who may appreciate them must understand, and they allude to yet further theories, ignorance of which impoverishes one's appreciation of these works. What point could there be, for instance, to the dots, were someone unaware of the role dots play in mechanical reproduction and to the role of mechanical reproduction in the life of our culture? The paintings are points of intersection of so many strands in contemporary culture that it is not only difficult to imagine what some stranger to our culture would make of them, but, consistent with the form of artistic experimentation that has characterized my analysis throughout, it is difficult to see what works exactly like these but painted, suppose, in the 1860s would have meant. And my argument has been that, whatever we are to say about aesthetic responses, it is possible to imagine that works with a common material counterpart elicit very different responses. *These* paintings are deeply theoretic works, self-conscious to such a degree that it is difficult to know how much of the material correlate must be reckoned in as part of the artwork; so self-conscious are they, indeed, that they almost exemplify a Hegelian ideal in which matter is transfigured into spirit, in this case there being hardly an element of the material counterpart which may not be a candidate for an element in the artwork itself. I shall return to a proper analysis of this subsequently, but for the present I mean only to stress that whatever the counterfactual nineteenth-century counterparts to the Lichtenstein paintings may have been about, they could not have been about what the Lichtenstein's are about. Even if they were in some mad way about brushstrokes, the brushstrokes they were about would not have connoted a set of associations only available to those who had known about the dense artistic controversies of the 1950s. Of course, those paintings could have been a kind of crystal ball through which the art of the future might be glimpsed, but what could anyone have made of what they saw there?

I am trying to state that the "aesthetic object" is not some eternally fixed Platonic entity, a joy forever beyond time, space, and history, eternally there for the rapt appreciation of connoisseurs. It is not just that appreciation is a function of the cognitive location of the aesthete, but that the aesthetic qualities of the work are a function of their own historical identity, so that one may have to revise utterly one's assessment of a work in the light of what one comes to know about it; it may not even be the work one thought it was in the light of wrong historical information. An object of the sort made by Tony Smith could have been made almost any time in modern times – at least the material correlate could have been made at any such time – but imagine one having been made in Amsterdam in the 1630s, set down where there is no room for it in the artworld of the times, the golden age of Jan Steen and Van Goyen, and it enters that world as the Connecticut Yankee does the court of King Arthur. What could it be, what could it be about, even if the possibility of its being an artwork could have arisen for those whose concept of art consisted in portraits of one another in ruffed collars and tables piled up with grapes and oysters and dead rabbits, or peonies with a single drop of dew, a convex mirror in which the whole world could be reflected as in the Arnolfini wedding portrait? And since, if I am right in supposing that it could not be about whatever Tony Smith is about, how could this object have had any structure other than the structure of so many big slabs of black plywood nailed together?

In *Sein und Zeit*, Heidegger speaks of tools as forming a kind of total system – a *Zeugganzes* – which is a complex of interreferential tools, not remarkably different from a language game, if we follow Wittgenstein in thinking of sentences as tools in their own right, to be brought out for various choreographed uses. There cannot, thus, just be nails. If there are nails, there have to be hammers to drive them and boards to drive them through; and changes at one point in the system entail changes at other points. You cannot imagine someone saying that the Etruscans were the first to have typewriter ribbons, not even if you find some carbon stretch of silk ribbon at Cerveteri, for that cannot have been a typewriter ribbon, not even if found wrapped round some bronze wheels that look like the spools in a bronze age typewriter, for the whole system has to be there at once: paper, metal, keys, and so on. Some while ago a cache of Da Vinci manuscripts was found which excited cartoonists to make drawings in the Da Vincian style of such things as lightbulbs and electric sockets, like a Renaissance form of the sorts of things we see in drawings by Claes Oldenberg. This is a parody of the idea we have of the genius "ahead of his time," for there are certain ways in which nobody can be ahead of his time: a notched bronze wheel exactly like a bicycle sprocket found in excavations in Tibet could not have been a precocious bicycle sprocket, whatever its identity as an artifact. And something like this is true of artworks as well: you can certainly have objects – material counterparts – at any time in which it was technically possible for them to have come into existence; but the works, connected with the material counterparts in ways we have hardly begun to fathom, are referentially so interlocked into their own system of artworks and real things that it is almost impossible to think of what might be the response to the same object inserted in another time and place. A portrait painted by a Jesuit artist of the favorite concubine of the emperor of China, which used shadows to round her lovely face, was rejected by her as hideous, since she believed she was being represented as half-black and that the painting was a joke, even if, to our eyes, it might have rivaled in sensitivity the Genevra da Benci of Leonardo. A painting by one of our contemporary artists in the style of Giotto simply could not be responded to the way a Giotto could, to its "touching naiveté," not unless the artist were ignorant of the history of art and in some miracle of coincident creation had reinvented a Quattrocento style. And this would be like someone who, in contrast with Menard and out of springs of invention one can hardly guess at, wrote in ignorance of the original something we might consider indiscernible from *Don Quixote*.

These are by now familiar extensions of Wölfflin's thought that not everything is possible at every time. I have reraised these points here because we now have at least this piece of theoretical apparatus to work with: if we may distinguish between the artwork and its material counterpart, then it is possible to imagine two works done at very different times – Lichtenstein's brushstroke painting of 1965 and an imaged painting exactly like it done in 1865 – which share a material counterpart but which *have* to be distinctive works of art since they cannot conceivably be about the same thing. I have tried to sketch the intricate tensions between subject and surface in Lichtenstein's painting, in a partial effort to say what they consist in (they consist in part in just these tensions). It cannot be true the painting of 1865 is about what Lichtenstein's is. The question before us, accordingly, is what connection there is between the artwork in either case and the common material correlate, and this is what I wish to address myself to now. It obviously involves something I shall term "interpretation," and it is my view that whatever appreciation may come to, it must in some sense be a function of interpretation. That in a way is not very different from the slogan in the philosophy of science that there are no observations without theories; so in the philosophy of art there is no appreciation without interpretation. Interpretation consists in determining the relationship between a work of art and its material counterpart. But since nothing like this is involved with mere objects, aesthetic response to works of art presupposes a cognitive process that response to those mere things does not – though the matter is inevitably complicated by the fact that once the distinction is available, and because of the fact that works of art may so closely resemble mere real things, an act of disinterpretation may be required in cases of inverse confusion, where we take a mere thing to be a work of art. Of course there doubtless are cases where this is not required: sunsets and the Evening Star are properly not regarded as works of art inasmuch as artistic intervention has not yet made artworks of things that have sunsets and the Evening Star as material counterparts. But the options are available if in fact unexercised.

In any case, aesthetic response presupposes the distinction and hence cannot *simply* enter into the definition of art. The matter is even deeper than that. As we shall see, aesthetic appreciation of artworks has a different structure from aesthetic appreciation of mere things, however beautiful and irrespective of whether the sense of beauty is innate. It is not a philosophical question, but a psychological one, whether indeed there is an innate aesthetic sense. What is philosophical is the question of what the logic of such appreciation may be, and what the structural differences are between responding to artworks and responding to mere things.

Tony Bennett

(1940–)

A follower of the eminent cultural materialist thinker Raymond Williams, the British critic Tony Bennett gives a more emphatically Marxist, specifically Althusserian, inflection to the practice of cultural materialist critique. This anthropologically inspired method of cultural analysis works at bridging the distance between aesthetics and politics by recourse to what is frequently called "a sociology of social forms." In other words, the critic pays attention to the ways in which cultural institutions determine and regulate individual and group practices. According to this view the embodied forms of everyday social life are thought to articulate a grammar of oppressive power relations. Those relations warrant a strict critical scrutiny if we are to avoid the ideological distortions of exclusionary politics that they invariably promote.

For Bennett, the field of literature is deeply complicit in promoting social exclusionary judgments based on elitist standards of taste. Pundits of literary taste preserve its authority by denying any links between literature and the forces of cultural production that animate social forms outside the sacred province of art. Bennett's work is a reaction against the tradition of art theory and aesthetics that posits the artwork as a site of transcendent values, free of the constraints of time, history, and the struggles of daily social practice. He lays the blame for this distorting and socially elitist proposition at the door of Kantian aesthetics. Bennett rejects Kant's characterization of the aesthetic as a unique modality of the human subject's mental rapport with reality authenticated, as it is, by a test of logical and empirical disinterestedness. Kant, in this way, endowed the aesthetic with a universal aura. He presupposed the existence of the faculty for judgment in all people as a natural property of the human subject. This assumption allowed one to conclude that anyone whose sensibility is unreceptive to a specific work of art, or to a specific "school" of taste is disqualified from judgment by an unanalyzable flaw in their individual nature. As Bennett states, "Within such discourse, the subject who fails to appreciate correctly is regarded as being incompletely human." Bennett is therefore committed to demystifying the idea that the artwork can be discussed and understood exclusively from within the hermetic space of the artist's or the critic's subjectivity. On the contrary, the critic who takes up a position *outside literature*, "writes its history as a history of functions, rules, techniques and institutions – in short, a history like any other . . ." (p. 46).

Bennett chooses to bracket altogether the proposition that literature is a single discourse that can only be thought about aesthetically. He thinks that the rarified categories and judgmental terms, the rhetorical features, and other earmarks of literary analysis, conspire to blind us to the social determinants of literature outside literature. Even more important, from Bennett's point of view: the strictly aesthetic features ascribed to literature insulate it from other modes of analytical discourse – chiefly Marxist analysis. Those discourses are, in turn proscribed from making productive social use of literature. Bennett is disappointed even with Marxist critics, such as Herbert Marcuse, who prove themselves seduced by the "classical" faith in the essence of art, and assign to it a transhistorical significance. Though Marcuse admits that artistic practices change with changing historical conditions, and thus are not exclusively aesthetically determined, he grants to the finished artwork an essential nature that transcends its production. From Bennett's point of view, this burdens Marxist analysis with the need to reconcile two contradictory positions: that art practices, techniques, styles, etc. might be socially determined but that art is not.

Bennett boldly takes up his own position *outside literature*, with the intent of correcting the mistakes of aesthetic idealists within and without the ideological bastion of the aesthetic. He insists upon redefining literature specifically in terms of its social *use value*. Use value is a key term of Marxist critique which insists upon pegging human valuations of the object world to the situations of real human need. This privileges the context of the subject's immediate social relations. Bennett spurns aesthetic judgments circumscribed within a universalized subjectivity as "really useless knowledge." For Bennett, such knowledge serves only to preserve canons of taste as a social privilege to be lorded over quotidian experience. The myth of "great art" perpetuates a political oppression which only the dismantling of the aesthetic can bring to an end. The corollary of this project, for the literary critic, is to theorize the relations of literature to society without indulging any aesthetic expertise.

Note: Pages cited are from the edition from which the following excerpt is taken, details of which are given in the footnote.

Really Useless "Knowledge": A Political Critique of Aesthetics

Aesthetics and the Reform of the Subject

In summary, then, the inconclusive conclusion of Kant's *Critique* can be reduced to the following questions: Will the universality of taste, once it has

Reprinted from: Tony Bennett, *Outside Literature*, London and New York: Routledge, 1990, pp. 162–6.

been produced, turn out to be a natural and original property of the human subject? Or will the subject to which a universality of taste can appropriately be attributed turn out to be the product of a process of cultural and historical unification? This Kantian cliff-hanger has provided one of the central cleavages within the history of aesthetics, and has been particularly influential in distinguishing between conservative and radical positions. It is, however, of quite incidental significance since, whichever position is adopted, the structure of argumentation employed is essentially the same. Each requires that some means be found of anticipating, to recall Alan Durant's phrase, the "discernments of a hypothetical posterity" and further, in order to validate this construct, of disqualifying those whose judgments do not agree with the yet-to-be announced, but constantly deferred, edicts of a unified valuing subject. In Lukács's man-centred aesthetics, in which the questions Kant leaves open are closed in the name of a historicised narcissism, the empirical failure of subjects in the present to anticipate the judgements that will be pronounced once the cultural and historical process of man's unification has been completed is attributed to the effect of false consciousness on social agents. But Peter Fuller, who espouses a form of historicised biologism, is obliged to resort to similar arguments. Although positing an aesthetic sense based on certain innate biological properties, Fuller – given that few people seem to be correctly appreciating as their biologies say they ought to – must project this 'natural and original' property as a post-historical construct, destined to realise itself only in culturally propitious circumstances. Meanwhile, by deploying a many-stranded discourse of disqualification, Fuller ensures that there is no need to take account of any contradictory evidence which might call this theory into question:

> But, of course, despite what some of my critics have said, my position is in no sense whatever ahistorical. I argue that – like so many human potentialities – this biologically given aesthetic potentiality requires a facilitating environment to develop, and to flourish. The trouble at the moment is that the decline of religious belief, and the change in the nature of work brought about by the rise of modern industrialism, and its subsequent development, have combined to erode the conditions under which this great human potentiality can flourish. That's why it is no use going to the man in the street.[1]

Moreover, it matters relatively little, practically speaking, whether the criteria of disqualification which accompany aesthetic discourse are malignant or benign. So far as questions of cultural policy are concerned, the orientation of aesthetic discourse predisposes it to generate proposals directed to the subject rather than the object side of the aesthetic relation, and to do so no matter what its political affiliations. Although in one respect tilted forward in anticipating "the discernments of a hypothetical posterity," aesthetic discourse is also obliged to be backward-looking since, as a condition of its construction, it must, at least to some degree, accept and endorse the dominant systems of evaluation handed down from the past. If the aesthetic is to be founded as a universally present mode of the subject's mental relation to reality, then, first, the objects valued in the past must be regarded as the right ones and, second, they must also be regarded as having been valued for the right reasons even if only, as Lukács argued, in limited ways, whose real meaning is to be progressively revealed. As a consequence – and Brecht's comments on Lukács demonstrate this most forcibly[2] – aesthetic discourse, when directed to the object side of the aesthetic relation, can result only in a politics of preserving what has already been preserved and consecrated in the judgements of the past, or of emulating, extending and adapting earlier aesthetic models to fit new circumstances. Since, for the reasons outlined earlier, value is ultimately fetishised as a property of the object, an inability to judge correctly must be attributed to a failing of the subject, a failing accounted for by a series of cultural impediments whose removal thus becomes the primary goal of cultural policy – through education in liberal bourgeois aesthetics or, more usually in Marxist aesthetics, through the transformation of social relations. It is not surprising, therefore, that the predominant tendency within Marxist aesthetics has been to constitute the members of oppressed social groups as subjects whose aesthetic judgement needs to be transformed by being conformed to some already elaborated aesthetic norm. There is, as Fuller puts it, no need, in such approaches, to go to the man in the street, no need to articulate a socialist cultural policy to the different discourses of value which circulate within and between oppressed strata. It is therefore small wonder that Marxist aesthetic discourse has proved quite irrelevant outside the academy since it impedes, in its very structure, an adequate theorisation of the field of social-cultural relations within which a socialist cultural politics must intervene.

And it does more than that. Earlier in his exchange with Terry Eagleton, Peter Fuller argues that "my aesthetics (though not my politics) are closer to those of Roger Scruton and the 'Higher Toryism' of Peterhouse than to all that discourse – semiotics and post-structuralist deconstruction – which goes on up the road at King's."[3] And with good reason, although he is mistaken to believe that aesthetic and political positions might be so clearly disentangled. Indeed, I have tried to show that the structure of aesthetic discourse is inherently suspect in its political leanings no matter how radical the political protocols displayed on its surface. Jan Mukarovsky, writing of the mutual intolerance

of aesthetic norms in polemical situations, succinctly summarises the consequences which discrepant judgements of taste bring in their tow:

> The aesthetic norm is replaced by another, more authoritative norm – e.g., a
> moral norm – and one's opponent is called a deceiver, or else by an intellectual
> norm, in which case the opponent is called ignorant or stupid. Even when the
> right of the individual to make aesthetic judgements is emphasised, one hears in
> the same breath the request for responsibility for them: individual taste is a com-
> ponent of the human value of the person who exercises it.[4]

In making this remark, Mukarovsky has in mind the relative intolerance produced by the functioning, within specific discourses of value, of ideals of personality that are identifiably socially specific in their articulations. In the case
of aesthetic discourse, obliged to operate at the level of universality in order
to establish the aesthetic as a distinctive mode of the subject's mental relation
to reality, such relative intolerance becomes absolute. Within such discourse,
the subject who fails to appreciate correctly is regarded as being incompletely
human rather than merely being excluded from full title to the membership of
a specific valued and valuing community. To fail to appreciate correctly as a
proletarian revolutionary, Scottish Nationalist, radical feminist, or, indeed,
Peterhouse Tory is one thing – a failure to take up a particular articulated aesthetic, social and political positionality. An aesthetic, by contrast, no matter
how benign the discourse of disqualification it deploys, must operate more far-
reaching and complete exclusions and do so by virtue of its very structure.

Notwithstanding the scientific claims which often accompany it, aesthetic
discourse is ideological in the Althusserian sense that it functions as a discourse
producing subjects. The universal valuing subject (man) it constructs inter-
pellates the reader into the position of a valuing subject who is defined, in relation to the valued object (man), within a mirror structure of self-recognition.
Yes, indeed, man is manifested in this object; yes, indeed, I recognise myself
in it; isn't it it/aren't I wonderful? – such is the effect of aesthetic discourse for
the subject who takes up the position it offers. As ideology, however, aesthetic
discourse is characterised by a number of contradictions and torsions, albeit
ones which vary in their consequences depending on the political articulations
of such discourse. In the case of bourgeois aesthetics, the production of a
unified valuing subject, although necessary in providing a theoretical legitimation for the re-presentation of class-specific aesthetic norms as universally
valid, is also, at another level, sham, and necessarily so. Such discourse *requires*
its ignorants if it is to fulfill its practical function of social differentiation. The
problem associated with attempts to appropriate aesthetic discourse for social-

ism are, in many respects, the reverse for, willy nilly, such discourse produces its ignorants and, however benign, an accompanying condescension which serve as a blockage to both political analysis and cultural policy formation.

"Shouldn't we abolish aesthetics?" Brecht asked in the title of an article he wrote in 1927.[5] His answer, of course, was: yes. As a producer, Brecht clearly found the prescriptions of aesthetic systems restricting. If you want an aesthetic, he asked two decades later (clearly implying that he didn't), it could be summed up in the slogan that socialists need "many different methods in order to reach their objective".[6] This did not imply any neutrality with regard to the question of value on Brecht's part, but his concern was always with political use-value – local, temporary and conjunctural – which he felt able to address without the need to develop any general, universally applicable theory of the aesthetic as a distinct mode. I think Brecht was right. The political utility of discourses of value operating via the construction of an ideal of personality to which broadly based social aspirations can be articulated is unquestionable. There is, however, no reason to suppose that such discourses must be hitched up to the sphere of universality in order to secure their effectivity. To the contrary, given the configuration of today's political struggles, it is highly unlikely that an ideal of personality might be forged that would be of equal service in the multiple, intersecting, but equally non-coincident foci of struggle constituted by black, gay, feminist, socialist and, in some contexts, national liberation politics. In particular conjunctures, to be sure, an ideal of personality may be forged which serves to integrate – but always temporarily – such forces into a provisional unity. But this is not the basis for a generalisable and universalisable cultural politics. Nor is this the time for such a politics.

Notes

1   Terry Eagleton and Peter Fuller, 'The Question of Value: A Discussion', *New Left Review* 142, (1983), p. 79.
2   Bertolt Brecht, 'Against Georg Lukács', *New Left Review* 84 (1974).
3   Eagleton and Fuller 1983, pp. 78–9.
4   Jan Mukarovsky *Aesthetic Function, Norm and Value as Social Facts*, Ann Arbor: University of Michigan Press, 1970.
5   John Willett (ed.) *Brecht on Theatre*, London: Methuen, 1978, p. 20.
6   Ibid., p. 112.

Pierre Bourdieu

(1930–)

Pierre Bourdieu was educated as a philosopher, but early in his academic career he turned his attention to research in sociology and has become France's best known and most controversial sociologist. His analysis of the institutions of education and art have been particularly influential. Like other French scholars who were educated in the years following the Second World War, he came of age in an academic culture dominated by Marxism, structuralism, and phenomenology. While Bourdieu finds none of these perspectives adequate by itself, he manages to borrow and synthesize elements of each as he develops his methods for studying culture. From Marxism he takes a special sensitivity to the way in which class relations structure society by creating various hierarchies of status and prestige. From structuralism, which was especially influential on his early work in sociology, he inherits the notion that social action may be structured by sets of unspoken rules in the same way that language is structured by the rules of grammar even when the speaker is unaware of those rules. Finally, his work reflects phenomenology's concern with the ways that people experience their lives and with the mental structures which give those experiences meaning. It is Bourdieu's ambition to combine the kinds of objective accounts of social action that are found in Marxism and structuralism with the kinds of subjective accounts of experience found in phenomenological accounts of experience. By combining subjective and objective perspectives on social life, he hopes to reveal the ways in which even the most mundane aspects of everyday life – speech patterns, facial expressions, and ways of dressing, for instance – are social markers which differentiate social groups from one another and further distinguish individuals within a group, all according to various objective rules or codes of behavior of which social actors may not even be aware.

According to Bourdieu's analysis, social activity is organized around *fields* in which individuals compete for various kinds of goods, including money, class standing, prestige, and power. Art, for instance is a field, as are various academic disciplines and industries such as film and fashion design. Bourdieu names the competitors within any given field the *habitus* (both singular and plural). A habitus is "a system of durable transposable dispositions, structured structures predisposed to act as

structuring structures" (1990: 53). That is, the behavior of each individual is structured by the social position into which that individual is born, but in acting out
the logic of his or her set of dispositions, the individual inevitably reproduces these
dispositions and further reinforces or modifies the rules of the fields of struggle.
Bourdieu insists that all of the inclinations and strategies of the habitus are the
product of social conditioning, but he admits that this socialization is very complex
and is open to creative modifications by various individuals. As a consequence, he
denies that human behavior can ever be completely predicted or explained by the
logic of the habitus. Bourdieu uses the term "capital" to describe the various kinds
of resources which people (habitus) hope to achieve in their struggle in a particular
field. These include economic capital (money invested in the market), symbolic
capital (prestige), and cultural capital (education and other markers of class status).

Two of Bourdieu's most important works, *Distinction* and *The Rule of Art* have
been devoted to extended analyses of the field(s) of art and literature. As the following excepts from *The Rule of Art* makes clear, Bourdieu analyzes art as a field that generates cultural capital or class status. Both the artist and the art consumer, he claims, are
driven by a need for social recognition, although they usually mistakenly believe that
the value of the art they produce and consume lies in the art object itself, and not in its
power to procure social recognition. Here he describes the way in which "high" art
(the subfield of restricted production) is related to popular art (the subfield of large-
scale production). As he points out, certain forms of high art derive their ability to
confer social distinction by the fact that they are *not* popular with the general public.

Reference

Pierre Bourdieu, *Logic of Practice*, trans. Richard Nice, Cambridge: Polity Press, 1990.

Suggested reading

Richard Harker, Cheleen Mahar, and Chris Wilkes (eds.), *An Introduction to the Work of Pierre
Bourdieu*, London: Macmillan, 1990.

The Author's Point of View

Some General Properties of Fields of Cultural Production

The science of cultural works presupposes three operations which are as
necessary and necessarily linked as the three levels of social reality that they

Reprinted from: Pierre Bourdieu, *The Rules of Art: Genesis and Structure of the Literary Field*,
translated by Susan Emanuel, Oxford: Polity Press, 1996, pp. 214–17, 231–2.

apprehend. First, one must analyse the position of the literary (etc.) field within the field of power, and its evolution in time. Second, one must analyse the internal structure of the literary (etc.) field, a universe obeying its own laws of functioning and transformation, meaning the structure of objective relations between positions occupied by individuals and groups placed in a situation of competition for legitimacy. And finally, the analysis involves the genesis of the habitus of occupants of these positions, that is, the systems of dispositions which, being the product of a social trajectory and of a position within the literary (etc.) field, find in this position a more or less favourable opportunity to be realized (the construction of the field is the logical preamble for the construction of the social trajectory as a series of positions successively occupied in this field). . . .[1]

Thus the real hierarchy of explanatory factors requires a reversal of the approach ordinarily adopted by analysts. On no account do we ask how such and such a writer came to be what he was – at the risk of falling into the retrospective illusion of a reconstructed coherence. Rather we must ask how, given his social origin and the socially constituted properties he derived from it, that writer has managed to occupy or, in certain cases, produce the positions which the determined state of the literary (etc.) field offered (already there or still to be made), and thus how that writer managed to give a more or less complete and coherent expression to the position-takings inscribed in a potential state within these positions (for example, in the case of Flaubert, the contradictions inherent in art for art's sake and, more generally, in the condition of the artist).

The Literary Field in the Field of Power

A number of the practices and representations of artists and writers (for example, their ambivalence as much towards the 'people' as towards the 'bourgeois') can only be explained by reference to the field of power, inside of which the literary (etc.) field is itself in a dominated position. The field of power is the space of relations of force between agents or between institutions having in common the possession of the capital necessary to occupy the dominant positions in different fields (notably economic or cultural). It is the site of struggles between holders of different powers (or kinds of capital) which, like the symbolic struggles between artists and the 'bourgeois' in the nineteenth century, have at stake the transformation or conservation of the relative value of different kinds of capital, which itself determines, at any moment, the forces liable to be engaged in these struggles.[2]

A real challenge to all forms of economism, the literary order (etc.) which was progressively instituted in the course of a long and slow process of autonomization presents itself as an inverted economic world: those who enter it have an interest in disinterestedness. Like *prophecy*, and especially the prophecy of doom, which according to Weber proves its authenticity by the fact that it secures no remuneration,[3] the heretical rupture with current artistic traditions finds its criterion of authenticity in disinterestedness. This does not mean that there is no economic logic in this charismatic economy founded on the sort of social miracle which is an act free of any determination other than the intrinsically aesthetic intention. We shall see that there are economic conditions for the economic challenge which leads to its being oriented towards the most risky positions of the intellectual and artistic avant-garde, and for the aptitude to maintain oneself there in a lasting way in the absence of any financial counterpart; and there are also economic conditions of access to symbolic profits – which are themselves capable of being converted, in the more or less long term, into economic profits. . . .

Because of the hierarchy established in the relations among the different kinds of capital and among their holders, the fields of cultural production occupy a dominated position, temporally, within the field of power. As liberated as they may be from external constraints and demands, they are traversed by the necessity of the fields which encompass them: the need for profit, whether economic or political. It follows that they are at any one time the site of a struggle between two principles of hierarchization: the heteronomous principle, which favours those who dominate the field economically and politically (for example, 'bourgeois art'), and the autonomous principle (for example, 'art for art's sake'), which leads its most radical defenders to make of temporal failure a sign of election and of success a sign of compromise with the times.[4] The state of relations of forces in this struggle depends on the autonomy which the field *globally* disposes of, meaning the degree to which its own norms and sanctions manage to impose themselves on the ensemble of producers of cultural goods and on those who – occupying the temporally (and temporarily) dominant position in the field of cultural production (successful playwrights or novelists) or aspiring to occupy it (dominated producers available for mercenary tasks) – are the nearest to the occupants of the homologous position in the field of power, and hence the most sensitive to external demands and the most heteronomous.

The degree of autonomy of a field of cultural production is revealed to the extent that the principle of external hierarchization there is subordinated to the principle of internal hierarchization: the greater the autonomy, the more the symbolic relationship of forces is favourable to producers who are the most independent of demand, and the more the break tends to be noticeable between the two poles of the field, that is, between the *subfield of restricted production*, where producers have only other producers for clients (who are also their direct competitors), and the *subfield of large-scale production*, which finds itself *symbolically* excluded and discredited. In the former, whose fundamental faith is independence with respect to external demands, the economy of practices is founded, as in the game of *loser takes all*, on an inversion of the fundamental principles of the field of power and of the economic field. It excludes the quest for profit and it guarantees no correspondence of any kind between monetary investments and revenues; it condemns the pursuit of honours and temporal standing.[5]

According to the *principle of external hierarchization* in force in the temporally dominant regions of the field of power (and also in the economic field) – that is, according to the criterion of *temporal success* measured by indices of commercial success (such as print runs, the number of performances of plays, etc.) or social notoriety (such as decorations, commissions, etc.) – pre-eminence belongs to artists (etc.) who are known and recognized by the 'general public'. On the other hand, the *principle of internal hierarchization*, that is, the degree of specific consecration, favours artists (etc.) who are known and recognized by their peers and only by them (at least in the initial phase of their enterprise) and who owe their prestige, at least negatively, to the fact that they make no concessions to the demand of the 'general public'. . . .

Position, Disposition and Position-Taking

The field is a network of objective relations (of domination or subordination, of complementarity or antagonism, etc.) between positions – for example, the position corresponding to a genre like the novel or to a subcategory like the society novel, or from another point of view, the position locating a review, a salon, or a circle as the gathering place of a group of producers. Each position is objectively defined by its objective relationship with other positions, or, in other terms, by the system of relevant (meaning efficient) properties which allow it to be situated in relation to all others in the structure of the global distribution of properties. All positions depend, in their very existence, and in the determinations they impose on their occupants, on their actual and potential situation in the structure of the field – that is to say, in the structure and distribution of those kinds of capital (or of power) whose possession governs the obtaining of specific profits (such as literary prestige) put into play in the field. To different *positions* (which, in a universe as little institutionalized as the literary or artistic field,[6] can only be apprehended through the properties of their occupants) correspond homologous *position-takings*, including literary or artistic works, obviously, but also political acts and discourses, manifestos or polemics, etc. – and this obliges us to challenge the alternative between an internal reading of the work and an explanation based on the social conditions of its production or consumption.

In the phase of equilibrium, the *space of positions* tends to govern the *space of position-takings*. It is to the specific 'interests' associated with different positions in the literary field that one must look for the principle of literary (etc.) position-takings, and even the political position-takings outside the field. Historians, who had the habit of going in the other direction, ended up discovering, with Robert Darnton, what a political revolution might owe to the contradictions and conflicts of the 'Republic of Letters'.[7] Artists do not really *feel* their relationship to the 'bourgeois' except through their relationship to 'bourgeois art', or, more generally, to the agents or institutions which express or incarnate the 'bourgeois' necessity at the very heart of the field, such as the 'bourgeois artist'. In short, the only way external determinations are exercised is through the intermediary of specific forces and forms of the field, that is, after having undergone a *restructuration*, and this restructuration is all the more major the more autonomous the field and the more capable it is of imposing its specific logic, which only represents the objectification of its whole history in institutions and mechanisms.[8]

It is thus only by taking into account the specific logic of the field as a space of positions and position-takings, actual and potential (the space of possibles or the problematic), that one may adequately understand the form that these external forms may take in the course of their translation according to this logic. This is so whether it is a matter of social determinations operating through the habitus of producers who have been durably fashioned by them, or the determinations exercised on the field at the actual moment of the work's production, such as an economic crisis or an expansionist movement, a revolution or an epidemic.[9] In other words, economic or morphological determinations are only exercised through the specific structure of the field and they may take completely unexpected routes – with economic expansion, for example, liable to exercise its most important effects through mediations such as a growth in the volume of producers or in the audience of readers and spectators.

The literary (etc.) field is a force-field acting on all those who enter it, and acting in a differential manner according to the position they occupy there (whether, to take the points furthest removed from each other, that of a writer of hit plays or that of an avant-garde poet), and at the same time it is field of competitive struggles which tend to conserve or transform this force-field. And the position-takings (works, political manifestos or demonstrations, and so on), which one may and should treat for analytical purposes as a 'system' of oppositions, are not the result of some kind of objective collusion, but rather the product and the stake of a permanent conflict. In other words, the generative and unifying principle of this 'system' is the struggle itself.

Notes

1   This chapter, which aims to draw out of the historical analyses of the literary field presented above some propositions which are valid for the whole set of fields of cultural production, tends to leave aside the specific logic of each of the special-ized fields (religious, political, juridical, philosophical, scientific) that I have analysed elsewhere and which will be the subject of a forthcoming book.

     . . . 'he' should be taken to refer to female agents as well [as male], and vice versa [Trans.]

2   The notion of field of power has been introduced (cf. P. Bourdieu, 'Champ de pouvoir, champ intellectuel et habitus de classe', *Scolies* 1 (1971): 7–26) in order to account for the *effects* which may be observed at the very heart of the literary or artistic field and which are exercised, with different strengths, on the ensemble of writers or artists. The content of the notion has been made gradually more precise, notably thanks to the research carried out on the Grandes Écoles and on the set of dominant positions to which they lead (cf. P. Bourdieu, *Noblesse d'État* (Paris: Minuit, 1989), pp. 375–6; in English as *The State Nobility* (Cambridge: Polity, 1995)).

3   Cf. M. Weber, *Ancient Judaism*, trans. Hans Gerth and Don Martindale (Glencoe: Free Press, 1952), pp. 278ff.

4   The status of 'social art', in this respect, is completely ambiguous: even if it refers artistic or literary production to external functions (for which the proponents of 'art for art's sake' do not fail to reproach it), it shares with 'art for art's sake' a radical challenge to worldly success and that 'bourgeois art' which recognizes it while looking down on the values of 'disinterestedness'.

5   It can be understood how by this logic, at least in certain sectors of the field of painting at certain times, the absence of any training and any scholarly consecra-tion may appear as a form of glory. [apparent]

6   There is nothing to be gained by replacing the notion of literary field with that of 'institution': besides the fact that it risks suggesting, by its Durkheimian connota-tions, a consensual image of a very conflictual universe, this notion causes one of the most significant properties of the literary field to disappear – its *weak degree of institutionalization*. This is seen, among other indices, in the total absence of arbi-trage and legal or institutional guarantee in conflicts of priority or authority and, more generally, in the struggles for the defence or conquest of dominant positions. Thus, in the conflicts between Breton and Tzara, the former, during the 'Congress for the determination of directives and the defence of the modern spirit' which he organized, has no other recourse than to anticipate the intervention of the police in case of disruption, and during the final assault to Tzara on the occasion of the

soirée at the Coeur à Barbe, he resorts to insults and blows (he breaks the arm of Pierre de Massot with a blow of his cane), while Tzara appeals to the police (cf. J.-P. Bertrand, J. Dubois and P. Durand, 'Approche institutionnelle du premier surréalisme, 1919–1924', *Pratiques* 38 (1983): 27–53).

7 Cf. especially R. Darnton, 'Policing writers in Paris circa 1750', *Representations* 5 (1984): 1–32.

8 As we have seen, that sociology which links the characteristics of works directly to the social origins of authors (cf. for example R. Escarpit, *Sociologie de la littérature* (Pairs: PUF, 1958)) or to groups to whom they were addressed, either real (patrons) or supposed (cf. for example F. Antal, *Florentine Painting and its Social Background* (Cambridge: Harvard University Press, 1986), or L. Goldmann, *Le Dieu caché* (Paris: Gallimard, 1956)), conceive of the relationship between the social world and cultural works in terms of the logic of *reflection*, and ignore the *refraction* exercised by the field of cultural production.

9 While an event such as the Black Death of the summer of 1348 determines the general direction of a global change in the themes of painting (the image of Christ, relations among figures, exaltation of the Church, etc.), this direction is reinterpreted and translated as a function of specific traditions, associated with local particularities of the field in the course of being established, as is shown by the fact that they appear in different forms in Florence and Sienna (cf. M. Meiss, *Painting in Florence and Sienna after the Black Death* (Princeton: Princeton University Press, 1951)).

Jean-Luc Nancy
(1940–)

Jean-Luc Nancy is a contemporary French philosopher teaching currently at the University of the Human Sciences in Strasbourg. He is a thinker dedicated to following out the consequences of phenomenological inquiry as initiated by Hegel and continued in the work of Heidegger and Derrida. Nancy's specific importance for literary aesthetics inheres in his ambition to employ the métier of deconstructive thought as a resource for linking aesthetics to politics. In his effort to debunk our traditional impulse to understand the aesthetic as a bracketing of the ordinary sense of the world, and hence as averse to the political, Nancy has recently focused quite literally on the irreducibility of the senses in the aesthetic.

In several previous works, *The Literary Absolute* (co-authored with Philip Lacoue-Labarthe, 1988), *The Birth to Presence* (1993) and *The Muses* (1996), Nancy has been seeking to throw off the fetters of a dichotomous western logic that makes thought and feeling, absolute and relative value, transcendence and immanence, and art and politics, mutually exclusive propositions. Nancy wants to think beyond the paradox that, by their incommensurability, such dichotomies foster *absolutely* relative values. For Nancy, a return to the experience of sense, and by extension *aisthesis* (the Greek source for the modern term "aesthetics"), is a hedge against this value relativism. Nancy views the aesthetic as a site of resistance to idealized meaning, at either pole of dichotomous logic. The aesthetic resists reductive rationalization in much the way that sense experience resists being colonized by concepts.

Rather than falling into the trap of reifying sense itself, however, Nancy asks us to see *aisthesis* as a border realm between opposed registers of experience. The aesthetic is a mobilization of sense that is neither sense nor Sense, neither percept nor concept. It is neither a counter of body nor of mind. It is neither present nor absent. Nancy asserts that if, in the context of this skepticism, one asks about the "sense of the world," one cannot solicit an adequate answer from the realms of Sense or the world. In other words, one must eschew both the rationalizing imperatives that make "Sense" of world at the expense of sensation, and the multiplicity of sense experiences that come at the expense of any possible generalizing beyond the immediate, physical, particular.

Following this logic, Nancy asserts that where there can be no absolute value, relative value will likewise cease to be a controlling conceit of human knowledge. Reality itself, as we know it in terms of our dichtomous logics, begins to fade. Hence Nancy's elusive formulation: "The sensible or the aisthetic is the outside-of-itself through which and *as* which there is the relation to itself of a sense in general, or through which there is the *toward* of sense." Within the constraints of this understanding, Nancy says that our grasp of the relation of sense to world becomes "fragmentary".

Indeed, Nancy characterizes his recent work in terms of an aesthetics of fragmentation. But we must consider closely what he means. We might be tempted to think that Nancy is privileging the fragment as a formal lever against the concepts of unity and totality that have such deep ideological roots in art theory. But Nancy is quick to admonish that *his* fragment is not the piece that is fallen away from a broken whole. Rather the fragment instances the "explosive splintering of that which is neither immanent nor transcendent. The in-finite explosion of the finite." The fragment is not Nancy's token of the incompleteness of art, which he thinks would be forever haunted by the ghost of totality, but an index of the artwork's relatedness to what is other than itself. Nancy insists that this is its political nature as well, in the sense that the fragment is, above all else, a mode of doing that escapes the limitations of sensuous *poiesis*, on the one hand, and rational *praxis* on the other.

Art, a Fragment

"Aisthesis"

It is a matter, then, of the relations between art and sense.[1] If the "absence" of sense – to take up Blanchot's word once again – defines the very sense of sense, and not its position or its modality, if this "absence" is nothing other than the sense of being insofar as it is in play *as the existence that is its own sense*, in other words – the words that have in the history of art a singular echo – if sense is the nudity of existing, in what way can this *nudity* be or become the *subject* of art? (In what way, perhaps, has it already become the subject of art?)

What we are asking here is thus what makes art apt to disengage sense in this way, this sense of sense: that existence is (the surprise of) sense, without any other signification.

Reprinted from: Jean-Luc Nancy, *The Sense of the World*, translated by Jeffry S. Librett, Minneapolis: University of Minnesota Press, 1997, pp. 128–34.

What we are asking here in the same movement is thus also if there is something in art that would be "essential," and how it might be "essential," to nude existence – and that would not come down to merely embellishing this existence. In other words, is art necessary to the articulation of sense in its "absence," in its "surprise"? Is it necessary to the thought of the sense of the world? And how does this involve fragmentation? . . .

The sensible or the aisthetic is the outside-of-itself through which and *as* which there is the relation to itself of a sense in general, or through which there is the *toward* of sense. But there is no sense "in general," nor is there a generic sense. There is sense only in local difference and differing division. Insensible différ*a*nce is sensible: it is the insensible in the completely sensible, infinitesimally sensible sense we give to the word when we speak, for example, of an "insensible diminution of the light." The five senses are not the fragments of a transcendent or immanent sense. They are the fragmentation or the fractality of the sense that is sense *only as fragment*.

Even if one affirms, with Aristotle, that there is no region of the sensible other than those by which our senses are affected, one will still not be able to produce the reality of a sensible Totality: the whole of the sensible owes its being only to its division, its dis-sent. But this is how it makes up the whole of this world here: nontotalizable totality and still without remainder – or at least without remainder that would not be in turn traced out along the surface of this world here. One should not even say that the "sensible whole" is *partes extra partes*, if this risks giving the impression that it is a matter of parts of a unity. The exteriority of sensible things is all there is of sensible interiority. In the same way, the reciprocal exteriority of the arts is the only interiority of their order, and the internal affinities of this order, Charles Baudelaire's "correspondences," always have the paradoxical character of affinities by incompatibility. The arts communicate only through the impossibility of passing from one to the other. Each one is at the threshold of the others.[2]

This fractality of (the) sense(s), exposed in the very place of the truth of sense, would be what is at stake in art, henceforth and for a long time to come – and perhaps also for a long time since.

This is indeed why aesthetics and art appear in our history (I mean appear as irreducible places of thought that seem necessary to the determination or to the problematization *of* sense itself) when the intelligibility of sense, in its cosmocosmetology, vanishes. This is what happens between the eighteenth century and Hegel. And this is why, when Hegel announces that art "is henceforth for us a thing of the past," he is announcing nothing other than the end of the beautiful (re)presentation of intelligible Sense – that is, of what he also calls "the religion of art" – and the sublation of this presentation in its modern mode of truth, the mode of the concept, philosophical "gray," the achieved immanence (without sensible difference) of a transcendence that has wholly come back to itself.

But at the same time, with exactly the same gesture, Hegel *delivers* art for itself: he delivers it from service to transcendence in immanence, and he delivers it to detached, fragmentary truth. Hegel, *volens nolens*, registers and salutes in fact *the birth of art*, the detachment of this "concept" that will henceforth be autonomous, exposed as the very detachment, separation, and fragmentation of sense.[3] Without a doubt, for Hegel, "the specific modes of the sensuous being of art are themselves a totality of necessary differences in art – the *particular arts*"; but this totality realizes itself only in maintaining its differentiation:

> What the particular arts realize in individual works of art is, according to the Concept of art, only the universal forms of the self-unfolding Idea of beauty. It is as the external actualization of this Idea that the wide Pantheon of art is rising. Its architect and builder is the self-comprehending spirit of beauty, but to complete it will need the history of the world in its development through thousands of years.[4]

Thus, the same Hegel who had presented the end of ancient religion[5] as the end of art in the death of the divine life that animated art (the "death of the great Pan") here presents art itself as the temple of all the gods, the numerous gods who are no longer gods but art itself in all its scintillating fragments – and this temple is on the scale of the history of the world. . . .

There remains then – what remains in the self-deconstruction to which the Occident has stubbornly and rigorously applied itself, precisely by reason of (and in proportion to) that nonpresentation of its Self to which it was destined from the beginning (to which it was destined by its own demand for truth, which for this reason can always dialecticize itself into "nihilism" as also into "nihilist" art). And what remains thus, or what is *coming* and does not stop coming as what remains, is what we call *existence*. It is "the existence of being," not in the sense of a predicate distinct from its essence, but in the sense of being that *is transitively* existence, or that *ex-ists*. Being exists the existent: it does not give the existent its sense *as* presupposition and end, but, rather, it is sense given with existence, as existence, more than a gift, being *toward* the world, where the world is not construed as a surrounding space, but as the multiple tracing out [*frayage*] of the singularity of existence. The world is multiple in regions and regimens of the existent, multiple in individuals and in events within each individual, but, first of all (and all the way to the end), it is multiple in materials, in material fragmentations of sense: sensible existence, fractal existence.

Fragment: no longer the piece fallen from a broken set, but the explosive splintering of that which is neither immanent nor transcendent. The in-finite explosion of the finite. Not the piece that has fallen, and even less the piece that has fallen into decay, but the piece that has *befallen*, that is to say, that has come by devolution. Devolution is attribution, division, destination, passing of contracts, transfer by unrolling (*de-volvere*), unfolding, and disintrication. World, fragment: being devolved.

Fallen pieces, waste, wreckage, jagged bits, remains, inner organs of slaughtered beasts, shreds, filth, and excrement, on which contemporary art – *trash art* – gorges itself (and of which it disgorges itself), are all posited, deposited, and exposed on the infinitely thin limit that separates falling-into-decay from befalling, loss from scintillating fragmentation, and abandon from abandon itself. Art vacillates here between its own decay and a future coming of its devolution. Between its failure and its chance, art begins once again. It was not really so naïve of Marx, after all, to be astonished at the effect and affect produced by the works of the Ancients, now that the myths that supported them have fallen into disuse; he understood this effect as the effect of a perpetual childhood freshness.[6] Perhaps art is the *infans* par excellence, the one who, instead of discoursing, fragments instead: fraying [*frayage*] and fracture of the access.

Art has hitherto been considered, in all possible ways, in terms of both "creation" (*poiesis*, genius, and so on) and "reception" (judgment, critique, and so on). But what has been left in the shadows is its befalling or devolving, that is to say, also its chance, event, birth, or encounter – which, in other terminologies, has been called the "shock," "touch," "emotion," or "pleasure," and which participates indissociably in both "creation" and "reception." Aesthetic pleasure (it is a pleonasm if one is indeed speaking of aisthetic pleasure, for "all pleasure is physical";[7] the sensing/sensed entelechy is always also that of a sentiment of pleasure or of pain) is still that with respect to which the discourse on art remains most discreet, distant, or distracted. At least, this is the case for the modern discourse on art. The classical discourse focused on how *to give pleasure* at least as much as on rules: but the aesthetics of rules and how to give pleasure (rules *for* and *of* giving pleasure) gave way to the aesthetics of *poiesis* and works. Nonetheless, the classical discourse generally contented itself with designating the giving of pleasure – being charming, touching, or graceful – as the goal, and barely touched on it, so to speak, any further.

No doubt, discourse, qua discourse, cannot avoid distance or distraction, as far as pleasure is concerned. Signification can *touch* on neither senses nor sense. One could also put it this way: *jouiscience is impossible.*[8] For pleasure – mixed up with displeasure in Edmund Burke's and Kant's versions of the "sublime," as also in Freud's "pleasure of tension," which is a subliminal or preliminary pleasure, a pleasure at the limit that is perhaps the essence of pleasure and that is for Freud the aesthetic "premium"[9] – pleasure does not take place except through *place*, touch, and zone. It is local, detached, discreet, fragmentary, absolute. A nonfractal pleasure, a pleasure without limits, fragmentation, arrival, or falling due, is not a pleasure at all: at most, it is satisfaction, approbation, contentment. Pleasure is not, for all that, "partial": the structure here is not the structure of a *pars pro toto*, but that of a singular totality.

Art is a fragment because it borders on pleasure: it *gives* pleasure [*il fait plaisir*]. It is made both out of and for the pleasure it gives, the pleasure thanks to which it touches – and with a *touch* that comprises its essence. What art does is to *please*: and so it is neither a *poiesis* nor a *praxis*, but another kind of "doing" altogether that mixes together with both of the other kinds an *aisthesis* and its double entelechy. By means of the touch of the senses, pleasure surprises and suspends the enchainment of signifying sense. Or, rather, what one calls in French the "*touche des sens*" (touch of the senses) consists precisely in this suspension and being-taken-by-surprise of signifying enchainment. A position similar to that of truth: the sensuous presentation of truth.[10]

Notes

1   I am keeping myself here in constant and problematic proximity to the stakes, or to the only stake, of the great modern philosophical statements on art, from Hegel (the sensible presentation of the Idea) passing by way of Nietzsche (the apotropaic access to the abyss of truth) to Heidegger (the *Dichtung* of truth).

2   Two remarks: (1) What is said here must be understood as applying to all that we call "sensible," starting beyond the mere "sensorial" sphere, which is itself nothing but an already abstract division; it is a matter of the sensual and the sentimental, of affect and sense in all of their extensions. Finally, it is a matter of *sense* insofar as it would be: being touched by existing. (2) One can imagine the consequences to be drawn concerning the desire for a "great art" as "total art," whether in the mode of a sublime synthesis from Kant to Wagner, or in the mode of a subsumption of all the arts beneath the art of "poesy," from Kant again and Hegel to Heidegger. I point here again to Lacoue-Labarthe's analyses concerning Wagner, Heidegger, and Mallarmé in *Musica ficta*.

3   This reading of the end of the "religion of art" in Hegel's *Phenomenology* is carried out and justified in "Portrait de l'art en jeune fille" (in Jean-Luc Nancy,

Le poids d'une pensée [Montréal and Grenoble: Le Griffon d'Argile, 1991], and in *L'art moderne et la question du sacré*, ed. Jean-Jacques Nillès [Paris: Cerf, 1993]). It goes without saying that a finer investigation would have to show precisely how art has not ceased to be born since Plato, Aristotle, and Plotinus, even when the subsumption of art beneath the intelligible is the organizing theme. Art appears as soon as sense makes itself atheistic: but this is no doubt as old as Lascaux. Art is more "primitive" than any schema of primitivity and progression, any schema of the advance of knowledge or the flight of the gods. And the same goes for the world.

4   Hegel, *Aesthetics*, vol. 1, trans. T. M. Knox (Oxford: Clarendon Press, 1975), pp. 73, 90. To be precise, one must add that the side of the "concept" can conquer for itself, in terms (and according to the general economy) of the *Aesthetics*, neither its autonomy nor its interior unity: it remains as such deprived of sensible life, color, and taste. This is, in the final analysis, what is at stake in the impossible dialectical step from "poetry" to "thought," as also in the nonsublatable contradiction within poetry itself, for poetry does not stop coming back to the sensible in the very moment when it is about to dissolve the sensible. The infamous "end of art" is at the very least, to put it quickly, only half of Hegel's thought here. The other half is the "vast Pantheon" of different arts, art as difference of presentation. And this itself belongs to the necessity of thought, for the latter "in a relative sense is indeed abstract, but it must be concrete, not one-sided" (p. 72). That concrete thought gives itself in a dialectical Christology does not prevent the latter from engendering "Christian art," which culminates, *never to finish*, in the intimate contradiction of poetry-thought (and/or poetry-prose), and consequently in the unachievable "Pantheon." I will show elsewhere how that can be read right off the page of Hegel's text.

5   In the text of the *Phenomenology*. This remarkable turn in Hegel escaped, in particular, Heidegger's notice, although the latter knew quite well that Hegel was not affirming the end of the production of art, but the end of the necessity of its presentation. But it is also this necessity that Hegel not only maintains but installs philosophically despite himself. By this very fact, Heidegger's interpretation of art finds itself at once in advance of and lagging behind Hegel's own account. A long analysis would be necessary, but I will note the principle of such an analysis briefly here: Heidegger's understanding of art is "in advance of" Hegel, insofar as it is an understanding of art as "opening of a world," that is, of the set of "relations" and their "joints" where "this being-open of the There is the essence of *truth*" (and my own approach owes much to this understanding: it is indeed a matter of a presentation of presentation or of coming). But Heidegger's understanding of art "lags behind" Hegel's to the extent that the relationship to the "earth" as "depth and closedness of the abyss," itself in a relationship to the divine that is implied by the paradigm of the "temple," seems to me to reenclose art within another sacredness that is also the same (to which is then added the assignation of the "people"). It is not that one must object to Heidegger that the world

is "pure" opening: in a sense, this world here is indeed "the earth." But it is the earth-world, and without gods, if not without places altogether. (Cf. Heidegger, "The Origin of the Work of Art," in *Poetry, Language, Thought*, trans. Albert Hofstadter (New York: Harper & Row, 1975).)

6   Marx, *Grundrisse: Foundations of the Critique of Political Economy*, III: "A man cannot become a child again or he becomes childish. But does he not find joy in the child's naïveté, and must he himself not strive to reproduce its truth at a higher stage?" Do this native truth of art and this return of sense-being-born have to do also with "emancipated labor"?

7   Immanuel Kant, *Critique of Judgment*, trans. Werner S. Pluhar (Indianapolis: Hackett, 1987), sec. 29, "General Comment on the Exposition of Aesthetic Reflective Judgments," p. 139. Kant picks up this point again with respect to Epicurus. Cf. sec. 54.

8   This is the reason why, when one speaks of such matters, the chances are that a poem rather than expository prose will be the result. Thus, to take an arbitrary example, Michel Butor writes (in 1973) about Pierre Alechinsky: "His soluble gaze surrounded / by the turban of exquisite odors / with the noise of his studio / and kisses on the windows" (*Pierre Alechinsky: Extraits pour traits*, ed. Michel Sicard [Paris: Galilée, 1989], 105). Still, it is too simple to deny *jouiscience*. Signification and discourse do not occur without pleasure or pain. But this is not my object here.

9   [Nancy examines this Freudian notion as it develops in *Jokes and Their Relation to the Unconscious* and in *Three Essays on the Theory of Sexuality* in "In Statu Nascendi," in *The Birth to Presence*, trans. Brian Holmes et al. (Stanford, Calif.: Stanford University Press, 1993), pp. 211–33. Trans.]

10 Which does not mean that pleasure and art are distributed simply in accordance with the five senses of an abstract sensoriality. Sensuality fragments otherwise, up to a certain point. But it fragments nonetheless.

Index

idealism, 57, 64–5, 109, 270
identity, identity formation, 28, 67,
    187–8, 315–16
ideology, 27, 53–4, 67–71, 73, 243,
    332–3, 336–47
image, images, 159–60, 165, 169,
    217–20, 223
imagination, 88, 103–8, 109–10, 114–15,
    136, 179, 259, 273–4
immanence, 246–51
incompleteness (in art), 179
"instrumentalist theory", 212
intellectual concept (*vis-à-vis* the
    artwork), 105–7
intentional fallacy, 212
internal (vs. external) sense, 21–3
interpellation, 67, 336
intuition, 217
Ionesco, Eugene, 59
Irigaray, Luce, 10
irony, 238, 265–6, 321–2

Jakobson, Roman, 223, 323
Jameson, Fredric, 5, 72–7
Jonson, Ben, 304
Joyce, James, 33, 138, 290, 292, 295, 311
judgment, judgment of taste, 103–4,
    332, 334–6, 350

Kant, Immanuel, 4, 6–7, 9, 61, 82,
    103–10, 135–7, 154, 163, 168, 191,
    197–8, 255, 265, 295, 316, 332,
    333–4, 351, 351 n. 2, 353 n. 7
katharsis, 206
Klopstock, Friedrich Gottlieb, 170, 286
knowledge, 67–71, 135, 143, 154, 180,
    257, 261
Kojève, Alexandre, 187
Kristeva, Julia, 315–18

Lacan, Jacques, 8, 67, 73, 134, 187–91,
    295, 315
Lacoue-Labarthe, Philip, 346, 351 n. 2

language game, 134–5, 283
Leibniz, Gottfried Wilhelm, 133, 157–8
Lenin, Vladimir, 69–70
Lessing, G. E., 191
Lichtenstein, Roy, 326–31
literariness, 323
Locke, John, 21, 98
Longinus, 5–7, 81–6
Lukács, Georg, 5, 33–41, 334–5
Lyotard, Jean-François, 7, 82, 104,
    134–9
lyricisim, 217–19

Macherey, Pierre, 69–70
MacLuhan, Marshall, 328
Malevitch, Kasimir, 136, 138
Mallarmé, Stéphane, 318, 351 n. 2
Marcuse, Herbert, 49–54, 55, 137, 333
Marx, Karl, 27–32, 38–41, 49, 255, 288,
    325, 332–8, 350, 353 n. 6
Marxism, Marxist criticism, 27–8, 33,
    38, 67–8, 71–7, 134, 195, 244, 288,
    290, 332–3, 335, 338
Mead, Herbert, 288, 290
medium, media, 277–9
Merleau-Ponty, Maurice, 61, 128–33
metaphor, 25, 149–51, 188, 205, 240
metonymy, 142
mimesis, imitation, 61, 64, 192–6, 205–9,
    259, 292
montage, 47–8
morality, moral truth(s), 17–18, 118,
    178, 276, 294–7
Moscow Linguistic Circle, 223
Mukarovsky, Jan, 335–6
music, 16, 29, 46, 65–6, 89, 118, 130,
    180, 212–14, 232, 247, 263, 324

Nancy, Jean-Luc, 346–53
narratology, 246–7
naturalism, 33
Nazism, 49, 122, 321
Neoplatonism, 87

360 Index

tragedy, 36, 205–10, 303
transcendentalism, 270
trope, 149–51, 169, 290
truth, 7–8, 16, 55–6, 84, 124, 144, 181,
    349

understanding, 103–7, 154

Veblen, Max, 290
Vico, Giambattista, 7–8, 110, 128,
    148–53, 168–9, 217, 260
Virgil, 26, 161, 218–19
virtue, 15–25, 116
Voltaire, 171

Warren, Robert Penn, 155
Wells, H. G., 311

West, Cornell, 270
Wilde, Oscar, 6
Williams, Raymond, 332
Williams, William Carlos, 293
Wimsatt, William, 104, 212
Wittgenstein, Ludwig, 9, 135, 282–7,
    326, 330
Wolf, Christian, 168
Wölfflin, Heinrich, 249, 330
Woolf, Virginia, 10–11, 311–14
Wordsworth, William, 119, 236–9

Xenophon, 85

Yeats, W. B., 293, 322

Zola, Émile, 33